# Readings in the Theory of Action

# Readings in the Theory of Action

Edited by

NORMAN S. CARE

and

CHARLES LANDESMAN

INDIANA UNIVERSITY PRESS

BLOOMINGTON & LONDON

Published in Canada by Fitzhenry & Whiteside Limited, Scarborough, Ontario

Library of Congress catalog card number: 68-27339

Manufactured in the United States of America

For Erica, Jennifer, and Peter,
And for Steven and Jennifer Lorraine

# Contents

## PART II. THE EXPLANATION OF ACTION



## PART III. THE CONCEPT OF ACTION IN HISTORY, ETHICS, AND LAW

# Preface

The philosophical problems which are posed by the fact that persons perform actions are not new, but the recent discussion of them has been fresh, intensive, and, we suggest, deserving of wide attention. This volume is a collection of important materials from the recent discussion. We hope it will be found useful by those attempting to understand the nature of human action, the logic of explanations and justifications of actions, and the bearing of views about these topics upon moral theory and conceptions of the nature of history and law.

Since the work collected here is meant to exhibit some part of a debate which is by no means finished, we do not suggest that this volume provides the final results of philosophical analysis of the concept of human action. Indeed, we recognize the evident danger in any attempt to sum up a philosophical discussion in progress. But we nevertheless believe it will promote the advancement of philosophical inquiry in this area to have these essays available together, for they seem to us to contain views and arguments that are essential to the present debate and to be uniformly carefully done.

It is necessary to mention that our way of grouping these essays is artificial, insofar as it is often the case that the contents of an essay make it a candidate for inclusion in more than one of our three sections. However, perhaps our introduction will show that our arrangement is not implausible, in light of the major concerns of each essay.

We wish to express our thanks to the authors for their generous cooperation in allowing us to present their work here. Formal acknowledgment and the original source of publication are given on the first page of each essay; the essay by James Bogen has not previously been published. We want to acknowledge as well the cooperation of Professor Tolman's family and the University of California Press in helping us include the essay by the late Edward Chace Tolman. For invaluable help in the preparation of the manuscript we offer special thanks to Mrs. Charlene Peterson and Mr. Paul C. Johnson, and to Oberlin College and to Hunter College of the City University of New York.

N. S. C.
C. L.

NORMAN S. CARE AND
CHARLES LANDESMAN

# Introduction*

1. *Action and behavior.* It would appear that no idea we have is more familiar than that of a human action, of something that someone does. Of course the notion expressed by the phrase "something that someone does" comprehends a wide variety of cases—it includes physical events such as walking, running, sitting, chewing; mental events such as thinking, imagining, calculating, judging, deciding; it encompasses "positive" actions such as talking to someone and "negative" actions or forbearances such as keeping still. But the essays presented in this volume will make clear that contemporary philosophers have found the idea of human action extremely puzzling, and not merely because of this variety of cases.

Not too long ago it was widely accepted that that view of the human person associated with the philosophy of Descartes, according to which a person is an amalgam of a physical substance (his body) and a mental substance (his mind), could be overcome by careful attention to the idea of action (or the idea of behavior, as it is more often expressed in the psychological literature). It was argued that those concepts which, in the Cartesian view, designated inner mental events could be defined or explained by reference to concepts designating behavior or be-

* For the complete citation of the books and articles referred to in this introduction but not contained in this volume, see the Selected Bibliography at the end of the volume.

havioral dispositions. More recently this alternative to the Cartesian view—sometimes called *behaviorism*—has been called into question on the ground that the very concept of an action cannot be analyzed satisfactorily without bringing in mentalistic terms, so if we take action seriously we cannot avoid accepting a dualism between mind and body analogous to that associated with Descartes' philosophy. It is thus the traditional problem of the relation between body and mind which has been one of the chief factors in the recent surge of interest in the concept of action. Another important factor is the recent turn that has been taken in ethics. It has been argued that the basic problem of philosophical ethics can be formulated as the question: What does it mean to justify an action? As the logic of justification has become one of the central topics of ethics, theorists have found it natural to believe that light can be thrown on it through an investigation of the nature of action itself.

The essays that follow may serve as an introduction to the theory of action for someone unfamiliar with recent work in this area of philosophical inquiry. Since each essay is intended as an original contribution to the theory, this volume can also serve as a collection of primary materials for those wishing to engage in research. In this introduction we shall demarcate and then survey those problems which make the concept of action an interesting and important topic of philosophical reflection.

The distinguished American psychologist E. C. Tolman once explained why he adopted behaviorism:

> The motives which lead to the assertion of a behaviorism are simple. All that can ever be actually observed in fellow human beings and in the lower animals is behavior. Another organism's private mind, if he have any, can never be got at. And even the supposed ease and obviousness of 'looking within' and observing one's own mental processes, directly and at first hand, have proved, when subjected to laboratory control, in large part chimerical.[1]

If one accepts, as Tolman here appears to, the rule of scientific procedure that the only entities which may be validly incorporated into a scientific theory are those that can be observed through the five senses, it follows that the psychologist studies not the alleged inner workings of the mind but the overt behavior or action of living organisms. What "can't be got at" is, according to this interpretation of science, equivalent to being nonexistent.

Behaviorism has very often been justified on the basis of this simple epistemological argument. But, as Tolman proceeds to point out,[2] behaviorism is not a unitary movement but one which breaks up into several interpretations that are often at odds with one another. A way of classifying these interpretations which reflects the differences among those predominantly espoused by philosophers and those predominantly espoused by psychologists is in terms of "descriptive" and "revisionary" behaviorism.[3] *Descriptive behaviorism* is the view that our existing conceptual scheme[4] is already behavioristic, i.e., the concepts we now use in everyday life to explain and describe the mental life of persons and animals can be defined, analyzed, and explicated by reference to behavior and behavioral dispositions. Terms such as "belief," "motive," "purpose," and "thought" designate not inner occurrences available only to introspection but tendencies to act under certain conditions. For example, a belief in a proposition may simply consist in a constellation of dispositions such as the tendency to assent to the proposition when asked if it is true, the tendency to act as if it were true, and so on.[5] *Revisionary behaviorism* claims that the scheme we ought to adopt and which psychologists ought to restrict themselves to developing is behavioristic. The revisionist is relatively uninterested in our existing everyday conceptual scheme; if it should turn out not to be reducible to a behavioral scheme, so much the worse for it; the part of it which fails to be reducible is on a par with traditional superstitions such as a belief in witches, elves, and demons.[6]

Problems begin to arise when we ask what is this *behavior* which has to bear such theoretical weight. Tolman points out that among psychologists there have been two competing definitions. According to the *molecular concept*, behavior consists of "the strict physical and physiological muscle-twitches which make it up," [7] or, more broadly, of the physical and physiological elements in an action. For example, when a driver uses his arm to signal a turn, his behavior according to the molecular concept consists of the motions of his arm through space together with the stretchings of the muscles and any other physiological changes involved. In contrast there is the *molar concept*, according to which behavior corresponds to our everyday notion of an action, of something that someone does. As examples of the molar concept Tolman mentions: "a rat running a maze; a cat getting out of a puzzle box; a man driving home to dinner; a child hiding from a stranger; a woman doing her washing or gossiping over the telephone; a pupil marking a mental-test sheet; a psychologist reciting a list of nonsense syllables; my friend and I telling one another our thoughts and feelings—*these are behaviors* (qua *molar*). And it must be noted that in mentioning no one of them have we referred to, or, we blush to confess it, for the most part even known, what were the exact muscles and glands, sensory nerves, and motor nerves involved." [8]

Another pair of definitions which cut across the molar-molecular contrast concerns whether the term "behavior" shall be restricted to designate only events observable on the outside of the organism—*peripheral behavior*—or shall be broadened to include events occurring within the organism, especially within its central nervous system—*central behavior*.[9] The interest of this second pair is that certain types of mental events—mental images, dreams, sensations, thoughts—resist reduction to peripheral behavior. For example, it seems implausible to consider a dream to be merely a disposition to tell a story upon awakening,[10] or an itch merely a disposition to scratch, or an orange after-image merely a disposition to report the presence of an orange object. Consequently, there is motivation for behavioristically oriented psychologists to classify events in the brain and central nervous system as behavior and to identify inner mental events with these. Consider, for instance, D. O. Hebb's assertion that "'mind' can only be regarded for scientific purposes as the activity of the brain."[11] Thus the contrast between observable outer events and private inner events which the early behaviorists thought could be overcome by insisting on observable criteria for psychological concepts reappears within the notion of behavior itself. If brain processes and like events are accepted as a form of behavior and thus incorporated into behavioristic psychology, then it is clear that psychological theories can no longer be restricted to entities which are observable by means of the five senses; they must now make use of theoretical terms descriptive of the microscopic processes occurring within the central nervous system. The simple empiricism and operationism upon which early behaviorism rested for its rationale and justification has, in recent years, been forced to make way for a theory of knowledge which allows for unobservables and which provides a rationale for new centralist versions of behaviorism.[12] With this development there has grown up in some quarters a renewed interest in the traditional Cartesian framework and the possibility of making it the basis of a science of psychology.[13]

2. *The theory of action.* We sometimes contrast an action, what a person does, with his thoughts and beliefs on the one hand and with things that merely happen to him on the other. Action in this sense is, by and large, molar peripheral behavior. It is more than mere thinking since, with the exception of forbearances and the like, it involves genuine physical interventions of a person in the world. And it is more than mere physical change such as the sneezes, coughs, twitches, and blinkings over which a person has no control. The title "the theory of action" has come, in recent years, to designate the inquiry into a set of problems specifically related to molar peripheral behavior. The discussion of mental actions such as thinking, deliberating, and imagining has usually been conducted under the rubrics of the philosophy

of mind and moral philosophy. The consideration of the relation of mental events to molecular central behavior, that is, the question of the identity of mind and brain, is usually classified as belonging to a discussion of the mind-body problem. In what follows we shall review the problems which are associated with the theory of action and which form the focus of discussion in the articles collected in this volume.

3. *Actions and movements.* An interesting question is whether actions which directly result in a physical intervention in the world necessarily involve movements of the agent's body. Some persons believe in the reality of psycho-kinesis, the ability to bring about physical changes in objects separated from one's body by directly willing them and without first moving one's own body or any of its parts. If a person can make an object fall to the floor in the same direct way he can move his arm, then he has an ability which is indeed strange. He can perform a *basic action,* i.e., an action which is performed without its being the result of a prior action, without moving his limbs.[14] The phenomenon of psycho-kinesis apart, molar peripheral behavior[15] usually involves movements of the body, particularly those movements which have been classified as molecular peripheral behavior. For example, when a person mails a letter, his arm travels from one point in space to another; his muscles expand and contract; his hand opens and closes; and so on. Some of Tolman's statements can be interpreted as asserting that there is a one-to-one correspondence between actions and the underlying molecular behavior. But he believed that the former had "emergent properties of their own" and that "descriptively they are different from the latter." [16] He is clearly wrong on the claim of one-to-one correspondence. For example, a person can mail a letter by using any one of a large number of different sequences of movements. He can use his right or his left hand; the letter may be gripped in a variety of ways; his hand may travel in one of any number of different paths to the mailbox. Between an

action and the associated physical movements there is often a one-many relation. Moreover, the same movement can accomplish different actions depending on circumstances—for example, gripping a piece of paper between thumb and forefinger and moving one's left hand along a certain path can have the result not only of a letter being mailed, but of a message being delivered, a bill being placed in a drawer, a driver's license being handed to an officer of the law, and many others. Between a physical movement and the resultant actions, there can be and often is a one-many relation.

Can actions be literally identical with the underlying physical movement? Tolman thinks they cannot, for if they have emergent properties of their own, then, by Leibniz' law,[17] they must be numerically different. Some philosophers have asserted that actions can be identified with movements. A. I. Melden, for example, claims[18] that the identification is possible provided we take into account the context of rules and practices in which the movement occurs. Actions are not movements *simpliciter* but are movements as occurring in a given context. Mailing a letter does not consist, as we have seen, merely of the associated movements, but, in this view, of this movement as occurring within a framework of such practices as writing and such institutions as a postal system and within an environment in which a mailbox is placed.

A view which comes close to reconciling this opposition between Melden and Tolman is implicit in a suggestion made by Donald Davidson.[19] He remarks that an action is something that can be described in a variety of ways—if "I flip the switch, turn on the light, and illuminate the room" and "unbeknownst to me I also alert a prowler to the fact that I am home" then "I do not do four things, but only one, of which four descriptions have been given." [20] One way of making this suggestion plausible is to think of the so-called emergent properties which Tolman believes distinguish molar behavior from the underlying molecular events as being properties of sequences of the latter. If we do this, then an action can be identified with a series of changes such that the series as a whole has attributes which cannot be logically derived from the attributes of the parts.

According to this way of reconciling the opposition it is also plausible to think of actions as particular events whose descriptions designate properties of which these events are instances. But once this idea is made explicit, an alternative becomes immediately available for consideration, namely that actions are not particular events at all but are rather properties or universals (like colors and shapes) whose instances are the agents who perform them. The two alternatives can be illustrated by reflecting on the statement "Jones flips the switch." According to the first, the predicate "flips the switch" is interpreted as designating a property which is instantiated by a particular sequence of events, namely Jones's action, and this sequence may also be an instance of properties designated by other descriptions such as "illuminates the room." According to the second, the predicate "flips the switch" is interpreted as designating the action itself which Jones performs. Jones is an instance of the action but so is anyone else who does the same thing.

Just as the first alternative makes it possible to argue that actions are numerically identical with the underlying physical movements, so the second makes it possible to argue that they are not. Given the widely accepted rule that logically independent predicates designate different properties and that predicates designating actions are logically independent from predicates designating the underlying movements, it follows, given that actions and movements are to be categorized as universals rather than particulars, that they are numerically different from one another. This question of how best to categorize actions belongs to the metaphysics of action, a topic which has not been explored to any significant extent. But this much is clear, that the outcome of the debate over the proper way of understanding the relation between actions and their underlying movements depends on further explorations along these lines.

*4. Actions and volitions.* On an intuitive basis, we have no difficulty in picking out cases of genuine actions and distinguishing them from things that merely happen. Take, for instance, the case of inanimate objects: when a billiard ball rolls across a table, its moving is nothing that *it* does; the manner and direction of its movement is not under its control; it does not choose to move nor does it deliberate whether or not it should move. And when we consider persons, we have no difficulty distinguishing an action, such as a teacher's lecturing to a class, from the things that merely happen to him while lecturing, such as his eyes blinking or his sneezing suddenly. Given that a consideration of particular cases establishes that there is a distinction to be drawn,[21] the question arises concerning its basis. Is there any characteristic possessed by everything which, on intuitive preanalytic grounds, we would unhesitatingly classify as an action, but which is missing in nonactions?

According to the *volitional theory* an action is an event which is caused by a volition or act of will. Suppose we take as a case of an action a person's walking out of a room of his own free will and contrast it with a mere happening such as his being thrown out of the room against his will. With respect to this particular example the fact that the action is voluntary whereas the happening is not suggests what some consider to be essential to the contrast between actions and mere happenings. Advocates of the volitional theory thus claim that (1) the defining feature of an action is that it is an event which is voluntary. They then go on to explain that (2) what makes an event voluntary is that it is something "willed" by a person in the sense that it is caused by that person's act of will or volition. Finally, (3) the term "volition" is explained by reference to such concepts as deliberation, choice, effort, and trying. Hobbes, for example, writes: "In *deliberation,* the last appetite, or aversion, immediately adhering to the action, or to the omission thereof, is *that* we call the *will.*" [22] And Jonathan Edwards asserts: "In every act of will there is an act of choice." [23]

Contemporary philosophers have been loath to accept the volitional theory as it stands. As against (2), and, for that matter, as against any view which ascribes a mental-process component to action, Melden writes: "The attempt to distinguish bodily movements that do, from those that do not, count as actions in terms of occurrent psychological processes is doomed to failure. What passes through my mind as I now act may be anything or nothing; it may be that all that happens is that without anything relevant passing through my mind, I just act."[24] On empirical grounds (2) can be attacked by pointing out that people sometimes act without any introspectable[25] antecedent deliberation or choice or mental effort—any impulsive act will serve as an example.[26] One way of sidestepping this type of criticism is to claim that volitions are theoretical entities which cannot be introspected by persons engaging in actions but which are essential in explaining why they do what they do.[27] This maneuver, however, has the disadvantage of making (3) more difficult to accept since such things as deliberations, choices, and efforts of will do seem to be the sorts of event which can be introspected. In brief, (2) and (3) are apparently incompatible.

(2) has also been criticized on a priori grounds. If a volition is itself an action (and note that deliberating, trying, and choosing seem to be things that people do) then it too must be caused by a volition, ad infinitum, and this is absurd.[28] Perhaps this attack can be blunted by claiming either that volitions are exceptions to (2) or that they are not actions but nonvoluntary mental states somewhat like desires and emotions. But the first alternative is arbitrary and gratuitous. And many philosophers[29] have rejected the second on the grounds that something which is not voluntary and is not subject to the agent's control cannot be the distinguishing feature of a free act.

It is also reasonable to be sceptical of (1). Consider the case of a man held up by a thief who threatens to take his life if he fails to hand over his money. After short deliberation and despite the fact that he does not want to hand it over, he does so anyway. His handing the money to the thief was not voluntary since he was forced to do it against his will; he was literally compelled to do something he did not want to do. Acts of this sort seem to be paradigm cases of acts done under duress and which hence fail to be voluntary. And yet what he did was done intentionally and purposely and after due deliberation; his movements in handing over the money were, unlike a sudden sneeze, fully under his control. His handing over the money was an action, and therefore the volitional theory fails to locate the distinctive feature of actions.

5. *Actions and intentions.* Attempts have been made to revise and qualify the volitional theory to avoid these sorts of objections. To take one example, John R. Silber thinks that there is a place for the language of volitions in at least those cases in which a person fails to do what he intends.[30] Suppose a person intends to raise his arm, tries to do so, but, because of a blockage of nerve impulse, his arm fails to rise. Silber claims that a mental act was performed; the person willed to raise his arm.[31] He is pointing out that there is a valid use for such concepts as "effort of will" which designate an inner act of a person and not merely observable behavior.[32] This is a fair point to make against behaviorism but it does not serve to reinstate anything like the volitional theory as a general analysis of the concept of an action.

D. W. Hamlyn argues for the stronger thesis that there is a mental element or "modification of consciousness," as he puts it, presupposed in action.[33] The element he fixes upon as being essential to many classes of action is intention. It is important to point out that intentions are not just the same sort of mental state as efforts of will or volitions. A man who has formed the intention to attend a lecture that he knows will bore him may have to make an effort of will to get himself there. The effort of will belongs to the stage of the execution of the intended action whereas the intention belongs to the stage of determining what action is going to get done. So the claim that it is the notion of intention that marks the differentiating feature of actions is more than a revision of the volitional theory; it is a new theory altogether.

The language of intentions has complications of its own. In the first place, to be very precise, a person's intention or purpose is something that lies in the future. If it is your present intention to go to the movies this evening, then your intention is simply going to the movies. And, unlike a volition or effort of will, this is not a present mental event since it is neither present nor mental. When we ascribe an intention as a modification of consciousness to a person, the mental element, strictly speaking, is the having of that intention or the having of that purpose in mind. However, with this understood, we shall from this point on use "intention" to designate the mental element.

In the second place, consider two statements such as the following:

(a) Jones intends to raise his arm.
(b) Jones raises his arm intentionally.

It appears that (b) could be true when (a) is false. If Jones raised his arm on impulse, this means that he did not, prior to the action, form an intention. A person's impulsive actions might, nevertheless, have been done intentionally or on purpose. Jones may be asked: "Why did you raise your arm?" and he might sensibly reply that he had no purpose or intention; he just felt like doing it. But since he did it because he felt like it, his doing it was fully intentional.

When we ascribe to someone an intention or purpose in doing a certain action we are usually claiming that he has in mind some goal which he wants to result from his action. Thus, when a person does something for its own sake, as Jones did in raising his arm, then, strictly speaking, he has no purpose or intention in doing it since he did not hope to accomplish anything thereby. A person may act intentionally without having a purpose or motive or reason in this strict sense. There is, of course, a broader use of "reason" in which "I just felt like doing it" gives a reason. But in the narrow sense, a reason is what someone hopes to accomplish. The question arises as to what features of an action the adverb "intentionally" designates. Daniel Bennett points out[34] that a person who does an act intentionally knows what it is that he is doing and knows those features of the context which are logically implicated in his act. If he, for example, intentionally lights a cigarette, then he knows he is lighting his cigarette and he knows his cigarette to be a cigarette. Thus "intentionally" at least designates a cognitive element, the knowledge and hence the belief of the agent.

Although knowing what one is doing is necessary for one's doing it to be intentional, it is certainly not sufficient. A person who unintentionally stumbles and falls may realize that he is stumbling and falling. What, then, is this further element, if there is any, which, when added to the cognitive component, yields an intentional act? To say that an intentional act is an action done on purpose or an action done with the agent's meaning to do it is perfectly correct, but it is also unhelpful since the concepts of purpose and meaning are just as problematic as intention.

Two of the theories which have been formulated to solve this problem are especially worthy of discussion here because of the widespread interest and comment they have elicited. One of them —*the ascriptive analysis of action*—is summed up by Fitzgerald in the following words: "In ordinary speech the word 'act', together with such allied expressions as 'A did it', is used not so much to describe what has happened, as to ascribe responsibility. . . . 'A's act caused B's death' is less a way of describing what has happened, than another way of saying that it was A's fault." [35] On this view, when a person is charged with doing an act and hence responsibility for it, he may defend himself by claiming that it was not voluntary or was not intentional. These defenses are ways of reducing or mitigating his responsibility. Now, H. L. A. Hart claims that "the word 'voluntary' [and, we may add, the word 'intentional'] in fact serves to exclude a heterogeneous range of cases such as physical compulsion, coercion by threats, accidents, mistakes, etc. and not to designate a mental element or state." [36] According to the ascriptive analysis, then, there is no further element which when added to the cognitive component yields an intentional act. There is, rather, a large variety of factors the absence of which "leaves" the action an intentional one.

A second approach, which can be extracted from some of the writings of Miss G. E. M. Anscombe,[37] is that an action is intentional only if it comes under a certain type of explanation, or a certain type of "Why?" question is appropriately asked of it. If a person involuntarily sneezes or blinks, then it would be wrong to ask him why he sneezed or blinked if what we were asking for was his reason for doing it. Although his sneezing, no doubt, had a cause or reason, *he* did not have a reason for doing it. In this view, if a person S does an action A intentionally, then:

(1) S knows that he is doing A,

and

(2) There is a reason R which S has for doing A.

Of course, for this theory to be plausible, we must interpret "reason" in the broad sense in which doing something for the pleasure of it is a reason. But still, (2) as formulated does not, when combined with (1), yield a sufficient condition of intentional action. For suppose S pushes against someone, knows that his body is pushing against him, and has a reason (e.g., wants to annoy him) for pushing against him. All this is compatible with S's being pushed and hence for his action being unintentional. What we need to add is that S did A because of R, or that R is the reason why S did A. Let us, therefore, modify (2) along these lines:

(2′) S does A because of R which is a reason he has for doing A.

Note that we can and need to distinguish between a reason a person has for an action and the reason why he acts. Not every reason he has need be the reason why he does what in fact he does.

Let us use the notion of wanting something in an extremely broad sense to represent, as Davidson suggests,[38] any pro or favorable attitude a person may have toward something. In this sense if a person feels obliged to perform some action, it follows that he wants to perform it, even though in a narrower sense we often allow that a person may feel obliged to do something he does not want to do. If we survey the sorts of things which people mention as being reasons they have for their actions, we can distinguish two types of case. In the case of actions performed for the sake of accomplishing some further goal of the agent, the agent's reason is simply what he wants to accomplish by that action together with his belief that he can accomplish it by doing just that thing. In the case of actions that people perform for their own sake such as playing games and taking walks, typical reasons are couched in such terms as "enjoyment" or "liking" or in general "wanting to do it for its own sake." So we can generalize and say that the sorts of things that count as reasons which people have for actions are their wants and their beliefs.[39] It follows, then, that an intentional action, in this analysis, is one which the agent is conscious of and which he does because of his wants and beliefs. Unlike the ascriptive theory, this analysis of intentionality makes essential reference to mental states, and therefore is incompatible with any of those simple peripheral versions of behaviorism which claim to be able to eliminate reference to mental states by means of a behavioral analysis.

*6. Action and explanation.* Explanations of actions which refer to the intentions, purposes, desires, and motives of agents are often called teleological explanations.[40] A common criticism of this type of explanation is that an agent's intention or purpose is a future state of affairs and what is future and thus does not exist (and may never exist) cannot explain a present action. This criticism may be blunted by recalling the distinction we made earlier between the intention as a future event yet to be realized and the intention as a present state of mind. It is the latter and not the former which does the explaining; it is not the end but the end-in-view which renders actions intelligible. Among those philosophers and psychologists who believe that in the long run a purely physiological account of the human makeup will turn out to be correct, teleological explanations, though common enough in everyday life, in psychology, and in history, are only provisionally acceptable and will not occur in the theory which is ultimately accepted as true. Thus W. V. O. Quine once wrote: "If we are limning the true and ultimate structure of reality, the canonical scheme for us is the austere scheme that knows . . . no propositional attitudes but only the physical constitution and behavior of organisms."[41] Other less austere behaviorists would be willing to allow teleological explanations provided that mental states such as desires and beliefs can be correlated and identified with physiological states.[42]

There is an ancient dispute in philosophy about the best way to describe and conceptualize the similarities and differences between human persons on the one hand and nonhuman animals (the brutes, as they were once called), biological organisms, and inanimate things on the other. In early modern philosophy those who wished to stress the similarities, such as, for example, Hobbes, liked to use the model of a machine: human beings are nothing but physical mechanisms differing from other things merely in the degree of complexity with which their parts are arranged. In part this meant that the principles and methods which are sufficient to understand and explain the behavior of nonhuman creatures are also sufficient to explain human action. Others, who were anxious to stress the differences, such as Descartes, replied by insisting that there was a nonmechanical principle, the soul or mind, which interacts with the human body and that reference to its activities (such as acts of will or volitions) are necessary to explain actions.

Contemporary psychologists and philosophers seldom discuss this issue in terms of whether or not there is, to use Ryle's phrase, a ghost in the machine. For psychologists, the dualistic hypothesis can provide no satisfactory explanation of behavior, since it would appear to make no sense to ascribe to an immaterial substance an internal structure and activity which could be causally linked to behavior. Among philosophers, A. J. Ayer has expressed a characteristic attitude in his admission that he does not find the hypothesis intelligible.[43] But even if there is no ghost in the machine, there still remains the question of whether persons are best characterized as machines in the first place. The current focus for this ancient dispute concerns the nature of teleological explanation. Among those who admit its legitimacy, the group whose views are analogous to traditional materialism—the physicalists, as they are sometimes called—want to insist that the sort of understanding of action it conveys is no different in principle from the understanding conveyed by explanation in the physical sciences. On the other hand, those whose views bear some analogy to traditional dualism—the new dualists, as we shall call them—argue that teleological explanation is unique.[44]

A form of explanation may be unique in a variety of ways. The type of uniqueness which has recently been discussed with reference to teleological explanation has to do with whether it comes under a certain general account of explanation called the covering-law model.[45] This model was first proposed as an analysis of explanation in science, particularly the physical sciences, and then was extended by Hempel and Popper to history and to human action in general. In its customary formulation its proponents assert that a satisfactory explanation meets the following formal condition: the event to be explained—the explanandum—is logically deducible from two statements—the explanans—one of which formulates a general law and the other of which states the antecedent conditions or causes from which the explanandum follows in accordance with the law. Thus a meteorologist might explain why it is raining by showing that the rain followed a prior condition of the weather in accordance with some law which asserted that rain invariably or usually follows such a condition.[46] Since an explanation shows how one event follows from previous events in accordance with a law of nature, then in at least one well-established sense of "cause," an explanation states the cause of the explanandum. There is implicit in the covering-law model an epistemological condition as well: since, in order to know an explanation for a given event, one must know or at least have good evidence for the existence of a law or regularity, and since such evidence consists of correlations observed to hold in the past, it follows that the knowledge upon which an explanation is grounded is based on inductive inferences.

This model has often been criticized on the ground that the kind of law appropriate to teleological explanation, a kind which connects the desires, beliefs, motives, and intentions of agents with their behavior, cannot or at least has not yet been found.[47] But even if the formal condition should be rejected [48] one may still adhere to the view that actions are caused by the desires and beliefs of agents provided that one rejects or at least qualifies the covering-law analysis of causality.[49] The epistemological condition has been criticized as well, most often on the grounds that a person can know his reasons for action by introspection in the same way he learns of his feelings and thoughts, and that inductive inference is not always necessary. In arguing against the Freudian notion of unconscious reasons, Peter Alexander claims[50] that a reason is always potentially conscious, that an agent can always call it to mind or recognize it when queried. If reasons for action can be known in the same sort of noninferential way that thoughts and feelings can be known, then knowledge of a covering law is not always necessary in order to know the causes of behavior. These doubts about the epistemological condition may show that the formal condition is problematic as well. It is, however, still possible to defend the causal character of teleological explanation provided we can sometimes know directly which condition causes what event.

There have been, however, attempts to criticize the causal character of teleological explanation on grounds other than a rejection of the covering-law model. An argument commonly offered [51] is that teleological states are logically connected to behavior and hence cannot cause it, given the assumption that effects must be logically independent from causes. The way, however, in which desires are often said to be logically connected to behavior is that the form of words used to describe the desire (e.g. "wanting to eat") is also used to describe the ensuing action ("eating"). But it is evident that this sort of connection may hold and yet the desire and action still be logically independent, i.e., it is surely possible for a person to want to eat and yet not eat or for him to eat and yet not want to.[52] Another line of argument against the causal character stresses the special function of reason-giving explanations. The way in which citing reasons functions to explain is that the reasons justify the action or show that it was the appropriate thing to do in the circumstances. Teleological explanations, it is claimed, reveal that, from the agent's point of view at least, what he does or intends to do is rational. Discourse about reasons belongs to the language of evaluation rather than the language of the objective, value-free description of natural events.[53] But even if the premise of the criticism is correct that the special function of reasons is to provide a rationale for actions, yet the conclusion that therefore reasons cannot be causes certainly does not follow. Although being a cause may not be sufficient for something to be a reason, its being a cause does not prevent it from being a reason either. Just as the same thing may be both blue and good, perhaps the same condition may be both a reason and a cause. As we have seen, a person may have a reason for an action without its being the reason why he acts. Given, then, that (1) a certain person has a reason for doing some action and (2) he does that action because of the reason, what additional claim does (2) make over (1)? The advocates of the causal character of teleological explanation claim that only the causal relation renders the "because" in (2) intelligible.[54] At the present time whether teleological explanation is causal is one of the key issues concerning the explanation of action. Although Hume's analysis of causality as a constantly occurring sequence of events, an analysis which is the ancestor of the covering-law model, had for a long time been widely accepted, the consideration of the concept of action is beginning to lead to widespread doubts of its validity.[55]

7. *Action and ethics.* Other issues that are discussed in some of the articles in this volume have to do with the bearing of an account of action upon ethics. It has been recognized since the beginning of reflection upon human life that actions are proper subjects of moral praise and censure and that such ethical concepts as being obligatory and being right or wrong apply to actions. And it has traditionally been supposed that the actions that are proper subjects of ethical concepts are such that the beings performing them are in some sense free agents. Recent inquiry has accordingly been directed to the basic question of whether or not persons may be said to act in a way that allows for the applicability of ethical notions. James Bogen, for example, entertains the view that no person so acts, and argues that recent work in the theory of action does not refute the "argument from physical determinism" which has this view as its conclusion.[56] Aside from this question of human action, but nevertheless presuming an affirmative answer to it, theorists have also claimed that the analysis of the concept of action itself has a bearing on the validity and applicability of certain principles of evaluation. For instance, John Rawls shows that certain types of actions such as punishing and promising which are important in the law and in ethics are constituted by the existence of legal and ethical rules, in the sense that it is the rules which make it possible for the actions to exist.[57] Examples of actions which cannot exist

outside of a system of rules are easily found in games. A batter may wave his bat three times, but this is not enough to strike out; he must be playing baseball, that is, he must be doing something as conforming to the rules of the game. Rawls claims that this fact about certain kinds of actions has important consequences in the procedures of justification and evaluation; specifically it implies the incorrectness of the unqualified assertion (sometimes associated with traditional utilitarianism) that actions can be evaluated as right or wrong by reference to their consequences. Those actions whose existence depends on a system of rules are to be evaluated by reference to the rules, and not by reference to their results. Rawls thinks that utilitarianism can be defended if considerations of utility are applied to the rules themselves rather than to the actions they regulate. B. J. Diggs, who builds on Rawls's work, suggests that if we examine closely just how the existence of moral rules do serve to make certain actions possible, we will see that utilitarianism cannot be saved even if Rawls's suggestion be adopted.[58]

## Notes

1. See p. 3 of this volume.
2. See p. 4 of this volume.
3. The contrast between descriptive and revisionary metaphysics is made by P. F. Strawson in *Individuals, an Essay in Descriptive Metaphysics*, p. 9.
4. By a conceptual scheme we mean a set of basic or fundamental concepts, categories, beliefs, principles, and rules which can be used in or presupposed in the construction of theories and the formulation of hypotheses.
5. The *locus classicus* of descriptive behaviorism is Gilbert Ryle, *The Concept of Mind.* A similar view that behavior constitutes the logical criteria for the application of mentalistic terms can be found in Ludwig Wittgenstein, *The Philosophical Investigations.* See the collection of essays *Wittgenstein, the Philosophical Investigations,* edited by George Pitcher, for further discussion.
6. Among psychologists those who espouse a revisionary position

are Tolman in *Purposive Behavior in Animals and Men* (see the chapter reprinted in this volume) and *Behavior and Psychological Man*, and B. F. Skinner in *Science and Human Behavior*. Among philosophers see the articles by Paul Feyerabend, "Materialism and the Mind-Body Problem," and Richard Rorty, "Mind-Body Identity, Privacy, and Categories." For a general discussion of the possible conflict between scientific and common sense conceptual schemes see chapter one of Wilfrid Sellars, *Science, Perception, and Reality*.

7. See p. 6 of this volume.

8. See p. 8 of this volume.

9. It is not obvious that all actions fit either into the peripheral or central categories. For example, are forbearances such as holding one's tongue events observable on the outside of the organism? We shall classify forbearances as cases of peripheral behavior when the act omitted would have been a case of peripheral behavior had it occurred. Thus holding one's tongue is peripheral because speaking is. In any case it is difficult to formulate a classification of behavior which is precise and exhaustive and exclusive.

10. See the monograph *Dreaming* by Norman Malcolm for a defense of the criteriological view of dreams.

11. D. O. Hebb, *The Organization of Behavior*, p. xiv. Among philosophers the thesis that mental events are identical with brain processes has recently acquired the title of "the neural identity thesis." See the articles by Feyerabend and Rorty (note 6) for a discussion of this view. A much cited defense is J. J. C. Smart's "Sensations and Brain Processes."

12. For critical discussions of the simple empiricism and operationism of early behaviorism see Carl Hempel, *Fundamentals of Concept Formation in Empirical Science*, Karl Popper, "Three Views Concerning Human Knowledge" in his *Conjectures and Refutations*, and Ernest Nagel, *The Structure of Science*, chapter 6.

13. The renewed interest in Descartes has been stimulated by certain developments in linguistics, especially the transformation approach. See Noam Chomsky's *Cartesian Linguistics* for the specific references to Descartes. See Jerrold J. Katz's *The Philosophy of Language* for a survey of the philosophical implications of this approach.

14. For a discussion of basic actions and their extent, see the articles by Arthur Danto reprinted in this volume.

15. We also need to make an exception here of forbearances. See note 9.

16. See pp. 7–8 of this volume.

17. By Leibniz' law we refer to the thesis that things differing with respect to any one of their properties must be numerically different from one another.

18. See the article by Melden reprinted in this volume.

19. See the article by Davidson reprinted in this volume.

20. See p. 180 of this volume.

21. The existence of a distinction is compatible with the existence of borderline cases which we cannot classify one way or the other on intuitive grounds. One way of dealing with the "grey" areas is to develop an explicit theory explaining the distinction in the easily classifiable cases and then use the theory to deal with the others.

22. *Leviathan,* chapter 6.

23. *Freedom of the Will,* Part 1, section 1.

24. See p. 33 of this volume. Chapter 5 of Melden's *Free Action* is also pertinent.

25. "Introspection" is the name given to that direct and noninferential way in which a person can become aware of his own thoughts, feelings, sensations, and, in general, mental states. That there is such a thing as introspection is beyond doubt, although how best to interpret it is a matter of controversy. The view held by Locke and many other philosophers was that introspection is a form of observation or perception whose objects happened to be mental rather than physical. An important contemporary view is that introspection is a type of direct knowledge not based on observation. For a survey of different theories see the article "Consciousness" in *The Encyclopedia of Philosophy,* edited by Paul Edwards.

26. See the article by P. J. Fitzgerald reprinted in this volume for a discussion and criticism of efforts to apply the volitional theory in the law.

27. The notion that those mental states which are involved in explanations of action are theoretical entities is explored for the case of wants in the article by Richard Brandt and Jaegwon Kim reprinted in this volume.

28. See Ryle, *The Concept of Mind,* p. 67. The whole of chapter 3 "The Will" is relevant. Also see the discussion "What is the Will?" by D. F. Pears, J. F. Thomson, and Mary Warnock in *Freedom of the Will,* edited by Pears.

29. See, for example, C. A. Campbell, "Is 'Free-Will' a Pseudo-Problem?".

30. See Silber's article reprinted in this volume.

31. See p. 87 of this volume.

32. This summary of Silber's thesis should be understood in the light of his remark that "I should resist any suggestion that volition can be understood in terms that are purely mental or spiritual or non-physical." Ibid.

33. See Hamlyn's article reprinted in this volume.

34. See p. 238 of this volume.

35. See the article by Fitzgerald reprinted in this volume, p. 373.

36. See H. L. A. Hart's paper "The Ascription of Responsibility and Rights" in *Logic and Language, First Series,* p. 153. This paper is the classical statement of the ascriptive theory. For another statement of it see J. L. Austin, "A Plea for Excuses" in his *Philosophical Papers,* p. 128. A critical discussion is contained in Joel Feinberg's "Action and Responsibility" in *Philosophy in America.*

37. See Miss Anscombe's *Intention,* section 5.

38. See p. 179 of this volume.

39. See the article by Davidson.

40. These are not to be confused with functional explanations. The question "Why does the heart beat?" may be answered by "To circulate the blood" or by "The purpose (or function) of the heart is to circulate the blood." Although reference is made to the function of the heart, there is no implication that the heart *has* any purposes, intentions, motives, or reasons for beating. A good discussion of functional explanation is in Nagel, *The Structure of Science,* pp. 401–28. Note that Nagel uses the term "teleological" where we have used "functional."

41. See Quine's *Word and Object,* p. 221.

42. For a discussion of this point see Charles Landesman, "The New Dualism in the Philosophy of Mind."

43. *The Problem of Knowledge,* p. 184.

44. For a survey of the new dualism see the article by Landesman mentioned in note 42. Examples of the new dualism are Charles Taylor, *The Explanation of Behavior,* A. I. Melden, *Free Action,* and Peter Winch, *The Idea of a Social Science.*

45. Standard accounts of the covering-law model are contained in Carl G. Hempel and Paul Oppenheim, "The Logic of Explanation," and Hempel, "The Function of General Laws in History." The term "covering-law model" is due to William Dray, *Laws and Explanation in History,* a selection from which is reprinted in this volume.

46. While this condition is often characterized as formal, it has been found difficult to formulate a satisfactory analysis of the concept of a law of nature in purely syntactic terms. In some accounts the

condition is weakened to allow nondeductive probability relations between explanans and explanandum. Explanations which lack explicit reference to a law or which contain only a rough and ready generalization have been called "explanation sketches" by Hempel.

47. See Dray's criticism of the model, especially chapters 2–4 of his book. Hempel has replied to Dray in the article reprinted in this volume. See also the article by Brandt and Kim reprinted in this volume for what might be interpreted as a limited defense of the model.

48. For an interesting general defense of the formal condition see May Brodbeck, "Explanation, Prediction, and 'Imperfect' Knowledge."

49. See the article by Davidson reprinted in this volume.

50. See the article by Alexander reprinted in this volume. For critical discussions see Theodore Mischel "Concerning Rational Behavior and Psychoanalytic Explanation" and J. Balmuth, "Psychoanalytic Explanation." For further discussion of an issue between Alexander and Mischel see Norman S. Care, "On Avowing Reasons."

51. See Taylor, *The Explanation of Behavior,* p. 33, and Melden, *Free Action,* p. 114, for examples of this type of argument.

52. Criticism of this form of argument is contained in the article by Davidson. See also Landesman, "The New Dualism in the Philosophy of Mind."

53. See the selections by Dray and Theodore Mischel for this viewpoint. Note also Hempel's reply. A. R. Louch's *Explanation and Human Action* is written entirely from this viewpoint.

54. See the article by Davidson in this volume for this argument.

55. See Davidson's article in this volume for a brief discussion of causality.

56. See the article by Bogen in this volume.

57. See the article by Rawls reprinted in this volume. Also, for a full discussion of the view that explanation itself, like punishment and promising, is an activity structured by rules, a view which is motivated in part by Rawls's account and which provides an interesting contrasting approach to the problem of the logic of explanation, see Theodore Mischel, "Pragmatic Aspects of Explanation."

58. See the article by Diggs reprinted in this volume. That acts should be judged by their consequences is called act or case utilitarianism. That they should be judged by rules which are themselves judged by the consequences of their being generally followed is rule utilitarianism. A spirited defense of act utilitarianism is J. J. C. Smart's *An Outline of a System of Utilitarian Ethics.*

# Part I ~ The General Theory of Action

E. C. TOLMAN

# Behavior, A Molar Phenomenon*[1]

## Prefatory Note

The motives which lead to the assertion of a behaviorism are simple. All that can ever actually be observed in fellow human beings and in the lower animals is behavior. Another organism's private mind, if he have any, can never be got at. And even the supposed ease and obviousness of "looking within" and observing one's own mental processes, directly and at first hand, have proved, when subjected to laboratory control, in large part chimerical; the dictates of "introspection" have been shown over and over again to be artifacts of the particular laboratory in which they were obtained.

The behaviorism here to be presented will contend that mental processes are most usefully to be conceived as but dynamic aspects, or determinants, of behavior. They are functional variables which intermediate in the causal equation between environmental stimuli and initiating physiological states or excitements, on the one side, and final overt behavior, on the other.

Further, it is to be pointed out that although behaviorism exerts an emotional appeal because it appears radical, modern and simple, actually we shall find it recondite, difficult, but, we may hope, scientific.

---

* Chapter I of *Purposive Behavior in Animals and Men* by Edward Chace Tolman. Copyright 1932 by The Century Company. Reprinted by permission of Appleton-Century-Crofts.

## 1. Mentalism vs. Behaviorism

The mentalist is one who assumes that "minds" are essentially streams of "inner happenings." Human beings, he says, "look within" and observe such "inner happenings." And although sub-human organisms cannot thus "look within," or at any rate cannot report the results of any such lookings within, the mentalist supposes that they also have "inner happenings." The task of the animal psychologist is conceived by the mentalist as that of inferring such "inner happenings" from outer behavior; animal psychology is reduced by him to a series of arguments by analogy.

Contrast, now, the thesis of behaviorism. For the behaviorist, "mental processes" are to be identified and defined in terms of the behaviors to which they lead. "Mental processes" are, for the behaviorist, naught but inferred determinants of behavior, which ultimately are deducible from behavior. Behavior and these inferred determinants are both objectively defined types of entity. There is about them, the behaviorist would declare, nothing private or "inside." Organisms, human and sub-human, are biological entities immersed in environments. To these environments they must, by virtue of their physiological needs, adjust. Their "mental processes" are functionally defined aspects determining their adjustments. For the behaviorist all things are open and above-board; for him, animal psychology plays into the hands of human psychology.[2]

## 2. Behaviorisms and Behaviorisms

The general position adopted in this essay will be that of behaviorism, but it will be a behaviorism of a rather special variety, for there are behaviorisms and behaviorisms. Watson, the arch-behaviorist, proposed one brand. But others, particularly Holt, Perry, Singer, de Laguna, Hunter, Weiss, Lashley, and Frost, have since all offered other rather different varieties.[3] No complete analysis and comparison of all these can be attempted. We shall here present merely certain distinctive features as a way of introducing what is to be our own variety.

## 3. Watson: The Molecular Definition

Watson, in most places, seems to describe behavior in terms of simple stimulus-response connections. And these stimuli and these responses he also seems to conceive in relatively immediate physical and physiological terms. Thus, in the first complete statement of his doctrine, he wrote:

> We use the term *stimulus* in psychology as it is used in physiology. Only in psychology we have to extend somewhat the usage of the term. In the psychological laboratory, when we are dealing with relatively simple factors, such as the effect of ether waves of different lengths, the effect of sound waves, etc., and are attempting to isolate their effects upon the adjustment of men, we speak of stimuli. On the other hand, when factors leading to reactions are more complex, as, for example, in the social world, we speak of *situations*. A situation is, of course, upon final analysis, resolvable into a complex group of stimuli. As examples of stimuli we may name such things as rays of light of different wave length; sound waves differing in amplitude, length, phase, and combination; gaseous particles given off in such small diameters that they affect the membrane of the nose; solutions which contain particles of matter of such size that the taste buds are thrown into action; solid objects which affect the skin and mucous membrane; radiant stimuli which call out temperature response; noxious stimuli, such as cutting, pricking, and those injuring tissue generally. Finally, movements of the muscles and activity in the glands themselves serve as stimuli by acting upon the afferent nerve endings in the moving muscles. . . .
>
> In a similar way we employ in psychology the physiological term 'response,' but again we must slightly extend its use. The movements which result from a tap on the patellar tendon, or from stroking the soles of the feet are 'simple' responses which are studied both in physiology and in medicine. In psychology our study, too, is sometimes concerned with simple responses of these types, but more often with several complex responses taking place simultaneously.[4]

It must be noted, however, that along with this definition of behavior in terms of the strict physical and physiological *muscle-twitches* which make it up, Watson was apt to slip in a different and somewhat conflicting notion. Thus, for example, at the end of the quotation just cited he went on to say:

In the latter case [that is, when in psychology our study is with several complex responses taking place simultaneously] we sometimes use the popular term 'act' or adjustment, meaning by that that the whole group of responses is integrated in such a way (instinct or habit) that the individual does something which we have a name for, that is, 'takes food,' 'builds a house,' 'swims,' 'writes a letter,' 'talks.'[5]

Now these "integrated responses" have, perhaps, qualities different from those of the physiological elements which make them up. Indeed, Watson himself seems to suggest such a possibility when he remarks in a footnote to his chapter on "Emotions":

It is perfectly possible for a student of behavior entirely ignorant of the sympathetic nervous system and of the glands and smooth muscles, or even of the central nervous system as a whole, to write a thoroughly comprehensive and accurate study of the emotions—the types, their interrelations with habits, their rôle, etc.[6]

This last statement seems, however, rather to contradict the preceding ones. For, if, as he in those preceding citations contended, the study of behavior concerns nothing "but stimuli as the physicist defines them," and "muscle contraction and gland secretion as the physiologist describes them," it certainly would *not* be possible for a "student of behavior entirely ignorant of the sympathetic nervous system and of the glands and smooth muscles, or even of the central nervous system as a whole, to write a thoroughly comprehensive and accurate study of the emotions."

Again, in his most recent pronouncement,[7] we find Watson making statements such as the following:

Some psychologists seem to have the notion that the behaviorist is interested only in the recording of minute muscular responses. Nothing could be further from the truth. Let me emphasize again that the behaviorist is primarily interested in the behavior of the whole man. From morning to night he watches him perform his daily round of duties. If it is brick-laying, he would like to measure the number of bricks he can lay under different conditions, how long he can go without dropping from fatigue, how long it takes him to learn his trade, whether we can improve his efficiency or get him to do the same amount of work in a less period of time. In other words, the response the behaviorist is interested in is the commonsense answer to the question 'what is he doing and why is he doing it?' Surely with this as a general statement, no one can distort the behaviorist's platform to such an extent that it can be claimed that the behaviorist is merely a muscle physiologist.[8]

These statements emphasize the whole response as contrasted with the physiological elements of such whole responses. In short, our conclusion must be that Watson has in reality dallied with two different notions of behavior, though he himself has not clearly seen how different they are. On the one hand, he has defined behavior in terms of its strict underlying physical and physiological details, i.e., in terms of receptor-process, conductor-process, and effector-process per se. We shall designate this as the *molecular* definition of behavior. And, on the other hand, he has come to recognize, albeit perhaps but dimly, that behavior, as such, is more than and different from the sum of its physiological parts. Behavior, as such, is an "emergent" phenomenon that has descriptive and defining properties of its own.[9] And we shall designate this latter as the *molar* definition of behavior.[10]

## 4. The Molar Definition

It is this second, or molar, conception of behavior that is to be defended in the present treatise. It will be contended by us (if not by Watson) that "behavior-acts," though no doubt in complete one-to-one correspondence with the underlying molecular facts of physics and physiology, have, as "molar" wholes, certain emergent properties of their own. And it is these, the molar properties of behavior-acts, which are of prime interest to us as psychologists. Further, these molar properties of behavior-acts cannot in the present state of our knowledge, i.e., prior to the working-out of many empirical correlations between behavior and its physiological correlates, be known even inferentially from a mere knowledge of the underlying, molecular, facts of physics and physiology. For, just as the properties of a beaker of water are not, prior to experience, in any way envisageable from the properties of individual water molecules, so neither are the properties of a "behavior-act" deducible directly from the properties of the underlying physical and physiological processes which make it up. Behavior as such cannot, at any rate at present, be deduced from a mere enumeration of the muscle twitches, the mere motions *qua* motions, which make it up. It must as yet be studied first hand and for its own sake.

An act *qua* "behavior" has distinctive properties all its own. These are to be identified and described irrespective of whatever muscular, glandular, or neural processes underlie them. These new properties, thus distinctive of molar behavior, are presumably strictly correlated with, and, if you will, dependent upon, physiological motions. But descriptively and per se they are other than those motions.

A rat running a maze; a cat getting out of a puzzle box; a man driving home to dinner; a child hiding from a stranger; a woman doing her washing or gossiping over the telephone; a pupil marking a mental-test sheet; a psychologist reciting a list of nonsense syllables; my friend and I telling one another our thoughts and feelings—*these are behaviors* (qua *molar*). And it must be noted that in mentioning no one of them have we referred to, or, we blush to confess it, for the most part even known, what were the exact muscles and glands, sensory nerves, and motor nerves involved. For these responses somehow had other sufficiently identifying properties of their own.

## 5. Other Proponents of a Molar Definition

It must be noted now further that this molar notion of behavior —this notion that behavior presents characterizable and defining properties of its own, which are other than the properties of the underlying physics and physiology—has been defended by other theorists than ourselves. In particular, acknowledgment must be made to Holt, de Laguna, Weiss, and Kantor.

*Holt:*

The often too materialistically-minded biologist is so fearful of meeting a certain bogy, the 'psyche,' that he hastens to analyze every case of behavior into its component reflexes without venturing first to observe it as a whole.[11]

The phenomena evinced by the integrated organism are no longer merely the excitation of nerve or the twitching of muscle, nor yet the play merely of reflexes touched off by stimuli. These are all present and essential to the phenomena in question, but they are merely components now, for they have been integrated. And this integration of reflex arcs, with all that they involve, into a state of systematic interdependence has produced something that is not merely reflex action. The biological sciences have long recognized this new and further thing, and called it 'behavior.' [12]

*De Laguna:*

The total response initiated by the distance receptor and reinforced by the contact stimulus (e.g., reaching out toward, pecking at, and swallowing) forms a functional unit. The act is a *whole* and is stimulated or inhibited as a whole . . . Where behavior is more complex, we still find a similar relationship.[13]

The functioning of the group [of sensory cells] as a whole, since it is a *functioning,* and not merely a 'chemical discharge' is not in any sense a resultant of the functioning of the separate cells which compose it.[14]

*Weiss:*

The investigation of the internal neural conditions form part of the behaviorist's programme, of course, but the inability to trace the ramifications of any given nervous excitation through the nervous system is no more a restriction on the study of effective stimuli and reactions in the educational, industrial, or social phases of life, than is the physicist's inability to determine just what is going on in the electrolyte of a battery while a current is passing, a limitation that makes research in electricity impossible.[15]

*Kantor:*

Psychologists are attempting to express facts more and more in terms of the complete organism rather than in specific parts (brain, etc.) or isolated functions (neural).[16]

Briefly, psychological organisms, as differentiated from biological organisms, may be considered as a sum of reactions plus their various integrations.[17]

## 6. The Descriptive Properties of Behavior as Molar

Granting, then, that behavior *qua* behavior has descriptive properties of its own, we must next ask just what, in more detail, these identifying properties are.

The first item in answer to this question is to be found in the fact that behavior, which is behavior in our sense, always seems to have the character of getting-to or getting-from a specific goal-object, or goal-situation.[18] The complete identification of any single behavior-act requires, that is, a reference first to some particular goal-object or objects which that act is getting to, or, it may be, getting from, or both. Thus, for example, the rat's behavior of "running the maze" has as its first and perhaps most important identifying feature the fact that it is a getting to food. Similarly, the behavior of Thorndike's kitten in opening the puzzle box would have as its first identifying feature the fact that it is a getting away from the confinement of the box, or, if you will, a getting to the freedom outside. Or, again, the behavior of the psychologist reciting nonsense syllables in the laboratory has as its first descriptive feature the fact that it is a getting to (shall we say) "an offer from another university." Or, finally, the gossiping remarks of my friend and myself have as their first identifying feature a set of gettings to such and such mutual readiness for further behaviors.

As the second descriptive feature of a behavior-act we note the further fact that such a getting to or from is characterized not only by the character of the goal-object and this persistence to or from it, but also by the fact that it always involves a specific pattern of commerce-, intercourse-, engagement-, communion-with such and such intervening means-objects, as the way to get thus to or from.[19]

For example, the rat's running is a getting to food which expresses itself in terms of a specific pattern of running, and of running in some alleys rather than in others. Similarly the behavior of Thorndike's kitten is not merely a getting from the confinement of the box but it is also the exhibition of a specific pattern of biting, chewing, and clawing such and such features of the box. Or, again, the man's behavior is not merely that of getting from his office to his be-wife-ed and be-pantry-ed home; it is also the doing so by means of such and such a specific pattern of commerce with the means-objects—automobile, roads, etc. Or, finally, the psychologist's behavior is not merely that of getting to an offer from another university; but also it is characterized in that it expresses itself as a specific pattern of means-activities or means-object commerces, viz., those of reading aloud and reciting nonsense syllables; of recording the results of these, and a lot of other bosh besides, in a *Protokoll,* and later in a typed manuscript, etc.

As the third descriptive feature of behavior-acts we find that, in the service of such gettings to and from specific goal-objects by means of commerces with such and such means-objects, behavior-acts are to be characterized, also, in terms of a *selectively greater readiness* for *short* (i.e., easy) means activities as against *long* ones. Thus, for example, if a rat is presented with two alternative spatial means-object routes to a given goal-object, one longer and one shorter, he will within limits select the shorter. And so in similar fashion for temporally and gravitationally shorter means-object routes. And what thus holds for rats will hold, no doubt, in similar and even more distinctive fashion for still higher animals and for man. But this is equivalent to saying that this selectiveness towards means-objects and means-routes is relative to the means-end "direction" and "distance" of the goal-object. The animal when presented with alternatives always comes sooner or later to select those only which finally get him to, or from, the given demanded, or to-be-avoided, goal-object or situation and which get him there by the shorter commerce-with routes.

To sum up, the complete descriptive identification of any behavior-act per se requires descriptive statements relative to (a) the goal-object or objects, being got to or from; (b) the specific pattern of commerces with means-objects involved in this getting to or from; and (c) the facts exhibited relative to the selective identification of routes and means-objects as involving short (easy) commerces with means-objects for thus getting to or from.

## 7. Purposive and Cognitive Determinants

But surely any "tough-minded" reader will by now be up in arms. For it is clear that thus to identify behaviors in terms of goal-objects, and patterns of commerces with means-objects as selected short ways to get to or from the goal-objects, is to imply something perilously like purposes and cognitions. And this surely will be offensive to any hard-headed, well-brought-up psychologist of the present day.

And yet, there seems to be no other way out. Behavior as behavior, that is, as molar, *is* purposive and *is* cognitive. These purposes and cognitions are of its immediate descriptive warp and woof. It, no doubt, is strictly and completely dependent upon an underlying manifold of physics and chemistry, but initially and as a matter of first identification, behavior as behavior reeks of purpose and of cognition. And such purposes and such cognitions are just as evident, as we shall see later, if this behavior be that of a rat as if it be that of a human being.[20]

Finally, however, it must nonetheless be emphasized that purposes and cognitions which are thus immediately, immanently,[21] in behavior are wholly objective as to definition. They are defined by characters and relationships which we observe out there in the behavior. We, the observers, watch the behavior of the rat, the cat, or the man, and note its character as a getting to such and such by means of such and such a selected pattern of commerces-with. It is we, the independent neutral observers, who note these perfectly objective characters as immanent in the behavior and have happened to choose the terms *purpose* and *cognition* as generic names for such characters.

## 8. The Objective Definition of Behavior Purposes

Let us consider these immediate dynamic characters which we call purpose and cognition in more detail; we begin with purpose. By way of illustration, take the case of Thorndike's cat. The cat's purpose of getting to the outside, by bursting through the confinement of the box, is simply our name for a quite objective character of his behavior. It is our name for a determinant of the cat's behavior which, it will now appear, is defined in the last analysis by certain facts of learning. Thorndike's description of the actual behavior reads:

> When put into the box the cat would show evident signs of discomfort and of an impulse to escape from confinement. It tries to squeeze through any opening; it claws and bites at the bars of wire; it thrusts its paws out through any opening and claws at everything it reaches; it continues its efforts when it strikes anything loose and shaky; it may claw at things within the box . . . The vigor with which it struggles is extraordinary. For eight or ten minutes it will claw and bite and squeeze incessantly. . . . And gradually all the other non-successful impulses will be stamped out and the particular impulse leading to the successful act will be stamped in by the resulting pleasure, until, after many trials, the cat will, when put in the box, immediately claw the button or loop in a definite way.[22]

We note two significant features in this description: (a) the fact of the behaving organism's readiness to persist through trial and error, and (b) the fact of his tendency on successive occasions to select sooner and sooner the act which gets him out easily and quickly—i.e., the fact of *docility*.[23] And it is these two correlative features which, we shall now declare, define that immediate character which we call the cat's purpose to get to the freedom outside. The doctrine we here contend for is, in short, that wherever a response shows docility relative to some end—wherever a response is ready (a) to break out into trial and error and (b) to select gradually, or suddenly, the more efficient of such trials and errors with respect to getting to that end—such a response expresses and defines something which, for convenience, we name as a purpose. Wherever such a set of facts appears (and where save in the simplest and most rigid tropisms and reflexes does it not?), there we have objectively manifested and defined that which is conveniently called a purpose.

The first clear recognition and pronouncement of this fact that the docility of behavior is an objective definition of something appropriately to be called its purposiveness, we owe to Perry. In an article published in 1918 he wrote:

If the kitten should be excited to effort by the mere appearance of a button in a vertical position; if these efforts should continue until a way was hit upon to turn it horizontally; and if the random efforts should then be replaced by a stable propensity to perform the successful act, then we could say that the kitten was *trying to turn the button*. . . . [i.e., purposing the turning of the button] In order that an organism may be said to act in a certain way because of [by virtue of purposing] a certain result, it is necessary that acts, proving themselves to have a certain result, should derive a tendency to occur from this fact; and that other acts, proving not to have the result, should derive from that fact a tendency to be excluded. It is necessary that acts of the eligible type and of the ineligible type should occur *tentatively*, and then take on a stable or dispositional character according to the result.[24]

Finally, it must be noted that McDougall has also sponsored a seemingly similar doctrine. For he, like Perry (and ourselves), finds that behavior, as such, has distinctive properties of its own, and these distinctive properties he cites as six: (1) "a certain spontaneity of movement"; (2) "the persistence of activity independently of the continuance of the impression which may have initiated it"; (3) "variation of direction of persistent movements"; (4) [the] "coming to an end of the animal's movements as soon as they have brought about a particular kind of change in its situation"; (5) "preparation for the new situation toward the production of which the action contributes"; (6) "some degree of improvement in the effectiveness of behavior, when it is repeated by the animal under similar circumstances." [25] And the first five of these, he says, indicate purpose. McDougall's doctrine also seems, therefore, at least superficially, very similar to ours.

It must be noted, however, that he does not particularly emphasize the sixth character, "some degree of improvement" —i.e., the "docility" of behavior which, as we see it, following Perry, is the crown and significance of the other five.[26]

And one further difference must also be emphasized. For whereas, for Professor Perry and for us, purpose is a purely objectively defined variable, which is defined by the facts of trial and error and of resultant docility; for Professor McDougall, purpose seems to be an introspectively defined subjective 'somewhat,' which is a something other, and more than, the manner in which it appears in behavior; it is a "psychic," "mentalistic" somewhat, behind such objective appearances, and to be known in the last analysis through introspection only. This difference between our point of view and McDougall's is fundamental and implies a *bouleversement complet*.[27]

## 9. The Objective Definition of Behavior Cognitions

Consider, now, the fact of cognition. The docility feature of behavior also objectively defines, we shall declare, certain immediate, immanent characters for which the generic name *cognitions* or *cognition-processes* is appropriate. More specifically, our contention will be that the characteristic patterns of preferred routes and of commerces-with which identify any given behavior-act can be shown to be docile relative to, and may *pari passu* be said cognitively to assert: (a) the character of a goal-object, (b) this goal-object's initial "position" (i.e., direction and distance) relative to actual and possible means-objects, and (c) the characters of the specifically presented means-object as capable of supporting such and such commerces-with. For, if any one of these environmental entities does not prove to be so and so, the given behavior-act will break down and show disruption. It will be followed by subsequent alteration. It is, then, such contingencies in the continuance of any given behavior-act upon environmental characters actually proving to be so and so, which define that act's cognitive aspects.

The fact of these cognitive aspects is readily illustrated in the case of a rat's behavior in the maze. After a rat has once learned a given maze his behavior is a very specific dashing through it. But the continued release upon successive occasions of this same very specific dashing can easily be shown, experimentally, to be contingent upon the environmental facts *actually proving to be so and so.* It is contingent upon the food at the goal-box actually proving to have such and such a character. It is also contingent upon such and such alleys actually proving to be the best and shortest way to that food. And, finally, this dashing is contingent upon these alleys actually being shaped the way they are. For, if any of these environmental facts be unexpectedly changed, i.e., no longer prove to be so and so, this given behavior, this given dashing, will break down. It will exhibit disruption. Its continuing to go off as it does constitutes, then, the objective expression of a set of immediate contingencies. Its continuing to go off as it does asserts that the environmental features have those characters for which such behavior does not break down. And it is such contingencies (assertions) for which the generic name cognitions seems appropriate.

## 10. The Organism as a Whole

The above doctrine that behavior is docile and, as thus docile, purposive and cognitive, also means, it should now be pointed out, that behavior is always an affair of the organism as a whole and not of individual sensory and motor segments going off *in situ,* exclusively and by themselves. For such docilities, as we have illustrated, mean shifts and selections and substitutions among motor responses and among sensory activities often widely distributed throughout the parts of the organism. The readiness to persist can involve wide shifts from one sensory and motor segment to another. Behavior as a type of commerce with the environment can take place only in a whole organism. It does not take place in specific sensory and motor segments, which are insulated and each by itself.

Indeed, this fact that behavior is an adjustment of the whole organism and not a response of isolated sensory and motor segments, going off, each in lonely isolation, can readily be demonstrated for organisms even lower in the scale than rats. Thus, for example, the behavior of crayfish in a simple T-maze led Gilhousen to conclude:

> No definite evidence was found to substantiate *any* doctrine of learning that would conceive it, even in the case of these relatively low animals, as primarily a reënforcement or inhibition of a particular reaction to a given stimulus. As has been illustrated . . . in the analysis of runs, the learning was characterized by continuously *differing* reactions to the maze situation. Intact crayfish which performed in a superior manner did so, *not by reacting invariably to the same specific*

*cues with some invariable reaction,* but, as far as could be observed, by *reacting in properly modified ways to different cues on different trials.*[28]

In this connection, it must be noted that certain behaviorists have tended to take this fact that behavior is of the whole organism as *the* fundamentally distinctive feature of behavior, as molar. For example, Perry, to whom we owe the original emphasis upon the docility of behavior, often tends to emphasize as the one distinctive thing about behavior the fact that it is of the *whole* organism. He writes:

> Psychology [i.e., behaviorism] deals with the grosser facts of organic behavior, and particularly with those external and internal adjustments by which the organism acts as a unit, while physiology deals with the more elementary constituent processes, such as metabolism or the nervous impulse. But in so far as psychology divides the organism it approaches physiology, and in so far as physiology integrates the organism it approaches psychology.[29]

He says further:

> The central feature of this conception of human behavior is that general state of the organism which has been termed a determining tendency. The organism as a whole is for a time preoccupied with a certain task which absorbs its energy and appropriates its mechanisms.[30]

And again:

> In proportion as the organism is unified and functions as a whole its behavior is incapable of being translated into simple reactions correlated severally with external events.[31]

Weiss and de Laguna also emphasize this same point.[32]

It may be noted finally, however, that from the point of view here presented the fact that behavior is of the whole organism seems to be derivative rather than primary. It is a mere corollary of the more fundamental fact that behavior *qua* behavior, as molar, is docile and that successful docility requires mutual interconnections between all the parts of an organism.

## 11. The Initiating Causes and the Three Varieties of Behavior Determinant

We have sought to show that immanent in any behavior there are certain immediate "in-lying" purposes and cognitions. These are functionally defined variables which are the last step in the causal equation determining behavior. They are to be discovered and defined by appropriate experimental devices. They are objective and it is we, the outside observers, who discover—or, if you will, infer or invent—them as immanent in, and determining, behavior. They are the last and most immediate causes of behavior. We call them, therefore, the "immanent determinants."

But these immanent determinants, it must now briefly be pointed out, are in their turn, caused by environmental stimuli and initiating physiological states. Such environmental stimuli and such organic states we designate as the ultimate or "initiating causes" of behavior. The immanent determinants intermediate in the causal equation between the initiating causes and the final resultant behavior.

Further, however, it must now also be made clear that beside the intermediating immanent determinants there are really two other classes of behavior-determinants intervening between stimuli (and the initiating physiological states) and behavior. They are to be designated as "capacities" and "behavior-adjustments." . . . For the present it must suffice to draw attention to the fact of them and to suggest a few preliminary characterizations.

First, as to capacities. It is fairly evident in these days of mental tests and the insistence upon individual and genetic differences that the nature of the finally aroused immanent determinants will themselves on any given occasion be dependent not only upon the characters of the initiating causes—stimuli and physiological states—occurring on that occasion, but also upon the capacities of the individual organism or species of organism in question. Stimuli and initiating states work through capacities to produce the immanent purposive and cognitive determinants and thus the final resulting behavior.

Second, as to behavior-adjustments. It must also be noted that in certain special types of situation it will appear that the immanent purposes and cognitions eventually allowed to function may depend for their characters upon a preliminary arousal in the organism of something to be called behavior-adjustments. Behavior-adjustments constitute our behavioristic substitute for, or definition of, what the mentalists would call conscious awareness and ideas. . . . They are unique organic events which may on certain occasions occur in an organism as a substitute, or surrogate, for actual behavior. And they function to produce some sort of modifications or improvements in what were the organism's initially aroused immanent determinants, such that his final behavior, corresponding to these new modified immanent determinants, is different from what it otherwise would have been.

To sum up. The first initiating causes of behavior are environmental stimuli and initiating physiological states. These operate on or through the behavior-determinants. The behavior-determinants are, it appears further, subdivisible into three classes: (a) immediately "in-lying" objectively defined purposes and cognitions—i.e., the "immanent determinants"; (b) the purposive and cognitive "capacities" of the given individual or species, which mediate the specific immanent determinants as a result of the given stimuli and the given initiating states; (c) "behavior-adjustments," which, under certain special conditions, are produced by the immanent determinants in place of actual overt behavior and which serve to act back upon such immanent determinants, to remould and "correct" the latter and thus finally to produce a new and different overt behavior from that which would otherwise have occurred.

## 12. Recapitulation

Behavior, as such, is a molar phenomenon as contrasted with the molecular phenomena which constitute its underlying physiology. And, as a molar phenomenon, behavior's immediate descriptive properties appear to be those of: getting to or from goal-objects by selecting certain means-object-routes as against others and by exhibiting specific patterns of commerces with these selected means-objects. But these descriptions in terms of gettings to or from, selections of routes and patterns of commerces-with imply and define immediate, immanent purpose and cognition aspects in the behavior. These two aspects of behavior are, however, but objectively and functionally defined entities. They are implicit in the facts of behavior docility. They are defined neither in the last analysis, nor in the first instance, by introspection. They are envisaged as readily in the behavior-acts of the cat and of the rat as in the more refined speech reactions of man. Such purposes and cognitions, such docility, are, obviously, functions of the organism as a whole.[33] Lastly, it has also been pointed out that there are two other classes of behavior-determinants in addition to the immanent determinants, viz., capacities and behavior-adjustments. These also intervene in the equation between stimuli and initiating physiological states on the one side and behavior on the other.

## Notes

1. Much of the argument of the present chapter has already appeared in the following articles:

E. C. Tolman, A new formula for behaviorism, *Psychol. Rev.*, 1922, 29, 44–53.

———, Behaviorism and purpose, *J. Phil.*, 1925, 22, 36–41.

———, A behavioristic theory of ideas, *Psychol. Rev.*, 1926, 5, 352–69.

2. It is obvious that we have oversimplified the views of both "mentalist" and "behaviorist." One ought no doubt to eschew any at-

tempt to envisage progress as a too simple contest between "movements" (cf. E. G. Boring, Psychology for Eclectics, *Psychologies of 1930* [Worcester, Mass., Clark Univ. Press, 1930], pp. 115–127). But the temptation is too great.

3. W. McDougall (Men or Robots, *Psychologies of 1925* [Worcester, Mass., Clark Univ. Press, 1926], p. 277) declares that he was the first to define psychology as the study of behavior. He says: "As long ago as 1905 I began my attempt to remedy this state of affairs [i.e., the inadequacies of an "Idea" psychology] by proposing to define psychology as the positive science of conduct, using the word 'positive' to distinguish it from ethics, the normative science of conduct." Cf. also, his *Psychology, the Study of Behavior* (New York, Henry Holt and Company, 1912), p. 19, "We may then define psychology as the positive science of the behavior of living things." But the credit or discredit for the raising of this definition of psychology to an *ism* must certainly be given to Watson (Psychology as a behaviorist views it, *Psychol. Rev.*, 1913, 20, 158–177; Image and affection in behavior, *J. Philos. Psychol. Sci. Meth.*, 1913, 10, 421–428). For the best analysis and bibliography of the different varieties of behaviorism extant to 1923, see A. A. Roback, *Behaviorism and Psychology* (Cambridge, Mass., Sci.-Art, 1923), pp. 231–242.

4. J. B. Watson, *Psychology from the Standpoint of a Behaviorist* (Philadelphia, J. B. Lippincott Company, 1919), pp. 10 ff. (References same for 1929 edition.)

5. *Op. cit.*, pp. 11 f.

6. *Op. cit.*, p. 195. (Reference for 1929 ed., p. 225.)

7. J. B. Watson, *Behaviorism* (New York, W. W. Norton and Company, rev. ed., 1930).

8. *Op. cit.*, p. 15.

9. For a very clear summary of the various different notions of "emergence" which are now becoming so popular among philosophers see W. McDougall, *Modern Materialism and Emergent Evolution* (New York, D. Van Nostrand Company, Inc., 1929). It should be emphasized, however, that in here designating behavior as having "emergent" properties we are using the term in a descriptive sense only. We are not here aligning ourselves with any philosophical interpretation as to the ultimate philosophical status of such emergents.

"Emergent" behavior phenomena are correlated with physiological phenomena of muscle and gland and sense organ. But descriptively they are different from the latter. Whether they are or are not ultimately in some metaphysical sense completely reducible to the latter we are not here attempting to say.

10. The distinction of molar and molecular behaviorism originates with C. D. Broad (*The Mind and Its Place in Nature* [New York, Harcourt, Brace and Company, 2nd impression, 1929], pp. 616 f.), and was suggested to us by Dr. D. C. Williams (A metaphysical interpretation of behaviorism, Harvard Ph.D. thesis, 1928). Broad intends primarily to distinguish behaviorism which appeals only to *some* gross observable activity, from behaviorism which must appeal to hypothetical processes among the molecules of the brain and nervous system.

11. E. B. Holt, *The Freudian Wish* (New York, Henry Holt and Company, 1915), p. 78.

12. *Op. cit.*, p. 155. The present chapter, as well as most of the subsequent ones, was written before the appearance of Holt's most recent book (*Animal Drive and the Learning Process* [New York, Henry Holt and Company, 1931]).

13. Grace A. de Laguna, *Speech, Its Function and Development* (New Haven, Yale Univ. Press, 1927), pp. 169 f.

14. Grace A. de Laguna, Sensation and perception, *J. Philos. Psychol. Sci. Meth.*, 1916, 13, 617–630, p. 630.

15. A. P. Weiss, The relation between physiological psychology and behavior psychology, *J. Philos. Psychol. Sci. Meth.*, 1919, 16, 626–634, p. 634. Cf. also *A Theoretical Basis of Human Behavior* (Columbus, Ohio, R. G. Adams Company, 1925), esp. chapter VI.

16. J. R. Kantor, The evolution of psychological textbooks since 1912, *Psychol. Bull.*, 1922, 19, 429–442, p. 429.

17. J. R. Kantor, *Principles of Psychology* (New York, Alfred A. Knopf, 1924), I, p. 3.

18. For convenience we shall throughout use the terms *goal* and *end* to cover situations being got away from, as well as for situations being arrived at, i.e., for *termini a quo* as well as for *termini ad quem.*

19. These terms, *commerce-*, *intercourse-*, *engagement-*, *communion-with,* are attempts at describing a peculiar sort of mutual interchange between a behavior-act and the environment which we here have in mind. But for convenience we shall hereafter use for the most part the single term *commerce-with.*

20. McDougall, in his lecture entitled "Men or Robots" (*Psychologies of 1925* [Worcester, Mass., Clark Univ. Press, 1926]), divided all behaviorists into "Strict Behaviorists," "Near Behaviorists," and

"Purposive Behaviorists." He classed the present writer and Professor R. B. Perry in the last group. It is then to Professor McDougall that we owe the title "Purposive Behavior," while it is primarily to Professor Perry (see below) that we are indebted for the original notions both of the immediate purposiveness and of the immediate cognitiveness of behavior.

Finally, it is to be noted that purposiveness and cognitiveness seem to go together, so that if we conceive behavior as purposive we *pari passu* conceive it also as cognitive. This complementary character of purpose and cognition has likewise been emphasized by McDougall (*Modern Materialism and Emergent Evolution* [New York, D. Van Nostrand Company, Inc., 1929], Chapter III); and by Perry, who also points out in some detail that "there is no purpose without cognition" (The cognitive interest and its refinements, *J. Philos.*, 1921, 18, 365–375). And that "all forms of purposive behavior depend on beliefs for the issue" (The independent variability of purpose and belief, *J. Philos.*, 1921, 18, 169–180). See also R. B. Perry, The appeal to reason, *Philos. Rev.*, 1921, 30, 131–169.

21. The term *immanent* is used by us in a purely colorless sense to mean merely directly in behavior.

22. E. L. Thorndike, *Animal Intelligence* (New York, The Macmillan Company, 1911), p. 35 f.

23. Webster defines *docility* as (a) teachableness, docileness; (b) willingness to be taught or trained; submissiveness, tractableness. We use it throughout in the sense of "teachableness."

24. R. B. Perry, Docility and purposiveness, *Psychol. Rev.*, 1918, 25, 1–20, p. 13 f. This emphasis upon the docility of behavior as the definition of its purposiveness (and also of its cognitiveness) has been expanded by Perry in other places, to wit: Purpose as systematic unity, *Monist*, 1917, 27, 352–375; and Purpose as tendency and adaptation, *Philos. Rev.*, 1917, 26, 477–495; A behavioristic view of purpose, *J. Philos.*, 1921, 18, 85–105; The independent variability of purpose and belief, *J. Philos.*, 1921, 18, 169–180; The cognitive interest and its refinements, *J. Philos.*, 1921, 18, 365–375; The appeal to reason, *Philos. Rev.*, 1921, 30, 131–169; and *General Theory of Value* (New York, Longmans, Green & Co., 1926), pp. 288 f.

25. W. McDougall, *Outline of Psychology* (New York, Charles Scribner's Sons, 1923), Chapter II, pp. 44–46; see also his Purposive or mechanical psychology, *Psychol. Rev.*, 1923, 30, 273–288.

26. In this connection it may be remarked parenthetically that we formerly tended to side with McDougall (E. C. Tolman, Instinct and

purpose, *Psychol. Rev.*, 1920, 27, 217–233; also Behaviorism and purpose, *J. Philos.*, 1925, 22, 36–41). That is, we then tended to hold that purpose might be said to inhere in mere trial and error and in mere persistence-until, irrespective of whether or not these tended to produce resultant learning. This seems to us now, however, an error. We have come to accept Professor Perry's *dictum* as to the need of *docility* for a true definition of purpose. It is only because there is implied in the category of trial and error and of persistence-until the further category of a resultant docility that trial and error and persistence-until have the meaning they do. Mere variability of response which involved no resultant selection among the "tries" would not be one's ordinary notion of "trial and error." Nor would mere keeping-on-ness seem a real "persistence-until." It is only when such variations and such persistences have implicit within them the further character of a resultant selection of the more efficient of the tries (i.e., *docility*) that they have their usual significance and are to be said to define purpose.

It should be noted that Singer also seems to hold much the same notion as that presented here of behavior as such and of purpose as one of its most fundamental characters. He says, to cite at random: "The history of my body's behavior reveals a purpose running through its various acts, a purpose quite like that which characterizes my neighbor, my dog, the moth which flutters by me." E. A. Singer, "Mind as behavior," *Studies in Empirical Idealism* (Columbus, Ohio, R. G. Adams Company, 1924), p. 59. See also E. A Singer, On the conscious mind, *J. Philos.*, 1929, 26, 561–575.

27. This was written before the appearance of McDougall's chapter entitled "The Hormic Psychology" in *Psychologies of 1930* (Worcester, Mass., Clark Univ. Press, 1930). In this latter place McDougall seems to deny any necessary connection between his doctrine of purpose and an animism.

28. H. C. Gilhousen, The use of vision and of the antennæ in the learning of crayfish, *Univ. Calif. Publ. Physiol.*, 1929, 7, 73–89. Final italics ours.

29. R. B. Perry, A behavioristic view of purpose, *J. Philos.*, 1921, 18, 85–105, p. 85.

30. R. B. Perry, A behavioristic view of purpose, *J. Philos.*, 1921, 18, 85–105, p. 97.

31. *Op. cit.*, p. 102.

32. A. P. Weiss, *A Theoretical Basis of Human Behavior* (Columbus, Ohio, R. G. Adams Company, 1925), p. 346. G. A. de Laguna,

*Speech, Its Function and Development* (New Haven, Yale Univ. Press, 1927), esp. Chapter VI.

33. It should be noted that both Koffka (*The Growth of the Mind*, 2d ed. rev. [New York, Harcourt, Brace and Company, 1928]) and Mead (A behavioristic account of the significant symbol, *J. Philos.*, 1922, 19, 157–163) have suggested the term *conduct* for much the same thing, it would seem, that we here designate as behavior *qua* behavior, that is, behavior as a molar phenomenon.

A. I. MELDEN

# Action*

We speak not only of the actions of infants, wild beasts, and lunatics but also of the actions of normal human beings in walking, talking, working, and playing. Yet we recognize an important difference between these two groups of cases. Infants, wild beasts, and lunatics may behave in ways that are fortunate or unfortunate to themselves and to others, but nothing done by such individuals is subject to moral criticism of any sort. Moral terms like "right" and "wrong" are appropriately applied only to the actions of normal and relatively mature human beings. In this paper I shall reserve the term "action" for the cases in which what an individual does can be in principle and in the appropriate circumstances the subject of moral review. This restricted usage of the term will enable us to avoid circumlocutions in addressing ourselves to the topic to be discussed: the relation between bodily movements and actions in the present restricted sense. When I perform an action, there is some bodily movement that occurs, but not every bodily movement counts as an action —not even those of normal adult human beings—since there are reflex movements, the activities of those who walk in their sleep, and the behavior of those under hypnosis. Hence it appears as though an action were a bodily movement of a special sort and that we need only specify the distinctive features of bodily movements that count as actions in order to elucidate the concept of

* Reprinted by permission of the author and the editors from *The Philosophical Review*, LXV (1956).

an action. We are inclined, accordingly, to look for certain psychological factors in order to mark off bodily movements that count as actions from all those that do not. I shall argue that the familiar programs of analysis suggested by this approach rest upon fundamental misconceptions concerning the logical features of the concept of an action, and I shall then go on to indicate in outline at least the manner in which the concept of an action is related to that of a bodily movement.

## I

It is difficult to resist the temptation to offer a simple summary formula in explanation of the concept of action, and, frequently, one of the first moves made in this direction is the suggestion that an action is a voluntary bodily movement. This, however, is to forget Aristotle's important reminder that the term "voluntary" does not help, since it is applied to a wide variety of bodily movements and serves only as a blanket term covering far too many different sorts of things.[1] Indeed, Aristotle regards the term "voluntary" as much too wide, since voluntary behavior is encountered in animals and small children who are exempt from moral criticism. And surely Aristotle is correct in rejecting the view that an action is a bodily movement that is chosen or deliberated, for "choice" and "deliberation" do not apply to spur-of-the-moment actions which we call "voluntary" and for which an agent is held responsible. When, for example, the traffic light turns red as I approach in my automobile, I do not in general deliberate and then choose to release the accelerator and apply the brakes. Indeed, most of the actions we perform are done without deliberation or choice. In most cases habits, desires, and impulses prevail—we act as we do as a matter of course, straight off, without reflection or pondering of any kind. But Aristotle's own elucidation of the term "voluntary" is wholly unilluminating; and the view which he seems to hold of the nature of action is less than satisfactory. Behavior is voluntary, he tells us, if "the moving principle is in a man himself." [2] What he means by a moving principle he does not say, and so far the formula adds nothing to the various examples he cites and would mean nothing apart from them. But since Aristotle recognizes that infants and animals who are not responsible for what they do engage in voluntary behavior, even an adequate account of the concept "voluntary" will need to be supplemented by a further condition. As I understand his doctrine, this condition is that there be rational choice; but since not all actions are deliberated and chosen, e.g., spur-of-the-moment or impulsive acts, rational choice is introduced in connection with the formation of the states of character from which such impulsive actions are alleged to spring. We are responsible for impulsive actions since we are responsible for the states of character from which they spring; and we are responsible for such states even though we are not now masters of them, because rational choice was exercised in the actions which led to their formation. Hence an action would seem to be a case of behavior which is voluntary and in which, either in cause or in actual occurrence, there is rational choice.

But not even this will do, if we reflect upon the simple case in which, on the spur of the moment, one stops one's automobile when the traffic light turns red. The attempt to read deliberation and choice into the many cases of which this is only one instance by reference to some earlier choice to obey the relevant law whenever any occasion arises to which it applies is as fanciful as the attempt to discover some original covenant into which each of us has entered before engaging in our normal political dealings or some omnibus choice in favor of morality prior to the acquisition of the moral habits we exhibit in our normal moral affairs. When we do decide to learn to drive an automobile, we do not in general decide, in addition, to obey the traffic laws. For most of us, at any rate, there is no option in favor of such obedience—to learn to drive an automobile is to learn to operate the conveyance as we see it operated in the normal sort of way by stopping at the red light, starting at the green light, and so on. Until such practices have been acquired, there is a failure to operate the automobile with the requisite skill. We can of course imagine cases in which people do learn to drive cars in happy isolation from all traffic regulations, and we can imagine people whose first desire is to operate the controls of a car and who, on learning that there are laws governing its operation in traffic, then decide that they will observe the law; but for most of us, at any rate, it would be far more correct to say that the decision to obey the laws occurs only after we have learned how to obey by repeated practice, and only in those occasional situations in which it is burdensome to obey and on considering briefly whether we should, we then decide after all to do so. There are, therefore, actions in which either in cause or in actual performance no rational choice is involved.

It is the enormous variety of cases that defeats any attempt to provide a summary account of the nature of action in terms of bodily and psychological factors. Some of my actions are deliberate. I weigh alternatives and choose. Some of my actions are done with a motive but without deliberation and choice. When I slam the brakes on as the car ahead of mine suddenly stops, I do so with a motive—in order to avoid a collision—but without the choice I exercise when I consider quickly whether or not to run through the light that has just changed to red and thus risk a traffic fine. Some things I do without any motive. I pass the salt to my dinner companion not in order to please him or with any other motive or purpose in mind, but because I am polite. I act out of politeness rather than for the sake of politeness. Some things I do simply because I want to, or on the spur of the moment, and for no reason at all. If we consider the mental processes attending the relevant bodily movements, we find an enormous variation in what transpires. The cases range from those in which nothing that seems at all relevant happens except the occurrence of the bodily movement—one responds to the situation in which one finds oneself almost automatically, guided as it were by habit and the whole accumulation of past experience—to the cases in which force of mind, great effort, or internal struggles are involved as habit is resisted or passions and temptations conquered (the sorts of cases by reference to which meaning can be given to Plato's expression "the spirited element" and Prichard's term "setting oneself"). The characteristic philosophic vice of generalizing from special cases is involved in the familiar summary explanation of the concept of action in terms of various psychological factors or processes. Perhaps the most frequent instance is the explanation given in terms of motives,[3] in which the preoccupation with the textbook examples of actions performed with ends in view leads the philosopher to ignore the very many sorts of actions in which no end in view is present at all.

There are still other formulae that need to be considered. Shall we say that bodily behavior is a case of action if it is free from compulsion? But animals and infants may move their limbs without compulsion. Indeed, there are internal compulsions that disqualify bodily movements as actions. Further, "compulsion" is as unilluminating as "voluntary." One is compelled by one's conscience (e.g., Luther's "Here I stand and can do no other"), but shall we say that there can be no conscientious action? One is compelled by hunger, but in different ways: the starving man reaches desperately for food, the hungry man steals a loaf of bread, and the man without any livelihood and faced with the prospect of hunger steals in order to avoid it—in all such cases one is compelled, but not in the same sense of the term. We need not multiply cases—what in one sense is compulsion is freedom from compulsion in another. The present formula is as unhelpful as Aristotle's "internal moving principle"; what is common to the great variety of cases that count as action is the verbal formula, and this, apart from a specification of the wide spectrum of cases falling under it, is wholly unilluminating.

When difficulties appear in the attempt to provide an analysis of an apparently categorical statement, the suggestion is often made that contrary-to-fact conditionals will do the trick. So in the present case it may be suggested that an item of bodily behavior is an instance of an action if the agent could have done otherwise, or if the agent could have done otherwise if he had chosen, or even if the agent could have done otherwise if he had chosen and he could have chosen. Here, again, the crucial phrase "could have done" provides us with only the semblance of an explanation. Consider the many different kinds of cases of which it would be true to say that a person could not have done otherwise. The man was insane, subject to compulsive desire, strong temptation, social pressure; or he was misinformed, responding through habit, unthinking, or even bound by conscience. What in one sense a person could have done, in another he could not. So too with "could have chosen." A person could not have chosen to ignore his conscience, but it is correct to say even of those in whom conscience prevails that in some sense they could have chosen to do other than what conscience demanded.

Finally I shall consider another and even more desperate measure. It might be thought that the problem of dealing with the great variety of cases falling under the term "action" could be disposed of in the following way: Instead of taking a simple statement about a physical movement and conjoining with it some psychological statement about a motive, choice, or so on, we might construct a disjunction, each disjunct of which is itself a conjunction of two statements, one reporting bodily movement, the other some psychological factor. Such a proposal would indeed meet the requirement that our account of an action must fit the wide variety of cases; it would fail nonetheless. Suppose one of the disjuncts to contain a statement about the presence of a motive, then any physical movement in respect of which the agent has a motive will count as a moral action. Are we, however, to deny that animals, children, and even those occasional men who are not responsible for their conduct and who are, therefore, not blamed but hospitalized or otherwise confined have motives for their conduct? Consider, too, the fact that an action may be one done impulsively, on the spur of the moment, without reflection, choice, or motive. As far as the psychological phenomena are concerned, there need be nothing to distinguish such actions from those for which no responsibility is incurred by the agent. It is for this reason that the proposed disjunction is unsatisfactory—it will fit the wide variety of cases called "action" only by failing to distinguish such cases from those clearly excluded by the term. This is not to say that it would be impossible in principle to discover a disjunctive formula that would fit all those cases we call "action" and no others. It is perhaps possible that some elaborate disjunctive statement in terms of gross physical movements, the actions of synapses, or even the presence of peculiar feelings could be contrived which would fit action and only action. But such an elaboration, even if it were successful, would be perfectly futile; for it would provide us with a true statement of the conditions present at the time any action occurred, not with an elucidation of the concept.

These are the results with which we are faced: (1) Any formula that fits the wide variety of actions turns out on inspection to be useless because the key term must be employed in a variety of ways. For the bodily movements that count as actions constitute a very complex range or family of cases, not a single group with its characteristic borderline fringe. (2) The attempt to distinguish bodily movements that do, from those that do not, count as actions in terms of occurrent psychological processes is doomed to failure. What passes through my mind as I now act may be anything or nothing; it may be that all that happens is that without anything relevant passing through my mind, I just act.

## II

If one considered the question "What is a chess move?" it is easy to see that each of the kinds of answers considered and rejected in the preceding section will not do at all. It may be, when I move my chess piece during a game, that all that happens is that my fingers push a piece from one square to another. As long as we confine our attention to bodily and psychological processes, there may be nothing to distinguish a chess move from the mere change of position of chess men resulting from an infant's random movements. And, clearly, the appeals to absence of compulsion (but consider the many sorts of moves called "forced"), to "could have beens," "would have beens," and even to the use of elaborate disjunctive functions, such as we considered in the preceding section, would be greeted with amusement. Nevertheless, to make a move in a game of chess is after all to engage in a bodily movement of some sort, so whatever else one is doing in saying that a move was made, is one not saying that a certain bodily movement took place? And, similarly, in the case of other actions, is it not a part of what one is saying, in saying that an action has taken place, that certain relevant movements of fingers, arms or legs, and so on, have occurred? Plausible as this may be, it is in my opinion mistaken.

1. If there were such a so-called descriptive component, then in order that I might know what I was doing in any given case, I would need to know what bodily movements took place, and this I could know only by observing my own movements. But if someone asks me, "Do you know what you have done?" the affirmative answer I give is in no way predicated upon any observation I may have made of my bodily movements. If my answer is in error (I gave the clerk a five, instead of a one, dollar bill), the error is not one of observation. When I do something and know what I am doing, it is not that I observe myself in action, and if I were to watch my arms, legs, and so on as I performed many of the familiar actions in which I engage, I would very likely fumble. But even when I take care in what I do, it is not that I observe my bodily movements and guide them as I would my child's movements as she learns to write, ride

a bicycle, or skate. If someone were to say to me reproachfully, "You did not watch what you were doing" as I drove my car, he would not be reproaching me for failing to observe my bodily movements, nor would he be urging me to watch them if he were to say, "Watch what you are doing!"

2. Consider third-person statements. Unless *A* had engaged in a bodily movement of some sort, he could not have done what he did, and unless I had used my eyes in observing what had gone on, I could not have described his action as I did. But from this it does not follow that in describing *A*'s action I am describing his bodily movements. For there are descriptions and descriptions, the physiologist's descriptions of muscle movements, my descriptions of the movements of arms and legs, and our familiar descriptions of actions—passing the salt hastily, paying one's bill distastefully, and so forth. To say that John paid his bill distastefully is not to say two things, one of which is that his body moved in a certain way, any more than to say the latter is to assert in part at least that such-and-such muscles were brought into operation. And because the latter must be true if his arms and legs moved as they did, it simply does not follow that in offering my description of the bodily movement, I am, among other things, offering a physiological description of what took place. But there is just as much reason for saying this as for saying that a third-person action statement is a blend of diverse things, one of which is a descriptive component about the occurrence of a bodily movement.

The truth is that in saying as we do that *A* paid his bill, performed the castling maneuver, or passed the salt to his companion, we are in no way interested in the minutiae of bodily movements that may have taken place, just as one interested in the movements of arms, legs, and fingers, e.g., a dancer, may be sublimely ignorant of the physiological and biochemical changes that take place. Consider the example of the chess move. One who knows no chess may see only the movements of arms and fingers as odd-shaped objects are moved about on a checkered surface; one who knows the game may see a given offensive or defensive move taking place. The former simply does not know what takes place during the game, and the latter, far from offering a description that overlaps the former's curious description of what takes place, is saying something radically different in character.

3. But suppose a statement describing an action were a blend of diverse items, one being a description of a bodily movement. How must this "descriptive component" be supplemented in order that we may be provided with the force of a statement about an action? It will be apparent that the attempt to provide a supplement by means of another "descriptive" statement, to the effect that the movement is voluntary, chosen, and so forth, must lead to one of two consequences. Either the crucial term (e.g., "voluntary," "chosen," "motivated") is much too restrictive or it is too broad, or if no change in the application of the term "action" is to ensue, a shift must be made in the use of the crucial term (e.g., voluntary) and all of the puzzles about action reappear once more in connection with this new usage. If, however, the supplementation is to be made by means of disguised contrary-to-fact conditionals, the same dilemma faces us in a new guise. It will not do to say, for example, that an action which took place is a certain kind of bodily movement that could have been other than what it was in the sense in which any physical occurrence could have been other than what it was, or in the sense appropriate to the familiar remark that a conscientious agent could not have acted otherwise. The sense of "could have been" required for the present purpose is just that sense involved in saying that the bodily movement counts as an action; but this does not help us.

It should not surprise us in view of these results to encounter even more drastic proposals. It has been agreed that the concept of an action is "fundamentally nondescriptive," [4] and among those to whom this proposal seems only to generate new paradoxes, it would not be unreasonable to expect to find representatives of the indefinability thesis. It would be dangerous to generalize, but the appearance of this familiar triad of theories is due to a familiar mistake—the failure to attend to the relevant context in which expressions have a use. The pattern of thought is as follows: "Actions are happenings. Statements describing actions are true or false. What happens is always some bodily movement and need be nothing more than this. Hence, whatever else a statement about an action may do, it describes such a movement." The underlying mistake is that what occurs when an action is performed can be understood independently of its context and hence need only be a bodily movement. How this is so I want to illustrate by reference to the analogous problem of the nature of a chess move.

## III

Consider the relatively artificial situation in which a chess move is made. Here there is an obvious change of context from the ordinary situation in which conduct occurs. There is little temptation to define a chess move in terms of bodily and psychological phenomena or to argue that the concept is "nondescriptive" or "indefinable." The concept is obviously social in character, logically connected with the concept of rules. How does this connection with the notion of rules enable us to distinguish between the random movements of an infant pushing chess pieces about on a checkered board and the chess moves of players? I want to argue that this distinction is intelligible only by reference to the notion of *following* or *observing* the given rules.

Central to the concept of a rule is the idea of obeying or following it. The notion of disobeying is dependent upon the more fundamental idea of obeying. Infants who push chess pieces about on a chessboard do not disobey or violate the rules of chess—they do not play chess at all. A chess player may violate the rule only after he has learned to obey. Without obedience there can be no disobedience, just as without the telling of the truth there can be no lying. Further, a rule is no mere statement which we can understand independently of the practice that is the obeying or the following of the rule. To understand the rule is to understand the kind of thing that would be obeying it, and it is only because we have followed or obeyed rules that any statement of a new rule, one we have not so far learned to follow, is intelligible. Again, to follow or obey a rule is not to repeat to oneself what the rule requires, reflect upon the situation in which one finds oneself in order to determine that it is one to which the rule applies, and then decide to obey it. Such an account, if it were true, would only serve to create a doubt that the person in question had learned the rule, for at best it could only describe the learner's fumbling, hesitating procedure.[5] Once we have learned the rules, we do not interpret the rule to apply to the given situation and follow this with a decision to obey—we simply obey.[6] And if in any given situation we choose to disobey, such choice is only parasitic upon the general practice in which no choice is exercised at all. Finally, obeying a rule is not something that can occur only once.[7] I do not mean that there may not be such a thing as a new rule which is such that only one occasion arises to which it applies and such that after it has been obeyed only once it is then set aside. If such a case should ever arise, it would happen only because one had already learned what rules were in other situations and in learning these rules had engaged in the practice of obeying them. The point is that to obey a rule is to acquire a custom, habit, practice, and if only one instance suffices, this is owing to the derivative function of habits established with respect to other rules. Again, this is not to say that every instance of acting from habit or custom is a case of obeying a rule. "This is our practice," "this is what we do," need only express the things we do *as a rule*, in general, and through social habit, not the things we do in *following a rule*. Nevertheless, the familiar cases of obeying a rule are the cases in which the agent has acquired a habit, practice, custom—that way of thinking and doing that characterizes the man who knows his way about in situations by following the relevant rules. We need, therefore, to distinguish between the case in which what someone does *accords* with the rule and the case in which someone *follows* the rule. A child may push a piece called "the knight" from one square on a chessboard to another in such a way that what it does accords with the rule governing the piece, but in reporting this fact we need only observe the single item of behavior of the child. In saying of a child that it followed the rule, much more is at stake, namely, the question whether the child has learned the rules of the game (including the one concerning the knight) and in doing so has acquired the specific way of thinking and doing which is the playing of chess.

To attempt to understand a move in a game of chess in terms of bodily and psychological processes occurring at the time the agent makes his move is to leave out what is essential to the move—the fact that what transpires in the way of such occurrent processes is a case of following the rules. Similarly, to attempt to understand the concept of a chess player in terms of occurrent psychological processes, the order of percepts, or some presumed psychical substance is once more to ignore that feature of the agent that consists in the fact that he has learned by repeated doings and hence has acquired the practice of acting as he does. In both cases the circumstances in which the bodily and psychological processes occur are crucial; for what makes the bodily movement a case of a move is the fact that movement of the piece on the board is a case of following a rule, and what makes the agent a chess player is that he has acquired that custom or practice—that way of thinking and doing—that characterizes those who follow the rules of chess. Chess player and chess move are thus correlative notions, and neither can be understood in terms of processes, bodily or psychological, viewed in isolation from the rules that have been learned and the characteristic ways of thinking and doing thereby achieved. Hence it is not that a piece has been pushed from one square to another that constitutes a chess move but that the bodily movement is that of an agent who, during the course of a game, exhibits the characteristic practice in thinking and doing that he has acquired. For someone who does not know what it is to make a move in a game, no report of what transpires at the times the moves were made would make any sense at all, and, observe as he would, such a being would have *no* idea of what was going on. For someone who knew no chess but did know what it was to follow the rules of *some* game, the reports of such activities would be understood only in the most fragmentary way; he might know that a game was being played but would not know what was going on. It is only because we ourselves have acquired that practice of following the rules of chess—the characteristic custom of doing things on a chessboard in a way that we understand because we share it with others who play chess—that the reports of a game are understood by us and recognized as true or false. The significance of the utterances we employ in reporting the activities on a chessboard is thus dependent upon the fact that we share with those involved in these activities the practices, in Wittgenstein's felicitous phrase, the form of life, of those who follow certain rules in the social transaction that is the playing of a game of chess.

Without this practice of obeying the rules, what we see is merely bodily movement. With it, we see this movement as a chess move, for we treat the physical movement made as a move in the play that takes place, and in our doing so, the physical movement that occurs takes on a wholly new aspect. It is because we supply this practical context of acquired skill that we can understand the descriptive accounts of those who report to us the progress of a game; without it such accounts are unintelligible.

All this may be granted; but it will be objected that a chess move is only one very special kind of action. We act in all sorts of ways, even in sweeping the chessmen off the board, thus bringing the play to an abrupt end. With this I should certainly agree, but the case of the chess move is nonetheless important, for the very artificiality of the example may serve to remind us of what is too easily forgotten in the case of other types of action, namely, the crucial importance of the practical context of common or shared practices involved in following rules, applying criteria, observing principles, acting on policies, and so on. Actions do constitute a whole family of cases, but in various respects this practical context is essential to an understanding of the distinction between a bodily movement and an action.

## IV

Consider some of the things we commonly do: we purchase food, drive automobiles, play, work, help and hinder our fellows. In all such activities, we have learned by imitating or following the instructions of others in obeying rules, employing criteria, following policies in the practices in which we engage. Thus in purchasing food our selection is guided by criteria for excellence, ripeness, and so on, and in paying for the items selected, our behavior is guided by various criteria and rules governing the use of currency. We act in such instances without reflection precisely because we have acquired the requisite skills. Or consider the enormously complex set of practices acquired by those driving their automobiles through traffic, responding to a variety of cues—the condition of the road surface, the sound of the motor, the presence of pedestrians and vehicles blocking the way, the signals of other motorists, the road signs, the traffic lights, and the instructions of the traffic police. In this complex set of practices we may recognize the observance of the rules, the application of criteria, the response to instructions, the following of policies of safe, economical, or efficient driving, and so on. These practices are supplemented by other complicating and even supervening practices. One may drive an automobile in order to make up one's mind whether to purchase it or in order to test it, and throughout one will be guided in general in one's thinking and doing by the observance of moral rules and principles. It is not that there are practices and practices, each independent of the other, so that at one time one is driving an automobile, at another making a purchase, at another responding to the moral requirements of the situation. It is rather that we have a blending of the practices we have acquired, in the activities in which we engage, where various practices are themselves affected by the general practice of observing moral rules and principles. It is this ability to carry out a complex and organized set of practices in which throughout the agent is guided without reflection by moral rules that marks the achievement of responsibility. Even in the relatively artificial case of a chess move, what takes place when the move is made has to be understood in terms of the practice of observing not only the rules of chess but also those of good conduct and good manners, for these are involved in the agent's way of thinking and doing.

It is equally important to bear in mind the enormous difference between the permissive rules of chess and the prescriptive and justifying rules of morality, between the justification of the rules of traffic and the justification of the rules of morality, between the inevitable conflicts of rules (and the resulting exceptions) in the field of morality and the occasional predicament that may arise when the ill-formed rules of a game are discovered to be in conflict. Understanding a moral rule does involve understanding the kind of cases which may be excepted, but there cannot be any exception to the rules governing the movement of the knight in chess. These differences are so important that it is misleading to speak of the term "rule" as univocal.

One more comment on important differences: If I do not play chess, I shall not understand what a chess player does as his fingers push a piece from one square to another, but if I do not drive a car, it does not follow that I am incapable of knowing what someone at the wheel is doing when I see his arm pulling at the handbrake. Here we need to recall the reference made earlier to the derivative effects of the mastery of rules in order to see that this difference, important as it is, is no objection to the general contention. For the practices we share with others need not coincide precisely, indeed they cannot if there is to be diversity in the activities of individuals, but there must be enough similarity between the practices involved in different activities in order to allow for an understanding of one kind of activity which derives from the practice involved in another. Where there is no such similarity, as in the case of one who has never seen or heard of any game or as in the case of a bushman who has never seen or heard of machines of any sort, there is no understanding of what is being done, no matter how carefully attention is paid by such individuals to the bodily movements of agents when they engage, respectively, in games of chess or in the driving of automobiles.[8]

It is impossible within the limits of this paper to guard against all of the misunderstandings to which the analogy I wish to draw between chess moves and other actions may give rise. Briefly, I am maintaining that just as in the case of the concept of a chess move, so in the case of the concept of any action the context of practices in which rules are obeyed, criteria employed, policies are observed—a way of thinking and doing—is essential to the understanding of the difference between such bodily movements and actions. Just as this way of thinking and doing marks in the one case the chess player, so it marks in the other the responsible agent, one who has acquired a complex of practices, among others the practice of observing moral rules and principles. The concepts "action" and "moral agent" or "person" are thus correlative.[9] Because we share so largely in our ways of thinking and doing, because in particular we are guided by moral rules and principles, we treat each other's bodily movements as actions, items of behavior for which the agent is responsible. Just as we supply a background of skills in understanding the bodily behavior of those engaged in playing chess, so we supply a complex background of skills in which rules are obeyed, criteria are employed, policies are observed, and so on, in understanding each other's behavior as action. This practical context—our common form of life—is crucial to our understanding. Without it we notice only bodily movements, and with it we see actions as we observe each other's behavior. Without it we employ the cool language of those who like coroners and physiologists are concerned to describe and explain bodily movements and effects, and with it we are enabled to participate in the use of discourse by which we impute responsibility to individuals when we treat them as persons or moral agents and their bodily movements as actions.

But this, it will be objected, is in effect to succumb to the philosophic vice of generalizing from very special cases—those actions performed in the social arena for which agents may be praised or blamed, such as cheating or dealing honestly in making purchases and driving with care or with unconcern for the safety of others. The very language employed for such conduct implies that the individuals referred to or treated are responsible moral agents and subject to praise or blame for what they do. But there are other cases of action, surely, with respect to which a specifically moral way of thinking and doing, the practice of observing moral rules, seems altogether out of bounds, so that the alleged correlativity of the terms "moral agent" and "person" is only evidence of unrestrained generalization from very special cases. My concluding remarks are directed at this objection.

In order to understand the concept of an action, we need to see how sentences in which typical action verbs are employed are used. Admittedly there is no single use. Some sentences are employed in praising or blaming (e.g., "*He* did it" uttered accusingly or "He *did* it" uttered exultingly by one watching a heroic rescue). Some sentences are employed with a view to determining whether blame is appropriate but where no blaming may actually occur (as in the hearings held in courts or during legislative fact-finding inquiries). Again, we may speak of actions where no verdict is anticipated, moral or legal. If my wife relates to me the various things she saw my neighbor doing, she might do so with a view to supporting the low opinion in which she holds him, but, equally, she may do so in order to make conversation or because she knows me to have a friendly interest in my neighbor's activities. And in giving me this information or in describing to me how he behaved, is she not speaking of just the sort of thing for which in appropriate circumstances any neighbor *can* be praised or blamed, action in the present sense of the term? For consider the remarks appropriate to such employments by my wife of sentences about the activities of my neighbor: "What on earth is he up to?" "I hope he will not leave the hole there; children may fall into it and hurt themselves," and so on. In reporting or describing as she does the actions of my neighbor, my wife does *not* employ the neutral language of those concerned to relate or describe bodily movements. It is rather to treat the bodily movements that did occur as behavior of a responsible agent, to impute to him not only the practices of those who have learned by imitation, following instructions, and so forth the ways in which tools are employed and activities of various sorts conducted but also the general practice of attending to the interests and well-being of others. If we consider the remarks appropriate to such employments of action sentences and contrast them with those appropriate to the behavior of lunatics, infants, and wild animals, it becomes clear that such normal uses of action sentences risk defeat on two quite distinct grounds: First, on learning that the individual engaged in the observed bodily movements is not responsible or morally competent and second, on learning that the alleged bodily movements did not occur (e.g., it was really someone else). For in such normal uses of action sentences, we ascribe responsibility to the individuals in question by treating the bodily behavior as action, and this we do by viewing it against the background of a set of practices, among others the practice of observing moral rules and principles. In short, we impute to the individual our common moral form of life.

There are cases, of course, in which sentences are employed in describing the behavior of our fellows and in which there is no ascription of responsibility. I have already mentioned the language of coroners and physiologists, in which a position of neutrality is taken with respect to the responsibility of the individual. But in what sorts of cases of an admittedly responsible agent would the question of common practices including that of observing moral rules be irrelevant? Would it be a case in which the individual raises his arm? But in that case we must not describe what the individual does as signaling, saluting, leading others in physical exercise drill, and so on. For these descriptions at once bring us within the social arena in which common forms of life have been achieved and by reference to which action statements can be understood and bodily movements treated as actions. No, we shall even have to deny that in raising his arm the individual was even pretending to engage in these activities, exercising, following the instructions of his physician, and so on. We shall have to rest content with the statement that he was simply raising his arm and never mind any further queries. But in that case, when the individual raises his arm what happens is that a bodily movement, not an action, occurs.

## Notes

1. *Nicomachean Ethics*, bk. III.

2. 1110a. The translation is by Sir David Ross.

3. See the latest instance in P. H. Nowell-Smith, *Ethics* (London, 1954), p. 114.

4. Cf. H. L. A. Hart, "The Ascription of Responsibility and Rights," in *Proceedings of the Aristotelian Society* (1948–1949). Although Hart does not discuss the relation between action and bodily movement, he seems to regard the term "descriptive" as properly applicable to bodily movements.

5. Compare this account of obeying a rule with Prichard's account in "Duty and Ignorance of Fact," of coming to "know" that one has a duty. It is small wonder that in Prichard's account every claim that one has obeyed the rule is only problematical.

6. See Wittgenstein's profoundly illuminating remarks in *Philosophical Investigations* on obeying rules, especially in § 219, "When I obey a rule, I do not choose, I obey *blindly*."

7. Cf. Wittgenstein, *op. cit.*, § 199.

8. It is for this reason that anthropologists often need to enter into the practices of primitive tribes in order to understand their activities, their language—in short, their culture.

9. Locke wisely rejects any attempt to define "person" in terms of ideas and an underlying immaterial substance. The concept, he tells us, is forensic and applies "only to intelligent agents capable of a law" and hence "concerned and accountable" (*Essay,* bk. II, ch. xxvii, sec. 26). It is this same correlativity of voluntary bodily behavior (i.e., action) and moral agent that leads Aristotle to remark about the individual whose unfortunate action was done by reason of ignorance that the terms "voluntary" and "involuntary" should not be applied to him in the event he does not repent, since such a being is a different sort of man and "should have a name of his own" (*Nicomachean Ethics,* 1110b).

D. W. HAMLYN

# Causality and Human Behaviour*

I do not think that any argument could be produced to show that it is impossible, in *any* sense of the word 'cause', for human actions to be caused. Nor do I think that the attempt to produce such an argument would be in any way an interesting philosophical exercise. It could hardly have any bearing on any further philosophical thesis, and would scarcely do much to cast light upon our concept of cause, if we have such a single concept. It is undoubtedly quite proper to ask what caused a man to do the things that he did, and equally proper to expect an answer. A thesis which is sometimes maintained in this connexion is that it is permissible to speak of the causes of a man's actions only when those actions are in some way abnormal—when, for example, they are involuntary or irrational. At other times, it is said, we speak of the man's reasons for what he did, and reasons are not causes. This is a thesis which has some appearance of being illuminating, and it is one to which in the past I have been inclined to give allegiance. Yet, we can undoubtedly ask what caused a man to act from a certain reason, and we can in principle say much about the causal conditions under which a man can act in the way in which he does, whatever be his reasons. The truth is, I think, that our tendency to ask for the causes of behaviour which is abnormal rather than normal, irrational rather

* Main paper of the symposium "Causality and Human Behaviour" in *Proceedings of the Aristotelian Society,* SV 38 (1964). Reprinted by permission of the author and the Editor of The Aristotelian Society.

than rational, is a function of the circumstances in which we demand explanations in this sphere, rather than indicative of something about the concept of cause. That is to say that since we find the actions which a man does voluntarily and from reason intelligible, we are naturally disposed to ask for the causes of behaviour which is the reverse of this. Nothing is implied by this about whether it is appropriate to speak, in any sense of the word 'cause', of the causes of normal, rational and voluntary behaviour. It is a function of what is often spoken of as 'causal explanation'—the fact that we explain phenomena by reference to causes when they deviate from some rule or law, a rule which is provided in the context of behaviour by what is normal. If there is an asymmetry in respect of our invocation of the concept of cause between normal and abnormal behaviour, it is an asymmetry due to the fact that it is normal, intelligent behaviour which we find intelligible, and not the reverse. That is not to say that there are no differences between the giving of reasons and the invocation of causes; it is to say that the latter cannot, without further argument, be limited to one sphere of behaviour.

If, then, there is to be a philosophically interesting and tenable thesis about the limitations of causality in respect of human behaviour, it must be a more precise and restricted thesis than that so far discussed. One possible thesis of this kind would be that no theory of behaviour can be produced which is expressible in physical terms of a more or less mechanical sort, or perhaps in psychological terms where the psychological theory in question is akin to one of a mechanical kind. It is not altogether clear, however, what this last would be, common enough though the conception has been, at any rate in the psychology of the past, if not the present. The conceivability of a physical theory of this sort may seem acceptable, since even if the physiological theory by reference to which explanations are given of bodily movement in general and muscular movement in particular may not be strictly mechanical, it is feasible to think of it in those terms.

And it might be held that behaviour just is bodily movement. The same is not true of any psychological theory. It is not sufficient to characterize such a view as one according to which psychological events are necessary and/or sufficient conditions of behaviour. It is quite possible for the occurrence of a certain state of mind, *e.g.*, an intention, to be a necessary condition of being properly said to have performed a certain action, *e.g.*, voting, without it being implied that the state of mind is the cause of the action. It is merely that it makes no sense to speak of an action of this kind being performed without there being at least some intention. It seems doubtful whether any state of mind could be, by itself, a sufficient condition of an action being performed, but, if it could be, it need not be the cause of the action. Whatever else is meant by 'cause', and the term may mean many things, it means more than necessary or sufficient condition.

It may be that light can be cast on this matter by considering the contexts in which the question whether human behaviour can be caused is naturally raised. One common context of this sort is provided by the problem of the freedom of the will and the question is discussed accordingly.[1] It is in fact by no means clear what relevance the thesis that behaviour cannot be caused has to that issue. Its possible relevance could come only through the supposal that the thesis that behaviour *can* be caused amounts to a form of determinism. Even so, it is by no means evident that it has any real relevance here (and I myself am still inclined to believe that it has none). Furthermore, the situation is often confused by the introduction of the issue whether the performance of *e.g.*, raising one's arm is mediated by some inner process, *e.g.*, willing. It is, in other words, asked whether in order to raise my arm I have to go through some inner process, akin to lever-pressing, which contributes to the operation of raising my arm. One argument used against this supposition is that it generates an infinite regress, since it then seems necessary to ask what further process again mediates the act of willing. The regress might indeed be blocked by insisting that the inner process is not of the kind which requires mediation. But while this issue may be of interest for its own sake, it is not strictly relevant to the determinism question; for there the appropriate matter to raise is whether actions can be caused by inner occurrences, not by inner performances, and to introduce the latter issue must inevitably be something of a red herring.

The same sort of considerations arise in a more complicated fashion if the problem is considered in another context—that of the body-mind problem. Here the situation is more complicated because, while it is conventional to speak of the body-mind problem, it is by no means clear that the criteria of mentality are single. That is to say that it is by no means evident that all those things which are spoken of as mental are alike; consider, for example, intentions, decisions, judgments, images and feelings. There may be some principle of unity here in that they may all be characterized as modifications of consciousness (where 'modification' is used in the sense common in 17th century Rationalism, meaning that they all depend for their existence on the existence of consciousness). Nevertheless, it may be better to speak of a cluster of mind-body problems unified in this way by the reference to consciousness, so that the fundamental issues stem from the division between what is conscious and what is not. When mind-body theories such as interactionism have been put forward, it has perhaps never been really clear what is supposed to interact with what—or what is supposed to cause what. Interactionists have commonly supported their view by the consideration that we can by forming an intention bring about certain bodily movements; but this is quite a different matter from the consideration that when we are, for example, worried, certain bodily effects are liable to occur. If we are concerned, in this issue, with the problem of the connexion, if any, between mental and bodily *events*, it is irrelevant to consider anything that *we do;* and *vice versa.*

Apart from considerations about mental events and acts, there are also problems about the notion of behaviour itself. The question whether behaviour may be said to be caused in any interesting sense (either in that it can be brought within a complete and uniform theory of physiology and bodily movement, or in that there is required in addition mental items linked to physiological events by links analogous to those which link physiological events themselves) cannot be decided until it is clear whether the concept of behaviour belongs on the mental or bodily side of the divide. My belief, as I shall indicate, is that there are good reasons for putting it on the mental side, implying that some modification of consciousness is presupposed in behaviour. If this is so, then anything that counts as action, anything that we *as persons* do, must be similarly conceived. In this respect, the bodily is that which needs no reference to *persons*, and its universe of discourse is restricted to that which simply occurs. It is nevertheless plausible to maintain that epiphenomenalism remains a possible thesis, in the sense that, as far as bodily movement is concerned, physiological theory is complete in principle, and that states of mind are, *qua events,* products of physiological processes. One reason for this belief is that while it seems fairly obvious that certain mental events—feelings, even the occurrence of images—may be set up by bodily stimulation of one kind or another, the reverse process does not occur. That is to say that mental *events* as such cannot be said to cause bodily occurrences, except where they occur in the context of intentions, wants, *etc.* The occurrence of a certain feeling could be said to have caused a man to do something only given some story about his intentions, wants etc. I shall insist in what follows on the quasi-Cartesian point that the rationale for the mind-body connexion is obscure; but the obscurity of the connexion between bodily stimulations and sensations is of a different order from that between intention [and] bodily movement. In the former case we have a causal connexion which admits no further explanation; in the latter case the whole idea that the connexion may be causal seems at fault. These points add up to the one from which

I started this discussion: Is the idea that it is possible to invoke a psychological theory of action or even bodily movement which is akin to a mechanical one really intelligible? That forming an intention can lead to certain bodily movements is, on the other hand, a very obvious point—but not a point which in any way implies the existence of causality.

Is it possible to produce, in principle, a uniform theory of physiology and bodily movement which will cover behaviour? One possible argument here is one which I used myself some ten years ago, but which I now think invalid.[2] This is to the effect that the bodily movements which may be involved in different instances of any one action may be at least indefinitely various. Hence any reference to a given action is tantamount to a reference to an indefinite disjunction of bodily movements. Hence again, whereas the causal processes underlying the bodily movements constituting any one instance of the action on a given occasion can be given, there are no causes of action as such. But such an argument could not show of itself that there are no causes of action; for similar situations arise elsewhere, even in physics, where a concept is 'open-textured' or indefinite in application. The motions of a physical body, for example, may be due to an indefinite range of movements of particles; this would not be reason for saying that its motion was not caused. Furthermore, it may be admitted that the movements of the body which constitute an action on one specific occasion may be explained in terms of their causes. What the argument seems to show is that the concept of action cannot be reduced to that of bodily movement. But if this is so, is it merely because the bodily movements involved in the performance of a certain action are indefinitely various, or is it for some further underlying reason? It is, I think, the latter.

The point which stands out about the explanation of behaviour and action is that the set of concepts in terms of which such explanations are naturally given is radically different from that in terms of which bodily movements are to be explained.[3] And here it is worth noting that when bodily movements are spoken of in this context, what is meant is those bodily movements which simply occur, not those which are *made* by the person in question. When someone makes a bodily movement, it is always true to say that a movement of the body occurs, although of course the reverse connexion does not always hold. But making a movement is really an instance of behaviour, and our explanations of such a movement would naturally be in terms of the person's intentions, reasons, purposes and so on, not in terms of the causal processes underlying the movements of the body which may be said to occur. It seems plausible to say that the set of concepts which surround those of action and behaviour, and in terms of which action and behaviour are to be explained, is radically different from any appropriate to the explanation of bodily movements *simpliciter*—the mechanism of nervous reaction to stimuli, of muscle contractions *etc.* Another way of putting the matter would be to say that while there are independent theories of action and bodily movement respectively, with their own peculiar logical characteristics, there is no allover theory into which they can both be fitted. Moreover, there is no prospect in practice of formulating bridging laws which will connect the two theories. This is in part due to the indefiniteness of application of behaviour concepts, but it is also due to the fact that, in the case of many actions at least, an intention is essential if the action is to be said to be performed at all (as I suggested earlier about voting). Hence, there is no possibility in these cases of formulating a principle to the effect that when certain bodily movements occur within a certain range then an action of a certain kind may be said to be performed. The range of muscle and limb movements which may be involved in punching someone on the jaw is indefinite, though presumably limited. But the same movements may be involved in an epileptic fit or simply in waving one's arm around with the accidental result of a hit on someone else's jaw. In such circumstances, what occurs can scarcely be treated as a punch on the jaw.

A possible objection to this point is that made by Williams in the Postscript to *Freedom and the Will.* This is to the effect that the claim that bridging laws are impossible here ignores the fact that it may be possible to connect descriptions of an action with descriptions of the total bodily situation, including what is happening in the brain. That is to say that it should be in principle possible to establish connexions between the total state of a man's body on a given occasion and what he is doing. This may be so, and if it is the case then empirical connexions will be establishable between the two theories—that of behaviour and that of the total physiological set-up. Nevertheless, there seems no prospect of these connexions being more than empirical; there is still no possibility of an all-over theory. (This is indeed a special version of the difficulties involved in the idea of a uniform theory of body-mind phenomena.) Yet, while this seems *prima facie* so, it is less easy to say why it must be so.

Among the necessary conditions of a set of bodily movements being counted as an action must be included the condition that the movements in question must fall within a limited range which constitutes the norm of the action. This point has been emphasised by Peters, and has been offered as the reason why the all-over theory in question is impossible.[4] Not *any* set of movements may be counted as an instance of any given action. This logical feature, however, is not peculiar to action. Nor is it peculiar to action that the norms in question may be conventional in nature. Social norms limit the possible variations in movement or nature which can be exhibited by anything which has essentially a social function. It is a simple empirical fact that horses cannot fly; it is not a simple empirical fact that cars cannot fly, for cars have an essential social rôle which limits the movements which they can make while still remaining cars. Similar things may be said about specific actions, such as crossing a road or signing a contract. It is not just an empirical fact that you cannot sign a contract with *any* set of movements of your hand; the range of possible movements is restricted by the conventions which govern contract-signing. But it is clear that the limitations on the possibilities here are significant only within the context of intentions. It is only if a man has some intention of signing a contract that there are limitations on the movements which he can significantly exhibit. It is here that the crucial point lies.

We are thus back again at the connexion between action and intention. Some actions presuppose actual intentions and, more important as will be indicated, an understanding of the notion of intention is a general prerequisite of an understanding of that of action. Once we begin to think of a man in terms of action or behaviour we involve ourselves in a conceptual scheme quite distinct from that in terms of which we conceive his physiological make-up. Intentions, reasons and purposes presuppose some awareness or consciousness on the part of the subject. The fact that awareness can be properly so called only if it is right, and that being right entails having reached the appropriate standard, means that is here, if anywhere, that it is relevant to mention standards or norms. The notion of intention could have arisen only for creatures within whose scheme of concepts that of a standard has a place. Given this and other features of the conceptual scheme which involves the notions of intention and action, it must be clear that the relation which we conceive as existing between action and intention is nothing like that between muscular movement and brain-state; and it is this which makes a unified conceptual scheme impossible.

It might still be held, however, that an intention might be simply correlated with or even identified with some state of the brain. Then, just as the brain-state might be said to be the cause of the bodily movements which follow, so the intention might be said to be the cause of those movements which we interpret, given the concept of intention in general and the concept of the specific intention in particular, as an action of a certain sort. In such circumstances we should be left merely with the problem of the exact connexion between the state of mind which is the intention and the brain-state—an orthodox body-mind problem. Otherwise the causal chain is complete.

One argument which has been used against the possibility of intentions being the causes of *actions* is that used by A. I. Melden in his *Free Action,* and it is an argument which is of interest for its bearings on the present question. Melden indeed employs the argument quite generally in connexion with motives, desires, decisions, *etc.* It is the argument to the effect that intentions cannot be said to be causes of action, since, in principle, no description of an intention can be given which is independent of the description of the action which is said to be its effect. That is to say, for example, that the only description which can be given of the intention to go for a walk is that it is just that intention. Thus there is an internal connexion between the intention and the action, and there cannot be a causal connexion between things which are internally related; for, if Hume showed anything at all, it was that the causal relation is a contingent one. This, as was ably pointed out by Rogers Albritton (in lectures on this subject given in London during 1963) is a form of what Quine calls 'essentialism'. It is to maintain that intentions are essentially the intentions to do certain things and can be characterized in no other way. The situation and a possible response to it can be put in another way as follows[5]:—To say that no independent description of the intention can be given is to say that there is an internal connexion between the concepts of intention and related action. But it by no means follows that where two concepts are internally related the things to which the two concepts may be applied cannot be contingently related. Thus, although the intention to write a letter can be described only as that intention, whatever goes on in the mind when the person has that intention might, *for that matter,* be represented as the cause of writing the letter—provided, of course, that anything does go on in the mind.

Sometimes it does seem possible to identify what goes on in the mind in these circumstances, if it is only, for example, that the person in question says to himself, "I will write a letter." Might not saying these words to oneself be the cause of the letter writing? Of course, anyone who knew that the person had said to himself, "I will write a letter" would not thereby necessarily know that the person had formed an intention. The words might have been said just to see how they sounded. For someone to have an intention, it is necessary, apart from anything else, that he should have the concept of something as an end or reason for action. However, when a man forms an intention to write a letter, he may, though he need not, express the intention to himself; he may say to himself, "I will write a letter." Nothing in Melden's argument shows that it is impermissible to say that his saying these words to himself caused him to write the letter. Indeed in many situations it would be very natural to say this, given that we understand the context. It may be admitted that if we interpret the man's saying these words to himself as the formation of an intention, then the intention itself, *qua* intention, can be defined only in terms of its object. On the other hand, what goes on in the man's mind is separately describable in terms of what he says to himself; and we are thus not forced, as Melden claims, to accept indefinable states of mind if we insist on causality here. It is a further question how we come by our concept of intention at all, but this question is not relevant to the present issue.

It might be objected that this does not justify the claim that the intention itself may be said to be the cause of the man's writing the letter. Yet, since the occurrence of the inner utterance happens on this occasion to be what goes on in the man's mind in forming the intention, and since the inner utterance is interpretable as the forming of an intention to write a letter, it seems quite permissible to say that the forming of the intention is the cause of the letter-writing; for this assertion may be understood in the terms which I have just outlined. Similar things might be said of having an intention, as well as forming an intention. And certainly it seems reasonable to say that my decision to write this paper was one of the contributory causes of my putting down the words which I have written. Whether this point has any long-termed interest is something which may well be doubted; for, in terms of the issues as I have presented them, the crux lies in the *connexion* between what goes on in the mind in having or forming an intention and the subsequent *bodily movements.*[6]

There can surely be no objection, on Melden's principle, to the assertion that intentions may be the cause of the bodily movements that follow. One consideration is that it seems possible to say that actions themselves are the causes of those movements. The fact that intention and action are internally connected makes it then possible to say that the intention may be the cause of the movements. The relation between action and movements is *prima facie* a contingent one, since, given that an action occurs, there is no necessity that any specific set of movements should occur. In many ways, however, this too is an uninteresting point. If intentions can be said to cause bodily movements only because the action which is the object of the intention causes the bodily movements to occur, no real light is cast upon the question of the possible connexion between intention and movement, or even upon that whether there is any such connexion. A further objection may be made as follows. First, performing an action cannot be said to *be* causing certain movements to occur. It has often been pointed out that my moving my arm is not the same as my causing certain muscle movements to occur, although when I move my arm certain muscle movements do occur. The criterion of identity of the action is given by the intention, and when I move my arm my intention is certainly not to bring about certain muscle movements, even if these are the result of my moving my arm. The thesis that the criterion of identity of an action is given by the intention is not one that can be maintained without qualification, for there are, of course, unintentional actions. Yet, even in these latter cases, the action which I in fact perform must be one which I could have intended, and where this is not so, we are inclined to say that the person concerned did not *do* the action in question. There is an oddity, however, about saying that the movements of my muscles are the unintended consequences of my moving my arm. This may be partly because in a certain sense the moving of the arm is a consequence of the muscle movements. But the real point is that, strictly speaking, the muscle movements are not consequences of my action at all, or are so only in the sense in which when I draw a square on the blackboard one consequence is that I draw lines on the blackboard. To say, furthermore, that the muscle movements are the *effects* of my moving my arm is even more extraordinary, since it is clear that in an important sense my action is not something that occurs independently of the movements, although it can certainly be described independently of a description of them.[7]

Yet, even if this consideration misfires, it still remains *conceivable,* on Melden's principle, that intentions should be regarded as the causes of bodily movements, and the same applies to volitions, decisions, wants *etc.* For, there is certainly no necessary connexion between *e.g.*, a decision to act in a certain way and the subsequent occurrence of any one set of movements. Yet, while the denial of a contingent relation between sets of events is enough to rule out causality, the acceptance of such a relation is not enough to substantiate causality. We should be inclined indeed to say that the occurrence of certain bodily movements was the result or consequence of a certain decision, rather than its effect. The reason for this is that we cannot see the *connexion* between the two; they do not form a unity intelligible in terms of any further model. Once again there is no unified conceptual scheme available, as there is in different ways between decision and action on the one hand and movement and physiological processes on the other.

It may be objected that whether or not such a unified theory can be provided, a physiological theory of bodily movement in human-beings is not complete. Given what we already know about physiology in general and neurology in particular, there would be a *prima facie* case for supposing such a theory to be complete in principle, unless anything about human action gave reason for a contrary view. This is equivalent to the question whether human-beings are in any way to be regarded as machines. That they are different in one respect is obvious; for human-beings are conscious, while machines, presumably, are not. The vital question is whether this makes any difference of importance, and it is to this question which I must now turn.

Some philosophers would maintain that the possession of consciousness by human-beings makes it possible for them to do things which no machine can do. Machines, of course, have to be programmed to do whatever they in fact do; but this is irrelevant to the present issue, since it is a feasible suggestion that human-beings can significantly be said to be programmed—by nature or by God.[8] Programming should be left out of consideration here. Now in a certain sense the possession of consciousness does make it possible for human-beings to do things which machines can never do, *i.e.*, those things which essentially involve consciousness. No mere machine could do such things as avoiding pain or taking pleasure in aesthetic objects, as long as it was non-conscious. This seems evident enough. If a non-conscious being appears to be indulging in activities which are essentially conscious or which essentially involve consciousness, this must be set down as appearance only and spoken of accordingly.

This point has, however, wider ramifications. If action and behaviour in general involve consciousness essentially in any way, then a non-conscious machine could not be said to act at all, properly speaking. If we speak of such machines doing various things, the word 'do' ought really to be in inverted commas. Granted that many of the things which human-beings do are done unconsciously, out of habit or unintentionally, the actions in question must be seen against those which are done intentionally, with some degree of awareness of what one is doing. A necessary condition, that is, of applying the concept of action and related concepts to anything is in general that the thing in question must be conscious. That is to say that it must at least be capable of doing things knowing what it is doing. While, therefore, not every action or item of behaviour is in itself essentially conscious, whatever may be said to act must in general be conscious. On the assumption that machines are not conscious they cannot be said to act in the proper sense. That is not to say that they perform what are merely analogues of human actions; it is to say that they do not act at all, whatever be the complexity of the movements which they produce and however much these look like actions. (And nothing, I suggest, in principle prevents them looking just like actions in all cases and in all respects.)

It might be said that this makes the whole business trivial and artificial. We have to talk in one way if the thing in front of us is conscious and in another way if it is not, and that is all there is to it. In a certain sense, that is indeed all there is to it, but it is scarcely a trivial matter. The possibility of a whole way of thought, the applicability of a whole set of concepts, with all its implications, is not a trivial matter. It can scarcely be said to be trivial even that some things are conscious while others are not, for this clearly makes a crucial division between things in the world. And whatever else be the case, we ought to behave towards conscious things differently in some respects from the way in which we behave towards non-conscious things, *e.g.*, in trying, in general, to avoid causing pain (although this raises a whole host of philosophical problems in its train, *e.g.*, about the importance of pain). However, when I said that it is a general necessary condition of applying to anything the conceptual scheme which centres round the concept of action that the thing in question should be conscious, I omitted to make an important qualification which was implicit but by no means explicit. The point is that not just any kind of consciousness will do. A creature which is conscious in the sense that it is a creature which is sensuous need not be said to act, even if its body exhibits movements which have the appearance of action. What is required is that specific kind of consciousness which is involved in being aware of what one is doing without, to use Miss Anscombe's not altogether happy phrase, observation. The knowledge in question must be practical. As I said earlier, to have an intention, it is at least necessary that one should have the concept of something as an end or reason for action.

It is not, therefore, right just to say that a condition of the application to anything of the scheme of concepts including that of action is that the thing must be conscious; for the thing in question must be capable of being conscious of what it is *doing*. To put the matter in a Pickwickian way, something can perform an action or do something only if it can know what it is doing. It is of no use, for example, to say that the thing in question need only be aware of the movements of its body; for we can be aware of movements of our body without acting, and we can act without being aware of any movements of our body. To act we must be able to be aware of ourselves *as acting*. It is not as if action just was bodily movement, the only condition being that we are not entitled to apply the concept to anything that is not conscious. The condition that the subject of action must be conscious is not an extrinsic condition, and hence is not one that can in any circumstances be dropped. It is for this reason that the concept of action must, if it is to be set on one side or other of the mental/physical fence, be set on the mental side of the fence. There are indeed purely mental actions, such as judging and considering. As far as the concept of action is concerned, bodily movements enter the picture of necessity only as providing those public criteria for the intelligibility of the concept upon which Wittgenstein rightly insisted. Just as we should have no proper justification for thinking that we have a concept of pain if there were no public expressions of pain, so we should have no justification for claiming a concept of action unless there were public expressions of action. Pain, however, is not identical with its expression; neither is action identical with bodily movement.

What this means is that we cannot stand in front of a machine and say, "Alas! Poor thing, it looks as if it is performing actions, but it is not. If only it were conscious!" We might as well say, "It looks as if it were conscious, but it is not. If only it were performing actions." Action and practical consciousness do not provide independent criteria for each other. We have, as indicated, public concepts of both, and their applicability in an objective way rests on the fact that we have ends to which action and intention are appropriate. For, just as there must be, as Wittgenstein insisted, agreement in judgments as well as in concepts if language is to have a purchase, so there must be some agreement over ends if practical thought is to have a purchase.[9] Given this, the only justification for attributing either to anything is that thing's similarity to ourselves. (I do not say that the only justification for *my* attributing them to anything else *but me* rests on this, for we have granted that the concepts in question are public concepts; hence, in speaking in this way at all, we presuppose already some interpersonal relations between conscious beings, *i.e.*, we presuppose a human society. The problems begin when we go beyond this, *e.g.* to animals. This differentiates what I have said from at least some versions of the traditional argument from analogy for other minds.)

Given this in turn, the question is how far the similarity must go. Anything that can act publicly must exhibit movement, and movement of some degree of complexity and plasticity; this at least is a necessary condition. But is anything else necessary? Does anything depend on what we are made of? It would clearly *make sense* to suppose that a machine made of wires, relays and transistors might be conscious in the relevant sense, but equally it might in fact only be manifesting all the appearances of consciousness in its movements without in fact being conscious. It is difficult to see how the problem could be solved except in the pragmatic way of saying that it would in practice make no difference how we decided.* (We cannot take the same line about ourselves, for, as indicated earlier, the present problem can arise only on the presupposition that we are conscious. But it can arise for any new creature which we come across which is sufficiently like us in some ways and unlike us in others. Science-fiction writers please note—although they have surely noted already.)

If all this is true, while consciousness is conceptually necessary for action, it need not be causally necessary for the production of any bodily movement or set of bodily movements whatever. In the circumstances, it is difficult to see what *a priori* argument to the contrary could be produced; for the lack of an all-over theory of body-mind phenomena prohibits it. Human behaviour has a causal underpinning but is not itself caused in any sense which has further ramifications of an interesting philosophical kind. For, even if intentions and the like may on occasion be said to be causes of bodily movements, this has no bearing on the question whether a physiological theory of bodily movement can be complete. My conclusion is that modifications of consciousness need not be considered as extra pieces of mechanism in our make-up. This is not the rôle which they play. To that extent, if epiphenomenalism can be interpreted as the theory that modifications of consciousness have of themselves no causal efficacy, epiphenomenalism remains a possible and even plausible thesis.

A final objection to this point of view would be that there is another and more plausible account of the relationship between physiological occurrences and states of consciousness. This is the view espoused by J. J. C. Smart, following U. T. Place[10]—that states of consciousness are strictly identical with brain processes. (Some form of parallelism is a further alternative, but not one,

* 1967. I now think that this is a very wrong thing to have said. Whether or not a thing is conscious, whether, for example, it can experience pain, clearly affects the issue of how we should behave towards it.

I think, which is ultimately intelligible.) The situation, it is said, is similar to the philosophically familar case of the morning and evening stars, which are in fact identical. There is, however, one important difference between the two cases—one in the conditions for making a justifiable identity statement. In the case of the morning and evening stars, we are entitled to make the identity statement because we know that there is a way of giving a separate identification of that which satisfies both descriptions, *i.e.*, Venus. There is nothing like this in the case of mental and bodily phenomena, nor is it easy to see how there could be such. If, therefore, it is a necessary condition of making a *justified* identity statement that the possibility exists of an independent identification of that which is said to possess both characteristics, it may make sense to suppose mental and bodily phenomena to be identical, but there could never be any justification for supposing them to be so in fact, as long as the condition remains unsatisfied. Moreover, as the condition has all the appearance of remaining unsatisfied necessarily, since one cannot conceive what such an independent identification might be in this case, it is scarcely plausible to characterize the identity theory as a scientific hypothesis, as Place, though not Smart, does.

Whatever other objections to this theory there may be, what I have said may be enough to suggest that it is more plausible to accept the slightly less radical thesis that epiphenomenalism provides. Smart holds that the identity theory is preferable on the grounds of parsimony and simplicity, since there is no other way of deciding between the two theories. On the other hand, it seems to me that the onus in this case is on anyone who holds that two such *prima facie* different things as physiological processes and states of consciousness are identical to prove his case. And this, I suggest, is just what cannot be done. Yet, whatever relation is accepted as holding between the two, it must be accepted that it is between *these* that the relation holds, and not between states of consciousness and action. For, these last two are fundamentally on the same side of the fence.

## Notes

1. *E.g.*, by A. I. Melden in his *Free Action* and by the contributors to the broadcast talks edited by D. F. Pears under the title *Freedom and the Will.*

2. In my article "Behaviour", *Philosophy* 1953, p. 135. The argument has in effect been re-invoked by P. F. Strawson in *Freedom and the Will,* pp. 64, 66.

3. *Cf.* Strawson again, *op. cit:,* p. 64.

4. R. S. Peters, *The Concept of Motivation,* pp. 5 ff.

5. Here and in many other places in this paper I owe much to discussion with Mr. G. C. Madell.

6. Melden, *op. cit.,* p. 16, says that he is concerned with the sense of the word 'cause' which is either the Humean sense, or if that is thought inadequate, the sense which is employed in physics or physiology. But what this sense is he does not elucidate. This is one of the defects of his treatment.

7. *Cf.* Melden, *op. cit.,* p. 85.

8. *Cf.* the articles by J. J. C. Smart and Ninian Smart, *Analysis,* April 1959.

9. *Cf.* also A. P. Griffiths, "On Belief", *P.A.S.* 1962/3.

10. J. J. C. Smart, "Sensations and Brain Processes", *Phil. Rev.* 1959; U. T. Place, "Is Consciousness a Brain Process?", *Brit. J. Psych.* 1956.

JOHN R. SILBER

# Human Action and the Language of Volitions*

Such phrases as 'acts of will', 'acts of volition', 'the act of a will' and 'he willed to do *x*', *etc.* have been interdicted by contemporary English philosophers. We have all been warned by Ryle that "the language of 'volitions' is the language of the para-mechanical theory of mind," and that if "a theorist speaks without qualms of 'volitions' or 'acts of will', no further evidence is needed in order to show that he swallows whole the dogma that a mind is a secondary field of special causes." [1] Since it is sometimes difficult to make clear the presence and intensity of one's qualms, many of us simply avoid phrases that might lead others to suspect us of holding the exorcised dogma.

In defence of the language of 'volitions', however, I wish in this paper to make two points: First, I shall show that the language of 'volitions' often conveys useful information without implying the acceptance by its users of metaphysical doctrines to which Ryle objects and that the assumption that the use of such language implies the acceptance of these doctrines is based on a mistaken and dogmatic view of the way language is to be interpreted. In the second place, and more importantly, I shall argue by means of an examination of human action that we need the

* Reprinted from *Proceedings of the Aristotelian Society,* NXV 64 (1964), by permission of the author and the Editor of the Aristotelian Society.

"language of 'volitions' ", at least some of it, in order to preserve in language the objective interiority and objective subjectivity of action and the moral perspective on it.

In order to avoid pointless misunderstanding let me state that I stoutly reject, without arguing the issue here, any theoretical separation of mind and body and any causal interpretation of their interrelation. On these issues I am in essential agreement with Ryle.

## I

When we speak of acts of volition we are not necessarily speaking of volition's acts or will's acts. Few indeed are the philosophers who have meant any such thing. In the phrase 'acts of volition' the use of the genitive is normally adjectival and not possessive; philosophers betray the shakiness either of their grammar or their intuitive grasp of the English language if they think that phrases of the form '*x* of *y*' necessarily or usually mean '*y*'s *x*'. When we speak of a robe of many colours, a house of seven gables, or acts of volition, we are not thinking of many colours' robe, seven-gables' house, or volition's acts. We are thinking rather of a many-coloured robe, a seven-gabled house, and volitional acts.

A similar point can be made regarding the phrase 'acts of will'. It need not and often has not been used to mean 'will's acts'. Usually it has meant either 'willed acts' or 'wilful acts'. Many persons whose command of English is exemplary might fail to distinguish between wilful and willed acts; yet others with equal mastery of the language might think that willed acts are intentional and voluntary while wilful acts are deliberate in addition to being intentional and voluntary. But persons who make this distinction might be totally unable to show the difference between 'intentional' and 'deliberate' such that an act might be one and not the other. They might even conclude that they were speaking pleonastically—a habit, not always without value or attraction, of some of the ablest English poets, novelists, rhetoricians, and philosophers.

But many a philosopher is prone to assume that whenever he hears a phrase like 'act of will' he has encountered a speaker who is clearly in need of his tutelage: the speaker must have hypostatized the concept of will since he has attributed agency to it. But unless he assumes that the genitive must be construed possessively he has no basis for finding fault with the speaker.

Suppose the philosopher asks the speaker, "When you said 'Lincoln's assassination was an act of will' did you mean that it was a wilful deed or that it was the act of *a* will?" The speaker replies, "I meant it was the act of a will." The philosopher, sure of his quarry now, asks, "Have you read *The Concept of Mind*?" But again the philosopher has concluded too hastily that the speaker has hypostatized 'will'. The speaker may have used the word 'will' in order to say emphatically that the act was the act of a person *as a person* and in order to contrast this act with those acts of persons that seem absent-minded, superficial, amenable to behaviouristic description, *etc.* And if the philosopher asks, "Well, if you meant 'person' when you said 'will' why did you confuse the issue by talking about the act of a will?", the speaker may reply, "Because I didn't mean 'person'. The word 'person' has been watered down too much. When a drunk asks for a hand-out we call that the act of a person, but Booth's act in killing Lincoln was nothing like that. His involvement was thorough and deep and introverted, and I wanted to emphasize this by saying his act was the act of a *will.*"

We may not particularly care for the speaker's choice of words, and we may think that philosophers like Kant and Strawson have adequately compensated for any watering of the meaning of the word 'person'; nevertheless, we cannot accuse the speaker of having hypostatized 'will'. Even his substantival use of the term does not imply that he thinks of will as some para-mechanical entity standing behind a person to make him do what he does.

There would seem to be, therefore, no philosophical objection to the employment of at least some of the language of 'volitions', unless philosophers feel empowered to dictate matters of style. But I should have thought that it is not the place of the philosopher to become either a philosophical Fowler of the Queen's English or a Fowler of the Queen's philosophical English. If my supposition is correct, then at least some of the language of 'volitions' will have to be acceptable, even if it is not preferred, usage.

## II

The more important question, however, is whether there are positive philosophical grounds for retaining the language of 'volitions'. An examination of action and of the language used to describe actions will provide this justification. Perhaps I should observe that although I am interested in the language used to describe actions, I am interested only in so far as the language helps to reveal the character of actions themselves. It might be necessary, moreover, to modify the language of action in order to convey linguistically the character of action.

But is it possible to separate actions from the verbal descriptions of them? In "A Plea for Excuses" J. L. Austin finds actions and descriptions of actions in something of a tangle. One reason why we have so much difficulty in deciding on the excuse we should use when we do something wrong is, says Austin, "because we do not take the trouble to state explicitly *what* is being excused. To do so," he adds, "is all the more vital because it is in principle always open to us, along various lines, to describe or refer to 'what I did' in so many different ways." [2] Apparently we have as much or perhaps more latitude in describing or referring to actions than we have in describing or referring to stable objects, such as houses, and stones: we are at liberty to proceed in a variety of ways according to our interests and points of view.

In describing a house, for example, a painter may note merely that the house is of brick with incidental wooden trim, twenty-five openings with twelve lights per sash, wood in firm condition, and old paint tight. Additional detail would be superfluous to a painter estimating the cost of painting the exterior. An estate agents' description, by contrast, may be full of almost empty words and phrases—a stately, elegant house in a substantial neighbourhood, *etc.* A better real estate description might include the number of rooms, total floor space, the architectural style if there were any, and the plot size. A legal description would disclose the network of legal claims upon and immunities enjoyed by the named owners of the property, state whether it was freehold or leasehold, and define its location by reference to a name or number on a surveyor's plan in some public office.

All of these descriptions and many others could be given of any one house. But the latitude of approach, while giving rise inevitably to partial descriptions distorted by perspective and interest, is not a licence for falsification. Finite descriptions can be true or false, and all true descriptions must be compatible—that is, they must be attributable without logical contradiction or factual conflict to the same house. And except for tendentious descriptions of the sort given by the real estate agent of our example, which often reveal more of the agent than the house, there are facts to confirm or discredit all descriptions.[3]

The possibility of describing an object in various ways that are all nonetheless ascribable to the object is not limited to houses; this condition is present in the description of plants, animals, people, scientific objects, *etc.*, and it seems to derive more from the nature of symbolic communication and truth than from the nature of the things described. Clearly the possibility of giving various descriptions attributable to one object is not a special problem encountered when we try to describe actions.

But Austin insists that "there are many special problems in

the particular case of 'actions'," and in support of this claim he says:

> Should we say, are we saying, that he took her money, or that he robbed her? That he knocked a ball into a hole, or that he sank a putt? That he said 'Done', or that he accepted an offer? How far, that is, are the motives, intentions and conventions to be a part of the description of actions? And more especially here, what is *an* or *one* or *the* action? For we can generally split up what might be named as one action in several distinct ways, into different *stretches* or *phases* or *stages*. Stages have already been mentioned: we can dismantle the machinery of the act, and describe (and excuse) separately the intelligence, the appreciation, the planning, the decision, the execution and so forth. Phases are rather different: we can say that he painted a picture or fought a campaign, or else we can say that first he laid on this stroke of paint and then that, first he fought this action and then that. Stretches are different again: a single term descriptive of what he did may be made to cover either a smaller or a larger stretch of events, those excluded by the narrower description being then called 'consequences' or 'results' or 'effects' or the like of his act.[4]

It is difficult, however, to find in this elaboration, or elsewhere in "A Plea for Excuses," any clearly formulated support for Austin's claim that there are special problems in the description of actions. His three pairs of descriptions pose many interesting problems, but the problems are unique to the description of actions only with respect to vocabulary. An object, such as a house, is characterized by legal conventions just as the action of knocking a ball into a hole is characterized by the conventions of golf. If I have clear and undisputed title in fee simple to a house, I cannot truly deny that the house is of freehold tenure; likewise, if I knock a ball into a hole while playing golf, I cannot truly deny that I have sunk a putt. In both cases, conventions must be part of any complete description of the object or action. We may generalize as follows: Conventions characterize some objects and actions; when this situation obtains conventions must be part of the complete description of such objects and actions; when conventions are a part of complete descriptions, they cannot be truthfully denied although actions or objects can be truthfully though partially described without reference to conventions.

Intentions and motives, unlike conventions, cannot be part of the description of things other than agents, actions or the products of actions. Whenever we attempt to describe something we must select our terms from a vocabulary appropriate to that which we are trying to describe; houses are not characterized by motives or intentions nor are actions by roofs or windows, and the terms of our descriptions of them must reflect these facts. But inasmuch as the problem of vocabulary selection is not peculiar to the description of actions, it cannot be the special problem to which Austin referred when he asked, "How far are motives, intentions and conventions to be a part of the description of actions?" Nor does this seem to be a special problem. In line with our generalization concerning conventions we hold: If an action is structured in part by motives and intentions, then a complete description of it must include motives and intentions as a part; partial descriptions of the action may be given without reference to motives or intentions provided none of the partial descriptions implies the absence of motive or intention in the action. We have, once again, the latitude to describe actions according to a variety of purposes and from a variety of perspectives, but we are still bound by the conditions that all true descriptions must be compatible, and that no true description can be denied.

We seem able, thus far, to resist the view that describing actions presents a special problem not found in describing generally and to maintain the distinction between the language used to describe objects and actions and the objects and actions themselves which provide the basis for judging the adequacy of descriptions.[5] Perhaps a special and insuperable problem for maintaining this position is encountered, however, when Austin asks: "What is *an* or *one* or *the* action? For we can generally split up what might be called one action in several distinct ways, into different stretches or phases or stages."

What precisely is Austin saying here? Does he suggest that when we describe an action in terms of various stages and phases and different stretches that we are at liberty to deny the unity of "what might be named one action"? Is he suggesting that there is no single action in reality to which our various descriptions refer but only a non-defined "what" that might, or might not, be named one action? Is his point that when we describe an action in terms of phases and stages, *etc.*, that we split—not the action, which may never have existed as a unity—but rather the *what* (that might be *named* one action) into parts that can function as independent descriptions, parts that are no longer dependent for their meaning and truth upon the possibility of their compatible attribution along with other descriptions to a single action? Is he proposing, in short, that the splitting of actions into phases and stages is not like describing either the parts of a house or the entire house from limited perspectives, but is rather like pulling down the house and giving independent descriptions of the materials that went into it?

If we take seriously Austin's choice of words—and how dare we do otherwise?—we must answer these questions affirmatively, for he says that in splitting the "what" into stages "we can dismantle the machinery of the act" and describe "separately" the planning, the decision, the execution, *etc.* In splitting the action into phases we can say that "he painted a picture" or that "he laid on this stroke of paint and then that." And in stretches a single term can be made to describe as one action a range of "events" that might also be described as the consequences or effects of an action. Nor is one word said by Austin to indicate that there is any limit imposed by the nature of actions on the way we can split up and describe them! Although Austin, in discussing his method, accepts the general proposition that "words are not facts or things" and that we must judge the adequacy of our words by considering them separate from but in relation to unnamed facts, he gives no indication of what the real characteristics of action are such that they may limit and give cognitive significance to our linguistic treatment of them.

That this position, which Austin seems to hold,[6] is untenable can be demonstrated by showing that the splitting up of actions into meaningful phases, stages and stretches is not possible unless there is a prior unity of action, real and not merely verbal, to be divided, and by showing the way in which the character of actions themselves set limits upon our division of them.

Unless there is real unity to the action of painting a picture, for example, there cannot be even a limited description of a phase of that action such as "he laid on this stroke of paint and then that." Admittedly, we can supply spatio-temporal co-ordinates for the event described by this phrase. But these are co-ordinates of the phase as an *event* but not as an act of painting. The description is merely that of an event unless and until it is understood as a partial description of an action to which descriptions of the painter's motives, intentions, and plans also refer. Only when it is recognized that the strokes of paint are laid down in the course of a temporally extended effort to objectify the painter's aesthetic interests do they take on the character of action and become a partial description of the action of painting the picture. Unless the phase is interpreted in light of the objective subjectivity of the painter, it cannot be described as an action. But once it is understood in the light of the painter's concerns, it is no longer a discrete event but merely a partial description of the action of painting the picture. Once the interior perspective of the painter is added, the spatio-temporal discreteness of the phase is compromised by its involvement in the creative process.

It is likewise self-refuting to suppose that we can *dismantle* the *machinery* of action into stages or *split* it by a variety of stretches.[7] The points just made to show the dependence of phases on a unitary conception of the act of which they are a part can be applied, *mutatis mutandis,* to prove that stages and stretches are similarly dependent. Further evidence of the conceptual and organic interdependence of the stages, phases and stretches of actions can be provided by means of the description and analysis of an action. By means of this examination we may also expose those characteristics of action which require the use of the language of 'volitions'.

## III

In light of the historical events of April 14th and 15th, 1865, in Washington, D.C., we should all agree that each of the following statements is a truthful answer to the question "What did Booth do?" [8]

1. He entered the State Box at Ford's Theater.
2. He aimed his gun at Lincoln.
3. He pulled the trigger.
4. He shot Lincoln.
5. He shot Lincoln at close range.
6. He shot Lincoln in the back of the head.
7. He deliberately shot Lincoln.
8. He leaped from the box to the stage of the theatre.
9. He broke his leg.
10. He mounted a horse and rode to Virginia.
11. He killed Lincoln.
12. He assassinated Lincoln.

If we were to deny the truth of any one of these twelve statements, we should thereby deny one or more of the facts of history. But are we committed to the view that Booth performed twelve different actions in connexion with his assassination of Lincoln? We could expand the list of descriptions until it numbered several hundred, but did Booth complete several hundred different actions? Although each of the twelve descriptions is a partial one, they vary considerably in scope and detail.

Does any one of them have the right scope to reveal one action to which it and all the other descriptions may be attributed? Can we answer the question "What did Booth really do?" in any simple, straightforward and yet accurate way?

If we examine the list of descriptions for logical interconnexions, we find surprisingly few. Either 5 or 6 or 7 implies 4, but 4 does not imply any other. Statements 11 and 12 could be true even if statements 1 through 10 were false. 12 could be false even if all of the others were true.[9] Statement 12, "He assassinated Lincoln," will be shown to be the central description, yet it is not implied by any one or by all of the other eleven, and it implies only 11. I think this exhausts the logical entailments between these twelve statements.

If there is any unity of action in this example, clearly it is not a logical unity: although all twelve descriptions are true and although all are partial descriptions of the activity of one man over a very short period of time, they are, with the very few noted exceptions, truth-functionally independent. The bond of action is not a logical one.

The interconnexion of these descriptions is not substantially increased, moreover, if we trace out all entailments that can be made with the aid of logic assisted by all the knowledge of science and common sense. Perhaps we could deduce 12 from 7 and 11; perhaps 2 from any one of 4, 5, 6 or 7. The descriptions still seem radically discrete.

We begin to get our first insight into the unity of these descriptions when we examine their positions in time and supplement our observer's view of them with the agent's point of view. The statements are already arranged so far as possible in the order of their commencement. Thus Booth entered the box before he aimed, aimed before he fired, fired before he shot Lincoln, leaped to the stage before he broke his leg, and rode to Virginia before Lincoln died. We can specify the precise moments at which Booth entered the box, aimed, and fired; the precise moments at which he leaped to the stage, broke his leg, mounted his horse, and crossed the Virginia state line. We can state precisely how long he remained in the box and in the saddle. On these points the facts are compelling; our descriptions and the ordering of them must conform to the facts.

But when was Lincoln shot? If by 'shot' we mean merely 'struck with a bullet', we can give the temporal co-ordinates for 4, 5 and 6. But by that definition shooting is not an action but only an effect of the firing of a gun. If instead of asking for the temporal co-ordinates of 4, 5, and 6 (which would appear to be identical) and 7,[10] we ask, At what time could we truly state 4, 5, 6, and 7?, we find that we should have to wait for the outcome of the flight of the bullet. Real time might be treated as an independent variable in the description of a sound house since a sound house is virtually impervious to time; but in the description of actions it is a constitutive element, because action has genuine duration and does not take on its fully determinate character except in the fullness of its time.[11] When the bullet struck Lincoln in the back of the head 4, 5, 6 and 7 could be truly asserted. Had the bullet struck Lincoln elsewhere, 6 would be false, and had the bullet missed him, none of them would be true in any literal sense.[12]

Although we stated that 4, 5 and 6 have the same temporal co-ordinates, we did not specify what they were. We know the moment at which 4, 5, and 6 could be truly asserted, but at what time did Booth shoot Lincoln? Are aiming and pulling a trigger part of shooting? Clearly they are. We find, therefore, that 4, 5, and 6 describe extended activity that includes within its duration the activity described by 2 and 3. Does this show the arbitrariness of our descriptions and their almost fiction-like independence from facts? On the contrary. Our actual experience of entering a room reveals the short duration of that action just as our experience of aiming and firing while thoroughly engaged in shooting reveals the inclusive duration of shooting. And the experience of shooting someone deliberately reveals an even greater duration and more complex interweaving of elements: in such an experience even the action of opening a door is contained within and coloured by the intent to complete the shooting, which has already been partially planned and is in process of execution. The concrete and highly complex experience of the enduring unity of shooting quickly disproves the view that the unity of action might be merely verbal and assigned according to convenience.[13]

Temporal co-ordinates can also be supplied for 8, 9, and 10. But 9 does not describe an action; it is rather a description of a consequence of 8. Here is a clear instance in which facts set limits to the stretch of a description. Description 8 cannot be stretched so as to include 9, nor can an alternative description achieve this stretch, because 8 describes an action in which the event described by 9 was neither the intended, desired, nor anticipated consequence. Their separateness is a far more obstinate fact than their interconnexion. Actually, 9 does not belong in a list of actions at all. A natural answer to the question, What did Booth do? is, He broke his leg. But the verb 'break' is ambiguous in ordinary usage; whether I break my leg purposely to collect insurance or accidentally by leaping, I can truthfully, and normally would, say "I broke my leg"; in the former case the breaking was a deliberate action, whereas in the latter it was an accidental occurrence. In 9 'broke' is used in the latter sense; hence, 9 should be removed from the list.

In the examination of 10 and 12[14] we confront once again the constitutive rôle played by time in the determination of action. 12 could not be asserted truly until several hours following the truthful assertion of 10. Booth had his leg set and was resting in Virginia before Lincoln died, and only thereafter could it be truly said that he assassinated Lincoln. Do we want, then, to say that Booth did not murder Lincoln until after he reached Virginia? Of course not. And this absurdity can be avoided if we recognize that the stretch of an action is determined in large part by the character of the action as seen and enacted by the agent. Once Booth leaped from the box he was done with the assassination of Lincoln. Thereafter his thought, purpose, intention, and movement—his action—was to escape and, curiously enough, to secure the public acclaim that he thought was his due and would be his reward when he arrived in Virginia. 10 describes an action right enough, but the action described is a distinct action rather than a stage or phase in the assassination of Lincoln. No essential facts of the assassination of Lincoln would have to be altered if Booth had broken his neck instead of his leg when he leaped from the box. The network of intentional and causal connexions between the escape and the assassination were few.[15]

By separating, for substantial reasons, the action of escape from that of assassination, we may avoid the absurdity that Booth did not murder Lincoln until after he arrived in Virginia, but other problems remain. Suppose Lincoln had recovered from the immediate effects of his wound only to die weeks later of lead poisoning? How long could the thread of Lincoln's life be stretched without snapping the ballistic link that binds his death to Booth's intentional action? To what extent, that is, did the determinate character of Booth's action depend upon the factual realization of his intention. Surely there is some part of Booth's action that would not have been altered whatever the course of his bullet. Could it be that what Booth *willed* would have remained unchanged?

## IV

The last question formulates the issue in such a way that an affirmative answer will provide a positive justification for some of the language of 'volitions'. The question has two facets: first, are we naming a distinct element in action when we refer to 'willing' or 'volition'; second, if there is such an element, can its character as revealed by action, or our assessment of it, be altered by events that take place after the action has been completed? The answer to this question in its various parts can be found by observing the effects on our descriptive and moral assessments of Booth's action and character when we introduce *seriatim* into our original list of twelve descriptions, either as additions or substitutions for one or more of them, each of the following six actions which are described in terms of characteristics observable either from the interior perspective of the agent himself[16] or from the exterior perspective of other persons:

*A.* Booth stands behind Lincoln, aims carefully, squeezes the trigger, and wounds Lincoln fatally.

*B.* Booth stands behind Lincoln, aims carefully, squeezes the trigger, but the gun misfires and Lincoln is not harmed.

*C.* Booth stands behind Lincoln, aims carefully, and does what he thinks is squeezing the trigger, but because of temporary paralysis or some blockage of nerve impulse, his muscles do not move. He puts the gun down, and Lincoln is not harmed.

*D.* Booth stands behind Lincoln, aims carefully, but at the last moment decides not to fire; nevertheless, his finger depresses the trigger and Lincoln is fatally wounded.

*E.* Booth stands behind Lincoln, aims carefully, but at the last moment decides not to fire; nevertheless, phosphorous in the powder ignites, the gun fires, and Lincoln is fatally wounded.

*F.* Booth stands behind Lincoln, aims carefully, but at the last moment decides not to fire, and does not pull the trigger. He puts the gun down and Lincoln is not harmed.

*A*, the only one of these six descriptions that does not alter the historical record, is merely a re-statement, within the limits of descriptive latitude, of 2, 3, 4, 7, and 11. It is not obvious that *A* adds additional interior insight to the original twelve descriptions. But there is not always a difference between descriptions based on interior views and those based on external views. In Booth's action the unity of intention, thought, motive, and bodily movement is so extensive and suppressive of conflict that data drawn from interior perspective duplicates what is already known from external observation. The action was wholly Booth's own, right down to his cry of *Sic Semper Tyrannis*. There appear to be no facts that mitigate his responsibility. It is not completely clear what his motives were or what he hoped ultimately to accomplish by his action; it is clear that nothing could have prompted him to say or justified him in saying of his action: "I didn't will to do it." [17] Rarely have will and action been so thoroughly one; how could one distinguish them sufficiently in the context of Booth's action to give meaning to such a statement? We have no reason to look for volition *as a distinct element* in this action nor do we find it there. If we insist on its being there as a distinct element despite our not finding it, it must be out of our concern to generalize the need we find for it when examining other and very different actions.

Had moral experience provided us with examples of only those unified actions in which no conflict or divergence between will and movement occurred, we should likely answer with a resounding "Nothing!" Wittgenstein's question, "What is left over if I subtract the fact that my arm goes up from the fact that I raise my arm?" [18] But the actions about which moral questions arise are rarely so unified (simple despite great complexity) as Booth's and are never so simple, motiveless, emotionless, and contextless as the act of raising one's arm. Naturally we can dispense with the language of 'volitions' when our examples are, by artifice, so simple and devoid of life that volitional tensions are absent.[19]

When *B* in turn, is added to our list of twelve, substantial and instructive revisions are required. 1, 2, and 3 can stand, and 8, 9, and 10 might still be true; all of the others are left in doubt by our assumption that *B* is true. Can we preserve the truth of 4, 5, 6, and 7 by inserting 'at' following each occurrence of 'shoot' in the list, *e.g.*, He shot at Lincoln? Can we say, following *B*, that 11 and 12 are clearly false? Far too many facts would be swept away if we did. He was not shooting *at* Lincoln:

How does one shoot *at* someone at point-blank range when he cannot possibly miss? And Booth did not miss Lincoln; his gun misfired. As far as Booth's action was concerned Lincoln was a dead man, for Booth's gun was well-aimed and he was not nervous. Nothing in Booth's action[20] spared Lincoln's life; an accident over which Booth had no control terminated some of the intended and expected consequences of an action that was already—in so far as the agent himself was concerned—complete and sufficient murder. The correct or most accurate description in *B* must be, although I grant its awkwardness, that Booth shot Lincoln unsuccessfully, killed him unsuccessfully, and assassinated him unsuccessfully. These statements have the advantage of preserving the descriptive integrity of Booth's action and its moral quality.[21]

In order to avoid the awkwardness of this suggestion (which may be unavoidable if we faithfully describe what Booth as a complete person, and not merely as a body, was actually doing), we may be tempted to say that Booth was *trying* to shoot and kill Lincoln. But Wittgenstein's objection that we cannot try to do something if there is no difficulty about it has merit. Although it took some effort and great daring to kill Lincoln, it was shockingly easy, and Booth moved successfully through all the stages of his crime that were difficult. Without effort he stood at Lincoln's back, put his gun to Lincoln's head, and calmly squeezed off his shot which (quite by accident but not by Booth's action, according to description *B*) never left the gun. Booth was not trying to shoot Lincoln; the accident aside, he was doing it.[22]

The least awkward yet accurate way to describe Booth's action in circumstance *B* is to say that Booth willed to shoot and kill Lincoln. This usage preserves in the description the volitional unity—the effect-producing unity—of the person as no other does.[23] Because I cannot explain and defend this usage of will now, I shall stand by the description that Booth shot and killed Lincoln unsuccessfully.

That, according to *B*, Booth missed Lincoln does not change Booth's personal moral quality. It does not make him a better person in the narrowly moral sense that is determined solely by consideration of his voluntary actions. Further, if Booth had not tried to escape after his gun misfired, but had crumpled to the floor, weeping and cursing himself for his treachery, and if he had used the knife he carried in reserve—not on Lincoln—but on himself, none of these facts would alter Booth's moral character at the time he fired. In these circumstances, however, both Booth and those who observed him should have to revise their assessment of his moral quality. We should have to admit that he was not so firmly set on his course of action as it seemed, hence that he was a better man than we thought. The latter events cannot alter the quality of the earlier ones, but they can radically alter our knowledge of the earlier ones.

The circumstances of *C*, whose truth we now assume, bring us to a test case of the need for volitional terms. In *A* and *B* the interior perspective of the agent and the external view of observers were in essential agreement; hence, they could be accurately described from the external perspective. But in *C* what is done and what appears to be done are radically different: unless we can speak about what Booth *willed* to do as opposed to what he *appeared* to do we shall have to use some special language or conclude absurdly that his action was the same both in *C* and in *F* and that his action in *C* was morally superior to his action in *D*.

According to *C*, Booth entered the box, aimed, and did what he had always done when firing at an object; the absence of the hammer click, report, and recoil first alerted Booth to the fact that his finger had not moved and the trigger had not been pulled. But from Booth's interior perspective his finger was pulled: he did *exactly* what he had done in *A* and *B*. If, as *C* requires, we subtract the closing of the finger on the trigger from Booth's squeezing the trigger and look for what is left, the answer cannot be nothing! Booth was doing unsuccessfully, or trying (in the sense of truncated or incomplete doing). As far as Booth's personal action is concerned, he pulled the trigger, but because of circumstances that cut short some of the effects (normally integral and organic parts) of his action, there was no movement in his finger. Surely the most natural, and also the most accurate, thing to say in these circumstances is that Booth willed to pull the trigger even though the trigger was not moved. That, I submit, is what Booth and most speakers of English would say. If some finger-wagging moralist said, "Booth's will was a murderous will," he should be saying nothing more ghostly than that in so far as Booth's volition (what he was *doing* unsuccessfully or what he was bent on achieving) is concerned, he killed Lincoln. And if we shift momentarily to the situation described in *E*, we should say that although Booth's gun shot Lincoln, Booth did not will to do it, *i.e.*, it was not done by his volition. This way of speaking is natural and its meaning is clear.

Two objections may be raised: first, one may argue that my conclusion has been drawn from *C*, that *C* is hypothetical, and therefore that my conclusion is hypothetical; second, one may object that my conclusion implies the para-mechanical theory of mind. Both objections, I think, can be overcome.

Godfrey Vesey, in a recent article, describes a medically confirmed report of William James that supplies factual support for circumstances similar to those in *C*. Vesey writes:

> [If] a patient who has lost sensation in one arm is asked to put the affected hand on top of his head while his eyes are closed, and is at the same time prevented from doing so, he will be very surprised on opening his eyes to find that the movement has not taken place.[24]

Recent experiments have shown, moreover, that the voluntary control of finger movements by a blind-folded patient, whose hand has been anaesthetized, are precise; that the patient makes exact movements on verbal command; that if his movement is prevented by the experimenter, he does not know and is surprised to discover that the movement has not taken place.[25] There is nothing hypothetical, then, about the conclusions we draw from *C*. They may be mistaken, but they cannot be dismissed on the ground that *C* is hypothetical.

If in situation *C* we had been able to remove Booth's brain case and insert into his brain at various points some fine electrodes, we could probably have detected neurological activity in Booth that was associated with his tightening of his finger muscles. If techniques were available for pinpointing neurological correlates of our higher decision processes, or if the abnormality that prevented Booth's action from being expressed in the movement of his finger were located in one of the effector nerve fibres, we could certainly verify the claim that Booth *willed* to pull the trigger,[26] that he did that which normally would have eventuated in his pulling the trigger.

When we say that Booth willed to pull the trigger, we are not denying that this was a mind-body action, an organic personal action. But we are saying that it was not the normal sort that can be read off and correctly interpreted from external appearances. And it is because the action in *C* is exceptional and because observers would be mistaken to judge the action on the basis of criteria normally applied in the exterior assessment of actions (criteria that were adequate in *A* and *B*) that we point out the inadequacy of these criteria by the use of volitional language.

I should resist any suggestion that volition can be understood in terms that are purely mental or spiritual or non-physical. Thus I should not accept Vesey's in other ways excellent suggestion for the interpretation of the patient's action in James's experiment. After rejecting a variety of possible interpretations, Vesey concludes, " 'So far as he, but not necessarily his arm is concerned, he moved his arm' or 'So far as the mental side of him as agent is concerned, he moved his arm.' "[27] The last description will not do. There is no reason to suggest that as agent a man has either a 'mental side' or 'a physical side'. Such usage might suggest the para-mechanical model that Vesey clearly rejects and effectively argues against. When Booth was doing what normally would have been observed as a movement in his trigger finger, there was doubtlessly a neurological-conscious action: there was personal action, and persons are mind-bodies, not mental and bodily parts united by some process of lamination. Much more remains unsaid about my use of 'will' and about its want of para-mechanical implications; enough has been said, nevertheless, to meet the second part of the objection to the conclusions drawn from my analysis of *C*.[28]

Limitations of time will not permit so much as a mention of the contributions to the argument of this paper that might follow from the analysis of situations *D*, *E*, and *F*. But I have not deleted them from the second list because the reader can follow for himself the method of successive assumption and analysis that I have been following and make the points for himself. Enough has been shown by the analysis of Booth's action under conditions *A*, *B*, and *C*, I think, to support my claim that there are positive philosophical grounds for the retention of some of the language of 'volitions', and that there is an organic unity and structure to human actions which can be discerned and which imposes limits upon our considerable latitude in the formulation of accurate descriptions of them.

## Notes

1. Ryle, G., *The Concept of Mind*, Peregrine Book Y 29, pp. 62–3.

2. Austin, J. L., *op. cit.*, *Proc. Arist. Soc.*, Vol. LVII (1956/7) p. 26, reprinted in *Philosophical Papers*, Oxford University Press, 1961, p. 148.

3. This is not to assume that all of the relevant facts are known.

4. Austin, J. L., *op. cit.*, p. 27; also pp. 4–5, and 19–20; repr. at p. 149; also pp. 126–7 and 141–2.

5. Austin unquestionably maintains as a general proposition the distinction between language and that to which it refers (p. 130); yet, as we shall see, he does not make clear what the non-verbal character of action is. Admittedly, this was not his objective in "A Plea for Excuses".

6. I should not assert that this is Austin's position, for his discussion of these issues is far too brief to justify a definitive statement of his view. Nor am I concerned in this paper with this historical question. Perhaps Austin would have placed very little emphasis upon the paragraph I have examined at length. I have done so because it is a very instructive paragraph with regard to the problem of describing actions whatever be its limitations as a statement of Austin's view.

7. The language is so grotesquely inappropriate to the discussion of action that sound doctrine could not possibly be conveyed in these terms. We can scarcely conceive of anything less like a machine than human actions. In conscious, voluntary action, for example, we have not merely the organic unity of the human body, but also the organic and conceptual union of mind-body engaged in coordinated, intelligent, volitional process. Strangely, perhaps for playfully perverse reasons (in order to be his own highly prized "eccentric talker"?), Austin liked the "machine" terminology. Not content to speak of "the machinery of action" he even spoke of "the machinery of doing actions" (p. 141) which, I suppose, is "the machinery of doing doings."

8. I had made this list for another purpose long before writing this paper; as far as I know, I have not made a selection of descriptions on the basis of any preconceived notion about the characteristics of actions. I did avoid descriptions which were either bizarre or required special insight into the historical events. The language of the descriptions, in so far as I can judge, is utterly common. I tried to order the descriptions chronologically.

9. It might seem that if 7 and 11 were true, then 12 must also be true. But this would be a reasonable rather than a logically necessary conclusion, for Booth might have deliberately shot Lincoln, wounding him slightly, and then killed him quite by accident. Or he might have killed Lincoln by accident and then deliberately shot him.

10. 7 does not have the same time of beginning as 4, 5, and 6 for the deliberateness with which Booth shot Lincoln was continually present in Booth's activity from the time he began to plan the assassination, hence, prior even to 1; *i.e.*, he was beginning deliberately to shoot Lincoln before he entered the box. Here the factual basis of the unity of Booth's action begins to obtrude.

11. I think this somewhat metaphysical language is perfectly clear in its meaning.

12. Thus we face the startling consequence, which we shall encounter again and discuss more fully at that time, that our descrip-

tions of Booth's activity might have required modification because of the course of events subsequent to his release of the hammer of his derringer. But was his activity altered, or did subsequent events provide us with sounder evidence on which to base our descriptions of his activity? In order to negative both possibilities and to avoid the implication that missing Lincoln could have altered the character of Booth's action, some moralists have argued that there is a moral sense in which 4, 5, 6, and 7 would still be true had Booth missed Lincoln. I do not accept this position, but it cannot be dismissed dogmatically; unfortunately, we shall not have time to consider it adequately.

13. I am not denying that actions can be 'split' arbitrarily and described according to convenience. But in such cases the arbitrariness of the description reveals its departure from, and hence the existence of, the real action.

14. We shall not have time to develop some of the important differences between 11 and 12. Because 12 is by far the richer and more inclusive description, I shall devote more attention to it.

15. Though *relatively* insignificant, there were doubtlessly some. Would Booth, vain and desirous of public renown as he was, have executed his plan to kill Lincoln had that plan omitted a realistic method of escape? Would Booth have done the deed had he not envisaged cheering throngs in Virginia?

The fact that Booth expected a hero's welcome in Virginia prompts me to suggest that the complete description of his action would have to include some mental elements of which Booth was probably not conscious. How could an intelligent man like Booth have expected to find safety in a Virginia occupied by Northern soldiers? How could he have been so blind that, while comparing himself to Brutus, he expressed surprise at being despised by the people? And is there significance in the fact that, as a boy, John Wilkes Booth killed pet animals just in order to distress his father, a famous actor, who had a reverence for living things, who opposed all violence, and whose middle name was Brutus?

16. There can be no objection in principle to the use of the data about actions supplied by the agent himself, since without making some use of such evidence we should have only a behavioristic conception of ourselves and no genuine conception of action.

17. This is not because such things are not said. Common folk, in America at any rate, say such things as 'It was his own volition' and 'He did it of his own volition,' and 'He willed to do it.' There is a

particularly interesting expression which, though shunned by the educated, enjoys wide circulation: 'I didn't go to do it.' A person who admits that he knowingly and intentionally killed a man may say by way of excusing his action, 'I didn't go to do it.' 'To go to do' seems very close in meaning to 'to will to do'. It might be construed to mean simply 'to do with premeditation,' but I doubt it.

18. Wittgenstein, L., *Philosophical Investigations,* Part I, 621.

19. Philosophers may be led astray by bloodless examples no less than by bloodless categories.

20. Had Booth failed to check his gun and his ammunition in advance, we might have to revise our estimate of his real intent, for an expert in the use of guns does not fail to check his weapons if he wants to shoot something.

21. The word 'rob' more naturally, but not more logically than 'shoot' or 'kill' conveys the idea of fully doing *X* even though unsuccessfully. Thus we say that the thief robbed the bank although he was captured before he left the bank. The robber does not cease being a thief when he is caught and the money is returned. There is a sense, too, in which Booth is a murderer even though, by the gun's misfiring, Lincoln's life "is restored" to him. [1967. In my essay "Being and Doing: A Study of Status Responsibility and Voluntary Responsibility," *The University of Chicago Law Review,* volume 35, No. 1, autumn, 1967, p. 77, I acknowledge the unnecessary confusion of statements such as "Booth shot Lincoln unsuccessfully" and find a less paradoxical way of retaining the important facts in such circumstances. (CF *Phenomenology in America,* Quadrangle Books, Chicago, 1967, p. 236.)]

22. And since Booth did all that he could have done and all that should have been necessary in order to kill Lincoln in these circumstances, we cannot say merely that he *attempted* to shoot and kill Lincoln. The description was true and its meaning exhausted by the time Booth entered the box. His aiming and pulling the trigger must count for something additional in an accurate description.

23. I confess my qualms at once; thus my use of 'will' is no shibboleth to prove me a metaphysical Ephraimite. When I say that a person is a volitional, effect-producing unity, I am not saying that a ghostly mental person produces effects in a physical person. I shall return to this conception later.

24. Vesey, G. N. A., "Volition", *Philosophy,* No. XXXVI, No. 138 (October, 1961), p. 352. In the formulation of *C*, I took care that it should fulfil the essential conditions of the situation James describes

and Vesey examines in this article. There are several possible interpretations of this situation which Vesey suggests. I cannot now consider each of them, but I recognize that my argument is incomplete, though not mistaken, until these other interpretations are considered.

25. There is no difference, so far as can be detected by the observer or the patient, in what the patient does when the motion is completed, with precision and what he does when the motion is restrained. But the patient, and sometimes the observer by means of electrodes attached to muscles or nerve fibres, can observe a difference between what the patient does when he moves (or because of restraint merely thinks he moves) his finger and what he does when he is not moving (nor thinks he is moving) his finger.

26. I do not claim that neurology could show that Booth willed to shoot Lincoln. The pinpointing of neurological correlates of intentions and purposes is not yet dreamed of by neurologists. At most it is their distant hope.

27. Vesey, *op. cit.*, p. 363.

28. I shall try eventually to meet successively all possible objections that Ryle or Melden or Wittgenstein might make against my use of "will" and "volition." The usage I have suggested avoids at least one of the pitfalls—the ideo-motor theory of the will's effect on action. In the examination of Booth's real and hypothetical actions, I have avoided the mistake of introducing the will as a third thing between mind and body which effects in bodily movement the intentions of mind.

ARTHUR C. DANTO

# Basic Actions*

"Well, why should we want to know?" said Verity, giving a yawn or causing herself to give one.
I. Compton-Burnett, *Two Worlds and Their Ways*

## I

"The man *M* causes the stone S to move." This is a very general description of a very familiar sort of episode. It is so general, indeed, that it does not tell us whether or not *M* has performed an action. The description holds in either case; so it *could* have been an action. Without pausing to inquire what further features are required for it definitely to have been an action, let us merely note that *there are* actions that fall under the general description of "causing something to happen." Yet, since this description leaves it unclear whether or not an action has been performed, performing an action cannot be one of the truth conditions for "causing something to happen." And since this description cuts across those two cases, we may assume we are employing the same sense of the expression "causes something to happen" in both. Presumably, we are using "causes" in just the same sense whether we say that the man *M* causes the stone S to move *or* we say that the stone S causes the pebble *P* to move. If it *is* clear from the latter sentence that an action has *not* been per-

* Reprinted by permission of the author and the editor from *American Philosophical Quarterly,* II (1965).

formed, this clarity will be due to certain facts about stones rather than to any difference in the concept of causality. It is commonly assumed that stones never perform actions, although men sometimes do. Hence the indefiniteness of our original sentence is not due to any ambiguity in the concept of causality, but rather to certain facts about men, or to certain assumed facts. The concept of causality allows us to ignore differences between men and stones, as well as differences between performing an action and not.

I shall persist in speaking of *individuals* (the man *M*, the stone S) causing things to happen, even though our concept of causality has been classically analyzed as a relationship between pairs of *events*. According to the classical analysis, the movement of the pebble *P* is one event, the effect of another event, which I shall, with studied ambiguity, simply designate an S-event, in this case its cause. Comparably, the movement of S in my other example is one event, the effect of another event, similarly and no less ambiguously to be designated an *M*-event, which is its cause. And this *M*-event, whether or not it is an action performed by *M*, is correctly (if rather generally) to be described as *causing something to happen*—namely, the movement of S.

I shall now suppose that my original sentence in fact describes an action performed by *M* (moving the stone S). Of this particular spatial translation of S we may say three distinct and relevant things: that it is (*a*) an action, performed by *M*; that it is (*b*) something that was *caused* to happen (in this case by *M*); and that it is (*c*) the effect of an event distinct from itself (in this case the *M*-event). That this event can be both (*a*) and (*b*) follows from the remarks in the first paragraph. That—disregarding the special information in parentheses—(*c*) must hold if (*b*) does—follows from the analysis of causality referred to in the second paragraph. That it is (*b*) follows, I suppose, from the fact that S is a stone: stones don't *just* start to move without something causing them to move.

We must now look into the *M*-event itself. Do all three characterizations apply to *it*? This, I fear, cannot be decided without investigation. Let us suppose, however, that the *M*-event is both (*a*) and (*b*), for it might well be. Then it must also be (*c*), and there must then be yet another event, distinct from it, which is its cause. This may be yet a further *M*-event, and about it we may raise the same question. It would be rash to claim that we have slid into an infinite regress, damaging or otherwise. But if a given *M*-event is both (*a*) and (*b*) and, hence, (*c*), then ultimately its being (*c*) must lead us to a further *M*-event, which is (*a*) and *not* (*b*). And unless some *M*-events are (*a*) and not (*b*), *no* *M*-events are ever (*a*). That is, if there are any actions at all, there must be two distinct *kinds* of actions: those performed by an individual *M*, which he may be said to have *caused* to happen; and those actions, also performed by *M*, which he cannot be said to have caused to happen. The latter I shall designate as *basic actions.*

In this paper, I shall defend (and explore the consequences of) four theses which I regard as fundamental to the theory of action:

(1) If there are any actions at all, there are basic actions.
(2) There are basic actions.
(3) Not every action is a basic action.[1]
(4) If *a* is an action performed by *M*, then either *a* is a basic action of *M*, or else it is the effect of a chain of causes the originating member of which is a basic action of *M*.

I wish first to make quite clear the sense in which an individual does not cause his basic actions to happen. When an individual *M* performs a basic action *a*, there is no event distinct from *a* that both stands to *a* as cause to effect *and* is an action performed by *M*. So when *M* performs a basic action, he does nothing first that causes it to happen. It will be convenient to consider two possible objections to this.

It may be objected, first, that there are or may be other senses of "causes" than the sense mentioned above, in accordance with which it would be proper to say that *M* causes his basic actions to happen. Thus, *if* raising an arm were an instance of a basic action, an individual who does this might still be said to cause it to happen in some sense of "cause" other than the sense that I reject in application to basic actions. I accept this objection: there *may be* such other senses of "cause." But (i) we should still require exactly the same distinction that I am urging within the class of actions, and I should therefore be defending the *verbally* distinct thesis that unless there were actions an individual causes to happen in this *new* sense, there would be no actions he caused to happen in the original sense, either. So, unless there were actions of the former sort, causing a stone to move would, for example, never be an *action* that anyone performed (although men might still cause stones to move, since performing an action is not a truth-condition for "causing something to happen"). And (ii) this new sense of "cause" would *not* apply *whether or not* an action had been performed. It should, indeed, be absolutely clear from the sentence "*M* caused *a* to happen"—using this special sense of "cause"—that *M had* performed an action. Those who find it convenient to maintain that the concept of causality is invariant to the distinction between performing an action and not, would have as little use for this new sense of "cause" as I do. Neither they nor I would want to say that *stones* cause *anything* to happen in this new sense of "cause." Not that I wish to restrict the performance of basic actions to men alone. Other individuals may, for all I know, perform them as well. Some theologians have spoken as though everything done by God were a basic action. This would prohibit us, of course, from saying that God caused anything to happen (the making of the Universe would be a basic action.) And, for reasons which will soon emerge, this would make the ways of God inscrutable indeed.

It may be objected, second, that if we take the absence of a cause to be the distinguishing mark of a basic action, then we must class as basic actions a great many events that we should be disinclined, on other grounds, to accept as actions at all, e.g., the uniform rectilinear motion of an isolated particle, or perhaps any instance of radioactive decay. This objection is readily deflected. I have not claimed that basic actions are not caused, but only that a man performing one does not cause it by performing some other action that stands to it as cause to effect. Moreover, the absence of a cause would not be a sufficient criterion for a basic action, even if basic actions *were* uncaused. It would serve only to mark off a special class of actions from the rest. Of course, only what is already an action can be a *basic* action. And I have not so much as tried to say what are the general criteria for actions.

## II

I have avoided citing unconditional instances of basic actions, in part because any expression I might use, e.g., "moving a limb," could also be used to designate something that was caused to happen, or something that was not an action, much less a basic one. I think there is nothing that is always and in each of its instances an unmistakably basic action. This is reflected by language in the fact that from the bare description "*M*'s limb moved," for example, one could not tell whether *M* had performed a basic action or even an action. Nor could one tell this by observing only the motion of the limb without bringing in differentiating contextual features. I have accordingly contented myself with the neutral expression "*M*-event," declaring it to be a basic action when I required an instance.

Now I wish to specify some of the differentiating contextual features, and I shall consider four distinct cases, all of which might indifferently be covered by the same description, so that the description alone leaves it unclear whether an action has been performed or not. Of the four cases, three (*C-1*, *C-2*, *C-4*) will indeed be actions, and of these one (*C-4*) will be a basic action. The four cases together might be termed a *declension* of the description. Not every such description admits of the full declension, for some appear never to be exemplified as basic actions at all. "Moving a stone," I should think, never, or not ordinarily, is exemplified as a basic action, though we have seen that it may be exemplified by an action. I want to begin with a deliberately controversial example and shall decline the expression "*M* laughs."

*C-1. M causes himself to laugh.* I am thinking here of cases where someone does something to make himself laugh, and does not simply laugh because of something he happens to do. Thus I may do something ridiculous and laugh because I find it so, but I did not do this ridiculous thing in order to make myself laugh. Again, I sniff a cartridge of nitrous oxide, not knowing it to be nitrous oxide, but just to find out what it is. But, since it is nitrous oxide, I laugh, though I did not sniff to make myself laugh. I wish to include only cases where I do something ridiculous or sniff from a private cartridge of nitrous oxide *in order to* laugh, perhaps because I think laughter good for the liver or because I just enjoy laughing and cannot always wait for someone or something to come along and cause me to laugh. I definitely want to exclude a comedian who laughs at some reruns of his antic films (unless he had them rerun for this special purpose), and definitely want to include someone who deliberately engages in auto-titillation to excite spasmodic laughter. Doubtless, episodes falling under *C-1* are rare in normal adults in our culture, but this is irrelevant. Also irrelevant is the fact that people don't laugh *at* the nitrous oxide they sniff, though they do laugh at the silly faces they pull, for their own delectation, in mirrors.

*C-2. Someone or something other than M causes M to laugh.* This is the typical case for adults and children in our culture. It is for my purposes again irrelevant whether the cause of *M*'s laughter is also its object, or whether it has an object at all (as it does not if he is tickled or submitted to nitrous oxide). Similarly, it is irrelevant whether, in case someone causes *M* to laugh, the former has performed an action or not, whether, that is, he did what he did in order to make *M* laugh. For it is what *M* does that uniquely concerns us here.

*C-3. M suffers a nervous disorder symptomized by spasmodic laughter.* This is comparable, say, to a tic: *M* laughs unpredictably, and for "no reason." Such laughter is mirthless, of course, but so are some instances falling under the two first cases. It may be argued that the entire case falls under *C-2*, and that in identifying it as the symptom of a nervous disorder, I have marked off a class of causes for *M*'s laughter. Still, the case requires special consideration, in that *M*'s laughing here is never an action, whereas his laughter under *C-2* sometimes *is*.

*C-4. M has the true power of laughing.* By this I mean that *M* laughs when he wants to without (in contrast with *C-1*) having to cause himself to laugh; without (in contrast with *C-2*) someone or something having to cause him to laugh; without, finally, as in *C-3*, suffering from the relevant nervous disorder. This does not mean that *M* is normal, but only that his abnormality is of a benign sort; i.e., it is by way of a gift. His laughing may have an object: he may, when he wishes, direct a stream of laughter at whom or what he chooses, without the chosen object ever being a *cause* of his laughing.

Instances falling under *C-4* are perhaps rare, but these alone would qualify as basic actions performed by *M* when "*M* laughs" is true. I have identified the case not so much by specifying what differentiating contextual features must be present, but by specifying what differentiating contextual features must be *absent.* Notice that *M*'s laughing here differs markedly from the ability most of us have of making laugh-like noises, e.g., for the sake of politeness, or to save our reputation for seeing a joke when we don't see it, or to play a mocker's role in an amateur theatrical. Most of us can pretend so to laugh: but I speak here of laughing, not of "laughing."

I want now to comment on these four cases.

When *M* laughs under *C-1*, we may say of his laughing three distinct things: that it is (*a*) an action of *M*'s; that it is (*b*) something that *M* causes to happen; and that it is (*c*) the effect of some event, distinct from itself (an *M*-event) which is its cause. *M*'s laughing here is an action in just the same sense in which his causing a stone to move is an action. Causing himself to laugh is the action he performed, though of course the description "*M* caused himself to laugh" leaves it unclear, as in the case of the stone, whether he performed an action at all. One could mark that difference only by bringing in the general differentiating features of action.

In *C*-2, *M* does not cause himself to laugh, and one may find reasons for balking at the claim that his laughing, in such a case, is an action of his at all. For consider this argument. When *M* causes a stone S to move, we may agree that the action is *M*'s. But we reject the claim that it is an action of S's. So parity suggests that when someone moves *M* to laughter, this may be an action performed by the former, but not an action of *M*'s.

What I must do is to show that parity is inoperative, and so justify my claim that instances of *C*-2 are actions in contrast with instances of *C*-3. Well, I shall somewhat artificially suggest that *M*'s action here requires this description: what he does is to *not not* laugh. The double negative is not, in the language of action, a triviality. Logically, of course, the double negative of a proposition is just that proposition, and from a strictly logical point of view, we could say the same thing, albeit more awkwardly, with "The man *M* causes the stone S to not not move" as we straightforwardly say with "The man *M* caused the stone S to move." I wish, in fact, to retain that regular inferential feature of double negation which allows us to proceed from not not *A* to *A*, but for the case of action I wish to exclude the reverse inference. For my double negative marks the case of *negligence*, and whether a negligence is to be ascribed to someone is a case for independent investigation. So, pending such investigation, we cannot say, on the basis of knowing that a man laughs, that he is to be charged with negligence. And for this reason we cannot automatically go from "laughs" to "not not laughs." Indeed, since we don't ascribe negligence to stones, it would be invalid, given my convention, to proceed from "the stone moves" to "the stone not not moves."

Do we quite want to say, then, that *C-2* is to be restated thus: *Someone or something other than M causes M to not not laugh?* Perhaps we would, in spite of flaunting usage. What we would be saying, however, is only this: that *M* was excited to laugh and did nothing to inhibit his laughter. And it is our common assumption that men are normally capable of doing something which, in effect, stops the flow of laughter from issuing forth in, say, public guffaws. Whether men are called upon to exercise these inhibitory practices varies from context to context: in the music hall there is license to suspend them, to "let oneself go," but at High Mass there is not. It is in such contexts only that laughter is *pronounced* a negligence, but blaming, surely, does not make of something an action when it would not otherwise have been so. It is only insofar as something is an action already that blaming it, or blaming someone for doing it, is appropriate.

With regard to *C-3*, however, the laugher stands liable to no special charge of negligence: his laughing fails to be a case of not not laughing, for identification of it as a nervous disorder, or in the syndrome of one, locates it beyond the control of the man who is so afflicted. It is, indeed, almost a paradigm case of this: like a hiccough. One *might* blame the man for being in a place where his symptom, easily mistakable as a negligence, might break out unpredictably. Or we might blame him again for a kind of negligence in "not doing something about it," viz., going to a nerve specialist, assuming there is a known cure. At all events, it is plain enough why *C-3* differs from *C-2*. The critical issue, of course, is the matter of *control,* and this brings us to *C-4*. And the rest of this paper is by way of a comment on *C-4*.

Most readers, I think, will resist the suggestion that *C-4* is a case of action. There is good reason for this. For most of us, laughing as a *basic action* is unintelligible. I shall hope to show why this is so, and showing it will involve a demonstration of thesis (2). Meanwhile, the reader might ponder the precise analogue to this in the case of *moving an arm,* which admits of a full declension. Thus *C-1*: *M* causes his arm to move, i.e., by striking it with his other arm; *C-2*: someone or something other than *M* causes *M*'s arm to move, e.g., by striking it; *C-3*: *M* suffers from a nervous disorder, so his arm moves spasmodically and unpredictably, as a kind of tic; and *C-4*: *M* moves his arm without suffering from a nervous disorder, without someone or something causing it to move, without having to do anything to cause it to move. Here, I am certain, *C-4* is the *typical* case. Moving an arm is one of the standard basic actions. If we now seek to determine in what way this behavior *is* intelligible, we should have no great difficulty in seeing why laughing under *C-4* is *not*.

## III

Suppose now that moving a stone is an action performed by *M*. It is difficult to suppose that *moving a stone* admits of a full declension, largely because it seems to lack cases for *C-3* and *C-4*. In fact there are difficulties in finding instances for *C-1* and *C-2* unless we change the sense of possession (*M*'s arm, *M*'s stone) from philosophical to legal ownership. But for the moment I shall be concerned only with the fact that we move stones only by causing them to move. This then means that, in order to cause the motion of the stone, something else must be done, or must happen, which is an event distinct from the motion of the stone, and which stands to it as cause to effect. Now this other event may or may not be a basic action of *M*'s. But if it is not, and if it remains nevertheless true that moving the stone *is* an action of his, then there must be something else that *M* does, which causes something to happen which in turn causes the motion of the stone. And *this* may be a basic action or it may not. But now this goes on forever unless, at some point, a basic action is performed by *M*. For suppose every action were a case of the agent causing something to happen. This means, each time he does *a*, he must independently do *b*, which causes *a* to happen. But then, in order to do *b*, he must first independently do *c*, which causes *b* to happen. . . . This quickly entails that the agent could perform no action at all. If, accordingly, there are any actions at all of the sort described by "causing something to happen," there must be actions which are *not* caused to happen by the man who performs them. And these are basic actions.

But this argument is perfectly general. If there are any actions at all, there are basic actions. This is a proof of thesis (1). Moreover, if *M* performs an action describable by "causing something to happen," he must also, as part of what he does, perform an action that he does not cause to happen. And this is a proof of thesis (4). It would be a proof of thesis (2) if in fact there were actions described as "causing something to happen." This would then require us to accept thesis (3) as true: for such an action would not be a basic action, and so not every action is basic.

I do not wish to suggest, however, that the only proof we are entitled to, for the existence of basic actions, is by way of a transcendental deduction, for I believe we all know, in a direct and intuitive way, that there are basic actions, and which actions are basic ones. To show that we do know this will clarify one of the ways in which laughing is a controversial instance of a basic action.

I must make a few preliminary remarks. First, every *normal person* has just the same *repertoire R* of basic actions, and having *R* is what defines a normal person for the theory of action. Second, persons may be *positively abnormal* when their repertoire of basic actions includes actions not included in *R*, and may be *negatively abnormal* when actions included in *R* are not included in their repertoire. Some persons may be both positively and negatively abnormal, e.g., someone who laughs as a basic action but who is paralyzed in one arm. If someone's repertoire is empty, he is capable of no basic actions, and hence of no actions. Such a deprived entity is a *pure patient*, e.g., like a stone. Plainly, our repertoire of actions is greater than our repertoire of basic actions, though a being who performed every possible action and all of whose actions were basic actions may be conceived of: such a being would be a *pure agent*. For the present, however, I am concerned with beings intermediate between pure patients and pure agents, and I want now to say that basic actions are *given* to such beings in two distinct senses, each of which bears a definite analogy to a sense that the term has in the theory of knowledge.[2]

(i) In the theory of knowledge, to say that $p$ is *given* is in part to point a contrast: one is saying that $p$ is not inferred from some other proposition. Analogously, when I speak of an action as given, I shall mean to say, in effect, that it is a basic action, and point a contrast with actions we *cause* to happen. The notion of givenness is understood this way: $p$ is a starting point for an inference to another and (commonly) different proposition $q$ for which $p$ provides at least part of the evidence. Analogously, an action $a$, if a basic action, is a starting point for the performance of another action $b$, of which it is at least part of the cause. "Is caused by" and "is inferred from" are analogous relations in the theories of knowledge and of action, respectively.

(ii) It has been argued that the distinction between *basic sentences* and sentences of other kinds is not ultimate, that a sentence which, in one context, is indeed a starting point for an inference to another, may, in a different context, itself be inferred to, and hence an end point in an inference.[3] Analogously, an action $a$ may, in one context, be a starting point and basic, while it may be caused to happen in a different one. There is some justice in this latter claim: as we have seen, one cannot tell from the bare description "moving an arm" whether a basic action is referred to, or even an action. But, thinking now of sentences, perhaps some restriction can be put on the *kind* of sentence which can be given in sense (i). If $p$ is given in one context and inferred in another, there might nevertheless be sentences which are never basic and always are inferred. And a corresponding restriction might hold in the theory of action: even if any action that is ever basic might, under a sufficiently general description, be caused to happen in another context, there might be actions that never are basic under any description. In the theory of knowledge, one such restriction is often defended, namely that basic sentences are those and only those which can be conclusively verified by sense experience, and that no other kind of sentence ever can be given. But within the class of potentially given sentences, a division might be made along the customary lines of sense-modality, i.e., those verified by seeing, or by audition, or by touch, etc. We might then define an *epistemically* normal person as one who experiences in all modes. A negatively abnormal person would then be deficient in at least one such mode, e.g., is blind; and a positively abnormal person then experiences in some mode outside the normal repertoire, e.g., has some "sixth sense." The analogy to the theory of action is obvious. But by means of it we may introduce our second sense of given: the normal modes of experience are "given" in the sense that they constitute the standard cognitive equipment. The normal person has various classes of starting points for inferences as he has various classes of starting points for actions. These are given in the sense that they are not for the most part *acquired.* Thus we speak of the "gift of sight," etc. This does not mean that there need be any sentences in the superstructure to which a negatively abnormal person might not infer: he is deficient only at the base: and then not *totally* deficient (or if he is, then he cannot have any empirical knowledge, is *cognitively impotent*). And similarly, *toutes proportions gardées,* with the negatively abnormal person as defined in the theory of action.

Now when a blind man says that he can know whether a certain object is red or not, there are two senses or uses of "can" that are compatible with his abnormality. He must mean either that he can *infer* to "*x* is red" from other sentences or that his case is not medically hopeless, that by means of a cure he may be restored to that state of normality in which such sentences may be known by him directly and not, as it were, *merely* by means of inference. Yet there is a true and in fact an *analytic* sense in which a blind man cannot know whether a certain object is red, nor, on certain accounts of meaning, so much as know what such a sentence *means* (the non-analytic senses are usually false). The situation of a *paralyzed* man is perfectly analogous. When he sincerely says that he can move his arm, he must mean either that he can *cause* it to move, or that his situation is not medically hopeless. But, in again a true and an analytical sense, he cannot move his arm and does not know, does not so much as understand, what it means to move his arm in the way in which a normal person understands this. For this is the kind of understanding that is alone given to those who have the power to move their arms in the normal, basic way. This kind of understanding cannot so much as be conveyed to a negatively abnormal person while he is so.

Some of the chief difficulties philosophers have encountered in the theory of action are due to their having approached it from the point of view of the negatively abnormal. From *that* point of view, basic action is hopelessly mysterious. There is, however, perhaps no better way of eliciting the quality of our knowledge of these things than to think of endeavoring to remove the mysteriousness surrounding these actions in the thwarted comprehension of the negatively abnormal person. We may achieve some sympathy for his plight by imagining *ourselves* similarly confronting someone who is *positively* abnormal, who can perform, as a basic action, what we at best can cause to happen, and then asking *him* to give us an understanding of his gift. The fact is that we cannot explain to the negatively abnormal, nor can the positively abnormal person explain to us, the way in which the basic action is performed (and this must be appreciated in the same way as the impossibility of explaining to a blind man what red literally looks like, or, if you wish, of our understanding what ultra-violet literally looks like). Suppose—just to take one case—a paralytic asks us what we do *first* when we raise an arm. We should be obliged to say we cannot answer, not because we do not know or understand what we do, but because we know and understand that there is *nothing* we do first. There is no series of steps we must run through, and since the request is implicitly for a *recipe,* we cannot say how we move our arm. A basic action is perfectly simple in the same sense in which the old "simple ideas" were said to be: they were not compounded out of anything more elementary than themselves, but were instead the ultimately simple elements out of which other ideas were compounded.

In one sense, then, we do, and in another we do not, know how we move an arm. But the sense in which we do not know is inappropriate. It is that sense which requires an *account,* and our incapacity for giving any such account is what has induced puzzlement, among philosophers and others, concerning the moving of an arm (and other basic acts generally). But this puzzlement should be dissipated upon the recognition that we have made a grammatical mistake in the inflected language of action. We have taken "moving an arm" as always a case of *C-1*, when *in fact C-4* is the standard case for normal persons moving normal arms normally. But having once committed this mistake, we look for a cause that is not there. And failing to find what we ought never to have expected to find, we complain that we do not know how we do move our arms. But of course we know. It is only that we cannot explain the manner of its doing. For there is no action, distinct from the action itself, to be put into the *explanans.* This is due to what I am terming the *givenness* of basic actions. Reference to basic actions belongs in the explanantia for explaining how things are done. So the paralytic, as long as he remains one, cannot understand: *Just raising the arm is what we do first.*

## IV

A paralytic might think there is some *effort* he is not putting forth, by which, if he did or could put it forth, he might as a consequence move his arm. But I want to say that he cannot try to move his arm if moving his arm is not already in his repertoire of basic actions. So in a sense he is right. If he could make the required effort, he could move his arm. But he cannot make that effort, cannot try, for he cannot in the only appropriate sense move his arm.

Consider the analogous situation with someone epistemically abnormal, say a deaf man. To ask a deaf man to try to hear a certain sound is rendered inappropriate by the fact that he is deaf. To try to hear, say, faint and distant music is to make an effortful listening. Only those who can already hear can make this effort. And what would count as trying (listening) in the deaf man's case? He could cup his ear, could place his ear to the ground, could contort his face and close his eyes. All this, however, is the pantomime of listening. Had he grinned or wagged a finger, it would have been as helpful. For there is no one thing that is better than any other in his situation. It is exactly this way with trying to move an arm. It is appropriate only to ask someone to try to move his arm when something externally inhibits normal movement, e.g., the arms are pinioned, and cannot be moved *freely* and *without effort.* But the paralytic cannot move his arm at all.

Consider these cases:

(*a*) I am a normal person who has swallowed a drug which gradually takes away the power to move an arm, rendering me, so long as it is in full effect, negatively abnormal. I make tests at five-minute intervals. It gets harder and harder to move my arm. And then I reach a point where I cannot move my arm and cannot *try* to. I have lost the power of trying, together with the power for doing.

(*b*) Someone thinks it would be spectacular to be able to extend and retract his fingernails, the way a cat does with its claws. We tell him it cannot be done, and he retorts that no one has ever tried, and he means to try. But in what should his trying consist? He could shake his fingers hard, could order them to extend, could pray, or could draw his soul up into a vast single wish. There is no rational way, for there is no way at all for a normal person. I don't mean that no one is or ever will be able to move his nails and to try to move them (e.g., with tight gloves on). If a man were prepared to suffer some sort of surgery, he might be able to cause his nails to go in and out, but we had not understood that he meant this by "trying." It is after all not the way cats do it. It is more the way we move a loose tooth.

(*c*) I am a normal person, challenged to move a normal stone. I take the challenge to imply the stone is not normal—perhaps it has some incredible density, or is fixed to a shaft driven deeply into the earth. But I decide to try, and the stone moves quite easily, having been a normal stone all along. So I conclude that the challenge was not normal. It turns out I was being asked to move the stone "the way I move my arm." But this is not something I even can try to do. I can, with ridiculous ease, cause the stone to move. So I can try to cause it to move as well. But I cannot try to move it as a basic action—that would be a proper encounter with nothingness.

One can do with effort only what one can do effortlessly; and "trying," the effort of will, is not something apart from the action that stands to it as cause to effect. It is the required action already being performed in untoward circumstances. Doing something with effort is not doing two things, any more than doing something gracefully is doing two things. Moving an arm is not then the result of an act of will: it *is* an act of will. But to speak of an act of will when the going is smooth is to behave a little like the dypsomaniac who wants to know what sorts of pink rats ordinary people see.[4]

It should be plain now why laughing, if performed as a basic action, is controversial. It is because whoever could so laugh would be positively abnormal, and we cannot understand what he does. In relation to him, we are in just the same position as the paralytic in relation to us. We lack a kind of gift.

## V

It is easy enough to sympathize with those who feel an action is not intelligible unless we can find a causal picture for it. But this is only because they have taken intelligibility to consist in having a causal picture. Dominated by this requirement, they may tend to invent some such picture, populating their inner selves with entities whose job it is to serve the automotive functions demanded by the causal model of intelligibility. But I am asking that we do not strain, and that we use the causal model only where it is natural to use it.

That there are actions, like moving an arm, which do not really require any other action as cause (and so no "inner" action as a cause) entails, I believe, no refutation of dualism. For all the distinctions I am thinking of are reproduced within the mental world, and cut across the distinction between body and mind. If, for instance, we take the description "*M* images *I*" where *I* is a mental image, then it is unclear, as it was in the case of "laughing" or "moves an arm," whether *M* has performed an action or not, or, if an action, then a basic action or not. The whole declension works, for *C-1*: *M* may cause an image to appear in his mind, perhaps by taking a drug; *C-2*: Someone or something other than *M* may cause an image to appear in *M*'s mind; *C-3*: *M* is haunted by an image which appears spontaneously, recurrently, and unpredictably—a symptom, of perhaps a psychic disorder; and *C-4*: *M* simply produces an image, as I and all those with the requisite alpha rhythms are able to do, i.e., as a basic action.[5]

I shall not press for a full parity, though I *am* prepared to defend the view that there is a problem of Other Bodies precisely analogous to the problem of Other Minds. All I wish to emphasize is that, whatever disparities there may be between the concept of mind and the concept of body, men may be said to act mentally in much the same way that they may be said to act physically. Among the things I take Descartes to have meant when he said that we are not in our bodies the way a pilot is in a ship, is that we do not always do things, as pilots must with ships, by causing them to happen. We do not turn, as it were, an inner wheel in order, through some elaborate transmission of impulse, to cause an external rudder to shift and, by so doing, get our boat to turn. We act directly. But then neither am I in my *mind* the way a pilot is in a ship. Or rather, I sometimes cause things to happen with my body and with my mind, and I sometimes just act with them directly, as when I perform basic actions. It is best, however, to avoid similes. Any philosophical problems we have with ourselves would only reappear in connection with anything sufficiently similar to us to be a suitable analogue. But if we find ourselves unintelligible, nothing sufficiently similar to us to be helpful is likely to be more clear.

## Notes

1. Thesis (3) is explored in detail in my paper, "What We Can Do," *The Journal of Philosophy,* vol. 60 (July, 1963), pp. 435–45. [Reprinted in this volume.]

2. The analogy between theory of knowledge and theory of action runs very deep indeed, almost as though they were isomorphic models for some calculus. Obviously, there are things we can say about actions that do not hold for cognitions, etc., but this means very little. Suppose we have two models M-*i* and M-*j* for a calculus C, and suppose that "star" plays . . . the same role in M-*i* that "book" plays in M-*j*. It is hardly an argument against their both being models for C that we don't print stars or that books are not centers of solar systems. I shall use theory-of-knowledge features as a guide for structuring the theory of action. When the analogy gives way, it will be interesting to see why it does.

3. Though not always without some awkwardness. Suppose it were

held that only sentences can be given which have the form of first-person reports of sense-experience, e.g., "I now see a reddish *x* . . ." Such a sentence is not easily rendered as the conclusion of an inference, though it can be so rendered, I suppose, if I both knew that something *x* had an unmistakable taste and that whatever has this taste is red. Then, by tasting *x* and seeing only its silhouette, I might feel secure in inferring that I was seeing a reddish *x*. Of course there are philosophically crucial senses of "see" which would rule this out, and make it, indeed, self-contradictory to say both "I see a reddish *x*" and "I see the black silhouette of *x*."

4. It is not difficult to see why it should be thought that there are two distinct things in the case of trying. It is because we often speak of trying and failing. So, if we can try and also succeed, trying is one thing and succeeding is another. And if succeeding consists in raising an arm, *trying* here must be something different, since failing consists in *not*-raising one's arm, and trying then could hardly consist in raising it. But this is not the important sense of the word for the theory of action.

5. But I am not sure whether *we* are positively abnormal, or those who have no images are negatively abnormal.

ARTHUR C. DANTO

# What We Can Do*

In this paper I shall presuppose the following notions:[1]

(1) *B* is a *basic action* of *a* if and only if (i) *B* is an action and (ii) whenever *a* performs *B*, there is no other action *A* performed by *a* such that *B* is caused by *A*.

(2) *B* is a *nonbasic action* of *a* if there is some action *A*, performed by *a*, such that *B* is caused by *A*.

(3) Whatever further may be said in the analysis of '*m* causes *n*', *m* causes *n* only if *m* and *n* are distinct events. There may be other senses of '. . . causes—' but this is the only sense I am interested in here.

(4) There is a basic repertoire *R* of basic actions such that *a* is a *normal person* only if *a* possesses *R*. *a* is *positively abnormal* if (i) *a* performs *B*, (ii) *B* is a basic action, and (iii) *B* is not included in *R*. *a* is *negatively abnormal* if (i) *a* cannot perform *B*, (ii) *B* is a basic action, and (iii) *B* is included in *R*. Any paralytic is negatively abnormal; anyone who can dilate his pupils "at will," i.e., without performing some action which causes them to dilate, is positively abnormal; raising an arm without performing some action that causes it to rise is included in *R*.

(5) If there are any actions at all, there are basic actions.

(6) There are basic actions.

(7) Not every action is a basic action.

(8) If *B* is an action performed by *a*, then either (i) *B* is a

* Reprinted by permission of the author and the editors from *The Journal of Philosophy*, LX (1963).

basic action or (ii) *B* is the terminal effect of a causal series the originating member of which is a basic action.

These notions taken together constitute a fragment of what I shall call a *theory of action.* It is not difficult to find a familiar analogue to this theory of action in a certain *theory of knowledge,* e.g., by substituting 'basic sentence' for 'basic action', 'is inferred from' for 'is caused by' 'sentence' for 'action', and by specifying a notion of "epistemic normality" for (4) (e.g., for 'paralytic' substitute 'blind man'; for 'can dilate his pupils . . .' substitute 'has a sixth sense'; and let "seeing" be the paradigm case of epistemic normality). One could retain 'distinct events' in (3) if one wished to keep the notion of performatives; otherwise one might give another interpretation for 'distinct events' or just drop (3) altogether. I am only indicating the analogue in a rough way, but there is, I think, a sufficiently plain structural parity for us to suppose that this theory of action and this theory of knowledge are, as it were, "models" for some uninterpreted and, I may say, heretofore unwritten calculus. If someone were to work the calculus out, he would have the logical armature for a whole class of philosophical theories, including the two I have mentioned. I am not to be concerned here, however, with issues in metaphilosophy. Instead, I want to give a highly informal gloss on (7).

# I

It is radically unclear from the *bare* description "*a*'s right arm rises at *t*" whether *a* performs here a basic action or, indeed, whether *a* has performed an action at all. We can determine this only by contextual specification. It will have been a basic action only if *a* raised his arm without causing[2] it to rise, and a non-basic action only if *a* caused it to rise by performing a basic action distinct from it, e.g., by pushing it up with his other arm. Otherwise it is not an action of his at all; e.g., if someone or something other than *a* caused the arm to rise, or if *a* suffers a special nervous disorder and has undergone a spasm, etc. On the other hand, it is commonly taken as clear from the bare description "*a*'s hat rises at *t*" that whether or not *a* has performed an action here, he has at least not performed a *basic action*. Any event that is sometimes a basic action admits of a description which leaves it unclear whether a basic action has really been performed. But some actions admit of comparable descriptions which, while they leave it unclear whether an action has really been performed, at least make it clear that a *basic* action has *not* been performed. So not every action is a basic action.

Nevertheless, some individuals are positively abnormal. So "*a*'s pupils dilate at *t*", while it normally leaves it clear that a basic action has *not* been performed, still leaves room for the possibility that *a* has performed a basic action if he is positively abnormal in the required way. Whatever we can do as a basic action, we can also cause to happen. But some things that normal persons can only cause to happen, some individuals can also perform as basic actions. *They* have, to put it platitudinously, two ways of doing what we can do in only one way.

I am to be concerned with the *limits* of positive abnormality, with actions that are *never* basic actions. This is a purely philosophical concern, I think, for so long as we can do a certain thing, it little matters practically whether we can in fact do it in only one way (and all ways of *causing* something to happen constitute, from my point of view, *one* way of doing it). Comparably, there may be many sentences that we can only know via inference, but this does not entail any ultimate ignorance—which is cognitive impotency—unless we have, unreasonably, restricted knowledge to direct, or noninferential knowledge.

Now raising a hat seems to be a natural candidate for an action which lies beyond these limits and which no individual, however otherwise positively abnormal, can claim as included in his repertoire of basic actions. The question is only whether this limit (and this 'can') is logical or factual. And this question may have some implications for philosophical theology. Does the alleged omnipotency of God require that whatever God can do as an action He also can do as a basic action? It is sometimes held that not only is God omniscient, but whatever He knows, He knows directly and noninferentially.[3] So I am considering the natural analogue to this in the theory of action. True, we would doubtless find it unintelligible were someone to claim that God can raise a hat without causing it to rise. But then we also find it unintelligible, *because we cannot do it ourselves,* that someone, e.g., Felix Krull, can dilate his eyes without causing them to dilate. And so, too, does a paralytic, for similar reasons, find it unintelligible when we claim to be able just to raise our arm. We cannot answer him when he asks us how we do it if, for instance, he expects a recipe. For there is nothing we do *first* in order to cause our arm to rise. Or rather, raising our arm is what we do first. And this is what he cannot understand.

## II

It is useful here to consider *telekinesis.* This is a possible view of how things might be moved, which arises, I think, only because people are dominated by a causal picture of action. Regarding an arm as, so to speak, an alien entity which, in its owner's case at least, is caused to move through the issuance of some inner summons, e.g., a volition, it becomes genuinely puzzling that we cannot, and genuinely possible that we might, through issuing an exactly similar summons, cause a similarly alien entity—a hat perhaps—to move. As though there were a kind of psychic energy which, since it undeniably (*sic*) causes some crass objects (arms) to move, might be harnessed and redirected to cause the movement of other crass objects (hats). And indeed this is a wholly plausible extension of an unfortunately wholly implausible theory of how men move their limbs.

Indeed, if those who believe in telekinesis were so much as able to find one man who moved his *arm* in the way in which they hope to be able to move *hats*, they would already have established their claims. The only thing is that they would have found a rare specimen, for I think few people, if any, move their arms by causing them to move through discharging psychic energy across whatever strange distance it is that supposedly separates them from their arms. Such rare specimens might move hats in much the same way. But the question I am concerned with is whether it is possible that we might move hats the way we do move an arm, *not* by causing them to move (and discharging psychic energy would only be a special kind of cause), but by *just* moving them—the way *we* move our arms: as *basic* actions.

A natural suggestion for answering "no" to this question is that hats are not parts of us, though arms are, and a man's repertoire of basic actions must be performed with parts of himself. But of course, there are parts of every normal person with which he cannot perform basic acts: fingernails, hair, teeth, not to mention the interior organs. So at best "*P* being part of *a*" is only a necessary condition for "*a* can perform basic acts with *P*." But it immediately follows that the latter is a sufficient condition for the former; so if I can perform basic actions with *P*, *P is* part of myself. If I then could move a hat as a basic action, that hat would be part of me. And so others could only cause it to move, for others have only one way of moving parts of me. This creates what I should call the Problem of Other Bodies.

I should in fact like to adopt as a *criterion* for something being a part of a man's self that he should be able to perform basic actions with it. This would suggest a form of metaphysical dualism not greatly in favor since, I believe, the vague days of German Idealism, a dualism far more interesting and rather more plausible than the customary dualism it intersects with, namely, the dualism of mind and body. Roughly, it would be a dualism with the self on one side and everything else on the other, and the self would consist in everything with which a man performs basic actions. The self would admit of increase and diminution, in the form of positive and negative abnormalities. When it diminishes to zero (death) a man is no longer able to act, for he is no longer able to perform basic actions: nothing is any longer part of him, because he is nothing. But this is in fact a digression, helping not at all with our problem. Or at all events, it merely restates it. For the limits of positive abnormality and the ultimate limits of the self are one and the same thing.

## III

Obviously, the normal man is not even in a position to *try*. For I understand by 'trying to do *B*' *not* "making a special effort in the hope of doing *B*, hoping that the special effort will cause *B* to happen," but instead "doing *B* with a special effort," e.g., in adverse circumstances—like moving one's arms against ropes that bind one. One *feels* the effort in doing *B* thus, and the temptation is to isolate the feeling, dignify it as "an act of will," then transfer it to the normal case, where circumstances are benign, and finally suppose that there are episodes of trying that cause the actions we perform. To try to move a hat as a *basic* action would then be to move it with effort, e.g., when it is nailed to the table, and this is already to have it in one's repertoire. So the normal man cannot try to move a hat as a basic action. But neither can he try to dilate his pupils or to retract his fingernails. Or to move his ears.

There are those who are positively abnormal in being able to move their ears as a basic act. They have that gift. And let us imagine that we, too, one day find ourselves with this gift, our self having become augmented in some dark way. How should a man know, on the very first occasion, that *he* is doing it, and that it is not just happening, that he has not been suddenly afflicted with a nervous spasm? Finding ourselves newly in control of a part of our body heretofore alien is not an experience most of us have this side of infancy, when, in time, it became clear that some things we could do directly, and some things we could only cause to happen. Perhaps the concept of cause only becomes clear when the limits of the self become clear. If so, then Hume was looking in just the wrong place when he sought to find the origin of our idea of causal power in our ability to move our limbs, for it is just there that causes are *not* to be found. If we did everything in the way in which we move our limbs (normally), we should have no notion of cause. So small wonder that Hume was disappointed.[4] Anyway, I am speaking of a man who has these concepts, and finds that he can do as a basic act what he before could only cause to happen. And I am asking how, the first time, he knows that *he* has done it.

I should think that the power and the knowledge of the power come at the same time. How does one, for example, know that one is raising one's arm when one does this as a basic action? This seems to be one of the things a man knows directly and not, as it were, on the basis of evidence. Nor is it something I know only because I notice it happening. That is, had I not noticed it (or had it brought to my attention because someone else noticed it and told me), I might not otherwise have known. If one day I should notice that my arm was rising and lowering, and then realize that, if I had not noticed, I would not have known it was doing this, this would be for me a terrifying experience, a sign that I had lost contact with part of myself, that my arm had become an alien entity. Now a man who looked in the mirror and found his ears moving in this way, that is, noticed that they were, would have hardly a less terrifying experience. It would be like finding that his face was covered with blotches he had had no suspicion of. So I am suggesting that even on the first occasion, when there has been the sudden acquisition of a new gift, this is not something a man would know about by only noticing that, say, his ear was moving.

I can imagine that one to whom this happened might rush to a mirror in order to check up. I should only find it hard to imagine him not finding what he expects. Largely because the gift consists in being able to start and stop the motion of one's ears without having to cause these things to happen, and checking up would consist in doing these things in front of the mirror; and if one does not know what to do, how can one check up? Notice that I might feel my ears moving and go to the mirror and check whether they were moving, but this will not tell me whether *I* was moving them. The mirror shows the same thing whether I am moving them or they are only moving. So I would have to know already if I were to know at all.

Do I after all know that I am seeing by *noticing* that I am? So that, had I not noticed, I would not have known? But in what should such noticing consist? Surely not in having some *auditory* experience.

## IV

Of course, one can sometimes notice that one's arm is moving, when one would not otherwise have known. Someone has anesthetized my arm, and sent a small electrical current through to some part of my brain. My mind is taken up with other things, and the experimenter cries out in great excitement: "Look! the arm is moving!" And I look and notice that it is moving, though I would not otherwise have known. The experiment is a success. I am in no special panic, for I know what is happening. It is not terrifying as it would have been had I not known what was happening, and awoke to see my alienated arm traversing space. In a case such as I have described, though, I have no better, and perhaps have a lesser authority for pronouncing on the motion of my arm than a favorably situated second person.

But is it possible that it should be brought to my attention, or that I myself should discover through noticing the fact, that my arm was *not* moving when I should have said, with my usual authority, that I was moving my arm? I am told to raise my arm, and then berated for not obeying, and I insist that I *have* obeyed, and then am told to look. I look. And there is my arm which I thought was aloft hanging instead at my side. Can there be such errors? Epistemologists often enough tell us of the strange cases of phantom limbs, where a man feels pains in limbs no longer his, where he would point to a space left empty by a sectioned arm if asked where the pain was. Had he not known the arm was gone, he would have said the hurt was there, so there might have been a point when he would have said the pain was there and *then* noticed his arm was gone. Might there not then be amputees who feel themselves to be raising an arm when they have no arm to raise? And then might there not have been that awful first moment when they noticed that they had no arm though they would have said they were raising it? And then might this not be our situation at any minute? One discerns here the first crack which can widen into a skeptical abyss, but I am less troubled by this than I am by the fact that my own position is threatened if not destroyed. For I have said that when one moves one's arm, one knows this, knows the thing itself, and not on the basis of some kind of evidence. But if illusions are possible, there must be space for them to enter, and if there *is* the required space, where, and between what, can it, on my account, be located? But if there is no room for a gap on my account, how can I be right?

It might then be thought that the correct account cannot be very different from one I shall now sketch.

If a man discovers, but would otherwise never have known, that his arm was not moving when he would have said that he was moving his arm, the question must be raised as to what his assertion would have been based upon. *Whatever* it would have been based upon, it could not have been based upon something different from what it would have been based upon in the normal case where a man would say that he was moving his arm and his arm in fact was moving, so that he would be saying something true. The two cases cannot differ except for the moving of the arm in the one case and its not moving in the other. For if what his assertion were based upon could be different, then the man would be able to tell, on the basis of this difference, whether his arm was moving or not, and the assumption is that he in fact finds this out only by noticing that the arm is moving or that it is not. So something must be invariant in the two cases, it must be this upon which his assertion is based, and plainly the behavior of the arm is *not* invariant in the two cases. This invariant factor, let us suppose, is a kinesthetic sensation, a feeling, perhaps, that one is moving one's arm. Call this *K*. Then the account —which I shall term the Inductivist Account—runs this way. A man associates *K*, over time, with the moving of his arm. At some time this noticed correlation becomes for him a habit of expectation. So whenever he has *K* he expects that his arm is moving, and commonly he is right, since his arm moves. But we all know how it is with inductions. It is possible at any point that *K* will fail to precede the arm motion it is taken to herald, it being only our man's great luck that it never actualizes. But we are thinking now of a case where it does become actual. By contrast, the normal case is this: (*a*) the man has *K*; (*b*) the man expects his arm to move; (*c*) the man's arm moves.

I am unable to accept the Inductivist Account of how we know that we move our arms. For I can imagine a case where (*a*), (*b*), and (*c*) all are true though the man does not move his arm. The two events "*a* has *K*" and "*a*'s arm rises" may be situated in parallel causal chains. Rather as though some metaphysical jokester were to sever the connections between pilot room and ship and reattach them elsewhere, so that the pilot, though he makes all the *right moves,* is not steering the ship, even though the ship behaves just as it would if he were in fact driving it. Knowing that he is making a turn and noticing that the ship in fact turns in the direction he wanted it to turn in, the pilot rests complacent in a sense of efficiency when credit ought properly to go to a pre-established harmony between pilot-moves and ship-moves. This difficulty cannot be forestalled by the Inductivist Account unless it adds a new truth condition: (*d*) the man moves his arm. But how can this be added when in fact it is supposed to be exhaustively analyzed as (*a*)–(*c*)? This cannot be an analysis, however, if (*a*)–(*c*) are true and (*d*) is false.

I should prefer to say that there is no connection between me and my body to be cut. There is that much point to the negative metaphor that I am not in my body the way a pilot is in a ship. There is no empty space between me and parts of me for a cartesian spirit to haunt. Which does not mean that the self, as I have characterized it, cannot admit of temporary or permanent diminutions, but only that it should know when this happens (barring the final diminution to zero).

There cannot then be errors of the kind I have been considering. My arm can move without my knowing it, but I cannot be moving it without knowing it. My arm can fail to move when I would have thought it was moving, but I cannot fail to move my arm without knowing that I have failed; and so I cannot be in a position to say that I am moving my arm and then find out, through noticing that my arm is not moving, that I was wrong. If, as a basic action, I could raise a hat, I would know.

## V

Wittgenstein speaks of someone locating his pain in a table. We might speak of locating a *K*-like kinesthetic sensation in a hat. So imagine that *a* feels *K* in his hat, and then notices that the hat moves. And over time a habit builds up, etc. Or let's not worry about whether *K* is located one place rather than another, but say only that one has some kind of feeling and then notices a hat move, and that, whenever one has the feeling, the hat moves, and this goes on. Would one ever say that one was moving the hat? If not, wherein does this case differ from the case of the arm? Are not (*a*), (*b*), (*c*) all satisfied? By opening a gap between ourselves and our arms, the Inductivist closes the gap between arms and hats. True, he might say we never do have the appropriate *K*. But suppose we did; would he not then have to say that we were moving that hat in just the same sense as he says we move our arm? The Inductivist can give only an inductive answer to the question, What are the limits of positive abnormality? It is just a matter of fact that we cannot move our hats in the way in which we move our arms. It is only that I have never had the right things to correlate with hat-moves.

I have challenged the Inductivist Account, but am I any better able than the Inductivist to show that the limits here are logical and not empirical? Someone may be able to show this, but I am not clever enough for that. True, at a certain level of description, hats are differently constituted than arms are, but this gives us only necessary conditions, for we have the case of negatively abnormal persons whose arms, like ours, are flesh and blood, but who cannot move their arms, and the case of positively abnormal persons whose eyes, like ours, are cells and nerves, but who can dilate their pupils. Nor would it help if there were hats made of flesh and blood and connected through nerves to someone's brain, *special* hats, so to speak, which were more like arms than hats. It is essential to our problem that we leave our criteria as they are. Or does this admit a trivial solution to the problem? For it might be our criterion, or part of our criterion, for a hat that a hat can move only when something causes it to move. The limits of positive normality then become logical by courtesy of the appropriate paradigm-case arguments.

Wrongly, perhaps, I am not satisfied with this. A man who could *just* dilate his eyes, without them being caused to dilate (by him or someone or something) would, by perhaps a similar appeal to paradigm usage, perhaps not be regarded as human. So whether or not a human can dilate his eyes that way admits of a final, logical answer. Our repertoire of basic actions *R* would specify the essence of being human. But by a comparable criterion, paralytics would not be human; and this is only a bitter piece of irony. If we relax these criteria, however, our problem once more becomes empirical. I don't say I would not be dubious if someone were to claim the hat-moving ability, even if his hat rose and fell: I should suspect fine wires or air jets. But I don't believe the thing is even physically impossible. Physics is concerned only with the way things move when they are caused to move (forgetting just now the First Law). But this, being quite another way of moving an object, would leave physics intact.

## VI

Besides, something may be a perfectly ordinary arm—and for all that we should be unable to move it as a basic action. Specifically, this is so when it is not *our* arm. This lies in the area of what I briefly indicated as the Problem of Other Bodies, which I cannot treat of here. But the fact that I can no more raise your arm than I can feel your feelings, so that privacy extends out into the world of crass objects, should serve to disabuse those who feel that the Problem of Other Minds is due to some logical feature peculiar to minds. The feature, which indeed marks the limits of what we can do, is peculiar rather to selves, and the distinction between a self and everything else cuts, I have suggested, across the distinction of mind and body. If someone could raise a hat as one of his basic actions, the hat would be his in a philosophical, rather than a legal sense: it would be part of him. So not just any hat would do.

The theological implications of all of this are rather hazy. Logical impossibility is alleged not to affect an ascription of omnipotence to God, but God could not even do some of the things that are done in the world; e.g., none of the basic actions that are performed by us are His actions. Unless He causes us to do them, in which cases not all His actions are basic actions. A believer might nevertheless take some comfort from the fact that "God made the world" and "The world was not caused" are quite compatible if the former describes a basic action.

## Notes

1. These notions are defended in "Basic Actions," in *American Philosophical Quarterly*, II (1965). [Reprinted in this volume.]

2. I take the expression "*a* causes *B*," when *a* stands for an individual, to be a shorthand way of saying that, if *B* is an event, then some other event in *a*'s biography stands to *B* as cause to effect. The relationship between this event and *a* is not easily analyzed, but for purposes of this discussion I shall leave it unanalyzed.

3. "The manner in which God knows the infinity of propositions is utterly more excellent than is the manner by means of which we know the few that we do. We proceed by argumentation, and advance from conclusion to conclusion, while God [apprehends] through a simple, sudden intuition." Galileo, *Dialogo Sopra i due Massimi Sistemi del Mondo*.

4. David Hume, *An Inquiry Concerning Human Understanding*, Sec. VII, Pt. 1.

JAMES BOGEN

# Physical Determinism

(1) A traditional argument against free will has the following as its premises.

(D1) Every physicial motion is made to happen by the operation of a physical cause.

(D2) All of the motions of and all of the motions caused by a man's body are physical motions (and are therefore made to happen by the operation of physical causes).

(D3) No man's body ever operates as a closed causal system. Although the motions which take place when we say a man acts may have proximate causes belonging to the man's body, their operation is always brought about by causes which are external to his body.[1]

The purpose of this article is to examine considerations (due primarily to Ryle and Melden) which are often said to invalidate this argument. I claim that they do not, and that the premises (D1)–(D3) are incompatible with libertarianism. If this is so, Aristotle was probably correct in holding that if a man acts, the source of his motion must lie within him. (*Nichomachaean Ethics* 1110a-5.) Whether or not Aristotle so intended, I shall take this to mean that the ascription of agency is falsified or rendered pointless if we assume that the physical motions which must occur in order for a man to act have causes which are external to the body of the putative agent.

(2) The argument sketched above may conveniently be la-

beled "the argument from physical determinism." Some contemporary libertarians have assumed that arguments of this kind are intended to show that every action has a physical cause. It has been objected that because human actions are not *just* physical motions, this does not follow from (D1)–(D3). Consider the move p-k4 in a chess game. The bodily motion which gets the piece of wood to the square marked "k4" does not secure the making of this move unless certain conventionally required conditions obtain. Since what causes the motion does not bring the game of chess or its rules into existence and does not bring it about that a game is going on, that the pawn is in a position from which it can be moved to k4, etc., it cannot be said to have brought about the move p-k4. The most we could say—so the argument runs—is that the cause of the player's movements was a necessary condition for the performance of the act. Related considerations are sometimes held to show that it is impossible in principle for any human action to have a physical cause.[2]

Even if (D1)–(D3) were intended to show that human actions have physical causes, the line of argument just sketched is far from convincing. For one thing, a determinist might claim that the existence of conventions and the fulfillment of the conditions they lay down are background conditions whose obtaining makes a physical cause sufficient for the performance of the action. For another, it is hard to see how such considerations could be applied to actions like walking, scratching an insect bite, hitting a man, or tearing a piece of paper, whose successful performances are not conventional in any obvious way.

But the physical determinist can make a stronger and more interesting reply. Physical motions are essential to the performance of the acts with which libertarians have traditionally been concerned. The import of (D1)–(D3) is that because they have causes external to his body, no man can be truly said to initiate the motions necessary for the performance of the actions ascribed to him. The moral to be drawn from this is not that the actions we perform are brought about by physical causes. It is that men should not be said to act at all because they do not initiate the motions required for the performance of an action. It is this radically antilibertarian position which I want to consider.

(3) In order to show why I think (D1)–(D3) lead to the conclusion that no man acts, it will be necessary to distinguish actions which consist of doing something in or by doing something else or something under a different description (e.g., signalling a waiter by crooking a finger, assassinating a president by setting a time bomb) from actions which consist simply of doing something (e.g., normal cases of moving a finger to signal or to connect wires). The former will be called "ø-acts" and the latter, "ψ-acts." Ignoring acts of omission and forbearance whose performance does not necessarily involve physical motion but whose consideration is of little interest for the purpose of examining the merits of libertarianism, ø-action is impossible without ψ-action, and we should not say that a man ψ-acted unless we thought he initiated certain physical motions. The determinist's position is that because the motions required for ψ-action are brought about by causes external to a man's body, a man cannot be said to initiate them and therefore cannot be said to ψ- or ø-act.[3] In order to introduce the distinction between ψ-acting and ø-acting upon which this depends, it will be necessary to say something about the term "action."

What philosophers call "actions" comprise a selection of the things it is natural to say (in various everyday circumstances) that a man does or is doing. Although "act" and "action" occur in ordinary speech, these words are seldom used by non-philosophers as often and in the same ways as in philosophical discussions. Philosophers tend to employ them as quasi-technical terms whose logic is guided roughly by certain ordinary language uses of the verb "to do." But not everything a man may be said to do in non-philosophical talk is or should be classified as an action.[4] Where is the line to be drawn?

In speaking of actions, philosophers usually have in mind things a man is said to do for which he may be held responsible.

They are what a man is praised or blamed for doing, what he is persuaded to do or dissuaded from doing, what he may be trained or educated to do, etc. Because of the way in which the notion of responsibility figures in praising, blaming, etc., and because the agent's intentions are often crucial in determining responsibility, it is tempting to reserve the term "action" for what a man does intentionally, on purpose, or deliberately. A philosopher who takes this line will be inclined to think that a man can be said to have acted—or to have acted freely—as long as he and his performance measure up to the standards by which we ordinarily determine whether he did what he did intentionally, on purpose, etc. Since we seldom consider the physical causes for a man's motions in deciding whether he acted intentionally, it becomes easy to think that the physical determinist's considerations are irrelevant to the question whether men should be considered capable of free action.[5] But this is surely a distortion. In setting out a distinction between the doings which are to be classified as actions and those which are not, the philosopher is trying to mark off such things as blushing, perspiring, falling, and waiting from such things as killing, stepping on a man's toes, and walking, as well as from murdering and stealing. The philosophically interesting differences between these cannot accurately be captured by saying that where V-ing is something a man does it is an action only if done intentionally, deliberately, or on purpose. The reason for this is that I cannot ask, e.g., if a man stepped on my foot on purpose unless I have established that he *did* step on it in the first place. The claim that he did step on my foot is not to be retracted (by saying that the man did nothing or did something else) simply because he did not step on it on purpose, intentionally, or deliberately. Unintentionally stepping on someone's foot is not like blushing, perspiring, or falling, and it is not something that merely happens to the man who does it —even though what makes him do it (e.g., being shoved or losing his balance) may be.

It would also be a mistake to say that a man does not act unless he is to be held responsible for what he did. We do not usually hold a man responsible for doing something if he has a reasonable excuse, but not all excuses are intended to show that he did not do it at all. Furthermore, there are many things which it is natural to treat as actions but for which there is normally no occasion to hold a man responsible. We do not ordinarily hold a man responsible for striking a match, scratching himself, or breathing unless all we mean by saying he is responsible for his V-ing is that he V-ed. But we could ask whether a man is to be held responsible for striking a match which touched off an explosion, for breaking a silence (in the course of a prison break, for example) by drawing a breath and even for scratching (when his scratching scores his skin and we wonder whether he couldn't have controlled himself). Thus if responsibility is required for the ascription of agency, we must accept the paradoxical conclusion that the very same performance (breathing, scratching, etc.) is sometimes an action and sometimes not.

Nevertheless, any account of action which ignores intention and responsibility is doomed to irrelevance. In order to insure that in talking about actions we shall be considering those things for which men can be praised, blamed, etc., I shall stipulate that where V-ing is what a man does, it is to be called an action only if the man who does it is able to V intentionally—whether or not he actually does so in the particular case under consideration and regardless of whether he is to be held morally, legally, or prudentially responsible for his V-ing.

More arbitrarily, I shall also stipulate that V-ing is an action only if its performance requires the occurrence of a physical motion of or caused by the agent's body. There are probably things which ought to be called actions and do not meet this condition. I do not consider them because a libertarian could not plausibly rest his case against physical determinism upon them.

Let us now distinguish $\psi$- from $\phi$-actions. When an agent, A, does something, V, we can often give a true statement of the form "A V-ed by ——ing" in answer to a question of the form

"How (i.e., by doing what) did he V?" where ——ing is something A is able to do intentionally and thus counts as an action under the stipulation just given. It is not necessary that A knowingly ——ed or was conscious of ——ing for the purpose of V-ing. For example, an experienced typist is seldom conscious of each motion his fingers make, even though he types by moving his fingers in certain ways.

In some cases ("A cleared the crossbar by pushing hard on the pole and jerking himself up") the blanks and the "V" position in the schema take descriptions of distinct happenings. In others ("He signalled the waiter by crooking his finger") they take logically independent descriptions of what is naturally considered one and the same happening. "He signalled" can be true when "he crooked" is not, and vice-versa, but when the signalling is done by crooking it is natural to say the signalling just is the crooking, and not a separate event which follows or accompanies it. I shall refer to a description which occupies the "V" position in a true answer to the question "how (by doing what) did A V?" as a "ø-description" providing that the description gives an act and is logically independent from the description which fills the blanks in the schema.[6] An act so described will be called a "ø-act" and the agent will be said to have "ø-done" whatever he did.

The blanks in the schema "A V-ed by ——ing" may be filled with another ø-description. For example, "A assassinated the president by setting a time bomb" tells us what A did in order to assassinate, but there is also an answer to "How did A set the bomb?" But consider the case in which an agent with normal—and no more than normal—control over his muscles signals a waiter by crooking a finger. Normally there will be no answer to the question "How did A move his finger?" which mentions anything A can be said to have done in order to move his finger and which he is able to do intentionally. (I am assuming of course that A did not move his finger by pulling it with his other hand, that he was not rigged to a machine by means of which he mechanically moved it, etc.)

The answer "A moved his finger by contracting such and such muscles" will not do. Suppose for simplicity's sake that the contraction of a single muscle causes the motion and call the muscle "MU." The only way in which a normal man could intentionally contract MU without resorting to electronic or mechanical devices would be to move his finger. This secures the contraction of the muscle if we know that when the finger moves the muscle must have contracted. But contracting MU in this way is not something a man can do to move his finger. To get his finger to move by contracting MU, the agent would first have had to move his finger in order to contract MU. Similar considerations rule out "A moved his finger by making such and such neurons fire" unless A has special equipment which enables him to get the neurons to fire without moving his finger in order to do so.

When, as in this case, we get no answer to the question "How did A V?" mentioning what A could intentionally do to bring off the V-ing, what replaces the "V" in the question will be called a "$\psi$-description," what is done under that description will be called a "$\psi$-act," and the agent will be said to have $\psi$-acted or $\psi$-done what he did.

The question whether or not a given description describes a $\phi$- or a $\psi$-act can be empirical rather than a logical matter. Although I cannot move my ears except by pulling them, some people can $\psi$-move their ears just as easily as I can $\psi$-wrinkle my nose. If a man claimed to be able to $\psi$-contract MU (i.e., to simply contract it instead of contracting it by moving his finger) in order to $\phi$-move his finger, I should be inclined to doubt him—especially if he told me that he was unable to $\psi$-move his finger, that he always had to contract MU to get it to move, but that it moved whenever he $\psi$-contracted MU. However, we may suppose it possible in principle that a man could $\psi$-contract MU just as we can flex a bicep, and my topic does not require an account of how we should determine whether the man crooks his finger by contracting his muscle or contracts his muscle by crooking his finger. On the other hand, it is reasonable to suppose that there are actions which, as a matter of logical rather than empirical fact, can only be ø-performed. Conventional actions such as moving a piece in a game or signalling a waiter are examples.

If questions of the form "How did A V?" always took ø-descriptions as answers, such a question would generate an infinite regress, and in order to ø-act, a man would have to perform an infinite number of different acts—or one or more acts under an infinite number of logically independent descriptions. As can be seen from the examples of ø-acts given so far, this is clearly not the case; we can always terminate an explanation of how a man ø-did something by giving a ψ-description. I am deliberately ignoring acts of omission, forbearance, etc., can think of no cases in which ø-acts are accomplished by purely psychical means, and do not consider covert "mental acts" as acts in any sense in which their consideration would be of interest in an assessment of libertarianism. Accordingly we may suppose that a series of "how did A . . . ?" questions can always be cut off by a ψ-description of an act whose performance requires the agent to move or bring about a physical motion. Normally, ψ-acts consist of the agent's moving his body or some part of it, but there are cases (breathing and spitting, for example) in which it may be more natural to say that what the agent ψ-moves is not part of his body. The physical determinist's argument amounts then to this: since every motion of or caused by a putative agent's body is caused by something external to his body, no man really initiates any of the motions whose initiation is required for ψ-agency. Therefore, no man ψ-acts. But since a man ø-acts only if he ψ-acts, no man ø-acts either.

(4) In order to assess the physical determinist's argument, we need to ask whether it follows from (D1)–(D3) that no man initiates any of the motions of or caused by his body.

Call the motion a man makes when he crooks his finger "mf."

The proximate cause of mf is the contraction of MU, and this in turn is caused by the firing of neurons, etc. According to (D3) a man's body never operates as a closed causal system and so we are to suppose that something which does not belong to the putative agent's body brings about the neural events which in turn cause the muscle contraction. If all of this is true, we cannot say that A *caused* mf, for the agent is not identical to the muscle which contracts, the neurons which fire, or the external causes of their operations. Thus (D1)–(D3) make it impossible to say that A initiated mf if "to initiate" means to proximately or indirectly cause the motion.

Is there any non-causal sense in which A could be said to initiate a motion whose cause lies outside of his body? If X is the external cause of mf, then (1) the operation of X made happen whatever made A's finger move, (2) under the physical conditions which obtained when mf was caused, nothing beyond the operation of X was required to bring about the sequence of events which produced the motion, and (3) under the conditions which then obtained, mf would not have occurred had X not brought it about.[7] From this it would seem to follow that if A were said to non-causally initiate or bring about mf, A's "initiation" of the motion would be neither necessary nor sufficient for its occurrence. That means that under the physical conditions which obtained when mf occurred, A's finger would have moved even if A had not "initiated" its motion. It also means that if A had been able to "initiate" without the operation of the external cause, his "initiating" would not have been enough to start the finger moving under those conditions. Assuming that "A $\psi$-moved his finger" means that A made the finger move (I shall argue for this contention presently) the fact that A non-causally "initiated" mf would seem a poor reason for saying that A acted.

But does it really follow from the fact that mf had an external cause that A's non-causal initiation of the motion was neither necessary nor sufficient to bring about its occurrence? Perhaps

"A moved his finger" is made true by a convention under which we say A initiated mf if or only if something, Y, occurs where the occurrence of Y is itself caused by the operation of X. It could be that Y occurs only if X causes mf. Thus if we suppose that the finger would not have moved had X not caused it to, then it would not have moved had Y not occurred. If A non-causally initiates mf only if Y occurs, then mf would not have occurred had it been false to say that A initiated his finger's motion.[8]

Someone who advocated this position would have to assume either that Y is itself a proximate or indirect cause of mf or that it does not cause mf but is made to occur by X in addition to something else which figures in the production of the motion. On the latter assumption, we must suppose that at some point in the sequence of events which terminates in mf, X produces at least two effects—the occurrence of Y and the occurrence of whatever plays a part in the production of the motion. There are cases in which a single cause has two effects (e.g., when a cue ball hits and moves two billiard balls simultaneously) but in such cases we need not suppose that the non-occurrence of one effect would guarantee the non-occurrence of the other. Thus if Y is not itself one of the causes of mf, there is no reason to say that had it not occurred X would not have brought about the motion of A's finger. And so we can still say that had A not "initiated" mf, mf would still have occurred given the operation of the external cause.

On the other hand, we know enough about what kinds of things cause the motions of a man's body to imagine what Y would have to be like if it were itself a proximate or indirect cause of the motion. If Y were not the contraction of a muscle or a neural or cerebral event, it would have to be the impinging of some sort of physical stimulus upon A's body, or the cause of its impinging. The suggestion to be considered is that by convention, Y's occurrence is a necessary condition for the truth of "A initiated mf." My objection to this is that native speakers of

English are woefully ignorant of the physical and physiological processes which lead to the motions figuring in the ψ-actions they report—so much so that under a convention of the kind suggested, the well-founded ascription of ψ-agency would be practically impossible under normal circumstances.[9]

A more important difficulty with the suggestion that the possibility of ψ-description rests upon the occurrence of what is brought about by a cause external to the agent's body is that it fails to do justice to the importance we attach to the agent. Suppose we are anxious to prevent the performance of a ø-act which would not be performed unless A ψ-moved something. If the causes of all of A's motions are external to A's body, why should we bother with A at all? And why should we attempt to dissuade him with arguments and entreaties if the workings of an external cause can produce not only the motion required for the ψ-action we wish to prevent but also the occurrence of Y upon which we are supposing the truth of the ascription of the ψ-act depends? Or suppose we are glad that a certain ψ-action occurred. Why should we feel grateful to a man who can be said to have acted only because the operation of an external cause brought about the required motion? Shouldn't our interest and concern center upon the external cause?

It will not do to reply that we can grant (D1)–(D3) without supposing we actually know what causes what must occur if we are to ascribe ψ-agency and therefore that we deal with A because we do not know what else to deal with. In asking whether the ascription of agency is incompatible with physical determinism, we want to know whether the discovery of an external cause for the motions a man was said to ψ-make would be grounds for retracting the claim that he acted. If all of our motions did have external causes the fact that we don't yet know what they are or how to deal with them has no bearing upon this question.

For these reasons, the view that what a man is said to ψ-move is moved by an external cause which also brings about what is necessary for us to say that he non-causally "initiated" the motion is implausible. It pictures our ascriptions of agency as depending upon physical and physiological knowledge which we do not in fact possess, and the "initiation" for which it allows is initiation in too weak a sense to explain the importance we attach to the agent whose actions concern us. But if we reject the view I have been considering and grant that under the conditions which obtained when A was said to move his finger, the operation of an external cause was enough to bring about the sequence of events which terminated in the motion and was necessary for its production, we can say that A initiated the motion only if we are prepared to admit that under the conditions which then obtained, A's "initiation" was not necessary for the occurrence of the motion and was not what made the motion occur.

If we admitted all of this, it is difficult to see how we could also claim that A had $\psi$-moved his finger. The suggestion that the action claim should be dropped in the face of all of this is intuitively plausible—especially in view of the fact that we do retract $\psi$-agency ascriptions when we discover that the crucial motion was externally caused. Suppose a man told us he was going to signal a waiter and then his finger crooked. Normally we should say he moved his finger. But what if we then discovered a fine wire tied to it and found out that his finger moved because the wire pulled it? Even if the man's finger moved just as he'd wanted it to and just when he intended to move it, we would not say he did move it. Why then should we think the discovery of external causes for all of the motions we say an agent makes in normal cases should be compatible with ascriptions of $\psi$-agency?

(5) I believe that a chief reason why many contemporary philosophers think that physical determinism is compatible with agency is a view about the language of action which derives from considerations raised by Ryle and Melden.[10] It is doubtful whether Ryle and Melden were directly concerned with the de-

terministic argument I have been considering. However, it is of interest to ask whether their views can be pressed into service against it, and regardless of their intentions, I believe that their work on action theory has contributed to our tendency to disregard the physical determinist.

Ryle and Melden suggest that if A moves his finger, we may describe the event which then occurs in either of two distinct languages or subdivisions of language—the language of physical events and the language of action. In physical-event language, the event is reported as the occurrence of a motion of A's finger. If, under this description, we ask why the event occurred or what brought it about, our "why" is a causal "why" demanding an answer in terms of physical causes of the motion.[11] But we may report the very same event in action-language as A's having moved his finger. In this case the question "why did it happen?" calls for an answer in terms of A's reasons, motives, etc. for acting instead of an answer in terms of physical causes for the motion. In action-language statements of the form "A moved X because . . ." what follows the "because" is not intended to tell us what causally initiated the motion.[12]

The following view which I shall label the "compatibility theory" (CT) represents the kind of position I take to have emerged as an extension of the considerations just sketched. According to CT, "A moved X" is a report by which we present the event in order to explain why it took place, and so it would be a mistake to think the action-language report explains the event by giving A as the cause of X's motion. It would also be a mistake to think that the truth of "A $\psi$-moved X" is excluded by the truth of "such and such caused the motion of X" because the former is not an explanation of X's motion and a fortiori, the two are not competing explanations of what brought about the motion. And so, the argument runs, there is no reason to think a causal explanation for the motion should preclude the truth of the action-language report "A $\psi$-moved X."

If someone thought there might be an incompatibility between the two reports, "A ψ-moved X" and "X moved," the CT theorist would tell him to consider the "forms of life" to which they belong and the practices and activities which give these reports their significance, claiming that an understanding of their interconnections will explain why our opting to report an event in action-language does not prevent us from reporting it in physical event-language as well and thus from treating the same event as the occurrence of a motion with a cause and an action with a reason.[13]

A serious objection to all of this is that we can imagine cases in which it would be perfectly natural to give a ψ-description as an answer to the question "what brought about such and such a motion?" It is because of this that the determinist can claim against CT theory that statements of the form "A ψ-moved X" are falsified by showing that the motion of X was not initiated by A.

Suppose an agent, A, has been rigged to a machine operated by an experimentor, B. When turned on, the machine temporarily debilitates all of the muscles in A's arm so that they can be bunched up or stretched out only mechanically and cannot expand or contract normally. As it debilitates the muscles, the machine also causes mf, a crooking motion of A's forefinger. Once the finger moves, the debilitator is automatically shut off so that A can again move as he normally does, but as long as it is in operation, A cannot move his finger unless he ø-moves it by pulling with his other hand or manipulating the machine himself. It is natural to say that while the machine is in operation A cannot ψ-move his finger even if it moves. We could imagine various sorts of experiments which might be run with such an apparatus. For example, B could explain the workings of the machine to A and tell him that he will be instructed at various times to crook his finger at the count of 5. At 5, B may turn on the machine, or may leave it off, and A is supposed to tell him whether he moved his finger.

What must be the case if it is to be true to say that A $\psi$-moved his finger? One condition of the truth of the $\psi$-report is that the motion occurs. But this is clearly not enough, for under the conditions just described, the motion always occurs after the count of 5 even though mf is caused by the machine and A cannot be said to have moved his finger. What then does "A $\psi$-moved his finger" commit us to which "A's finger moved" does not?

Since we are deliberately considering a case in which A does not move his finger unless he $\psi$-moves it, we cannot say he moves his finger just in case he performs some other action to get it to move. Nor can we say the $\psi$-report is true just in case mf occurs when A wants his finger to move and intends to move it. There is surely a distinction between moving one's limbs and having them moved for one by happy coincidence just when one wanted or intended them to move. Nor can we say that A $\psi$-moves in case his finger moves when he wants (intends) it to and he tries to move it. Trying to move it could mean attempting to beat the machine at the count of 5, or exerting some sort of effort as the machine goes into operation (in the way in which a paralyzed man can sometimes strain to move a limb over which he has little or no control). If A's trying consists in attempting to move his finger before his muscle is debilitated, we must say that he tried and failed if the muscle is debilitated and the finger moved before he can do it. If he exerts effort as the machine is actually causing his finger's motion, it makes sense to ask whether the motion was due to his trying or to the machine's acting. To show that the motion was caused by the machine is to show that A did not move it.[14] (Consider the case in which a paralyzed man just gaining control over his limbs complains about the exercise machine which moves his legs for him when he is trying to move them himself.)

It could be suggested that a man never $\psi$-moves his finger at all—that the only $\psi$-act an agent ever performs is a special mental act of willing by means of which he $\phi$-moves his limbs. The difficulties involved with this are too well known to require fresh enumeration, and the suggestion therefore need not be considered here.

"A moved his finger" is false in the case we have been considering just in case mf either fails to occur or is caused by the workings of the experimentor's machine. I can see no other way of accounting for this except on the grounds that CT is incorrect and "A ψ-moved his finger" claims that the motion was due to A and therefore that the action claim does give an explanation for the motion which is incompatible with its explanation in terms of an external physical cause. If this were not so, it would be impossible to explain the difference between "A's finger was moved by the machine" and "A ψ-moved his finger"; no further difference is to be found in the situation under consideration.

Suppose that a third party, C, observed the motion of A's finger, did not know whether the machine was working or not, and asked "why did A's finger move that time?" Couldn't this question be taken as a serious request for an account of the origin of the motion, and wouldn't "A moved it" be a straightforward answer to it? If so, the ψ-description does function as an explanation for the finger's motion which is clearly incompatible with "mf was caused by the machine."

It will be objected that this is a bizarre case which is so strikingly different from the situations in which we normally ask for and give action-language reports that it provides no basis for a general denial of the CT claim that ψ-descriptions are always compatible with explanations of motion in terms of physical causes. It is worthwhile to examine this objection in some detail, for it embodies much of what makes CT theory appear to be plausible.

Part of the plausibility of the CT theory derives from the consideration that not all causal explanations are incompatible with ψ-descriptions. Where A does ψ-move his finger mf is caused by a cerebral event, muscle contraction, etc., and these are clearly physical causes. Why should "A ψ-moved his finger" be true when mf has a physical cause? It is tempting to think that if the ψ-description did purport to explain what brought about the motion, it would be falsified by the explanation in terms of muscle contraction. The next step is to conclude that it is not so falsified because it did not purport to explain the occurrence of mf at all. And the next step is to seize upon the theory that ψ-descriptions only redescribe and never explain what brought about physical motions as a way of making sense out of this.

The possibility of accepting this line depends I think upon the fact that when (as is seldom) we actually concern ourselves with ψ-descriptions in daily life, we usually have no interest in what brought a motion about. Typically, we ask for ψ-descriptions to find out how a ø-action was brought off. For example, a student trying to learn a difficult instrumental passage might ask if his teacher moved his hand in a certain way in order to find out how the passage can be executed. Given this interest, the question what brought about the motion his teacher made has little chance of becoming relevant. Or suppose a psychiatrist has observed a patient moving his hands in a curious way, the same way he once moved them just before the onslaught of a severe fit of depression. If he asks a nurse if she noticed the patient moving his hands in that way, it is not because he knows a motion occurred and wonders if the patient brought it about; it is because he wants, e.g., to keep a record of the ψ-movements of his patient when he is out of the room in addition to those he observes himself. I conjecture that what makes it plausible to say with the CT theorist that ψ-descriptions merely describe and do not explain is the fact that our mundane interests in ψ-actions usually lead us to mention them for reportorial rather than explanatory purposes as in the cases just sketched.

But the purposes for which a statement is made do not necessarily determine its truth conditions. Even if a man says "the shortest girl in the chorus line is my sister" in order to tell someone who knows he has a sister who his sister is, his statement still commits him to the truth of "I have a sister" and can be made for the purpose of informing someone of this in other contexts. Similarly, the fact that we do not ordinarily report a $\psi$-action in order to explain why a motion occurred does not establish that the $\psi$-description cannot be used to say that a given motion was brought about by an agent or that the falsity of this claim would not falsify the $\psi$-description given for purely reportorial purposes.

Furthermore, the CT theorist's use of the distinction between reporting and explaining an event is an arbitrary one, since explanations of occurrences always or almost always report whatever is said to have brought the occurrence about. Consider the statement "the contraction of MU caused a rapid motion of A's finger" in the mouth of someone who knows what makes fingers move but who had suspected that the administration of a certain drug weakened the muscle sufficiently to prevent it from causing a rapid motion. He has given the drug and reports the causing of a rapid motion by the muscle as a piece of evidence against his theory. Is his statement then reportorial or explanatory? If he regularly made the statement for this reportorial purpose, could we conclude that it is not fit for explanation but only for reporting?

The moral of these examples is that making a statement for reportorial purposes does not preclude its employment in other contexts for explanatory purposes, and that there is no reason to think that the same statement must have different truth conditions when used reportorially than when used to explain an occurrence. The plausibility considerations outlined above for CT are thus inconclusive, and I think the bizarreness of the psychological experiment case can be easily discounted. Its bizarreness consists solely in the fact that in the context of this case the $\psi$-description "A moved his finger" is given to explain the occurrence of a finger motion whereas in a normal case, we should be unlikely to use the description at all and would probably use it—if we did—for some reason other than to explain why a finger moved. In the psychological experiment case, one of the truth conditions for the ψ-description was that the motion of A's finger have no external physical cause. The fact that such descriptions are seldom given for the purpose of explaining what brought about a physical motion is no reason to think the ψ-description would not have the absence of an external cause as a truth condition in a normal case.

But all the same, don't "A moved his finger" and "A's finger moved" refer to one and the same event? If so, how could the former possibly explain the occurrence of the latter? We can't say that something, X, brought about something, Y, unless X and Y are different items.

Someone who thought that one event (the motion of A's finger, in this case) must always be brought about by another *event* would have difficulty accepting the explanation "A's finger moved because A ψ-moved it," for in this case A's moving his finger and his finger's moving are one and the same event under different descriptions. However, events are commonly said to be brought about by persons or things as well as by other events. There is nothing wrong with saying for example that Amy stiffened the eggs by beating them even though the stiffening and the beating are one and the same event. "A ψ-moved his finger" may be taken to say that A brought about mf, and it is clear that when taken in this way the explanation gives one item (the motion of the finger) which was brought about and another quite distinct item (the agent whose finger moved) as its initiator.

(6) I have been attempting to discredit the claim (that ψ-descriptions are always reports and never explanations of motions) by which the CT theory attempts to reconcile the thesis that we sometimes ψ-act with (D1)–(D3), the premises of the physical determinist. Now I want to argue quite apart from this, the strategy by which the CT theorist seeks to make his peace with physical determinism is wrongheaded because it makes it impossible to explain the point of our uses of action-language.

If the CT theorist takes seriously his idea that ψ-reports of the form "A moved X" do not explain what brought the motion about and are therefore compatible with the claim that the motion was made to happen by an external cause, he cannot maintain that A initiated the motion in any sense in which A's initiation could be called a necessary condition for the motion's occurrence. In order to see what is wrong with this—and why I claimed earlier that we should not ascribe $\psi$-agency to a man who had failed to initiate a motion in some stronger sense—consider actions like theft and murder which concern us mainly because of non-conventional consequences and effects of the motions the agent $\psi$-makes in order to perform them.

When we accuse a man of murder, we do not describe his crime as consisting solely of his having $\psi$-moved his limbs in certain ways. But all the same, we should have no interest in the crime if the motions did not cause the death of the agent's victim, and this is why an accusation of murder is defeated if we can show that the accused did not make the crucial motions. Similarly, even though to steal is not just to make certain motions, the damage done by a thief involves transportation of goods which our accusation assumes would not have taken place without the motions he was supposed to have made. That is why we can defeat an accusation of theft by showing that the accused did not make the motions required for the transportation.

But CT theory allows us to say that if a man $\psi$-moves in such a way as to cause a death, his motions were brought about by an external cause whose operation was necessary and sufficient to produce them under the physical conditions which then obtained. If that is so, we cannot say that had the action-language report "A $\psi$-moved in such and such a way" been false, those motions would not have occurred. How could the truth of an action-language report justify punishing or blaming a man for a death caused by certain motions if those motions would have occurred under similar physical conditions even if the action-language report were false?

Suppose we rehabilitate a thief and as a result, it is no longer true to say that he steals or that he ψ-makes the motions which must occur in order for a theft to be committed. On the CT view, this is not nearly as heartwarming as it might seem, because the effects of the rehabilitation need not amount to anything more than that certain ψ-descriptions will no longer be true of the thief. Unfortunately, that is no guarantee that the external causes which once brought about the motions which figured in his stealing will not continue to bring about similar motions of his limbs resulting in the removal of jewels from shop windows, money from vaults, and wallets from other men's pockets. Surely rehabilitation is meant to accomplish more than a change in the language we shall use in the future to describe events in which the agent's limbs move in the same ways and produce the effects we wanted to prevent by rehabilitating him.

Next consider ø-acts involving motions whose significance is conventional. In chess we usually draw a sharp distinction between A moving p-k4 and A having his arm shoved in such a way as to get the pawn to k4 when it is A's turn and the pawn can legally be moved to that square. If p-k4 was the move A intended to make when he was shoved, he would agree to let the pawn stand. But if we know his arm was shoved, we would have to ask what his intentions were—not to determine whether he actually made the move (as he clearly did not), but in order to find out whether he wants us to proceed as though he had. And so we do not say that A moved when what he intended to ψ-do was brought about by something shoving his arm even though what happened may later be counted as a move. If all of our motions were made to happen by external causes, the distinction we draw between the case where A moves and the case in which his arm is shoved would seem to be a distinction without a difference.

Finally suppose that someone teaches me to execute enormously difficult passages on the guitar. That should mean that I can now make ψ-motions I was unable to make before. But what sort of accomplishment would this be for me or my teacher if

CT were correct? Well—we might say I had learned to non-causally initiate certain motions, but if these motions all had an external cause, they could have occurred under similar physical circumstances whether I had non-causally initiated them or not.

What these examples suggest is that the use of an action-language would be pointless unless we thought that in $\psi$-acting the agent initiated motions which would not have occurred if he had not initiated them. Because CT fails to account for this, it cannot do justice to the significance of the action-language we use or the rationality of the practices and activities (punishing, rehabilitating, teaching, encouraging, deliberating, etc.) to which it belongs.

(7) The failure of CT suggests that when we treat a man as an agent, we must suppose that he initiated the motions he $\psi$-made in a sense in which "A initiated such and such a motion" is false if the motion would have occurred without his initiating it. To suppose this would be, I think, to suppose that (D3) is false—that when A $\psi$-moves X, the motion has no external cause. As I suggested earlier, this supposition is a version of the Aristotelian dictum that when a man acts the source of his motion lies within him.

In order to avoid misunderstandings which have resulted in mistaken criticisms of the Aristotelian and related positions, the following observations need to be noted. First of all, it would be a mistake to object to the Aristotelian dictum on the grounds that it does not by itself tell us what an action is. Melden's observation that it does not constitute a full account of human agency is undoubtedly correct, but there is no reason to suppose that it should.[15] The import of the physical determinist's argument is not that "A $\psi$-moved X" should be *analyzed* as claiming merely that X moved and that the causes of the motion belonged to A's body. There are all sorts of movements of a man's internal organs, as well as spasms, twitches, and tics involving motions we should not say a man $\psi$-made even if we did discover that they had no external causes. The lesson to be learned from the physical determinist is that whatever our concept of $\psi$-agency may be, its application *presupposes* the absence of external physical causes for the crucial motions. The importance of the Aristotelian position is that it articulates a supposition we must make in ascribing agency; that is not to say that it provides an analysis of our agency ascriptions.

Secondly, it will not do to object that the Aristotelian dictum does not supply us with a criterion we can apply in order to determine whether a man $\psi$-moved what we know to have moved. The case of Ryle versus Descartes is instructive here. In a famous passage, Ryle complains that upholders of the Cartesian theory of volition

> should have noticed the simple fact that they and all other sensible persons knew how to decide questions about the voluntariness and involuntariness of actions . . . before they had ever heard of the hypothesis of the occult inner thrusts of actions. They might then have realized that they were not elucidating the criteria already in efficient use, but tacitly assuming their validity, trying to correlate them with hypothetical occurrences of a para-mechanical pattern. Yet this correlation could . . . be of no practical or theoretical use, since it would not assist in our appraisals of actions . . . Nor would it elucidate the logic of those appraisal concepts . . . which antedated the invention of this causal hypothesis.[16]

It would be more charitable to read Descartes as claiming that our concept of agency would not apply to human beings if all of their motions had external physical causes than as claiming that we make our ascriptions on the basis of criteria which require us to determine the cause of the motions of the agent. The para-mechanical side of Descartes' theory is open to independent and extremely serious objections, and I do not mean to defend the theory in this regard. The point I want to make is that the objection that we do not actually ascribe agency on the basis of a determination of the causes of a motion of the putative agent's body is irrelevant to the claim that our concept of action (together with the criteria it involves) would be inapplicable if every motion of or caused by a man's body had an external physical cause. The Aristotelian dictum (of which I take the Cartesian theory to be a perhaps unfortunate elaboration) holds simply that the sources of an agent's movement must lie within him if there is to be human action; it does not purport to offer this as a criteria for determining agency in daily life any more than it purports to provide an exhaustive analysis of the concept of action.

Finally, it is important to resist the suggestion that the claim that libertarianism is compatible with physical determinism commits one to a priori physical or physiological pronouncements. (D3), the contention that no man's body functions as a closed causal system, may be treated as a contingent statement subject to verification or falsification by empirical means in the case of a given motion. So far as I know, there is no conclusive argument to show that (D3) must be false in principle, and there is surely no reason to think that the determinist's claim is necessarily true. Someone who thought the statement "some men $\psi$-move their limbs" could be established a priori would have to deny (D3) a priori if he believed that physical determinism is incompatible with libertarianism. But it is easy to imagine worlds in which no man $\psi$-acts. The most he could plausibly maintain is that men could in principle $\psi$-act if their motions are not brought about by external causes. This leaves the question whether (D3) is true open to empirical examination.

(8) Since the purpose of this article was the negative one of objecting to a kind of libertarian response to physical determinism and arguing that libertarianism and physical determinism are incompatible, I do not propose to offer a positive account of the concept of an action. However, it will be necessary to consider briefly how the Aristotelian dictum (as I have been interpreting it) might figure in an account of human agency to relieve the difficulties raised by the physical determinist. If what I have been arguing is correct, the possibility of $\psi$-agency (and hence of $\phi$-agency) depends upon the falsity of the assumption that no man's body ever acts as a closed causal system and the

truth of the contention that in some cases, the causes of a man's movements are to be found within his body. How might this position be developed?

One possibility would be to say with Chisholm that A $\psi$-moves X only if A himself causes X's motion.[17] Where A is said to $\psi$-move his finger, we know that the proximate cause of its motion is the contraction of some muscle. Since no man is a muscle, there seems to be little plausibility in the suggestion that A proximately causes the muscle. In order to cause the motion indirectly, A must bring about the contraction, and we may assume that in order to do this, he must proximately cause the neural or cerebral event, ce, which makes the muscle contract. But it is difficult to see how such an hypothesis could be maintained. The reason for this is that it would seem impossible to accept the causal explanation "A caused ce" unless there could be an answer to the question how (by doing or suffering what) A brought about the cerebral or neural event. If there were no answer to be found, A's causing ce could amount to no more than the occurrence of ce in the presence of A, for *ex hypothesis,* A does or suffers nothing in causing ce and thus nothing happens when A is said to cause the cerebral event except the event itself. Thus we cannot claim that A caused ce unless we are prepared to admit that A does or undergoes something, V, to make ce happen. This presents Chisholm with the following dilemma. If he claims that A causes ce by V-ing, the determinist will argue that the V-ing of A is an event and that unless it is an event of a remarkably mysterious and unique kind, it—like every other physical event—should have a cause. If something caused A's V-ing, then it and not A is what initiated the motion A was said to have $\psi$-made. On the other hand, if Chisholm maintains that A caused ce without doing or suffering anything, we must object that we have no way of distinguishing between A's causing ce and ce's happening in the presence of A.[18]

It seems to me unlikely that this kind of difficulty can be surmounted, and at this point it would be overly optimistic to proceed on the assumption that it will be. And so let us consider an alternative to Chisholm's application of the Aristotelian dictum.

Let us suppose that an agent ψ-moves something, X, if and only if he initiates the motion of X, there is no action he performs by which he does so and that he initiates the motion of X only if it is caused, but not caused by the operation of what does not belong to the agent's body. We cannot say that the absence of an external cause is *sufficient* for A's initiation because that would lead to the conclusion that a tic or twitch caused by what belongs to A's body constitutes a ψ-action. Can the assumption that the absence of an external cause is a necessary condition for ψ-agency avoid the difficulties which led us to say that agency was incompatible with physical determinism?

To say that A initiated the motion of X will not mean that A caused its motion. However, we are supposing that A can be said to have initiated the motion only if it had a cause belonging to his body, and hence, only if a cause was in operation and its operation was necessary and sufficient (under the obtaining physical conditions) to bring about X's motion. Thus we can say that had A not initiated the motion, it would not have occurred, and that the truth of "A initiated the motion of X" secures the operation of the cause that was necessary and sufficient to guarantee the occurrence of the motion.

But won't this involve the same difficulties we encountered earlier in considering the view that the operation of an external cause brings about the motion of X as well as what justifies our ascription of ψ-agency? One of the difficulties with this view was that it led to the conclusion that the ascription of ψ-agency depends upon a knowledge of the physical causes of a motion which we do not possess. The view I am now suggesting has no such consequence. According to it the ascription of ψ-agency is falsified by the discovery of an external cause for the motion A is supposed to have ψ-made, and in the absence of evidence for an external cause, we say that A ψ-moved X—even though subsequent developments could falsify our claim by showing it had an external cause. That is different from the view I rejected earlier. The rejected theory made it look as though our $\psi$-ascriptions depended upon our knowing or assuming the occurrence of some particular physical event in the sequence of causal events which led to the motion of X.

More importantly, the view that when A $\psi$-moves X, its motion is brought about by an external cause which also produces the occurrence of what is necessary or sufficient for the truth of a $\psi$-description failed to explain why we deal with the agent whose actions concern us. The view I am now proposing avoids this difficulty. We are now supposing that A $\psi$-moves X only if the causes for the motion belong to A's body. This together with the fact that the agent is where body is and that to deal with an agent is always *inter alia* to do what affects his body (though of course it is often more than *just* affecting his body) makes it possible to explain why we deal with an agent instead of directing our efforts to something external to his body; we do so because to deal with the agent is to deal with the source of the crucial motions—the body in which the causes which produce them are located. This does not, of course, explain why we sometimes treat a man as a rational agent (e.g., in reasoning with him to encourage or discourage some course of action) instead of a mechanism (as when we perform surgery to stop the shaking of his hands or the muscular spasms which cause them). Nor does it guarantee that a comprehensive knowledge of the internal causes for $\psi$-made motions might not lead us to treat men more and more like machines and less and less like rational agents. All we can hope for from the Aristotelian dictum is an account of a presupposition required to justify our uses of action-language and the dealings with agents which the truth of the physical determinist's assumptions would render pointless.

One final word. It is commonly said that the question whether men can act freely is an a priori one, and that the suggestion that action might be impossible can be dismissed as somehow unintelligible or incoherent. A result of this examination of physical determinism would seem to be that in at least one version, the free will question is an empirical one, and that to show what it would be like for a man to be unable to act freely all that would be needed would be to demonstrate that the physical determinist's premises, (D1)–(D3) are in fact true. However, if it could be shown that (D3) is necessarily true, I take it that this would establish a priori that human action is impossible.

## Notes

1. I am indebted to Robert Grimm for this formulation of the determinist's argument, to Norman Care and Daniel D. Merrill for helpful discussion of various issues involved with it, and to a number of students at Oberlin College, Robert Stone and Stephen D. Stitt in particular, for drawing my attention to its importance.

2. S. I. Benn and R. S. Peters, *The Principles of Political Thought,* 1964, pp. 18, 234 ff.

3. This distinction is roughly similar to Arthur Danto's distinction between "basic" and "non-basic" acts. [See the article "Basic Actions" by Danto, reprinted in this volume.] However, I do not wish to claim, as does Danto, that to $\psi$-move X is to be the cause of X's motion. Cp. Arthur Danto, "Freedom and Forbearance," in *Freedom and Determinism,* ed. Keith Lehrer, pp. 47–50.

4. Answers to the question "what is A doing?" can include "blushing," "perspiring," "falling," "thinking," "worrying," "waiting," "shivering," and "sleeping," none of which would normally be considered an action.

5. This is part of what I think lies behind Ryle's treatment of the distinction between "voluntary" and "involuntary" and the importance he attaches to this with regard to the topic of freedom and the will. See *Concept of Mind,* Ch. III, sections 3 and 4.

6. Although we can answer the question "How did A V?" by redescribing what was described as A's V-ing (as in "A signalled by crooking his finger") it would be a joke to say "A beckoned B by signalling for him to come," "A took B's life by killing him" or "A yelled by shouting." That is why we must say that the descriptions which fill the "V" and "——" positions in "A V-ed by ——ing" must be logically independent.

7. My reason for saying that X caused mf only if mf would not

have occurred without the operation of X is simply that we reject claims of the form "X caused Y" if we discover that under similar conditions Y would have occurred without X. As an example, consider our rejection of a witch doctor's claim to have caused an explosion by doing a dance where we know that in addition to doing the dance, he lighted the fuse on a charge of dynamite. This point is argued in detail by Morton O. Beckner in "Aspects of Biological Explanation" in *Philosophy of Science Today*, ed. Sidney Morgenbesser, 1967.

8. This point was brought to my attention by Keith Donnellan.

9. One other possibility should be considered. Suppose Y is a physical occurrence which could be identified, e.g., with A's wanting to, having a reason to, or deciding to move his finger. Then, even though we were not aware of the occurrence of Y under its description as a physical event, we might be aware of the occurrence of the mental event to which Y happens to be identical. If we supposed the occurrence of the mental event to be sufficient to justify the claim "A ψ-moved his finger" (assuming of course that mf occurred), couldn't we say that A ψ-moved his finger even though mf had an external physical cause? Perhaps, but I submit that there is no mental event whose occurrence is either sufficient or necessary for the truth of a ψ-description. The mere fact that A's finger moves and he intends, decides, wants to, or has a reason for moving it does not by itself establish the truth of "A ψ-moved his finger." And the fact that it moved when he did not intend to move it, etc., is not by itself enough to establish that he did not ψ-move it. Furthermore, if we assume an identity between a mental and a physical occurrence, it is difficult to avoid the conclusion that what causes the event under the physical description also causes the event under the mental description (providing that certain other conventionally required conditions obtain). This raises fresh difficulties for libertarianism which are beyond the scope of this paper. Finally, as I shall argue in the main body of this paper, the theory that ascriptions of ψ-agency are made true by the occurrence of what is brought about by an external physical cause makes it impossible to understand the importance we attach to the agent in considering what he has done. This argument is independent of the considerations against which the psycho-physical identity hypothesis might be directed.

10. See A. I. Melden, *Free Action*, 1961, and "Action" in *The Philosophical Review*, LXV (1956). [The latter is reprinted in this volume.] See also Ryle, Ch. III.

11. For a classical statement of this position, see Ryle, Ch. III, section 5.

12. See Melden, *Free Action,* Ch. 4–9.

13. Cp. Melden, "Action."

14. In any case, it would be a mistake to say that trying is something we $\psi$-do in order to do something else. Where "trying" means "exerting effort," the $\psi$-moving of a finger is seldom difficult enough to require any effort. Where it is difficult enough to require effort, "A is trying to move his finger" is better understood as meaning that he is going about $\psi$-moving his finger and having some difficulty doing it, than that he is performing an action called "trying" in order to get his finger to move. Where "trying" means "is going about," often what one does in trying to V is to V. The only cases in which one tries to V and succeeds in ø-V-ing are those in which the trying consists in performing or attempting to perform some other act in order to V. For example, the $\psi$-acts one performs when he tries to pole-vault are such things as pushing down on a pole (or moving one's arms for that purpose)—not acts called "tryings."

15. Melden, "Action."

16. Ryle, pp. 67–68.

17. Roderick Chisholm, "Freedom and Action" in Lehrer.

18. Chisholm (in Lehrer, pp. 19–20) responds to this sort of objection by suggesting that the difficulty of distinguishing between "X caused Y" and "Y occurred in the presence of X" infects the notion of causality in general and is therefore not a difficulty generated by any detail peculiar to his own theory. The suggestion is that an adequate general account of causality will clear up the difficulty without affecting his account. This seems to me to be incorrect. Where X is a thing (rather than an event) we can always show that X's causing of Y amounted to more than Y's occurrence in X's presence by determining what X did or suffered to bring about Y. Thus, for example, the difference between the wheelbarrow moving in my presence and my causing its motion would be my pushing on it to make it move.

# Part II ~ The Explanation of Action

PETER ALEXANDER

# Rational Behaviour and Psychoanalytic Explanation*

## I

It is often said that psychoanalysis has drawn our attention to the irrational springs of human behaviour. Recently, however, I have heard it said [1] that, on the contrary, psychoanalysis has revealed that our behaviour is more rational than we usually suppose it to be. The neurotic, according to this view, is radically misinformed but on the information he has he behaves rationally and if he discovers, or is supplied with, information he lacks he does the rational thing and alters his behaviour accordingly. This is a tempting and persuasive view but, it seems to me, a misleading one which calls for a detailed examination. I shall first show why the view appears to have some force, then discuss the notion of rational behaviour and finally raise some objections to the view.

In *The Psychopathology of Everyday Life,* and many other places, Freud argued that many pieces of apparently accidental, haphazard or purposeless behaviour could be explained in terms of unconscious wishes or purposes. I give three of his examples which will be convenient for testing the view in question.

(1) A woman patient always read "storks" instead of "stocks"

* Reprinted by permission of the author and the editor from *Mind,* LXXI (1962).

and did not know why she did so. Freud explained this by discovering that she had no children but badly wanted them.

(2) Freud found that on a sheet of notes about his daily engagements he had himself written the correct date, September 20th, and, under it in brackets, October 20th. He could not remember doing this and was, at first, completely mystified by it. He finally explained it in terms of an unconscious wish. He had just returned from a holiday, feeling fit and ready for work, but he had very few patients. He had, however, a letter from a patient saying that she would come to see him on October 20th. He concluded that his mistake sprang from a wish that the intervening month had passed. He accounts for his easy discovery of the explanation by the fact that the "disturbing thought" was not unpleasant.

(3) A young woman with a jealous husband danced a can-can at a party. Everyone was full of praise except the husband who accused her of behaving like a harlot ("once again"). The next day she went driving in a carriage, jumped from the carriage because, she said, she was afraid that the horses were going to bolt, and broke her leg. Her unconscious purpose, Freud says, was to punish herself for her forwardness and make it impossible for her to dance the can-can in the immediate future. (There is a good deal more supporting evidence for Freud's explanation.)

The idea that apparently purposeless and innocent slips of tongue and pen can be explained in terms of unconscious wishes and purposes is connected with the Freudian theory of the generation and cure of neuroses. Even the simple examples I have quoted involve minor neurotic symptoms but in the full-blown neuroses greater stress is laid on the unconsciousness of the purposes and wishes and the difficulty of discovering them. The general theory is, briefly, that a person who has desires of which he is ashamed or frightened protects himself from them by "pushing them into the unconscious", forgetting them beyond all normal power of recall, and substituting for the behaviour which would satisfy them some more innocent behaviour which, however, is mysterious both to himself and to the ordinary observer. Such behaviour is often referred to as a "symbolic" satisfying of the forbidden desire and is also regarded as inflicting a punishment for the repressed wish. It is mysterious because it does not appear to serve any purpose and no adequate reasons for it are obvious.

The view I am considering stresses the central assertion of the Freudian theory that it is possible to explain much of our behaviour in terms of unconscious wishes, purposes, and so on. The behaviour which we usually call "irrational" can be shown to be based on reasons which can be unearthed by psychoanalysis. The examples I have given show typical, though elementary, explanations of this sort. At first sight it seems plausible to say that since reasons can be given for pieces of behaviour we usually call "irrational", even this behaviour is, after all, rational, but at the unconscious level. It is a short step to the conclusion that Freud has shown irrational behaviour to be "really" rational and that we are, therefore, more rational than we usually suppose. I am inclined to think that the step, though short, is in the wrong direction.

The view is connected with a general account of human behaviour according to which the only way to explain an *action,* as distinct from a mere physical movement, is by showing that it was the rational thing to do. Attempts to explain actions in terms of physical causes are, at best, no more than explanations of physical movements: attempts to explain them in terms of forgetfulness or clumsiness, or some other such factor, amount to admissions that the actions cannot be explained or to assertions that they were not actions at all. I do not intend to discuss, here, this general view but only its application to psychoanalytic explanation.

It is important, here, to mention the distinction, to which I shall return, between rational *beliefs* and rational *behaviour*. It may be rational or irrational to hold a given belief but given that I hold it, I may act rationally or irrationally on its basis. If I firmly believe, falsely and on insufficient evidence, that my neighbour is planning to poison me, that is irrational. But it is rational, *given* my firm belief, to avoid drinking tea in his house and to instruct my wife not to leave him alone in our kitchen.

The view in question is that the neurotic behaves rationally in this sense. He unconsciously holds a number of irrational beliefs but, given these beliefs, he behaves rationally. Psychoanalytic explanation, it is argued, involves discovering these beliefs. The theory of cure is that if the neurotic discovers, or is provided with, the information he lacks he will abandon these beliefs because he will see that they are irrational. He will, in consequence, stop behaving in a neurotic way. It is sometimes even argued that to dispel these beliefs, and to bring about a cure, it is *sufficient* to bring them to light, when their absurdity will be evident to the patient.

I am concerned chiefly with the alleged rationality of the behaviour rather than the unquestioned irrationality of the beliefs, and with psychoanalytic explanation rather than cure. It is necessary for my purpose to examine the distinction between rational and irrational behaviour and to say something about explaining behaviour. These topics are the subjects of my next two sections.

## II. Rational and Irrational

It may well be that there are various senses in which the word "rational" is used in connection with behaviour. I shall discuss here what appears to me to be a central and important sense in which it is commonly so used and try to show that, at least in this sense, the view I am considering is mistaken or misleading.

There is a difference between saying that a given piece of behaviour would be rational in a given situation and saying that *A*'s behaviour in that situation was rational. What makes a given piece of behaviour rational in a given situation is that there are good reasons for behaving thus; what makes *A*'s behaviour rational is that he behaved in the way he did *for* those good reasons. The good reasons were *his* reasons. He *had* those reasons for behaving thus. I shall mainly be working towards a closer analysis of what it is for a given person's behaviour to be rational. I shall not, I am afraid, arrive at a complete analysis of rational behaviour in this sense; but it will be sufficient for my purpose if I can correctly establish certain of its characteristics.

As a first approximation I might suggest that *A* behaved rationally if he behaved thus for a reason. But this clearly will not do because we should not say this if *A*'s reason was a bad one. I may do something for a reason without its being the reasonable thing to do or, *a fortiori*, rational. This is implicit in the fact that I can correctly say that *y* was *my* reason for doing *x* while admitting that *y* is not *a* reason or *a good* reason for doing *x*. I may, for instance, have done *x* because I thought it would achieve *y* but now I see that it could not possibly have done so.

Thus we must add to the first suggestion that the reason was a *good* reason. But this is still inadequate since any reason *for* doing *x* cannot be a very bad reason and a reason for doing *x* may be good without being sufficient. One good reason for doing *x* may be outweighed by several good reasons against doing *x* or it may not *by itself* (*i.e.* without other good reasons) constitute a sufficient reason for doing *x*. In order for *x* to be rational I must have sufficient reason for doing *x*, that is, a reason or collection of reasons which is strong enough to stand even after weighing the important reasons for and against doing *x*. There may be a reason, a good reason or good reasons for doing *x* without there being sufficient reason. So we have at least one further necessary modification of the original suggestion. Let me say that *a piece of behaviour was rational if it was done for reasons which constitute a sufficient reason.*

I must now consider what it is for something to be a reason and to be a sufficient reason for certain behaviour. If I say that *y* is a reason for doing *x* I imply that *x* will achieve, or help to achieve, *y*, that the behaviour is somehow appropriate to what it is intended to achieve; if I say that *y* is not a reason, or is a bad reason, I imply that *x* will not achieve or help to achieve, *y*, *or* that it is unlikely to do so *or* that it will not do so as economically as some other behaviour would *or* that it will also produce other undesired consequences. If *x* is very unlikely to achieve *y* or could not possibly do so we could not correctly say "*y* is a reason for doing *x*" although *I* could still say "My reason for doing *x* was *y*". If I say that *y* (which now may be complex) is sufficient reason for doing *x* I mean that *x* is likely to achieve *y* and that *y* is valued above all other things which may be brought about by doing *x* but which I do not want to bring about or which I want *not* to bring about.

There are some difficult cases which do not at first sight seem to fit into this account of reasons. It might be said, for example, that when I thank someone for a present I do not aim to achieve anything and even that it is not correct to say that I had any reason. I think that there are perhaps cases in which thanking someone for a gift is just a spontaneous gesture which would appear to be too calculated if we said it was done for a reason.[2] I doubt if this behaviour would be said to be either rational or irrational, but I am very unsure about this. Of other cases it might be said that the fact that someone gave me a present was a reason, and perhaps sufficient reason for thanking him, and that no mention need be made of my wishing to achieve anything. But in such a case I think we can always say that a reason for thanking him was that I wanted to show him that I was pleased, or grateful (or that I wanted to conform to convention or . . .). The question "Why did you thank him?" can be answered by "Because he gave me a present", but it can then be asked again in expectation of some such answer as "because I wanted to show my gratitude". I am inclined to think that whenever it is appropriate to ask for a reason for a piece of behaviour, it is possible to give a reason in terms of someone's wanting or intending to achieve something, even if in certain cases what it is intended to achieve is consistency or appropriateness or a state of mind in someone else.

I can now expand my account of rational behaviour. A piece of behaviour was rational if it was done for reasons which constitute a sufficient reason, that is, if it was likely to achieve what was intended and unlikely to lead to other consequences whose undesirability outweighs the desirability of what it was intended to achieve. It was irrational if it was not done for reasons which constitute a sufficient reason, that is, if it was unlikely to achieve what was intended, or less likely to achieve it than some other piece of behaviour, or was likely to lead to other consequences whose undesirability outweighs the desirability of what it was intended to achieve.

There is, of course, a scale of rationality between the most rational and the most irrational. Clearly it is irrational to do something which cannot possibly achieve what is intended and clearly it is rational to do something which is very likely to achieve it without any unwanted side-effects. In between we often have to contrast alternative ways of behaving between which it is not easy to decide. In a given situation, other things being equal, it is rational to behave in a way which is more likely to achieve what is intended, less rational or irrational to behave in a way which is less likely or unlikely to achieve it.

There may *be* a sufficient reason for behaving in a certain way in a given situation but if this is not my reason for behaving in that way then I cannot be said to have behaved rationally, by reference to *that* reason. It is therefore necessary to be clear about what it means to act *for* a reason or with a reason in mind, to *have* a reason or to say that a given reason was *my* reason. An inarticulate person may sometimes be said to behave in a certain way for a reason, and even for a good or sufficient reason even though he is unable to say what this reason was. Habitual actions and those performed during the exercise of a craft may be done for good reasons and constitute rational behaviour although the agent was not conscious of the reasons before, during or after the actions. I may have a reason in mind without attending to it. However, I think that it is a necessary condition of my acting for a reason that I should be able to become aware of my reason if I think about my behaviour, although I need not be able to state it. To say that a given reason was *my* reason is to imply that, if I think of that reason or someone suggests it to me I can recognize it *as my* reason, or one of my reasons, for that behaviour (or as having influenced my behaviour). I doubt if it is correct to say "I acted for a reason" and at the same time to confess that, however hard I think about it, I cannot discover the reason and that, however many possible reasons are put to me, I cannot recognize any of them as *my* reason. If this is true of having a reason it is true of having a good or a sufficient reason. Having a reason, at least in this sense, is a necessary condition of behaving rationally.

It would be as well to mention here a consideration which will become important later. There is a perfectly ordinary, everyday sense of "unconscious" in which while I am not thinking of something I may be said to be unconscious of it. I am at the moment unconscious of what I had for breakfast this morning because I am not thinking of it or trying to recall it, but if I did try I could probably recall it. Similarly I may have a reason for behaving in a certain way and yet be unconscious of my reason at any given time. This is to be distinguished from the technical sense in which "unconscious" is used in psychoanalysis, according to which what is unconscious is beyond all our normal powers of recall.

If what I have said so far is correct, both rational behaviour and irrational behaviour are such that they could have been consciously planned even if they were not. My account allows, as I think we normally would allow, that some habits and learned skills may be said to be rational. Irrational behaviour resembles rational behaviour in the sense that it is the sort of behaviour which it is possible to give reasons for and against.

I have used the words "intention" and "intend" because I wish to exclude from both categories such things as reflexes and sheer accidents. For these, if we are to call them "behaviour", we need a third category which may be called "non-rational" and includes any behaviour of which it does not make sense to say either that it was or was not done for a reason. Non-rational behaviour could not be intended; for example, fainting or jumping when startled (*real* fainting and *real* jumping), or sheer accidents involving unforeseeable events, like unavoidably running over someone who runs out in front of a car. I cannot intend to faint or run a person over unavoidably.

It might be thought to be an objection that doubt can be cast upon the rationality of behaviour which tends to achieve what is desired, by questioning the rationality of seeking to achieve the particular thing desired. Behaviour which, in a narrow context, looks rational may be regarded as irrational in a wider context. Given that I wish to commit suicide it is rational to choose the gas oven rather than the electric oven but there may be more rational ways out of my difficulties than self-destruction. This is not, however, an objection to my view since suicide would be judged to be rational or irrational in the light of yet other things desired and the criteria I have outlined would simply be applied in the wider context.

Similarly, it may be rational to behave in a particular way given the beliefs I have about certain matters of fact but these beliefs may be irrational because they conflict with the evidence I have or evidence I could easily get or are based on careless or mistaken reasoning. But if I believe that $w$ is the case and that, in consequence, I ought to aim to produce $y$, then behaviour that tends to produce $y$ may be rational, within the narrower context, no matter how wrong is my belief about $w$. The rationality of behaviour is relative to context.

This bears obliquely on my reason for *not* saying that behaviour which is rational must achieve what is intended *in the way the agent thinks it does*. Suppose that we have discovered empirically that railway lines buckle in hot weather when gaps are not left between them, although we know nothing about the relation between heat and expansion. Then it is rational to leave gaps between them so that they do not buckle, even if we think we do this in order to appeal to the aesthetic senses of the gods so that they will refrain from bending the rails and even if, when we have learnt about heat and expansion, we no longer think it is rational to leave gaps *because* the gods prefer it.

## III. Explaining Behaviour and Justifying Behaviour

It is easy to mistake a justification for a piece of behaviour for an explanation of it and I suspect that such a mistake is involved in the view I am considering. The mistake may arise in this way. A person behaves in an unusual way and, without consulting him, we ask ourselves why he behaved as he did. That is, we look for reasons for his behaviour. If we are able to find a sufficient reason we may think we have explained his behaviour, but the most we can be sure we have done is to justify behaviour of this sort in this kind of situation. We have not explained *his* behaviour until we have discovered what *his* reasons were. We have discovered something that would explain it but not necessarily what does explain it. We may justify such behaviour by showing that it achieved something of which *we* approve but we can explain it only by showing what *he* intended to achieve.

Suppose, for example, that for a month our friend eats and drinks nothing but milk. We cast about for explanations and decide, since he has shown some interest in nutritional problems, that he wished to show that milk is a complete food for an adult. (There are, of course, several other reasonable conclusions we might reach.) This would be a good reason for his behaviour and sufficient, we think, to justify it. But if we are ignorant of our friend's reasons we cannot say that this was his reason and although we have justified such behaviour to ourselves we have not explained it. We have shown how behaviour of this sort might be shown to be rational but we have not shown that he behaved rationally. The most we can say is that if this *was* his reason it would both explain and justify his behaviour.

He may now deny that we have found his reason. There are two possibilities. First, he might give another good or sufficient reason, which would both explain and justify his behaviour. Second, he might give another reason which was a bad one. This would explain his behaviour but not justify it or show it to be rational, just because it was a bad reason. Thus to explain a piece of behaviour is not just to show that it was a rational thing to do and to show that it was a rational thing to do is not necessarily to explain it. To explain a piece of behaviour we have to show what reasons the agent had: to show that he behaved rationally we have also to show that these reasons were sufficient. We may therefore justify such behaviour as *A*'s without either explaining it or showing that he behaved rationally and we may explain his behaviour without showing that he behaved rationally.

There is an ambiguity about the word "reason" which I should perhaps get out of the way. I refer to the fact that we occasionally use "reason" in the sense of "cause". There is sometimes a difference between saying "My reason for doing *x* was *y*" and "The reason why I did *x* was *y*". The second form may be used to indicate causes as well as reasons in the strict sense I have been using. I can correctly say "The reason why I fainted was that insufficient blood was getting to my brain". Thus a statement of the form "The reason why I did *x* was *y*" may be used either to reinforce the assertion that my behaviour was rational or for the different purpose of giving a causal account of what I did. It would be odd to say "My reason *for* fainting was that insufficient blood was getting to my brain", because it suggests that on discovering the physiological fact I realized that the appropriate thing to do, finding no reasons against, was to faint, so I fainted. I can, however, say either "The reason why I bought a thermometer was that I *wanted* to measure my temperature" or "My reason for buying a thermometer was that I wanted to measure my temperature". The need to include the word "wanted", or some such word, in the description of the reason, in the strict sense, is important.

## IV. Criticisms

When we are considering behaviour in the ordinary way, and not theorizing about it in the manner of psychoanalysis, we find two sorts of behaviour which are conveniently labelled "rational" and "irrational". It is helpful, or sometimes essential, to contrast these with one another and with the sort of behaviour which can be called "non-rational". But psychoanalytic theory implies that all the behaviour which we call "irrational" can, at least in principle, be explained in terms of unconscious purposes, and so on. If we go on to say that this shows such behaviour to be rational we blur these distinctions. There would be nothing wrong with this if it were accompanied by arguments showing these distinctions to be inaccurate or unnecessary, but such arguments do not seem to be forthcoming. As we shall see, nothing of this sort follows from psychoanalytic theory, so it is difficult to see how such arguments could be upheld.

Here it is sufficient to note that if we say that our irrational behaviour has been shown to be "really" rational we allow "rational" to be used only in contrast to "non-rational". It is not very instructive merely to distinguish our faintings and unavoidable accidents from all the rest of our behaviour, and to make no further distinctions. In making moral judgments, ascribing responsibility, assessing intelligence, cleverness, reliability and a host of other activities it is essential to make finer distinctions. Moreover, the problems in which psychoanalysis originated depend upon this distinction. The meaning of "rational" in such contexts involves the contrast with both "irrational" and "non-rational". If this is so, to assert that our irrational behaviour has been shown to be rational is to use "rational" in a new sense while pretending to use it in the familiar sense, for it leaves us no behaviour which can be said to be, either consciously or unconsciously, irrational.

This frustrates any attempt to make the view more acceptable by saying "Freud has shown us that behaviour which is consciously irrational is unconsciously rational". This is not to say that he has shown us that we behave more rationally than we usually suppose, for it is not to say anything about the rationality about which we usually suppose. We usually, I claim, suppose people to be rational to the extent to which their behaviour fits the criterion I have outlined, or something like it: we do not, without benefit of Freud, entertain ideas about unconscious rationality. This formulation does, indeed, leave the distinction between consciously rational and consciously irrational behaviour but it weakens it by suggesting that unconscious rationality differs from conscious rationality only in being unconscious. This is misleading because Freud has not left us any behaviour which is unconsciously irrational with which to contrast that which is unconsciously rational. "Rational", I suggest, is being used in such different senses at the conscious and unconscious levels that we must be very careful how we draw an analogy between them.

We might, in an attempt to save the view, retreat still further and claim that Freud has shown our irrational behaviour to be *more like* our rational behaviour than we supposed, since whereas we formerly thought that we could not give good reasons for it we now find that we can. This is to draw an analogy between psychoanalytic explanations and certain ordinary explanations of behaviour in terms of reasons for it. The value of this analogy depends on the extent to which the good reasons for "irrational" behaviour are like the good reasons for rational behaviour. A more detailed examination will show that the reasons adduced in psychoanalytic explanations are very unlike what we would normally regard as good reasons and consequently that the behaviour in question is shown to be rational only in a new and unfamiliar sense.

I shall come to this more detailed examination by recapitulating three points I made earlier and applying them to psychoanalytic explanations. In ordinary circumstances (1) we may explain a piece of behaviour by showing that it was done for a reason or with a reason in mind and showing what that reason was; (2) to explain a piece of behaviour is not necessarily to show that it was rational; (3) to show that somebody's behaviour was rational it is necessary to show (*a*) that the agent had reasons and (*b*) that the reasons were sufficient reasons.

Thus the fact that a psychoanalytic explanation can be given for a piece of otherwise unexplained behaviour does not show that behaviour to be rational unless (*a*) the reasons given were the reasons for which the agent behaved as he did and (*b*) they were sufficient reasons. It seems to me that there is some doubt about the possibility of satisfying the first condition and that the very nature of the typical psychoanalytic explanation makes impossible the satisfying of the second. This is not to claim that psychoanalytic explanations are not explanations or are useless but only that they are of a very different kind from everyday explanations of rational behaviour. I shall discuss these two conditions separately.

(*a*) I have argued that when we say that I did something for a reason or with a reason in mind we imply that I must be able to discover that reason or recognize it when it is suggested to me as having influenced my behaviour. It must, at least in this sense, be *my* reason. I may recognize a suggested reason as a good reason without recognizing it as *my* reason and I may have to admit, if I am being honest, that *my* reason is not to be found among the good reasons.

The sense in which we normally allow that a person may be unconscious of his reasons for acting demands that he should be able to discover them by everyday methods of self-questioning or at least to recognize his reasons when they are suggested by others using similar everyday methods. But the special sense in which "unconscious" is used in psychoanalysis may make all the difference, since a person's unconscious reason, in this sense, is *ex hypothesi* beyond his power to discover without the assistance of special techniques and, usually, another person trained in these special techniques, working on the basis of a special theory. Neurotic behaviour is mystifying to both the neurotic and the ordinary observer. The discussions and other transactions necessary to dissolve the mystery are very unlike the discussions we normally go through in finding explanations for normal behaviour.

The nature of the techniques employed is very important in the present context. Are they such that the patient can be said, when he has accepted the explanation, to have *recognized the reasons* as those which in fact influenced his behaviour? This I doubt. Case histories show, again and again, that the patient meets the suggested reason as a stranger, failing to recognize it or resisting it violently, until a good deal of preparatory work, including the expounding of bits of theory, has been done by the psychoanalyst. Is this preparatory work correctly described as showing the patient that these were in fact his reasons rather than showing him that, given the theory, these reasons are "good", *i.e.* fit the theory? Is his acceptance more correctly described as seeing what his reasons were or as seeing what his reasons *must have been*? ("must" not, of course, implying *logical* necessity). Of course, his resistance to the reasons is explained by the theory. We are all familiar with our own inner struggles not to admit a disreputable reason for which we have acted but we are also familiar with our own reluctance to admit a disreputable reason which we are sure did not influence our action. Moreover, the importance of the transference situation suggests, very strongly, I think, that the processes involved are not just those associated with intellectual conviction.[3]

When the patient accepts or "discovers" unconscious reasons he may be saying "Now I see what my reasons must have been, though I did not suspect it" or he may be saying "Now I see what my reasons were but I had forgotten them". It is easy to suppose that the alleged reasons were not in fact effective reasons, did not in fact influence the behaviour, but rather that the behaviour can be interpreted *as if* they were and, moreover, that the cure can be achieved if this interpretation is accepted, whether or not it is correct. I am suggesting that the *process* may be more like the normal justifying of an action than the normal explaining of an action even though what issues from it is not very like a justification for the action. There is, of course, the connected problem of how it is possible to discover that we are remembering reasons we had forgotten, especially when the forgetting is of the Freudian type.

(*b*) Compared with the ordinary acceptance of reasons for behaviour, the acceptance of the psychoanalytic kind of reason for behaviour which before looked irrational is odd in another way, because we can never have been conscious of having *such* reasons for *such* behaviour. The theory holds that unconscious reasons are effective only because they are repressed and so unconscious in the technical sense. In the ordinary way, before we say that a piece of behaviour was rational we demand that a sufficient reason be given for it. A sufficient reason is such that we can see that it could have been a reason for this particular behaviour and, I think, that we can conceive of ourselves as behaving thus with this reason in mind. We demand appropriateness.

I doubt if the typical Freudian reason can satisfy this condition. Such a reason is a reason for this behaviour only because it was unconscious. We can never know what it would be like to act thus with this reason in mind since it does not make sense to talk of acting with unconscious (in the technical sense) reasons in mind. The typical unconscious reasons are not the sorts of reasons which would lead to that sort of behaviour if we were conscious of them. The shocked reaction "Good gracious, is that why I did it? I should never have done it if I had known" is typical and says more than the speaker, and perhaps Freud, usually realizes. The whole point of the theory is that neurotics behave as they do because they fool themselves completely about certain things; but we cannot fool ourselves completely and be aware that we are fooling ourselves. Unconscious reasons are not just possible conscious reasons for the behaviour in question: they would not be regarded as reasons for it if they were conscious.

This does not mean simply that the patient would see the reasons as disreputable if they were conscious but that he would see them as inadequate. For example, suppose that my lunging at lamp-posts with my umbrella is explained by referring to my Oedipus Complex. My alleged reasons for behaving as I do are:

(i) I feel that my father hates me because we are rivals for my mother's love and I therefore wish to kill my father so that I do not have to share her love;

(ii) I am ashamed of and feel guilty about this wish so I conceal it from myself;

(iii) it is still effective so I "satisfy" it without realizing that this is what I am doing by some substitute activity such as lunging at lamp-posts;

(iv) I want to punish myself for having this wish.

Now if my wish to kill my father were conscious it would be obvious to me that it was not adequately satisfied by my lunging at lamp-posts. If my wish to protect myself from my own guilt were conscious it would be obvious that such behaviour would not help. That is, these "reasons" can be reasons for this behaviour only if they are unconscious for they would not look like reasons if they were conscious. The fourth reason looks, at first sight, more convincing. By behaving in an odd way I upset my relations with society by leading people to treat me as odd and so punish myself for my guilty wishes. However, this is not a very effective way of punishing myself as I would no doubt see if I were conscious of my guilty wishes and my desire to punish myself for them. The reasons would not appear to be appropriate to the form of my behaviour and we might further question the belief that the mere having of certain wishes merits punishment. It is not satisfactory, moreover, to regard all these factors taken together as constituting good reasons in the ordinary sense; even if they were all conscious the behaviour would not appear to be appropriate.

It is true that if my father hates me this may be a sufficient reason for protecting myself against him, but is it a sufficient reason for the neurotic behaviour in which I indulge? Only, I suggest, in conjunction with the theory. The relation between the reasons and the behaviour is not such that we would normally say that this was a sufficient reason for this behaviour. The relation needs explaining in terms of more theory. These considerations suggest that "reason", "good reason" and "sufficient reason" are used in this context in senses very different from their usual ones. In their ordinary senses, something which would not look like a sufficient reason for doing *x*, if we were conscious of it, is not a sufficient reason for doing *x*.

I can now return to the examples I quoted from Freud. In each of these, the behaviour does not seem to be related to the alleged reason in the way in which ordinary behaviour is related to ordinary good reasons for it. The woman who read "storks" for "stocks" does not appear, by so doing, to have furthered either the end of obtaining children or of concealing from herself her own unhappiness and it is doubtful if she or others could have seen the behaviour as achieving anything except with the help of the Freudian theory.

Freud's own mistake about the date did not make the wished-for day come more quickly, nor bring him more patients, nor conceal from himself that he was short of patients. If he had been convinced that it was the correct date it might have done the last, but he was not. His behaviour would have been perfectly rational if he had meant merely to remind himself that he had no important engagements until October 20th, but he neglects entirely this possibility. If he had not been so interested in explanations which fitted his theory might he not have thought that this was his reason? Moreover, it is easy to suppose that he did not recognize the reason he gives as his reason but inferred that it was his reason because it was the kind of reason he was looking for—and, indeed, he introduces the reason by saying "It was not difficult to explain . . ." (*i.e.* in terms of the theory).

The woman who jumped from the carriage could hardly have

regarded her desire not to dance the can-can again or her desire to regain her husband's respect as good reasons for breaking her leg if she had been aware of them. She did, of course, punish herself for dancing the can-can and losing her husband's respect but I doubt if she would have found it the appropriate kind of punishment if she had been conscious of all this. It is true that the punishment does, in a sense, fit the crime but I doubt if many of us would regard our having danced the can-can as constituting sufficient reason for, and as being suitably punished by, the wilful breaking of our legs. Moreover, the husband's loss of respect here was due, Freud darkly hints, to more serious offences for which this is not a punishment with even this macabre kind of appropriateness.

In general, similar things can usually be said about Freud's explanations of neurotic symptoms. If I am said to do $x$ for unconscious reason $y$, it is nearly always the case that $y$ is not the sort of thing which we would normally consider a good reason for $x$. The theory is, of course, that $y$ leads to $x$ because it is repressed. The repression of the guilty thoughts is prior to the behaviour so that the behaviour cannot be thought of as fulfilling a wish to deceive oneself but only as fulfilling the repressed wish in spite of its being repressed or as punishing oneself for having the wish at all. The punishment itself seems always to be too severe, or not severe enough, or inappropriate in some other way.

It might be said that the reason given for the behaviour is the whole complex repressed-guilty-desires, that is, that the fact of repression is part of the reason. But the same arguments apply since if the neurotic could be conscious of having repressed his guilty desire this would still not look like a good reason for this behaviour. Moreover, this begins to look like an account in terms of causes rather than reasons, similar to "The reason why we hear scufflings is that there are mice in the cellarage". It seems more accurate to say "The reason why he did this was that he had repressed certain desires of which he felt guilty" than to say "His reason for doing this was that he *wanted* . . ." . I cannot discuss this here but wish merely to point out that there is a danger of confusing these two senses of reason in this situation. I have argued elsewhere[4] in favour of a causal interpretation of psychoanalytic explanations and cure but this would clearly be incompatible with the view I have been examining.

It seems to me that we can say that Freud has shown that it is possible to construct a theory on the basis of which irrational behaviour can be interpreted *as if* it were the outcome of given unconscious reasons. There is an apparent analogy between psychoanalytic explanations of irrational behaviour and ordinary explanations of rational behaviour. But the analogy can be pushed so little that it seems more of a hindrance than a help to use "explanation" and "reason" as if these words were used in the same senses in the two contexts. I have tried to show that unconscious reasons are very unlike conscious reasons and especially unlike what we normally call "good reasons" or "sufficient reasons" for behaviour. If we do call them "good reasons" it is clear that we use these words in an unusual sense and are therefore not entitled to go on to say that such explanations show our irrational behaviour to be really rational. This would be warranted if we added that "rational" was being used in a new sense but then the original statement would lose its point. I have no objection whatever to the use of words in new or unusual senses as long as it is clear that this is what we are doing and that it is in some way helpful or illuminating.

## Notes

1. By Mr. J. W. N. Watkins and others, in discussion and conversation.

2. My thanks are due to Paul Ziff for convincing me of this.

3. Patrick Mullahy, in *Oedipus, Myth and Complex*: "Nor does enlightenment *per se* concerning the causative relation of [such] experiences to his illness effect cure."

4. *Arist. Soc. Supp. Vol.*, 1955.

DONALD DAVIDSON

# Actions, Reasons, and Causes*

What is the relation between a reason and an action when the reason explains the action by giving the agent's reason for doing what he did? We may call such explanations *rationalizations,* and say that the reason *rationalizes* the action.

In this paper I want to defend the ancient—and common-sense—position that rationalization is a species of ordinary causal explanation. The defense no doubt requires some redeployment, but not more or less complete abandonment of the position, as urged by many recent writers.[1]

## I

A reason rationalizes an action only if it leads us to see something the agent saw, or thought he saw, in his action—some feature, consequence, or aspect of the action the agent wanted, desired, prized, held dear, thought dutiful, beneficial, obligatory, or agreeable. We cannot explain why someone did what he did simply by saying the particular action appealed to him; we must indicate what it was about the action that appealed. Whenever someone does something for a reason, therefore, he can be characterized as (*a*) having some sort of pro attitude toward actions of a certain kind, and (*b*) believing (or knowing, perceiving, noticing, remembering) that his action is of that kind.

* Reprinted by permission of the author and the editors from *The Journal of Philosophy,* LX (1963).

Under (*a*) are to be included desires, wantings, urges, promptings, and a great variety of moral views, aesthetic principles, economic prejudices, social conventions, and public and private goals and values in so far as these can be interpreted as attitudes of an agent directed toward actions of a certain kind. The word 'attitude' does yeoman service here, for it must cover not only permanent character traits that show themselves in a lifetime of behavior, like love of children or a taste for loud company, but also the most passing fancy that prompts a unique action, like a sudden desire to touch a woman's elbow. In general, pro attitudes must not be taken for convictions, however temporary, that every action of a certain kind ought to be performed, is worth performing, or is, all things considered, desirable. On the contrary, a man may all his life have a yen, say, to drink a can of paint, without ever, even at the moment he yields, believing it would be worth doing.

Giving the reason why an agent did something is often a matter of naming the pro attitude (*a*) or the related belief (*b*) or both; let me call this pair the *primary reason* why the agent performed the action. Now it is possible to reformulate the claim that rationalizations are causal explanations, and give structure to the argument as well, by stating two theses about primary reasons:

1. For us to understand how a reason of any kind rationalizes an action it is necessary and sufficient that we see, at least in essential outline, how to construct a primary reason.
2. The primary reason for an action is its cause.

I shall argue for these points in turn.

## II

I flip the switch, turn on the light, and illuminate the room. Unbeknownst to me I also alert a prowler to the fact that I am home. Here I do not do four things, but only one, of which four descriptions have been given.[2] I flipped the switch because I wanted to turn on the light, and by saying I wanted to turn on the light I explain (give my reason for, rationalize) the flipping. But I do not, by giving this reason, rationalize my alerting of the prowler nor my illuminating of the room. Since reasons may rationalize what someone does when it is described in one way and not when it is described in another, we cannot treat what was done simply as a term in sentences like 'My reason for flipping the switch was that I wanted to turn on the light'; otherwise we would be forced to conclude, from the fact that flipping the switch was identical with alerting the prowler, that my reason for alerting the prowler was that I wanted to turn on the light. Let us mark this quasi-intensional[3] character of action descriptions in rationalizations by stating a bit more precisely a necessary condition for primary reasons:

C1. *R* is a primary reason why an agent performed the action *A* under the description *d* only if *R* consists of a pro attitude of the agent toward actions with a certain property, and a belief of the agent that *A*, under the description *d*, has that property.

How can my wanting to turn on the light be (part of) a primary reason, since it appears to lack the required element of generality? We may be taken in by the verbal parallel between 'I turned on the light' and 'I wanted to turn on the light'. The first clearly refers to a particular event, so we conclude that the second has this same event as its object. Of course it is obvious that the event of my turning on the light can't be referred to in the same way by both sentences, since the existence of the event is required by the truth of 'I turned on the light' but not by the truth of 'I wanted to turn on the light'. If the reference were the same in both cases, the second sentence would entail the first; but in fact the sentences are logically independent. What is less obvious, at least until we attend to it, is that the event whose occurrence makes 'I turned on the light' true cannot be called the object, however intensional, of 'I wanted to turn on the light'.

If I turned on the light, then I must have done it at a precise moment, in a particular way—every detail is fixed. But it makes no sense to demand that my want be directed at an action performed at any one moment or done in some unique manner. Any one of an indefinitely large number of actions would satisfy the want, and can be considered equally eligible as its object. Wants and desires often are trained on physical objects. However, 'I want that gold watch in the window' is not a primary reason, and explains why I went into the store only because it suggests a primary reason—for example, that I wanted to buy the watch.

Because 'I wanted to turn on the light' and 'I turned on the light' are logically independent, the first can be used to give a reason why the second is true. Such a reason gives minimal information: it implies that the action was intentional, and wanting tends to exclude some other pro attitudes, such as a sense of duty or obligation. But the exclusion depends very much on the action and the context of explanation. Wanting seems pallid beside lusting, but it would be odd to deny that someone who lusted after a woman or a cup of coffee wanted her or it. It is not unnatural, in fact, to treat wanting as a genus including all pro attitudes as species. When we do this and when we know some action is intentional, it is empty to add that the agent wanted to do it. In such cases, it is easy to answer the question 'Why did you do it?' with 'For no reason', meaning not that there is no reason but that there is no *further* reason, no reason that cannot be inferred from the fact that the action was done intentionally; no reason, in other words, besides wanting to do it. This last point is not essential to the present argument, but it is of interest because it defends the possibility of defining an intentional action as one done for a reason.

A primary reason consists of a belief and an attitude, but it is generally otiose to mention both. If you tell me you are easing the jib because you think that will stop the main from backing, I don't need to be told that you want to stop the main from backing; and if you say you are biting your thumb at me because you want to insult me, there is no point in adding that you think that by biting your thumb at me you will insult me. Similarly, many explanations of actions in terms of reasons that are not primary do not require mention of the primary reason to complete the story. If I say I am pulling weeds because I want a beautiful lawn, it would be fatuous to eke out the account with 'And so I see something desirable in any action that does, or has a good chance of, making the lawn beautiful'. Why insist that there is any *step*, logical or psychological, in the transfer of desire from an end that is not an action to the actions one conceives as means? It serves the argument as well that the desired end explains the action only if what are believed by the agent to be means are desired.

Fortunately, it is not necessary to classify and analyze the many varieties of emotions, sentiments, moods, motives, passions, and hungers whose mention may answer the question 'Why did you do it?' in order to see how, when such mention rationalizes the action, a primary reason is involved. Claustrophobia gives a man's reason for leaving a cocktail party because we know people want to avoid, escape from, be safe from, put distance between themselves and, what they fear. Jealousy is the motive in a poisoning because, among other things, the poisoner believes his action will harm his rival, remove the cause of his agony, or redress an injustice, and these are the sorts of things a jealous man wants to do. When we learn a man cheated his son out of greed, we do not necessarily know what the primary reason was, but we know there was one, and its general nature. Ryle analyzes 'he boasted from vanity' into "he boasted on meeting the stranger and his doing so satisfies the lawlike proposition that whenever he finds a chance of securing the admiration and envy of others, he does whatever he thinks will produce this admiration and envy" (*The Concept of Mind*, 89). This analysis is often, and perhaps justly, criticized on the ground that a man may boast from vanity just once. But if Ryle's boaster did what he did from vanity, then something entailed by Ryle's analysis is true: the boaster wanted to secure the admiration and envy of others, and he believed that his action would produce this admiration and envy; true or false, Ryle's analysis does not dispense with primary reasons, but depends upon them.

To know a primary reason why someone acted as he did is to know an intention with which the action was done. If I turn left at the fork because I want to get to Katmandu, my intention in turning left is to get to Katmandu. But to know the intention is not necessarily to know the primary reason in full detail. If James goes to church with the intention of pleasing his mother, then he must have some pro attitude toward pleasing his mother, but it needs more information to tell whether his reason is that he enjoys pleasing his mother, or thinks it right, his duty, or an obligation. The expression 'the intention with which James went to church' has the outward form of a description, but in fact it is syncategorematic and cannot be taken to refer to an entity, state, disposition, or event. Its function in context is to generate new descriptions of actions in terms of their reasons; thus 'James went to church with the intention of pleasing his mother' yields a new, and fuller, description of the action described in 'James went to church'. Essentially the same process goes on when I answer the question 'Why are you bobbing around that way?' with 'I'm knitting, weaving, exercising, sculling, cuddling, training fleas'.

Straight description of an intended result often explains an action better than stating that the result was intended or desired. 'It will soothe your nerves' explains why I pour you a shot as efficiently as 'I want to do something to soothe your nerves', since the first in the context of explanation implies the second; but the first does better, because, if it is true, the facts will justify my choice of action. Because justifying and explaining an action so often go hand in hand, we frequently indicate the primary reason for an action by making a claim which, if true, would also verify, vindicate, or support the relevant belief or attitude of the agent. 'I knew I ought to return it', 'The paper said it was going to snow', 'You stepped on *my* toes', all, in appropriate reason-giving contexts, perform this familiar dual function.

The justifying role of a reason, given this interpretation, depends upon the explanatory role, but the converse does not hold. Your stepping on my toes neither explains nor justifies my stepping on your toes unless I believe you stepped on my toes, but the belief alone, true or false, explains my action.

## III

In the light of a primary reason, an action is revealed as coherent with certain traits, long- or short-termed, characteristic or not, of the agent, and the agent is shown in his role of Rational Animal. Corresponding to the belief and attitude of a primary reason for an action, we can always construct (with a little ingenuity) the premises of a syllogism from which it follows that the action has some (as Miss Anscombe calls it) "desirability characteristic." [4] Thus there is a certain irreducible—though somewhat anemic—sense in which every rationalization justifies: from the agent's point of view there was, when he acted, something to be said for the action.

Noting that nonteleological causal explanations do not display the element of justification provided by reasons, some philosophers have concluded that the concept of cause that applies elsewhere cannot apply to the relation between reasons and actions, and that the pattern of justification provides, in the case of reasons, the required explanation. But suppose we grant that reasons alone justify in explaining actions; it does not follow that the explanation is not also—and necessarily—causal. Indeed our first condition for primary reasons (C1) is designed to help set rationalizations apart from other sorts of explanation. If rationalization is, as I want to argue, a species of causal explanation, then justification, in the sense given by C1, is at least one differentiating property. How about the other claim: that justifying is a kind of explaining, so that the ordinary notion of cause need not be brought in? Here it is necessary to decide what is being included under justification. Perhaps it means only what is given by C1: that the agent has certain beliefs and attitudes in the light of which the action is reasonable. But then something essential has certainly been left out, for a person can have a reason for an action, and perform the action, and yet this reason not be the reason why he did it. Central to the relation between a reason and an action it explains is the idea that the agent performed the action *because* he had the reason. Of course, we can include this idea too in justification; but then the notion of justification becomes as dark as the notion of reason until we can account for the force of that 'because'.

When we ask why someone acted as he did, we want to be provided with an interpretation. His behavior seems strange, alien, outré, pointless, out of character, disconnected; or perhaps we cannot even recognize an action in it. When we learn his reason, we have an interpretation, a new description of what he did which fits it into a familiar picture. The picture certainly includes some of the agent's beliefs and attitudes; perhaps also goals, ends, principles, general character traits, virtues or vices. Beyond this, the redescription of an action afforded by a reason may place the action in a wider social, economic, linguistic, or evaluative context. To learn, through learning the reason, that the agent conceived his action as a lie, a repayment of a debt, an insult, the fulfillment of an avuncular obligation, or a knight's gambit is to grasp the point of the action in its setting of rules, practices, conventions, and expectations.

Remarks like these, inspired by the later Wittgenstein, have been elaborated with subtlety and insight by a number of philosophers. And there is no denying that this is true: when we explain an action, by giving the reason, we do redescribe the action; redescribing the action gives the action a place in a pattern, and in this way the action is explained. Here it is tempting to draw two conclusions that do not follow. First, we can't infer, from the fact that giving reasons merely redescribes the action and that causes are separate from effects, that therefore reasons are not causes. Reasons, being beliefs and attitudes, are certainly not identical with actions; but, more important, events are often redescribed in terms of their causes. (Suppose someone was injured. We could redescribe this event "in terms of a cause" by saying he was burned.) Second, it is an error to think that, because placing the action in a larger pattern explains it, therefore we now understand the sort of explanation involved. Talk of patterns and contexts does not answer the question of how reasons explain actions, since the relevant pattern or context contains both reason and action. One way we can explain an event is by placing it in the context of its cause; cause and effect form the sort of pattern that explains the effect, in a sense of 'explain' that we understand as well as any. If reason and action illustrate a different pattern of explanation, that pattern must be identified.

Let me urge the point in connection with an example of Melden's. A man driving an automobile raises his arm in order to signal. His intention, to signal, explains his action, raising his arm, by redescribing it as signaling. What is the pattern that explains the action? Is it the familiar pattern of an action done for a reason? Then it does indeed explain the action, but only because it assumes the relation of reason and action that we want to analyze. Or is the pattern rather this: the man is driving, he is approaching a turn; he knows he ought to signal; he knows how to signal, by raising his arm. And now, in this context, he raises his arm. Perhaps, as Melden suggests, if all this happens, he does signal. And the explanation would then be this: if, under these conditions, a man raises his arm, then he signals. The difficulty is, of course, that this explanation does not touch the question of why he raised his arm. He had a reason to raise his arm, but this has not been shown to be the reason why he did it. If the description 'signaling' explains his action by giving his reason, then the signaling must be intentional; but, on the account just given, it may not be.

If, as Melden claims, causal explanations are "wholly irrelevant to the understanding we seek" of human actions (184) then we are without an analysis of the 'because' in 'He did it because . . .', where we go on to name a reason. Hampshire remarks, of the relation between reasons and action, "In philosophy one ought surely to find this . . . connection altogether mysterious" (166). Hampshire rejects Aristotle's attempt to solve the mystery by introducing the concept of wanting as a causal factor, on the grounds that the resulting theory is too clear and definite to fit all cases and that "There is still no compelling ground for insisting that the word 'want' *must* enter into every full statement of reasons for acting" (168). I agree that the concept of wanting is too narrow, but I have argued that, at least in a vast number of typical cases, some pro attitude must be assumed to be present if a statement of an agent's reasons in acting is to be intelligible. Hampshire does not see how Aristotle's scheme can be appraised as true or false, "for it is not clear what could be the basis of assessment, or what kind of evidence could be decisive" (167). Failing a satisfactory alternative, the best argument for a scheme like Aristotle's is that it alone promises to give an account of the "mysterious connection" between reasons and actions.

## IV

In order to turn the first 'and' to 'because' in 'He exercised *and* he wanted to reduce and thought exercise would do it', we must, as the basic move,[5] augment condition C1 with:

C2. A primary reason for an action is its cause.

The considerations in favor of C2 are by now, I hope, obvious; in the remainder of this paper I wish to defend C2 against various lines of attack and, in the process, to clarify the notion of causal explanation involved.

A. The first line of attack is this. Primary reasons consist of attitudes and beliefs, which are states or dispositions, not events; therefore they cannot be causes.

It is easy to reply that states, dispositions, and conditions are frequently named as the causes of events: the bridge collapsed because of a structural defect; the plane crashed on takeoff because the air temperature was abnormally high; the plate broke because it had a crack. This reply does not, however, meet a closely related point. Mention of a causal condition for an event gives a cause only on the assumption that there was also a preceding event. But what is the preceding event that causes an action?

In many cases it is not difficult at all to find events very closely associated with the primary reason. States and dispositions are not events, but the onslaught of a state or disposition is. A desire to hurt your feelings may spring up at the moment you anger me; I may start wanting to eat a melon just when I see one; and beliefs may begin at the moment we notice, perceive, learn, or remember something. Those who have argued that there are no mental events to qualify as causes of actions have often missed the obvious because they have insisted that a mental event be observed or noticed (rather than an observing or a noticing) or that it be like a stab, a qualm, a prick or a quiver, a mysterious prod of conscience or act of the will. Melden, in discussing the driver who signals a turn by raising his arm, challenges those who want to explain actions causally to identify "an event which is common and peculiar to all such cases" (87), perhaps a motive or an intention, anyway "some particular feeling or experience" (95). But of course there is a mental event; at some moment the driver noticed (or thought he noticed) his turn coming up, and that is the moment he signaled. During any continuing activity, like driving, or elaborate performance, like swimming the Hellespont, there are more or less fixed purposes, standards, desires, and habits that give direction and form to the entire enterprise, and there is the continuing input of information about what we are doing, about changes in the environment, in terms of which we regulate and adjust our actions. To dignify a driver's awareness that his turn has come by calling it an experience, much less a feeling, is no doubt exaggerated, but whether it deserves a name or not, it had better be the reason why he raises his arm. In this case, and typically, there may not be anything we would call a motive, but if we mention such a general purpose as wanting to get to one's destination safely, it is clear that the motive is not an event. The intention with which the driver raises his arm is also not an event, for it is no thing at all, neither event, attitude, disposition, nor object. Finally, Melden asks the causal theorist to find an event that is common and peculiar to all cases where a man intentionally raises his arm, and this, it must be admitted, cannot be produced. But then neither can a common and unique cause of bridge failures, plane crashes, or plate breakings be produced.

The signaling driver can answer the question 'Why did you raise your arm when you did?', and from the answer we learn the event that caused the action. But can an actor always answer such a question? Sometimes the answer will mention a mental event that does not give a reason: 'Finally I made up my mind'. However, there also seem to be cases of intentional action where we cannot explain at all why we acted when we did. In such cases, explanation in terms of primary reasons parallels the explanation of the collapse of the bridge from a structural defect: we are ignorant of the event or sequence of events that led up to (caused) the collapse, but we are sure there was such an event or sequence of events.

*B*. According to Melden, a cause must be "logically distinct from the alleged effect" (52); but a reason for an action is not logically distinct from the action; therefore, reasons are not causes of actions.[6]

One possible form of this argument has already been suggested. Since a reason makes an action intelligible by redescribing it, we do not have two events, but only one under different descriptions. Causal relations, however, demand distinct events.

Someone might be tempted into the mistake of thinking that my flipping of the switch caused my turning on of the light (in fact it caused the light to go on). But it does not follow that it is a mistake to take 'My reason for flipping the switch was that I wanted to turn on the light' as entailing, in part, 'I flipped the switch, and this action is further describable as having been caused by my wanting to turn on the light'. To describe an event in terms of its cause is not to identify the event with its cause, nor does explanation by redescription exclude causal explanation.

The example serves also to refute the claim that we cannot describe the action without using words that link it to the alleged cause. Here the action is to be explained under the description: 'my flipping the switch', and the alleged cause is 'my wanting to turn on the light'. What possible logical relation is supposed to hold between these phrases? It seems more plausible to urge a logical link between 'my turning on the light' and 'my wanting to turn on the light', but even here the link turned out, on inspection, to be grammatical rather than logical.

In any case there is something very odd in the idea that causal relations are empirical rather than logical. What can this mean? Surely not that every true causal statement is empirical. For suppose '*A* caused *B*' is true. Then the cause of $B = A$; so, substituting, we have 'The cause of *B* caused *B*', which is analytic. The truth of a causal statement depends on *what* events are described; its status as analytic or synthetic depends on *how* the events are described. Still, it may be maintained that a reason rationalizes an action only when the descriptions are appropriately fixed, and the appropriate descriptions are not logically independent.

Suppose that to say a man wanted to turn on the light *meant* that he would perform any action he believed would accomplish his end. Then the statement of his primary reason for flipping the switch would entail that he flipped the switch—"straightway he acts," as Aristotle says. In this case there would certainly be a logical connection between reason and action, the same sort of connection as that between 'It's water-soluble and was placed in water' and 'It dissolved'. Since the implication runs from description of cause to description of effect but not conversely, naming the cause still gives information. And, though the point is often overlooked, 'Placing it in water caused it to dissolve' does not entail 'It's water-soluble'; so the latter has additional explanatory force. Nevertheless, the explanation would be far more interesting if, in place of solubility, with its obvious definitional connection with the event to be explained, we could refer to some property, say a particular crystalline structure, whose connection with dissolution in water was known only through experiment. Now it is clear why primary reasons like desires and wants do not explain actions in the relatively trivial way solubility explains dissolvings. Solubility, we are assuming, is a pure disposition property: it is defined in terms of a single test. But desires cannot be defined in terms of the actions they may rationalize, even though the relation between desire and action is not simply empirical; there are other, equally essential criteria for desires—their expression in feelings and in actions that they do not rationalize, for example. The person who has a desire (or want or belief) does not normally need criteria at all—he generally knows, even in the absence of any clues available to others, what he wants, desires, and believes. These logical features of primary reasons show that it is not just lack of ingenuity that keeps us from defining them as dispositions to act for these reasons.

*C.* According to Hume, "we may define a cause to be an object followed by another, and where all the objects similar to the first are followed by objects similar to the second." But, Hart and Honoré claim, "The statement that one person did something because, for example, another threatened him, carries no implication or covert assertion that if the circumstances were repeated the same action would follow" (52). Hart and Honoré allow that Hume is right in saying that ordinary singular causal statements imply generalizations, but wrong for this very reason in supposing that motives and desires are ordinary causes of actions.

In brief, laws are involved essentially in ordinary causal explanations, but not in rationalizations.

It is common to try to meet this argument by suggesting that we do have rough laws connecting reasons and actions, and these can, in theory, be improved. True, threatened people do not always respond in the same way; but we may distinguish between threats and also between agents, in terms of their beliefs and attitudes.

The suggestion is delusive, however, because generalizations connecting reasons and actions are not—and cannot be sharpened into—the kind of law on the basis of which accurate predictions can reliably be made. If we reflect on the way in which reasons determine choice, decision, and behavior, it is easy to see why this is so. What emerges, in the *ex post facto* atmosphere of explanation and justification, as *the* reason frequently was, to the agent at the time of action, one consideration among many, *a* reason. Any serious theory for predicting action on the basis of reasons must find a way of evaluating the relative force of various desires and beliefs in the matrix of decision; it cannot take as its starting point the refinement of what is to be expected from a single desire. The practical syllogism exhausts its role in displaying an action as falling under one reason; so it cannot be subtilized into a reconstruction of practical reasoning, which involves the weighing of competing reasons. The practical syllogism provides a model neither for a predictive science of action nor for a normative account of evaluative reasoning.

Ignorance of competent predictive laws does not inhibit valid causal explanation, or few causal explanations could be made. I am certain the window broke because it was struck by a rock—I saw it all happen; but I am not (is anyone?) in command of laws on the basis of which I can predict what blows will break which windows. A generalization like 'Windows are fragile, and fragile things tend to break when struck hard enough, other conditions being right' is not a predictive law in the rough—the predictive law, if we had it, would be quantitative and would use very different concepts. The generalization, like our generalizations about behavior, serves a different function: it provides evidence for the existence of a causal law covering the case at hand.

We are usually far more certain of a singular causal connection than we are of any causal law governing the case; does this show that Hume was wrong in claiming that singular causal statements entail laws? Not necessarily, for Hume's claim, as quoted above, is ambiguous. It may mean that '*A* caused *B*' entails some particular law involving the predicates used in the descriptions '*A*' and '*B*', or it may mean that '*A* caused *B*' entails that there exists a causal law instantiated by some true descriptions of *A* and *B*.[7] Obviously, both versions of Hume's doctrine give a sense to the claim that singular causal statements entail laws, and both sustain the view that causal explanations "involve laws." But the second version is far weaker, in that no particular law is entailed by a singular causal claim, and a singular causal claim can be defended, if it needs defense, without defending any law. Only the second version of Hume's doctrine can be made to fit with most causal explanations; it suits rationalizations equally well.

The most primitive explanation of an event gives its cause; more elaborate explanations may tell more of the story, or defend the singular causal claim by producing a relevant law or by giving reasons for believing such exists. But it is an error to think no explanation has been given until a law has been produced. Linked with these errors is the idea that singular causal statements necessarily indicate, by the concepts they employ, the concepts that will occur in the entailed law. Suppose a hurricane, which is reported on page 5 of Tuesday's *Times*, causes a catastrophe, which is reported on page 13 of Wednesday's *Tribune*. Then the event reported on page 5 of Tuesday's *Times* caused the event reported on page 13 of Wednesday's *Tribune*. Should we look for a law relating events of these *kinds*? It is only slightly less ridiculous to look for a law relating hurricanes and catastrophes. The laws needed to predict the catastrophe with precision would, of course, have no use for concepts like hurricane and catastrophe. The trouble with predicting the weather is that the descriptions under which events interest us—'a cool, cloudy day with rain in the afternoon'—have only remote connections with the concepts employed by the more precise known laws.

The laws whose existence is required if reasons are causes of actions do not, we may be sure, deal in the concepts in which rationalizations must deal. If the causes of a class of events (actions) fall in a certain class (reasons) and there is a law to back each singular causal statement, it does not follow that there is any law connecting events classified as reasons with events classified as actions—the classifications may even be neurological, chemical, or physical.

*D.* It is said that the kind of knowledge one has of one's own reasons in acting is not compatible with the existence of a causal relation between reasons and actions: a person knows his own intentions in acting infallibly, without induction or observation, and no ordinary causal relation can be known in this way. No doubt our knowledge of our own intentions in acting will show many of the oddities peculiar to first-person knowledge of one's own pains, beliefs, desires, and so on; the only question is whether these oddities prove that reasons do not cause, in any ordinary sense at least, the actions that they rationalize.

You may easily be wrong about the truth of a statement of the form 'I am poisoning Charles because I want to save him pain', because you may be wrong about whether you are poisoning Charles—you may yourself be drinking the poisoned cup by mistake. But it also seems that you may err about your reasons, particularly when you have two reasons for an action, one of which pleases you and one which does not. For example, you do want to save Charles pain; you also want him out of the way. You may be wrong about which motive made you do it.

The fact that you may be wrong does not show that in general it makes sense to ask you how you know what your reasons were or to ask for your evidence. Though you may, on rare occasions, accept public or private evidence as showing you are wrong about your reasons, you usually have no evidence and make no observations. Then your knowledge of your own reasons for your actions is not generally inductive, for where there is induction, there is evidence. Does this show the knowledge is not causal? I cannot see that it does.

Causal laws differ from true but nonlawlike generalizations in that their instances confirm them; induction is, therefore, certainly a good way to learn the truth of a law. It does not follow that it is the only way to learn the truth of a law. In any case, in order to know that a singular causal statement is true, it is not necessary to know the truth of a law; it is necessary only to know that some law covering the events at hand exists. And it is far from evident that induction, and induction alone, yields the knowledge that a causal law satisfying certain conditions exists. Or, to put it differently, one case is often enough, as Hume admitted, to persuade us that a law exists, and this amounts to saying that we are persuaded, without direct inductive evidence, that a causal relation exists.[8]

*E.* Finally I should like to say something about a certain uneasiness some philosophers feel in speaking of causes of actions at all. Melden, for example, says that actions are often identical with bodily movements, and that bodily movements have causes; yet he denies that the causes are causes of the actions. This is, I think, a contradiction. He is led to it by the following sort of consideration: "It is futile to attempt to explain conduct through the causal efficacy of desire—all *that* can explain is further happenings, not actions performed by agents. The agent confronting the causal nexus in which such happenings occur is a helpless victim of all that occurs in and to him" (128, 129). Unless I am mistaken, this argument, if it were valid, would show that actions cannot have causes at all. I shall not point out the obvious difficulties in removing actions from the realm of causality entirely. But perhaps it is worth trying to uncover the source of the trouble. Why on earth should a cause turn an action into a mere happening and a person into a helpless victim? Is it because we tend to assume, at least in the arena of action, that a cause demands a causer, agency an agent? So we press the question; if my action is caused, what caused it? If I did, then there is the absurdity of infinite regress; if I did not, I am a victim. But of course the alternatives are not exhaustive. Some causes have no agents. Primary among these are those states and changes of state in persons which, because they are reasons as well as causes, make persons voluntary agents.

## Notes

1. Some examples: G. E. M. Anscombe, *Intention,* Oxford, 1959; Stuart Hampshire, *Thought and Action,* London, 1959; H. L. A. Hart and A. M. Honoré, *Causation in the Law,* Oxford, 1959; William Dray, *Laws and Explanation in History,* Oxford, 1957; and most of the books in the series edited by R. F. Holland, *Studies in Philosophical Psychology,* including Anthony Kenny, *Action, Emotion and Will,* London, 1963, and A. I. Melden, *Free Action,* London, 1961. Page references in parentheses will all be to these works.

2. We would not call my unintentional alerting of the prowler an action, but it should not be inferred from this that alerting the prowler is therefore something different from flipping the switch, say just its consequence. Actions, performances, and events not involving intention are alike in that they are often referred to or defined partly in terms of some terminal stage, outcome, or consequence.

The word 'action' does not very often occur in ordinary speech, and when it does it is usually reserved for fairly portentous occasions. I follow a useful philosophical practice in calling anything an agent does intentionally an action, including intentional omissions. What is really needed is some suitably generic term to bridge the following gap: suppose '*A*' is a description of an action, '*B*' is a description of something done voluntarily, though not intentionally, and '*C*' is a description of something done involuntarily and unintentionally; finally, suppose $A = B = C$. Then *A*, *B*, and *C* are the same—what? 'Action,' 'event,' 'thing done,' each have, at least in some contexts, a strange ring when coupled with the wrong sort of description. Only the question "Why did you (he) do *A*?" has the true generality required. Obviously, the problem is greatly aggravated if we assume, as

Melden does (*Free Action,* 85), that an action ("raising one's arm") can be identical with a bodily movement ("one's arm going up").

3. "Quasi-intentional" because, besides its intensional aspect, the description of the action must also refer in rationalizations; otherwise it could be true that an action was done for a certain reason and yet the action not have been performed. Compare 'the author of *Waverly*' in 'George IV knew the author of *Waverly* wrote *Waverly*.'

4. Miss Anscombe denies that the practical syllogism is deductive. This she does partly because she thinks of the practical syllogism, as Aristotle does, as corresponding to a piece of practical reasoning (whereas for me it is only part of the analysis of the concept of a reason with which someone acted), and therefore she is bound, again following Aristotle, to think of the conclusion of a practical syllogism as corresponding to a judgment, not merely that the action has a desirable characteristic, but that the action is desirable (reasonable, worth doing, etc.).

5. I say "as the basic move" to cancel the suggestion that C1 and C2 are jointly *sufficient* to define the relation of reasons to the actions they explain. I believe C2 can be strengthened to make C1 and C2 sufficient as well as necessary conditions, but here I am concerned only with the claim that both are, as they stand, necessary.

6. This argument can be found, in one or more versions, in Kenny, Hampshire, and Melden, as well as in P. Winch, *The Idea of a Social Science,* London, 1958, and R. S. Peters, *The Concept of Motivation,* London, 1958. In one of its forms, the argument was of course inspired by Ryle's treatment of motives in *The Concept of Mind.*

7. We could roughly characterize the analysis of singular causal statements hinted at here as follows: '*A* caused *B*' is true if and only if there are descriptions of *A* and *B* such that the sentence obtained by putting these descriptions for '*A*' and '*B*' in '*A* caused *B*' follows from a true causal law. This analysis is saved from triviality by the fact that not all true generalizations are causal laws; causal laws are distinguished (though of course this is no analysis) by the fact that they are inductively confirmed by their instances and by the fact that they support counterfactual and subjunctive singular causal statements.

8. My thinking on the subject of this section, as on most of the topics discussed in this paper, has been greatly influenced by years of talk with Professor Daniel Bennett.

RICHARD BRANDT AND
JAEGWON KIM

# Wants as Explanations of Actions*

Some features of the concept of a want, and of the explaining relation in which a want may stand to an action, have not received sufficient attention. In what follows we shall offer some suggestions and descriptions which may be one step toward remedy of this situation. We shall be at pains to point out the extent to which the features we describe fit in with a conception of the explanations of actions conforming to the inferential (deductive or inductive) and nomological patterns of scientific explanation, and also to point out where perhaps the fit is not so snug.

Some philosophers may not be very sympathetic with our contentions. Some philosophers think that a want is not the sort of thing that could explain an action at all, at least in any way at all similar to that in which natural phenomena are explained in the empirical sciences. They regard it as a certainty that wants are not causes of actions—and indeed often think that deliberative actions do not have causes in the sense in which natural events do. Moreover, they think that the usual nomological scheme of explanation, in general, does not apply to actions, even if there are some events to which it does apply.

We are not aiming primarily to reply to the contentions of these philosophers. We do believe, however, that what we have to say may serve to allay some doubts of this sort, by making

* Reprinted by permission of the authors and the editors from *The Journal of Philosophy,* LX (1963).

clearer the details of what an inferential-nomological explanation of an action might be, in which reference to the agent's wants figured prominently.

## I. Wanting

If wanting were a special sort of conscious occurrence, introspectively identifiable whenever it occurred, like itches and sinking sensations, philosophers might feel fewer qualms about regarding wants as partial causes of behavior or about accepting in principle the idea of laws relating them to actions or decisions. For various good reasons, however, this conception of wanting has all but disappeared today; we propose to ignore it.

The word 'want' has many distinct but related senses in English. Sometimes it is used in the sense of 'ought', as in 'You want to eat before you go'; sometimes it means 'need', as in 'He wants a spanking'; and it means still different things in 'The police want him' or 'You are wanted by the boss'. We wish to attend, however, to the sense that the word has in statements like 'He stole the money because he badly wanted a new car for his honeymoon'. This sense of 'want' is the one in which wants are important for understanding action. 'Wants' in this sense doubtless differs in subtle ways from 'desires' and 'wishes', but we shall not attempt to explore this. In what follows we shall use the locution '*x* wants *p*', understanding by this '*x* wants that *p*' in the above sense (and where '*p*' is some appropriate sentential clause). This is a convenient substitute for the normal idiom using the infinitive. Thus, instead of saying "*x* wants *y* to be elected president" we shall say "*x* wants that *y* be elected president." By using this locution we avoid expressions in which 'want' is followed simply by a noun or a noun phrase, as in 'He wants a meal', locutions which can be ambiguous outside the particular contexts of their utterance. What people want is that something should be the case, so that, in the case of the meal, what the person wants is, presumably, that he eat a meal or that he be served a meal. '$x$ wants $p$' does not, of course, imply that $p$ is wanted *for itself*. Among the things a person can want is that he himself do a certain thing, but we should notice that a person can be motivated, e.g., by considerations of duty, to do something we should not say he *wanted* to do.[1]

Now '$x$ wants $p$' has the meaning it does have for us because we believe roughly the statements listed below. Perhaps other statements should be added to the list. Furthermore, some of the listed statements may not be exactly true. But adult speakers of English *believe* that most of them are approximately true, and if anyone disbelieved all of them this would be excellent reason for doubting that he understood the meaning of '$x$ wants $p$'. Some of these statements give a necessary condition for '$x$ wants $p$', others a sufficient condition, and no doubt some of them could be strengthened, with additional qualifications, so as to state a necessary and sufficient condition; but this detail is of no great importance.

(a) If, given that $x$ had not been expecting $p$ but now suddenly judged that $p$ would be the case, $x$ would feel joy,[2] then $x$ wants $p$.
(b) If, given that $x$ had been expecting $p$ but then suddenly judged that $p$ would not be the case, $x$ would feel disappointment, then $x$ wants $p$.
(c) If daydreaming about $p$ is pleasant to $x$, then $x$ wants $p$.
(d) If $x$ wants $p$, then, under favorable conditions,[3] if $x$ judges that doing $A$ will probably lead to $p$ and that not doing $A$ will probably lead to not-$p$, $x$ will feel some impulse to do $A$.
(e) If $x$ wants $p$, then under favorable conditions,[3] if $x$ thinks some means $M$ is a way of bringing $p$ about, $x$ will be more likely to notice an $M$ than he would otherwise have been.
(f) If $x$ wants $p$, then, under favorable conditions,[3] if $p$ occurs, without the simultaneous occurrence of events $x$ doesn't want, $x$ will be pleased.

To accept the above explanation of the connection between believing these statements and the meaning of 'wants' is, of course, to accept for 'wants' the proposal that many philosophers of science have made about "theoretical constructs"—that the meaning of a "theoretical construct" is given, at least partially, by the laws and "correspondence rules" in which it appears. It may be helpful, then, to construe 'wants' as a theoretical construct. Thus statements (a) to (f) can be viewed as a small-scale psychological theory which is implicitly embedded in our everyday understanding of events or processes involving wanting, feelings of joy and disappointment, and the like. The meaning of 'wanting' is anchored in this theory. It may seem paradoxical to say both that these statements give the meaning of 'wanting' and that they are synthetic, corrigible, and probably incomplete. But what is shown by this apparent paradox is that the concept of wanting in everyday life is not precise and clear-cut and that its meaning is not now fixed, but may change as theoretical knowledge in psychology grows.

In support of this view of 'wants' is the fact that not all of the above statements *can* be viewed as analytic. Any *one* can be so viewed, but not the whole set. For, to take an example, the joint assertion of (c) and (f) entails 'If daydreaming about $p$ is pleasant to $x$, then, under favorable conditions, if $p$ occurs . . . $x$ will be pleased'. This statement is obviously synthetic, one in which the word 'want' does not even appear. Since it is synthetic and entailed by (c) and (f), it is impossible for both (c) and (f) to be analytic. It is possible that after suitable modification each of the statements (a) to (f) could be rewritten as an equivalence, with '$x$ wants $p$' on the lefthand side and the related expression on the right. In this case all the righthand statements could be grouped together in a conjunction or as a disjunction or, more plausibly, as some disjunction of conjunctions. In that case the statement obtained could not be denied analyticity on the foregoing ground. But it could not plausibly be regarded as analytic, given the somewhat vague and open-ended everyday concept of wanting.

Neither can statements (a) to (f) reasonably be regarded as *simply* synthetic. It is true that further observations and requirements of theoretical simplicity might induce us to modify them or even abandon some of them. But, to see their special status, consider the following possibly true statement:

(g) If events like *p* have in the past been associated with the reduction of drive-stimuli in the agent, the agent will tend to want *p* for itself.

No one would be accused of failing to understand 'wanting' on the ground that he did not believe or even understand (g), whereas this question would arise for one who disbelieved (a) to (f). It need not be claimed that a person does not understand 'wanting' if he does not subscribe to *every* one of (a) to (f), much less if he subscribes to a slightly altered version of the set. But if he subscribes to *none* of the set, or only to a few of them, we would think he did not have the ordinary concept of wanting. However, the acceptance or rejection of (g) by itself would seem to have no such effect. It seems, then, that (a) to (f) are *central* to the meaning of 'wanting', whereas (g) is only peripheral, in the present state of psychological concepts. Indeed, even among (a) to (f), some seem more central to the meaning of 'wanting' than others. Intuitively it seems that (a), (b), and (f) are more central to the meaning than the rest. In particular (e) is rather like (g); normally it would require some psychological sophistication to believe (e).

It is sometimes said that the meaning of a theoretical term should be associated with the totality of the empirical statements we accept in which that term appears. It should be noticed that we are not endorsing this claim in its full generality. For, as things stand now, the addition or deletion of (g) has nothing to do with the meaning of 'wants'. We can distinguish, if only roughly, centralities of statements with respect to their association with the meaning of the terms that appear in them.

We wish to make a few further observations about 'wanting':

First, we have used the terms 'pleasant' and 'unpleasant' in our explanations of 'wanting'. But 'pleasant' and 'unpleasant' do not denote directly observable qualities; they are relational terms which themselves have to be explained, probably, in terms of the concept of wanting. For example, 'pleasant' probably has to be explained as meaning something like 'an experience that the person would like (wants) to prolong or repeat'. Thus there is a kind of circularity in some of the statements (a) to (f), considered as explanations of the meaning of 'wanting'. But there is nothing objectionable in this. On the contrary, it only confirms our view that the statements (a) to (f) represent a small common-sense theoretical network which interrelates wanting and experience of pleasure and displeasure among other things. The circularity only serves to enrich the scope of the scheme. One would find oneself in difficulty over this only if one wished to assert that the statements (a) to (f) were definitionally analytic. It is true, however, that one who wishes to give an explanation of psychological concepts, beginning with "observation terms," will wish to ascribe a certain reconstructional priority to terms like 'joy' and 'disappointment' and 'impulse to do'.

Second, there is the question whether, if 'wanting' is construed as outlined, a person can always know what he wants. It is clear that, if our account is correct, there are circumstances in which a person can know that he wants something. Suppose he notices he is overjoyed at a certain piece of news or that another piece of news causes acute disappointment. Then he can know that he wants a certain thing. But according to our analysis there can be situations in which one wants something but does *not* know that one does. Suppose one wants $p$ but the conditions in (a) and (b) are in fact not realized; then so far the person has no reason to judge that he does or doesn't want $p$. This situation is like the case in which a person does not know he is courageous until he encounters a situation that calls for courageous action. Now, a person can try, say, tests (c) or (d). But, if he is excited or tired, the thought of $p$ occurring may leave him cold. Statements (e) and (f) give tests we are often in no position to apply. Presumably a person can usually apply (c) and (d); but (c) does not establish that one doesn't have a want, and (d) does not establish that one does, unless we change the implication to an equivalence, as perhaps we should. In any case, (d) still contains the "under favorable conditions" clause, as a consequence of which the test is not always conclusive. This outcome seems to us intuitively correct. For instance, we think a person may believe he doesn't want prestige, whereas in fact he does. Or a person may think he wants a good character, whereas in fact he only has an aversion to having a bad reputation.

Third, the account we have offered for 'wanting' is very much the account that must be given for some other psychological terms. Perhaps 'believing' is among these. It is more certain that the names of character and personality traits are among them. Indeed, the explanation of some of these involves the concept of wanting. For instance, 'sympathetic' seems to imply readiness to want relief or succor for a person in distress. 'Inquisitive' implies a readiness to want to know at least certain kinds of things in certain situations. Indeed it seems likely that all names of character traits are of this sort.

## II. Wanting and Action

What is the relation between wanting and doing, deciding, or choosing?

Sometimes the relation seems relatively direct and simple. One is thirsty, and suddenly finds oneself on the way to the tap, still thinking about the problem on which one was concentrating; there was no deliberation whether to get a drink. Or one is offered a box of chocolates; one's hand reaches for one, almost automatically. One didn't argue: I'd like to have a chocolate; here are some chocolates; so I'll take one. Or, one wants to impress a person, and one finds oneself boasting; there was no conscious reasoning. Or, one would like to go sailing, so one finds oneself daydreaming about sailing; there was no decision to daydream about sailing. In such cases there is no weighing of pros and cons or reflection as to the best strategy to be adopted. Sometimes there is not even awareness that one does want something:

when one wants *p* and sees that doing *A* would produce *p*, one often automatically does *A*, without reflecting that one did want *p*. Let us call such actions *nondeliberative.*

In what way do wants explain nondeliberative actions? By the synthetic but quasi-analytic principle (d), above, a person who wants *p* and who judges that doing *A* will probably lead to *p* and that not doing *A* will probably lead to non-*p* will feel *some impulse* to do A. Of course, to feel an impulse to do *A* is not necessarily to do, or to be following by doing, *A*; some impulses are consciously suppressed, others are too weak to move us, and so on. So, if wanting is to imply even nondeliberative action, it must be by virtue of some further principle connecting impulses to do with doing. Presumably this principle will be one according to which impulse becomes action depending on certain general features of the situation, such as the strength of the impulse, the kind of action required, the personality and character traits of the agent, and the sociopsychological situation in which the action is to be performed. In fact no such law or set of laws is known. Evidently a full statement of such a true principle would be a complicated business, even if we were content with principles of a statistical form. The psychology of action has not gone that far.[4] There is also the possibility, parallel to a problem for the explanation of deliberative action which we shall discuss below, that there is no true *general* principle here at all, but at best only restricted "law-like" principles (in Ryle's sense) in which there is essential reference to specific individuals. However, we take for granted in everyday life that a proper combination of the requisite factors occurs quite often, and so, when nondeliberative action occurs, we properly explain it by reference to what the agent wanted, *via* some such general statement as (d) above.

In *deliberative* actions, the relation between wanting and doing is relatively indirect and complex. It is obvious that very often, when a person in fact wants *p* and believes that doing *A* will lead to *p*, he does not do A, for any one of several reasons. First, obviously, doing *A* may be expected to lead to other consequences he doesn't want, as well as *p*; or there may be some conflicting act that he thinks will lead to results he wants more than *p*. Second, when a person is making a serious decision, he will usually pay no attention to the fact that doing *A* will lead to *p*, despite his wanting *p*, unless he knows that he wants *p*. (Conversely, if a person sincerely but wrongly believes that he wants *p*, this fact is apt to be a relevant factor in his deliberative process.) In making a decision, a person will often line up the pro points and the con points, but unless he recognizes that he wants *p* he may not count it as a pro point for *A* that doing *A* will lead to *p*; in this case the fact that he really wants *p* will not influence his decision insofar as his decision is "rational." Again, a person may know that he wants *p*, but think it a bad thing that he does and refrain from doing what he thinks will lead to *p* on that account. Similarly, he may count it as a pro point for doing *A* that it will lead to *p*, although *p* is something he does not think of himself as wanting but rather as something he ought to want—such as the public good or conformity to some moral standard. A person need not always do what he does because he wants it or its consequences in our sense of 'want', or even because he thinks he does.

The implication of these facts is this: When action is deliberative, it is one thing to want *p* and believe that doing *A* will lead to *p*; it is quite another to choose, decide to do, or do *A*. The one does not necessarily lead to the other. So far, then, wants do not yet fully explain action. For the purpose of explanation, if we are to follow the standard pattern of explanation in science, we need an empirical law (perhaps only something like the "law" relating wanting and disappointment along the lines of (b) above) or something like an empirical law. What kind of law might this be?

We know of no reasonably well-confirmed law that connects wants, beliefs, and actions for all persons in every choice situation, for the case of deliberative action. But, in the case of some individual we know well, we can sometimes know some statement like this to be true of *him:* 'At any time *t, he* will perform that action among those he believes possible which he *thinks* will maximize expectable utility for him', where 'utility' is defined in some way in terms of the agent's intensity of want for any event in question. To make this sort of statement about a person, or about a person at a particular time, would be to classify him as a *rational* agent, in one possible sense of 'rational'. Evidently, not everyone is rational in this sense, and in fact probably no one is rational at all times. Hence we cannot assert something corresponding to the above statement, as a general law true for everyone. What we can know is a "law-like" fact about some particular individual over some period of time, much as we can know of a particular piece of substance that it is fragile or conducts electricity without knowing that it is glass or copper. The law-like statement in question characterizes what we might call the "choice-habits" of some people, describes how they come out in action, as a result of deliberation.

Whether one asserts laws or only law-like statements like the above, however, the principle does not yet relate *wants* to action. It relates judgments about wants—in the form of estimates of expectable utility—to action. In order to have a continuous connection between wants and action, we need still another law or set of laws, relating a person's wants to his estimates of expectable utility. We have already said something relevant to this, in our discussion of whether a person always knows what he wants. (Obviously the measurement of wants for this purpose would require a sophisticated psychological theory and technique. The statements (a) to (f) are clearly insufficient for this task; they do not even enable us to make *comparative* judgments concerning the relative strength of two or more wants. Also, how accurate are one's judgments of the relative strength of his wants, and how do people estimate the probability of an outcome? Then, too, people make mistakes in arithmetic.) Obviously there is not at present any known law about this, although recent empirical studies contain interesting results.

How then, it may be asked, in the absence of known laws, can it be claimed that there are explanations of actions on the basis of wants, of the usual nomological form? The answer to this question is simple: There is at present *no theoretical* explanation of action on the basis of wants; there is simply no theory to do the job. We can and do have, however, *nontheoretical* common-sense explanations which ordinarily satisfy us and which are based upon such empirical assumptions as that people do act according to some rational calculation and that people do not often make simple logical or arithmetical mistakes; we also have a good deal of knowledge about preference scales of people, both collectively and individually. (A given agent, of course, is favorably placed to have particularly accurate information about himself.) These assumptions, which enjoy a broad factual warrant in our experience, can be listed along with the statements (a) to (f) to make the scheme more comprehensive for explanatory (and predictive) purposes, although these assumptions do not enjoy the quasi-analytic status of (a) to (f). So it is proper to say that we do have explanations of actions on the basis of wants; but these everyday common-sense explanations, whether of deliberative or nondeliberative actions, on the basis of wants, presuppose and derive their explanatory force from an everyday common-sense scheme of psychological knowledge of people in general or of the preference scale (etc.) of a given agent in particular, which can be unpacked in more or less precise statements, some of which we have tried to sketch. Thus, when we say "He stole the money because he badly wanted a new car for his honeymoon," we are using information about the agent's preference scale (etc.) and general propositions about what people ordinarily do in certain circumstances, inferring deductively or inductively the explanandum statement, very much as we do when we offer the explanation, "The radiator leaks because the temperature fell to 10° last night and there was no anti-freeze in the radiator." Explanations of this kind may not have much theoretical power or interest; but to grant this is only to concede that they *are* common-sense explanations. Trivial and obvious as they seem, these explanations are not fundamentally different in logical and methodological requirements from their counterparts in natural science. Truly deductive explanations of actions may be difficult and even impossible to attain, but we must remember that even in physical science deductively complete explanations are often found only among theoretical explanations of laws and theories and seldom among explanations of specific events and states.

It may be said that the analysis of 'wanting' that we have offered is largely dispositional, and it may then be argued that the effect of this is that explanations of action on the basis of wants, as we have outlined them, are no more than trivial, just like explanations of a lump of sugar dissolving in water on the basis of its being soluble in water or of opium putting people to sleep on the basis of its soporific power. While the two examples just cited are indeed trivial explanations, this is not because they appeal to dispositions. They are trivial because the dispositional statements invoked as explanations are logically entailed by the explanandum statements: that a lump of sugar dissolves in water at a certain time logically entails that it is soluble in water at that time, and that opium puts people to sleep entails that it has soporific power. For this reason the alleged explanations do not provide any new enlightenment about the situations to be explained; they do not set them in a lawful pattern. But when, for instance, we explain why a person notices a restaurant at a street corner where he had never noticed one before, by pointing out that he is *hungry*, that is, that he *wants* to eat, the situation is quite otherwise. Clearly, the statement that he noticed a restaurant does not logically imply that he is hungry; further, the assertion that one wants something implies many other things than just noticing via some of the statements (a) to (f) or, presumably, other similar true statements we might have listed. So, when we say that the person noticed the restaurant because he wanted to eat, we are setting the event to be explained in a wider pattern of lawful regularities.

Are the explanations of action on the basis of wants as we have outlined them "causal explanations"? There is the extreme view, endorsed by many philosophers, which categorically denies that they are causal explanations—and indeed that any alleged explanation of action on the basis of wants could succeed in being a genuine causal explanation. However, what these philosophers mean by "causal explanation" is often unclear, and, when it is clear, it is not at all certain that all the familiar explanations found in the natural sciences are "causal" in any single required sense. Sometimes these philosophers seem to have in mind something analogous to the *mechanical* model of classical physics; sometimes, *deductive* explanations with *general* laws and *antecedent* conditions; sometimes any explanation in which reference is made to *antecedent* events or states; sometimes an explanation in which the explanans includes facts that are occurrents in a sense in which wanting, at least as we have explained it, is not; and so on. We find it hard to attach much importance to this issue, in the absence of a generally accepted and methodologically interesting conception of "causal explanation" that is appropriate to the issue at hand.[5] What we think clear and important in this dispute is the question of whether or not sensible explanations of human actions exhibit the appropriate inferential and nomological pattern of explanations found in physical and biological sciences—in other words, whether explanations of action form a unique type of explanation with special logical and methodological requirements distinct from those of explanations in natural science. Obviously, if our analysis of wanting and of explanations of action in terms of wants is plausible, at least in basic outline, it is one good reason for thinking that explanations of action do not differ from explanations in natural science, in inferential nomological pattern.

## Notes

1. It might be thought that '*x* has an aversion to *p*' means the same as '*x* wants non-*p*' and that the following statements could therefore be accepted, with suitable modifications, as an explication of '*x* has an aversion to *p*'. This proposal, however, is mistaken, and we are not making any claim to explain the meaning of 'aversion to'. Wants and aversions differ in structure, and although a parallel could be worked out, we prefer to avoid this complication. For some differences, see Stephen Pepper, *The Sources of Value* (Berkeley: University of California Press, 1958), chap. 10.

2. We here ignore the question whether 'joy' and 'disappointment' are properly construed as "observation terms" or as "theoretical terms" which we know how to apply because of laws or rules connecting them with publicly observable behavior. If one adopts the latter view, one must at least allow these terms a rather special status on account of our experiences of states of joy and disappointment in ourselves. In this respect these terms are different from 'wants', which does not denote an experience.

We also ignore the question whether 'joy' and 'disappointment' must be taken to refer to some physiological fact, at least as used by some persons.

3. The vague escape clause 'under favorable conditions' is essential to the truth of some of the above statements. For example, such conditions as extreme fatigue, emotional excitement (e.g., grief), or the temporal remoteness of the event judged about must count as unfavorable conditions, for when they obtain the consequent will not hold even if the antecedent does. In the present state of psychological knowledge no exact account of the scope of 'favorable conditions' can be given.

Psychologists' discussions of some or all of the foregoing statements include Karl Duncker, "Pleasure, Emotion, and Striving," *Philosophy and Phenomenological Research*, 1, 415–425; A. F. Shand, *The Foundations of Character* (London: Macmillan, 1920), *passim;* and F. Heider, *Psychology of Interpersonal Relations* (New York: Wiley, 1958), chaps. 4 and 5.

4. For a model of such a principle or set of principles, see E. C. Tolman's "A Psychological Model" in Parsons and Shils (eds.), *Towards a General Theory of Action* (Cambridge: Harvard University Press, 1951), pp. 279–354.

5. We also agree, on all essential points, with W. P. Alston's recent able criticisms of some philosophers' arguments for the thesis that explanations of actions are not causal explanations, in his paper "Wants, Beliefs, and Action," read to a conference at Wayne State University in April, 1963, of which he kindly furnished us a copy.

THEODORE MISCHEL

# Psychology and Explanations of Human Behavior*

Empirical psychologists are often deeply suspicious of the "understanding" of human behavior which novelists and playwrights can give us. As one recent book puts it

> Shakespeare and Dostoevsky may be "better psychologists than the psychologists" in their ability to touch closely and movingly on some widely held prototheory of behavior; they may even provide a prodigality of plausible initial statements in their building of convincing portraits, but they and the non-empirical psychologists in general, apparently never feel the sharpest goad of the research psychologist—to find out by looking whether or not he is right.[1]

On this view, explanations like those given by Shakespeare and Dostoevsky are "nonempirical" in a very damaging sense—they are based on some "prototheory" of behavior, and one gives them without bothering "to find out by looking whether or not he is right."

What leads these writers to think that Shakespeare's explanations are based on a "prototheory" is their belief that all "explanations share the characteristic of making the statement to be explained an instance of some wider generalization. They all involve in a more or less rigorous way the *deduction* of the statement to be explained."[2] If this is what it means to explain,

* Reprinted by permission of the author and the editor from *Philosophy and Phenomenological Research,* XXIII (1963).

then what Shakespeare tells us about human behavior can be an "explanation" only insofar as it tacitly assumes some generalizations or laws about human behavior. Since Shakespeare neither formulated nor tested any such laws, it is held that he must have taken them for granted—they constitute his "prototheory." This view is also supported by methodologists primarily concerned with the natural sciences, like C. G. Hempel and E. Nagel. These writers claim that we can explain an action in terms of the agent's motives only by virtue of an empirical generalization linking the motive to the ensuing action. In other words, the motive is taken to be an initial condition which can explain the action only when the latter can be deduced from the motive by means of an appropriate general law. In this way explanation in terms of motives are assimilated to the pattern of explanation characteristic of the physical sciences—i.e., to explanations which subsume what is to be explained under some law or law-like regularity.[3]

In contrast to this, I want to defend the view that novelists, playwrights, and other students of distinctively human behavior, can give us responsible, empirical explanations without using any generalizations, laws, or theories. For when they explain what men do in terms of their "motives" they are not explaining in terms of regularities or patterns of behavior; their explanations differ in type from those based on laws, law-like statements, or theories. After defending the use of such explanations, I will try to show that at least some of the explanations actually given in psychology are similar to those given by novelists and playwrights, rather than to those given by physical scientists when they explain things other than human actions. Finally, I will suggest that recognition of this difference in explanation type allows us to see what is valid in the "existential" approach to psychology without committing us to excess metaphysical baggage.

# I

How does Shakespeare explain behavior? Why, for example, is Iago plotting against Othello? Well, he resents Othello for having appointed Cassio to the lieutenancy, he suspects the "lusty Moor" of an intrigue with his wife, and he sets out to serve his turn upon him. By leading Othello to think that Cassio is too familiar with Desdemona, Iago can gain his revenge, become the logical candidate for the lieutenancy, and yet remain "honest Iago" to all the world. But even when his profit in Cassio's ruin has been achieved, Iago continues to plot against Othello. What motivates him now is a desire to reduce the nobility that confronts him to baseness. To strip Othello of his self-respect, to harry him until he collapses at his feet, and thus to demonstrate his own superiority and power—this is Iago's aim when he plots against Othello.

No doubt, much more needs to be said in elucidating Shakespeare's explanation; but this may suffice to show that while his explanation involves reasons, aims, motives and intentions, it does not seem to involve any theory, or general laws, of behavior. Shakespeare is explaining why Iago acted in this way, but he is not saying anything about how all men, or all men of a certain kind, act under specified circumstances. To think that Shakespeare must have assumed that all men, or all vain, envious men, will act as Iago did under the circumstances would be silly—for such an assumption is patently false. We could, of course, improve our generalization by replacing "all vain, envious men" with a more and more detailed statement of Iago's character and background. But in order to get a generalization which we can assert with confidence we will have to fill in more and more detail until only someone "just like Iago" would fit. And in that case our "generalization" pertains to an individual rather than a class and thus is not a "general law" in the required sense. That is, when we explain Iago's action in terms of *his* particular character and background, we subsume that action under the pattern of an individual's past behavior, but not under a pattern that holds for all people of a certain kind. Consequently, the regularity in terms of which the explanation is given is not a "law" in the sense in which experimental psychologists claim that explanations of human behavior must be based on empirically tested "laws." [4]

When we explain what someone does in terms of a pattern in his past behavior, the regularity we appeal to is more like what Ryle calls a "dispositional statement of a law-like kind." According to Ryle motive explanations are of this dispositional type. For in his view, to say that someone is, e.g., envious, is to say that he is inclined to do and say certain sorts of things, to make certain sorts of plans, to feel certain sorts of feelings in certain situations. And "to say that he did something from that motive is to say that his action, done in its particular circumstances, was just the sort of thing that that was an inclination to do. It is to say 'he *would* do that.'" [5]

Now such dispositional explanations share one crucial characteristic of explanations based on general laws: both explain by showing that what happened is not surprising in view of what happened in the past. But while we often explain behavior in that way, there are times when such explanations completely fail to tell us what we wanted to know in asking "Why did he do it?" For we may ask this question because we do not understand the agent's *reason* for acting that way. Why, for example, did the driver fail to stop at the red light? If we were to ask him, *he* could not reply by citing a disposition to drive recklessly. To explain his action he would have to represent it as the right, the appropriate, thing to do under the circumstances—e.g., he had to get home in a hurry, it was late at night and he had looked ahead to see if anyone was coming, etc. Though we might not accept the explanation he gives us, we would at least begin by looking for his reasons when we are trying to understand why he did it. If we cannot find a satisfactory explanation in term of reasons we may alleviate our surprise by pointing to a disposition: one could have expected this in view of his past, it is the sort of thing he would do. But we might still wonder what the point of his doing it was.

Since most human actions are intentional, they puzzle us when we fail to understand the agent's intentions. Usually the puzzle is solved, the action explained, when we succeed in discovering something about the agent, or the situation confronting him, which brings out the reason for his action. This may involve discovering the agent's goals and these may, of course, be odd ones; or his beliefs, including, possibly, mistaken ones, about the situation confronting him. And since the way in which people seek their goals is often regulated by rules, the reason for an action may become clear when we understand the rules—be they social and legal norms or individual rules (e.g., the strategy of a chessplayer or a general)—which the agent was following. Ordinarily, when we ask for the explanation of an intentional action we are asking for the "calculation" [6] which shows the considerations that lead the agent to decide on this as the right, the appropriate, thing to do under the circumstances. Understanding this, we understand why he did it.

When we explain an action in this way we make a judgment to the effect that, given the agent's goals, etc., this was the thing for him to do. The explanation "justifies" the action in the sense that it represents it as the appropriate thing to do from the agent's point of view. But to show that an action was right *given* the agent's goals and beliefs, the rules he was following, etc., is not to justify his holding these beliefs and goals, or his adherence to these rules. Consequently, to explain in terms of reasons is not to certify the agent's "rationality," but only to show that this would seem the right (reasonable, appropriate) thing to do *if* one held the agent's beliefs, etc.

It should also be noted that in giving such explanations we are not implying that the agent actually went through such a calculation. For an explanation in terms of reasons can be given for any purposive, or intentional, action and a man may act intentionally without doing any mental planning—e.g., I drive my car without thinking what to do next, but my actions are purposive and if asked I could give reasons for what I did. Moreover, it is not only our words but also our actions that reveal our intentions. Because the pattern of my behavior may reveal a purpose different from the one I profess, it is possible for someone (including myself) to doubt that my professed intention is my real one. Nevertheless, though we may ascribe an intention to someone who in fact denies having it, it must be logically possible for the agent to acknowledge his own intention. So while intentional actions are not necessarily accompanied by bits of mental planning, they do involve a purposive pattern of behavior and the possibility of acknowledging the intention (at least in the "long run").

Explanations in terms of reasons thus differ in type from explanations based on laws or dispositions. While the latter explain by showing that what happened is not surprising in view of past regularities, the former explain by showing that what was done is intelligible because, from the agent's point of view, it was the thing to do. When we explain human behavior in terms of laws or dispositions we explain from "outside," in terms of regularity rather than rationale, in a way similar to that in which we explain the behavior of animals and things. But when we explain in terms of reasons we take the agent's point of view and look for the considerations which lead him to choose this deed as the right thing to do under these circumstances—in this sense we explain his behavior from "inside."

Before asking whether such explanations can be scientifically acceptable—a question I will consider in the next section—let us note that this, surely, is the kind of explanation Shakespeare and Dostoevsky give us. To assume that they must have written their characters on the basis of "some widely held prototheory of behavior" is *prima facie* absurd since it is a commonplace of criticism that a character whose development is a mere illustration of some theory about human behavior is a poor creation.

What distinguishes "wooden," "mechanical" characters from those which seem to "live" is precisely that the former keep on doing what that sort of character *would* do, while the latter surprise us with each new turn in their development. But, though the development of a character like Othello is unexpected, it is also "inevitable." Killing Desdemona is clearly not the sort of thing Othello would do; but when he does it it seems the only thing for him to do. We are surprised because this is a genuine development and not the sort of thing we could have expected from the start. Yet we understand it because Shakespeare has made it possible for us to see the considerations which lead Othello to decide on this as the only thing to do. Seeing this we see that he could do no other—it was "inevitable." But saying that Othello could do no other is not like saying that the glass could only shatter when the stone hit it. It is more like saying "I cannot betray my friend" and explaining why we cannot. There are reasons, not causes or dispositions, why he could do no other. We understand the inevitability of the action from "inside" rather than "outside."

If Shakespeare and Dostoevsky can teach us something about human psychology, this is not because they have discovered surprising *laws* or *regularities* in human behavior, but because they have discovered the surprising *reasons* why some people do the things they do.

## II

While explanations in terms of reasons differ in type from explanations in terms of dispositions, laws or theories, they are not "unscientific" or "unempirical" in any damaging sense. For in explaining an action by representing it as the right thing to do from the agent's point of view, we are ascribing certain beliefs and intentions to the agent. We are saying something about him which is either true or false; we are making claims which have to be supported by evidence. And the evidence consists of some of the things the agent says and does, or some of the things he would do or say under certain circumstances. Sometimes it is very hard to find out what a man's motives and intentions really are—in word and deed, men sometimes deceive others and sometimes deceive themselves. But no matter how much deception or self-deception may be involved, a man's actions and words are always in some way significant for seeing what he really has "in mind." And in practice skilled observation—the sort of observation at which clinical psychologists and psychoanalysts are especially good—can often, though not always, bring us to the point where we can assert with confidence that this or that is what the agent really had "in mind." Moreover, when we fail to reach this point the difficulty is empirical, not logical—we fail because we lack relevant evidence, not because it is logically impossible for one person to "inspect the contents" of another person's mind.

So explaining an action in terms of the agent's reasons for acting is certainly not something one can do without bothering "to find out by looking whether or not he is right." But the place to look is not the psychologist's "laboratory" where empirical generalizations are tested, but the individual's behavior—what he says and does, what he would say and do under certain circumstances. And when we are dealing with the explanations which Shakespeare and Dostoevsky give us, there is no place to look other than the play or novel—since they construct all the things their characters say or do, it is only an examination of their constructions that can tell us whether they have really explained the things they make their characters say and do.

In sciences like physics the claim that we cannot adequately explain without using laws is plausible. For suppose we try to explain one event (e.g., the bursting of the radiator) in terms of another (e.g., a fall in temperature). How could we know that one event really explains the other, or even that it has anything to do with the other, without knowing that these two events are "connected?" And what connection can there be between events other than a law which enables us to predict the occurrence of one of the events from the occurrence of the other? So the statements offered in explanation of the bursting of the radiator must meet two conditions: (1) they must be *true,* and (2) they must *really explain*—i.e., the fact being explained must be "connected" with the facts offered in explanation. Unless our explanation includes a law connecting the two sets of facts, we cannot know that one really explains the other. This is what leads Hempel to claim that:

> The use of universal empirical hypotheses as explanatory principles distinguishes genuine from pseudo-explanation . . . [pseudo-explanations] are based on metaphor rather than laws; they convey pictorial and emotional appeals instead of insight into factual connections.[7]

But the situation is radically different when we explain a human action in terms of the agent's reason for doing it. To use a trivial example: suppose we explain why a man took a taxi by saying that it was raining, the taxi was most convenient, he could afford the fare, and he did not want to get wet. Clearly, one could challenge the truth of this explanation. But would it make any sense to grant the truth of the facts cited, and then to ask whether these facts can really explain why he took the taxi? Do we need some sort of empirical law asserting a "factual connection" in order that our explanation be "genuine" rather than "pseudo?" Surely not. For when we explain in this way we are not offering one set of facts (e.g., rain and a desire not to get wet) as conditions from which to predict, on the basis of some general law, the occurrence of another fact (e.g., taking the taxi). A man who says "I will take a taxi because it is raining" is not *predicting* what he will do; he is *justifying* what he intends to do as the right thing to do in view of an end. So when we explain an action by representing it as the right thing to do, from the agent's point of view, the "connection" between the action and the reasons which explain it is not a "factual connection." We do not need to be empirical scientists in order to know that taking a taxi is the thing to do when it is raining.

Of course, an empirical connection which the agent knows, or believes, to be true *may* be what makes something relevant as a reason—e.g., the chemist's decision to put litmus paper into a solution in order to test its acidity depends on his knowledge of an empirical regularity. If we did not understand that the chemist knew this regularity, we would not understand why he regarded what he did as the right thing to do. But in explaining his action we are showing the point of what he did, the reasons which led him to decide on this as the right means to his end. And a false empirical belief held by the agent—e.g., a criminal's belief that he would not be caught because . . . —may do this as well as a true one.

That the connection between an action and the reasons which explain it is not a "factual connection" certainly does not imply that anything and everything can be cited as a reason for the action. For something is not a reason simply because a man says it is. If a New Yorker were to say that his reason for taking a taxi is that it is raining in China, we would ask "What has that to do with it, how is that relevant to your decision?" He might be able to show its relevance, but the possibility of this depends on the fact that in any given context certain things are accepted as evidently related to others as reasons for action. Only the relation is one of *relevance* rather than *regularity*.

So Nagel misses the point when he tries to support the claim that explanations in terms of reasons require generalizations about human conduct by arguing that even if we have shown that certain factors were in fact present, this

> clearly does not establish *which* of these factors (or for that matter, whether any of them) was the actual reason for the actor's conduct . . . Thus the fact that a person on trial for murder is known to have hated the victim does not suffice to show that he committed the mur-

der . . . *because* of his hatred—for . . . he may have killed the deceased by accident, because he was paid to do so, or for a number of other reasons.[8]

Of course, showing that the murderer hated his victim does not suffice to show that this was his reason for killing him. But it is not true that we can support the claim that F was the "actual reason" for the murder only if we assume that "when the given factor is a circumstance under which men act, they *generally* conduct themselves in a manner similar to the particular action described in the imputation, so that the individual . . . presumably also acted the way he did because the given factor was present."[9] Instead of appealing to such "generalizations," what we ordinarily do when we want to know what the "actual reason" was is to find out all we can about the agent's relevant aims and beliefs, the "strategy" he was following, etc.—an empirical inquiry in the course of which we may appeal to dispositions or draw inferences from laws.[10] On the basis of what we so discover, we try to construct a calculation which makes the crime intelligible by showing that *if* one had held these beliefs, etc., then committing the crime would have seemed the thing to do under these circumstances. And if we succeed in showing this, then we can properly claim to have found the "actual reason" for the crime. Surely something like this is what actually happens in a court of law when the prosecution tries to establish the accused's "motive." No generalizations are required because we don't need them in order to understand how the accused's hatred *could* "really explain" why he killed the victim—as could money, or "a number of other reasons." Generalizations are not needed because reasons for murder are not, as Nagel seems to think, causal "factors" in whose presence people will, generally, kill. They are considerations relevant to a decision to kill, and they do not need to be "factually connected" with murdering—as a fall in temperature does have to be synthetically "connected" with the bursting of the radiator—in order for us to understand how one *could* explain the other. To show that R was the "actual reason" for the murder is not to show that one can predict that people will, generally, kill in the presence of R; it is to show that R is the consideration which led this particular man to decide that killing the deceased was the thing for him to do under these circumstances.[11]

But the action is not entailed by the calculation; the explanans cannot be logically deduced from the explanandum. How then do we know that we have "really" explained the action? In general terms one could say that a good explanation in terms of reasons is one in which the explanandum can be used to "justify" the explanans. That is, R is a good explanation of why A chose to do X if, given A's beliefs, aims, etc., it is a good reason for doing X. But how do we know that the considerations adduced in our explanation really constitute "good reasons," how do we know that they really suffice to "justify" the action as the right one from the agent's point of view? One cannot and need not specify in advance the criteria which any and every explanation in terms of reasons must meet in order to be a good one. This is not because there are no criteria, but because the criteria are contextual so that it is only within a specific explanatory context that we can decide when the considerations adduced "really" explain the action. For example, why does Iago "look dead with grieving" and make a show of not wanting to say anything against Cassio when Othello asks who began the brawl? (*Othello*, II, iii). Because it was essential to his plot that he maintain the role of "honest Iago," because he could count on Othello to "compel" him to tell the "truth" and thus get Cassio disgraced anyhow, and because this stratagem enabled him to make further use of Cassio in his plot—as a "good friend" he could easily suggest to Cassio that he ask Desdemona to intercede with Othello. And then "I'll pour this pestilence into his ear/That she repeals him for her body's lust." This is why Iago, who really hated Cassio, decided to put on this show of friendship. Of course, Iago's action cannot be logically deduced from this explanation. But if someone were to greet it with "Yes, but why did he do it?", we would not understand what he is asking for. What other, or better, reasons could Iago have had? The question may not be senseless, but it makes sense only if the questioner has something in mind which casts doubt on our explanation—either some evidence against the truth of one of the explanatory premises, or some consideration which we have overlooked and which may throw the "justification" out of joint, i.e., require us to revise the judgment that, from Iago's point of view, this was "good reason," this was the right thing to do under the circumstances. Barring this, one cannot, in this context, go on asking "Why did he do it?" We have found a good explanation of Iago's behavior—it is based on the evidence and, in its context, it leaves no further room for "Why did he do it?"—though it does not, of course, logically entail Iago's action. Why should it when we are explaining in terms of reasons rather than by deduction from a general law? One could not claim that the action has not "really" been explained because it cannot be deduced from the explanans without begging the question of what it means to explain.

The logical possibility of error does remain—an explanation in terms of reasons may have to be revised in light of new evidence. But surely this is no argument against such explanation. After all, explanations in terms of empirical laws and dispositions are not infallible either. Why should we expect logical certainty when dealing with question of fact?

In sum, we can give responsible, empirical explanations of intentional actions in terms of the agent's reasons without using any generalizations or theories about human behavior in our explanation. For when we explain in this way there is never any problem about whether explanans and explanandum are connected in fact; the only problem is that of discovering what, as a matter of fact, the agent's reasons were. Discovering this is an empirical process which may involve inference based on laws and dispositions. But explaining the action by showing that the agent decided that this was the right, the appropriate, thing to do for such and such reasons is a rational process which requires no empirical laws or theories of behavior.

## III

I now want to show that some of the explanations given in psychology are also of this type. While I think that many of the approaches developed by clinical psychologists who stress the importance of understanding the patient's point of view—Kelly's *Psychology of Personal Constructs* is one example[12]—are best construed as attempts at explanation in terms of reasons, I will here confine myself to the sort of explanation psychoanalysts often give in terms of the patient's unconscious motives (e.g., she acted this way because of an unconscious hatred of her mother). I choose this illustration because it is familiar and because it may help to show that it would be a mistake to think that explanations in terms of reasons can only apply to a limited range of "rational" behavior.

As a number of writers have pointed out, Freud's explanations often shift between talk about the neurotic's unconscious purpose and intentions and talk about the causes of his acts.[13] For example, in explaining a woman's obsessive behavior Freud tells us that "the deepest secret of her illness was that it enabled her to shield him [i.e., her husband] from malicious gossip, and to make a comfortable existence apart from her possible for him." [14] This certainly sounds as if the "secret of her illness" is that her obsessive behavior has a point to it, just as if it were something she decided to do for a reason. This is also suggested when Freud tells us that "the purpose she had in performing the action . . . was to correct a painful event of the past." [15] But while this sounds like an explanation in terms of reasons, it is odd because her behavior is obsessive—she could not help doing it, so how could it be something she "decided" to do?—and because she did not know that she had any such "reason" —since this was not a consideration for her when she acted that way, how could it be her "reason?" This oddness, as well as the fact that Freud often speaks of psychic "forces" and "mechanisms" causing various kinds of behavior—e.g., in connection with the same case he says "it took a long time and much effort for her to grasp and admit to me that such a motive as this could alone have been the driving force behind her obsessive act" [16] —has led many students to regard his explanations in terms of unconscious motives as explanations in terms of causes, laws and theories, rather than reasons.

Now the neurotic's behavior obviously differs in at least two important ways from that of a person who acts intentionally (i.e., for a reason). In the first place, it is "obsessive"—the woman cannot control her own behavior in the way someone who acts purposively can. Secondly, she does not know her "reason" for acting and the "not knowing" is dynamic—in contrast to someone whose motive is "preconscious" rather than "unconscious," she can be brought to admit her "reason" only after "a long time and much effort" in analysis. These differences between normal and neurotic behavior clearly call for explanation in terms of laws and theories. Why does this happen to some people under some conditions and not to others? Freud's answer is his theory about repression and the way in which neurotic symptoms can be produced by unconscious conflicts. By means of this theory Freud traces the obsession to its causes in the patient's past—i.e., the scene on the morning after the unhappy bridal night. Insofar as Freud gives us such theories about symptom formation, they are similar to those used in the physical sciences and their merits can be discussed in much the same way.

But what of Freud's explanation of, e.g., the obsessive ritual, in terms of the agent's unrecognized purpose? Is it logically dependent on his causal explanation of why people of a certain kind develop neurotic symptoms under conditions of a certain kind? It seems that Freud is here raising an entirely different kind of question, namely: What "reason" did she have for using this stratagem? What did she "achieve" by her obsession?

Why did she "decide" to be ill? No doubt these are very odd-sounding questions. But Freud seems to be asking and answering just such questions when he tells us "the purpose she had in performing the action" or claims that "her symptoms enabled her to continue her relationship with him." [17] Could we not make better sense of these explanations in terms of unconscious motives if we regarded them as extensions of explanations in terms of reasons rather than as odd, speculative and, probably, unwarranted explanations in terms of laws and theories? Though neurotic actions differ significantly from normal, intentional ones, the differences may not be such as to preclude the possibility of explaining the former in a way analogous to that in which we typically explain the latter. After all, as we noted earlier, a man may act intentionally without doing any "calculating" beforehand. And it is also true that a man may sincerely think that he has acted for one reason but, after searching his own conscience or probing his motives with the help of another, he may see quite clearly that he really acted for a different reason. No doubt this is a case where the motive is "preconscious" and so it differs importantly from that of the neurotic who has repressed his motives and can admit them only after "a long time and much effort" in psychotherapy. Yet the neurotic's actions do show a purposive pattern—what he does loses its puzzling character and becomes intelligible when we see him as trying to achieve this and to avoid that. And when the analyst proceeds to ascribe an "unconscious motive" to the patient, though the latter's denial of this motive does not overthrow the analyst's interpretation, if the interpretation is correct it is expected that the patient will, at least ideally, come to agree with it in the end. Surely what the psychoanalyst does when he gives such an interpretation of the patient's unconscious motives is more like what the trial lawyer, or the man of affairs, does when he tests his "interpretation" of another person's reasons for acting, than it is like what the physicist does when he tests his hypothesis about the cause of a certain phenomenon. When

Freud's patient finally admits that this was the motive for her obsessive acts, is she giving assent to theoretical considerations which show that this was the "driving force" causing her behavior? Clearly she is in no position to do that. But she, and only she, can finally admit that this really was the "reason" for her curious actions.[18]

The compulsive character of the neurotic's behavior does, of course, make it odd to say that she "decided" to do what she apparently does not want to do (i.e., suffer from her obsession and other neurotic symptoms). Yet psychoanalysts contend, e.g., that the neurotic "became so ill in order to be unable to marry and so to remain with her father,"[19] or, more generally, that neurosis is "precisely the method the individual uses to preserve his own center, his own existence."[20] Surely this implies that in their view neurosis is not just something that happens to a person (like infection caused by a germ), but is something he does; that there is some sense in which one can adduce "considerations" relevant to the neurotic's "decision" to be ill. Moreover, it is hard to see how the difference between compulsive and free behavior—i.e., the obsessive ritual vs the freedom achieved when the patient rids himself of the obsession through analysis—can be made out without the introduction of unconscious "purposes," etc. For the difference between them is not that in one case behavior is caused while in the other it isn't; causal explanations can, presumably, be given in both cases. To say that the causes are different is true, but fails to bring out the point of the distinction between "compulsive" and "free" behavior. For the difference is that while the normal person does what he wants and knows (or can easily become aware of) the reasons why he does it, this is not true of the neurotic. And one of the contentions of psychoanalysis seems to be that there is a sense in which the neurotic does what he (unconsciously) "wants" to do, that there are (unconscious) "reasons" for his actions—but he has repressed these wishes and purposes and cannot become aware of them without psychotherapy. The difference between free and compulsive behavior might then be construed as the difference between acting in accordance with one's aims and intentions, and being "driven" by aims and intentions which one cannot (without therapy) acknowledge as one's own.

Thus the behavior of Freud's patient seems mad and unintelligible—what possible "reason" could she have for having to run several times a day into another room and having to stand there in a certain position, by the table with a spot on it, until the maid appears on the scene? But then Freud sees a purposive pattern in her actions: if she identifies herself with her husband and identifies the table bearing the spot with her wedding bed, then we can see that "the obsessive act thus says: 'No, it is not true, he was not disgraced before the servant, he was not impotent'." [21] The obsessive act becomes intelligible—there is a "reason" for her action—when we see that "it serves the purpose of restoring her husband's credit after that unfortunate incident." [22] Though it will take "a long time and much effort" in analysis before the patient can admit to having this motive and be cured of her obsession, all of her symptoms become *meaningful* when we "perceive in them the voices which pleaded for him, excused him, exalted him, lamented his loss." [23] So we come to see that there really is a point to the obsessive ritual and the other symptoms; given her unconscious "aims" and distorted "beliefs" about the situation this would seem to her the thing to do.

Psychoanalysis thus makes it possible to see that while the neurotic's behavior is irrational, it is not a-rational: there is method in the madness. What seems a-rational becomes intelligible in terms of unconscious "purposes" and "intentions." For in terms of these the psychoanalyst can construct a "calculation" which shows us that from the neurotic's distorted "point of view" this strange behavior would seem "justified," would seem the "right," the "appropriate," the "rational" thing to do; and the patient can, at least ideally, be helped to see that he has really been operating in terms of this distorted "rationale" whose nature he has been hiding from himself. Irrational actions can thus be explained by extending the model used in explaining rational actions. This, I suggest, is why "Freudian psychology is exactly the stuff upon which the poet has always exercised his art . . . Yet the relationship is reciprocal, and the effect of Freud upon literature has been no greater than the effect of literature upon Freud." [24]

## IV

Recognition of the role of rational explanations sheds some light on the "existential" approach to psychology with its insistence that "the present dominant images of man in psychology and psychiatry are inadequate." [25] Writers who champion this view hold that we must develop a "psychology that will be relevant to man's distinguishing characteristics as man," a psychology which sees man as a unique individual who makes real decisions and acts responsibly with a view to the future.[26] This approach appeals to clinical psychologists who think that there is a conflict between what they believe as "scientists" and what they do as therapists. As Carl Rogers formulates the issue, to be "scientific" one has to understand the person as an "object" that is "manipulated" in therapy; but to be an effective therapist and understand one's patients one cannot do this.[27] As a result, there is said to be a conflict in psychology between the "objective" view that "the way to understand is from the outside" and the "existential" view that "the way to understand is from within." [28] And Rogers has suggested that this conflict might be reconciled by a "changed view of science" which recognizes that "science too, at its inception, is an 'I-Thou' relationship with the world of perceived objects, just as therapy at its deepest is an 'I-Thou' relationship with a person." [29]

But surely one can do justice to the legitimate concern of psychologists like Rogers, May and Maslow, without adopting the desperate expedient of a Buberian interpretation of physics. What is distinctive of man as man is his developed capacity for using language. This capacity makes it possible for man to act intentionally (i.e., for a reason). For even though a man may do something intentionally without ever formulating his reasons for doing it, we would not describe men as acting intentionally if they could never put into words what they are doing and why they are doing it. To talk of a stone's reason for falling is to talk nonsense, and to speak of a rat as moving "in order to" avoid an electric shock is to speak in a weak, analogical sense. But the descriptions which we ordinarily apply to characteristically human activities—i.e., he telephoned, signed, plotted, paid, bought, married, etc.—are descriptions of intentional actions and the agent, typically, has a reason for doing them.

Now consider an intentional action like Iago's plotting against Othello. No doubt Iago makes various movements and sounds, and these are "hard data" of direct sense perception which can be described from "outside" without any reference to what is going on in Iago's mind. Psychologists who claim that "the behavior of the subject, verbal or not, is an event in the external world of the scientist, just as is the behavior of a rat" [30] are claiming that psychology, as a science, must confine itself to this external, spectatorial point of view. But if it does, then it is not dealing with "verbal behavior" if this means more than the emission of sounds. For if we describe men as "speaking" then our description presupposes that they are using words which have meanings, words which are combined in accordance with a system of rules. But meanings and rules are not "events in the external world." So if we describe what happens from a purely external point of view as the mere occurrence of events (i.e., the emission of certain sounds), we cannot at the same time describe it as "speaking."

Nor can we confine ourselves to the "outside" if we are to describe what Iago does *as* plotting. For "plotting" is not logically equivalent to a physical description of some complicated series of movements and sounds. If Iago is really plotting then he must *understand* what he is doing, he must be aware of the relation between what he does now and the consequences this will have for Othello. His action is purposive, he is using means to attain an end, and we can ask whether what he did was the right, the appropriate, the rational thing to do—questions which make no sense when asked of a purely physical description of his movements. If Iago's actions were not intended to have certain consequences in the future, then we could not describe what he does as "plotting." So if we describe Iago in this way, we take his words and deeds to have a significance which is not open to direct sense inspection, a significance which is understood only when we understand his intentions. But intentions are not merely "events in the external world." [31]

To be sure, when we describe Iago as "plotting" (or performing some other intentional action), we are not asserting the occurrence of any events other than, or additional to, those referred to in a physical description of the movements and sounds he makes. The same activity can be described in a number of ways, and what a man does when he plots can also be described as a complicated series of movements and sounds. Insofar as we describe what happens in this way we are dealing with "events in the external world" which can be explained from the "outside," perhaps in terms of some neuro-physiological theory. But when we do this we are not dealing with what concerns students of distinctively human behavior—e.g., plotting, marrying, etc.—but are dealing instead with what concerns the physiologist—i.e., the movements and sounds made by human organisms under certain conditions. If, on the other hand, we are concerned with intentional actions, then we are concerned with behavior that is described as having a point to it, a point that can only be understood from "inside" in terms of the considerations which lead the agent to decide on this as the right thing to do. Neuro-physiological talk cannot tell us why Iago plotted against Othello, but "to get the lieutenancy" can. And when we explain in terms of reasons our "image of man" is the one championed by the existential approach—here we see the responsible agent who makes choices and acts with a view to the future.

Because men alone can act rationally, they alone can act irrationally. And their irrationality, like their rationality, can be explained in a way in which the behavior of things that never act for reasons cannot be explained. This, I suggest, is the valid insight of "existential psychology."

## Notes

1. Mandler and Kessen, *The Language of Psychology,* p. 250.
2. *Ibid.,* p. 217; their italics. See also Chpts. XI–XIII, *passim.*
3. See Hempel and Oppenheim, "The Logic of Explanation" in Feigl and Brodbeck, *Rdgs. in Philo. of Science,* pp. 319–352; Hempel, "The Function of General Laws in History" in Feigl and Sellars, *Rdgs. in Philosophical Analysis,* pp. 459–471; E. Nagel, *The Structure of Science,* pp. 551–563. Hempel and Oppenheim say that "There is no formal difference on this account between motivational and causal explanations," *op. cit.,* p. 328.
4. "Scarcely anyone would be interested in a recitation of the doings of Rat A, then Rat B, then Rat C . . . Scientific statements are made about "rats", not about "Rat A", about "people", not about "Miss A", usually with reference to the behavior of groups of organisms." Mandler and Kessen, *op. cit.,* p. 167.
5. G. Ryle, *The Concept of Mind,* pp. 92–93. See also pp. 83–93 and 123–124.
6. I take this concept from W. Dray to whose excellent analysis of "rational explanations" in history my discussion is indebted. See W. Dray, *Laws and Explanation in History,* esp. Chpt. V. [Reprinted in this volume.]
7. C. Hempel, "The Function of General Laws in History," *op. cit.,* p. 461. In the same vein, E. Nagel, in discussing one of Maitland's explanations, argues that only if "Maitland tacitly assumed some sort of generalization about human conduct" is there any ground for holding that his explanation "had anything to do" with the matter being explained. (Nagel, *op. cit.,* p. 553).
8. E. Nagel, *op. cit.,* p. 555; his italics.
9. E. Nagel, *op. cit.,* p. 555; his italics.
10. Laws and dispositions may thus be evidence supporting the

premises used in our explanation. But this in no way shows that we are "really" explaining in terms of them rather than in terms of reasons. For if we explain something by deducing it from a law, the evidence which justifies our use of this law as an explanatory premise is no part of the explanation, nor is the explanation "really" given in terms of it. If it were, we could not explain anything without explaining everything.

11. Of course, I am not denying that there may be cases where we cannot find an explanation in terms of reasons—e.g., "There was no reason in it; he was driven by a mad fit of passion."

12. Kelly explains a person's actions in terms of the "constructs" he uses to "anticipate" what will happen if he acts one way or another; his psychology is thus an "*anticipatory* rather than a *reactive* system" of explanation. (*op. cit.*, p. 170, his italics). Unfortunately, Kelly fails to see that explaining in terms of "constructs" is explaining in terms of reasons rather than in terms of "predictive hypotheses." See my "Personal Constructs, Rules and the Logic of Clinical Activity," *Psychological Review*, v. 71, 1964.

13. See the articles by S. Toulmin and A. Flew in *Philosophy and Analysis* (M. Macdonald, ed.), A. C. MacIntyre's *The Unconscious*, and A. Flew, "Motives and the Unconscious," *Minnesota Studies in Philo. of Science*, vol. I, pp. 155–172.

14. S. Freud, *General Introduction to Psychoanalysis*, Permabook Ed., p. 274.

15. *Ibid.*, p. 288.

16. *Ibid.*, p. 288.

17. *Ibid.*, p. 284.

18. Kelly asks clinical psychologists to follow this adage: "If you do not know what is wrong with a person, ask him; he may tell you. The clinician who asks such a question will have to be prepared to do some careful listening." Kelly, *op. cit.*, pp. 322–323.

19. Freud, *op. cit.*, p. 285.

20. R. May, "Existential Bases of Psychotherapy," in R. May, ed., *Existential Psychology*, p. 76. Freud's claim that "symptoms are actually substitutes for the missing satisfaction" (Freud, *op. cit.*, p. 353) seems to involve a similar point.

21. Freud, *op. cit.*, p. 274.

22. *Ibid.*, p. 274.

23. *Ibid.*, p. 284.

24. L. Trilling, "Freud and Literature," *The Liberal Imagination*, p. 44.

25. R. May, ed., *Existential Psychology*, p. 7.

26. R. May, *op. cit.*, pp. 39–51; see also, in the same volume, A. H. Maslow, pp. 55–58, and G. Allport, p. 95.

27. C. Rogers, "Persons or Science? A Philosophical Question," *American Psychologist*, v. 10, 1955, pp. 267–278.

28. C. Rogers, "Two Divergent Trends," in R. May, *op. cit.*, esp. pp. 86–88.

29. C. Rogers, "Persons or Science?," *op. cit.*, p. 278. In a similar vein Maslow calls for a "revolution in the theory of science . . . (which) will affect not only the science of psychology but all other sciences as well"; in R. May, ed., *op. cit.*, p. 58.

30. Mandler and Kessen, *op. cit.*, p. 37.

31. Of course, I am not denying that we discover his intentions from the things he says and does, or would say and do under certain conditions. But then the things he says and does are not *merely* "events in the external world."

DANIEL BENNETT

# Action, Reason, and Purpose*

Someone does something, i.e., he acts, only if he causes (determines, makes) some object or objects to have some property or properties. When you subtract the fact that my arm went up from the fact that I raised it, part of what's left is the fact that I caused an event. But, even were the concept of cause involved in our idea of action, unique in its application to action (a question I will not discuss in this paper), our idea of action would contain other important, and difficult, elements. Our paradigm of acting is doing something intentionally or on the basis of a reason. That is, basic to our idea of action is the idea of agency somehow modified by intention and reason. The question for which I want to suggest an answer in this paper is: How do intention and reason modify agency to yield our basic idea of action?

## I

The difficulty in the ideas of intentional and rational agency that I want to discuss can be stated fairly precisely.

If *S* causes the cigarette in his hand to be lit, then

1. There is something which he causes to be lit and which is a cigarette;[1]
2. If the cigarette in his hand is identical with the cigarette-bomb in his hand, then S causes the cigarette-bomb to be lit.

* Reprinted by permission of the author and the editors from *The Journal of Philosophy*, LXII (1965).

(A cigarette-bomb is merely a cigarette with explosives in it.)

These entailments hold in virtue of the *transparency* of unmodified agency. But,

If S causes the cigarette in his hand to be lit *intentionally* or *on the basis of a reason* (e.g., to smoke), then, although

1. There is something which S causes to be lit intentionally or on a reason and which is a cigarette; and
2. If the cigarette in his hand is the cigarette-bomb in his hand, it does not follow that S causes the cigarette-bomb to be lit intentionally or on a reason.

We may suppose S causes the cigarette-bomb to be lit unwittingly or by mistake; that he had no reason for causing a cigarette-bomb to be lit.

The first entailment holds and the second fails in virtue of what I will call the apparent *translucency* of agency modified by intention and reason.[2]

If intentional and rational agency are apparently translucent, then so are unintentional and nonrational agency.

If S causes the cigarette-bomb to be lit unintentionally or not on a reason, then

1. There is something that S causes to be lit unintentionally or not on a reason, and it is a cigarette-bomb; but
2. If the cigarette-bomb is the cigarette in his hand, it does not follow that S causes the cigarette in his hand to be lit unintentionally or not on a reason.

We thus seem to be justified in attributing contrary properties to a thing. The cigarette, i.e., the cigarette-bomb if it is one (it remains the same object no matter how you describe it), seems to have the property of being caused by S to be lit intentionally or on a reason, and also at the same time the property of being caused to be lit by S unintentionally or not on a reason.

Such an attribution, clearly, will not do. Either intentional and rational agency are not properties of objects at all, or they are more complex in their structure than grammar suggests.

It has been held[3] that the expression 'does intentionally' does not express a property, but is (in a once popular phrase) a non-descriptive expression, used to ascribe responsibility or excuse or to block an excuse. On this view, there would not be the difficulty I have outlined above, since it would be false that there is any object in the world such that it is intentionally caused by someone to have some property. This view is, in its effect, an emotive theory of action; I will not try to form an estimate of it in this paper.

It has also been held [4] that causing intentionally and causing rationally are relative properties, as follows: The full description of a man's intentionally or rationally causing a cigarette to be lit is, "S causes the object in his hand (be it cigarette-bomb or a mere cigarette) to be lit intentionally *under the description* 'causing a cigarette to be lit' " or "S causes the object in his hand to be lit on a reason *under the description* 'causing a cigarette to be lit.' "

This is a way out of the difficulty, for it renders causing intentionally and on a reason transparent.

> If S causes the object in his hand to be lit intentionally (or on a reason) *under the description* 'causing a cigarette to be lit', then
>
> 1. There is an object that has the property of being caused to be lit intentionally (or on a reason) *under the description* 'causing a cigarette to be lit', and
> 2. If the object in his hand is a cigarette-bomb, then S causes the cigarette-bomb to be lit intentionally *under the description* 'causing a cigarette to be lit'.

This view also works to make unintentional and nonrational causing transparent.

But the view that intentional and unintentional, rational and nonrational agency are, thus, relative to descriptions amounts to the view that these basic modifiers of action are quasi-linguistic properties. Therefore, that agency is sometimes thus modified entails the existence of a language. This seems counterintuitive.

Furthermore, if the expression 'under the description' has the sense it *seems* to have, an action would be intentional or done for a reason, on this view, only if it were actually described.

The expression seems to be, in fact, the formal-mode descendant of expressions like 'qua', as in "man qua man has an essence," and 'under its aspect as', as in "I am determined under my aspect as phenomenon," expressions which dot the history of philosophy with obscurity. We need an account of intentional and rational agency that does not have to rely on such obscure expressions but also does not allow us to infer that objects have incompatible properties.

As a preliminary to giving such an account I want to consider two questions: (1) What must an agent know about an object when he intentionally causes that object to have some property? and (2) What makes a desire and a belief in accordance with which an agent acts a reason *on the basis* of which he acts?

## II

We should distinguish the following two claims: that S causes the cigarette in his hand to be lit intentionally (1) entails that S knows the object in his hand to be lit, and (2) entails that S knows the object in his hand to be a cigarette.

Here the verb 'to know' is used in a sense that allows for substitution within its scope and for quantification from outside. The expression 'the object in his hand' occupies what Quine calls a "purely referential" position. 'Know' in this usage is transparent. Being *known* by S to be lit is a property of the object in S's hand.

This usage of 'know' seems appropriate when it is perceptual knowledge we want to express. Thus, if S perceives the object in his hand to be lit and if the object in his hand is identical with the cigarette-bomb, then S knows the cigarette-bomb to be lit. Or if the object in his hand is the cigarette-bomb and if S perceives the object in his hand to be a cigarette, then S perceives the cigarette-bomb to be a cigarette. It does not follow, of course, that S perceives the object in his hand to be a cigarette-bomb.

Corresponding to this usage of 'know' is a usage of 'belief' that is also transparent. If we wish to express the fact that someone has made some sort of perceptual mistake, then we would say not that S perceives the object in his hand to be *F*, but that S *takes* it to be *F*. Suppose the object in S's hand is a firecracker. He may take it to be a cigarette.

If a person knows some object to have some property, then he also takes it to have that property. The sort of knowledge we are considering can be thought of as, simply, correct taking.[5]

The knowledge expressed and the belief implied in claim 1 have to do with the *outcome* of an intentional action. S's knowledge that the object in his hand is lit is his knowledge of an achievement. But the knowledge expressed in 2 has to do not with the outcome of the action, but with its setting. So far as the act of lighting a cigarette is concerned, the cigarette might as well be a permanent feature of his hand.

Knowledge of the outcome and knowledge of the setting of an action are, strictly, independent. S might know the object in his hand to be lit and not know that the object in his hand is a firecracker. He might take it to be a cigarette. In such a case we would say that S caused the firecracker in his hand to be lit by mistake or unwittingly. Furthermore, S might know the setting of the action, but not its outcome. He might know the object in his hand to be a cigarette, but not know it to be lit. For example, he might take it to be not (yet) lit.

Must an agent know the setting of his action if the action is intentional? It seems clear that he must. If S causes the cigarette in his hand to be lit intentionally, then it follows logically that he knows the cigarette to be a cigarette. If he mistakes it for a firecracker, then he has not caused the *cigarette* in his hand to be lit intentionally, though, if he takes it to be a firecracker, he also, probably, takes it to be an ignitable, and he has, therefore, caused the ignitable in his hand to be lit intentionally.

Must he know the outcome if the action is intentional? It seems clear that he need not.

S may aim to light a cigarette, correctly taking it to be a cigarette, cause the cigarette to be lit, but not know that he has, and furthermore, cause it to be lit intentionally. This would be unusual, of course. But, there are analogous cases where it is more usual.

S may aim to wiggle his ears, and wiggle them, and not know he has. He may need a mirror or a witness to tell. However, S would have wiggled them intentionally.

It is more obvious when the action's completion is remote. S may fling a rock at the king as the latter rides by on horseback, aiming to raise a lump on the king's head, and he may succeed, but the king may be obscured by the crowd, and S may be unable to appreciate his achievement. However, he would have raised a lump on the king intentionally.

It appears, then, that when S causes the cigarette in his hand to be lit intentionally, he must know the object in his hand is a cigarette, but he need not know it is lit.

## III

"Smoke!" says appetite.

I take *this* to be a cigarette (in the sense of being one of the smokable things); straightway, I cause *it* to be lit.

This, according to one of Aristotle's accounts, is a piece of practical reasoning. The most puzzling thing about it is the word 'straightway'. Does it mean 'causes'? That is, do appetite and perceptual belief cause the agent to cause the object to be lit? Or does it mean 'therefore' or 'it follows that'? That is, do the propositional objects of the desire and the belief jointly entail that the agent acts? Or does it mean both? I want to say it *cannot* mean either.

Desiring to smoke and taking an object to be a cigarette are or might be reasons on the basis of which an agent causes the object in his hand to be lit. I want now to consider the question: What are the necessary and sufficient conditions for the desire and the taking (together) to be a reason on which the agent acts?

The most obvious proposal, probably, is the following:

> Desiring to smoke and taking the object in his hand to be a cigarette (which together I will call *R*) is a reason on the basis of which S causes the object in his hand to be lit if and only if *R*, in the prevailing conditions, causes S to cause the object in his hand to be lit (or, simply, causes the object in S's hand to be lit; I will not try to choose between these alternatives).

I will call this the *causal thesis.*

The causal thesis at best gives necessary conditions for *R*'s being a reason on which S acts.

That S causes the cigarette to be lit is, as we have seen, transparent. That *X*, in the prevailing conditions, causes *Y*, where *X* and *Y* are events, is also transparent. If the match's being struck, in the prevailing conditions, causes the match to light and if the match is identical with the match-bomb, then it follows logically that the match's being struck, in the prevailing conditions, causes the match-bomb to light.

If the causal thesis were true, therefore, the fact that S causes the object in his hand to be lit on the basis of the desire and the taking ought to be transparent. But it is not. It is apparently translucent. If the object in his hand is a cigarette-bomb, it does not follow that S causes the cigarette-bomb to be lit on the basis of his desire and perception. He has, we may suppose, *no* reason on which to light a cigarette-bomb.

Furthermore, causation is transitive. If *X* (either an agent or an event) causes the cigarette to be lit and if the cigarette's being lit, in the prevailing conditions, causes the cigarette to explode, then *X* causes the cigarette to explode.[6]

But S's causing the object in his hand to be lit on the basis of his desire and belief is not transitive. S may cause the object in his hand to explode, by causing it to be lit, but he will not have caused it to explode on the basis of desire and belief.

The causal thesis does not, therefore, state sufficient conditions for acting *on* the desire and belief. Whether it states necessary conditions I will not discuss in this paper. The question is central to the problem of freedom. My argument, however, is independent of this problem.

Consider next the following thesis:

> *R* is a reason on the basis of which S causes the object in his hand to be lit if and only if (1) the propositional objects of the desire and the belief entail that S causes the object in his hand to be lit, and (2) S causes the object in his hand to be lit.

I will call this the *entailment thesis.*

One might weaken it to state merely necessary conditions for acting on the desire and the belief, and conjoin it with a similarly weakened causal thesis, to get the combined *causal-entailment thesis:*

> *R* is a reason on which S causes the object in his hand to be lit if and only if (1) the propositional objects of *R* entail that S causes the object in his hand to be lit, and (2) *R* in the prevailing conditions causes [S] to cause the object in his hand to be lit.

The difficulties I will now discuss are common to the entailment thesis and the combined causal-entailment thesis.

The propositional object of the belief is the singular, true or false, proposition that the object in S's hand is a cigarette. How would we have to construe the propositional object of the desire to make the entailment come out?

One might try the following: S desires the object in his hand to be smoked by way of being caused to be lit by S.

S's "practical premises" [7] would then be (1) the object in my hand being smoked by me by way of being caused to be lit by me, and (2) the object in my hand being a cigarette.

Here, the desired entailment follows from the propositional object of the desire alone.

The desire, on this representation of it, is a property of the object in S's hand. This desire is completely transparent. If the object in S's hand is a firecracker or a cigarette-bomb, then S's desire to smoke would be his desiring that the firecracker or the cigarette-bomb be smoked. There may be cases where we want to take desire as transparent, but, surely, typically, the desire to smoke is not the desire to cause some concrete determinate object to be lit, but is the desire that something smokable (i.e., a cigarette, cigar, pipe, etc.) be lit. Similarly, the desire to drink is not the desire to down some determinate volume of water, but the desire that there be some volume of water that is downed.[8]

The entailment will not come out, however, if we make the propositional object of S's desire existential. Let us suppose S's desire to smoke is his desire that there be an $x$ such that $x$ is a cigarette and $x$ is smoked by S by way of being lit by S. S's practical premises will then be (1) there being an $x$ that is smoked by way of being caused to be lit by me, and (2) this being a cigarette.

These premises do not entail that S causes *this* (the object in his hand) to be lit.

We might try to turn S into a Kantian, and make his desire to smoke have something like the following form: S desires that, for all $x$, if $x$ is a cigarette and is within his reach (say in his hand), then S smokes $x$ by way of causing $x$ to be lit. This, conjoined with the propositional object of the belief, does entail that S causes the object in his hand to be lit, but it may be at the cost of making S's desire insane, as Anscombe puts it. If this is S's desire, it wouldn't do to let him hold your carton of cigarettes.

There is a deeper difficulty with the entailment thesis, however. We may, if we like, suppose that we have hit on a sane representation of the propositional object of S's desire, which, together with the propositional object of belief, entails that S causes the object in his hand to be lit. The fundamental difficulty with the entailment thesis stems not from the practical major, however, but from the minor and the conclusion, both of which are singular.

The minor is the singular proposition: the object in S's hand is a cigarette. The conclusion is the singular proposition: the object in S's hand is caused by him to be lit. Now, the object in S's hand may be a firecracker. If it is, then from the sane propositional object of the desire and the proposition that the firecracker in S's hand is a cigarette, which is the (false) propositional object of the belief, we can infer that S causes the firecracker to be lit. But it is false that S causes the firecracker in his hand to be lit on the basis of his taking it to be a cigarette and his desiring to smoke. S causes the firecracker to be lit not on the basis of any reasons.

The difficulty cannot be avoided if we insist that the practical minor be true. For the object in S's hand may be a cigarette-bomb, in which case the minor: the object in S's hand is a cigarette, is true. But, it is false that S causes the cigarette-bomb to be lit on the basis of his taking it to be a cigarette and his desiring to smoke.

The difficulty with the entailment thesis is the same, at bottom, as the difficulty with the causal thesis. Neither is sufficiently strong to account for the apparent translucency of causing rationally. Perhaps Aristotle was right after all in suggesting that there is a distinctive sort of relation between the reasons on which an agent acts and his acting, a distinctiveness which stems from the fact that *action,* as Aristotle puts it, is something "particular," i.e., concrete or singular.

The following thesis is evidently true:

> *R* is a reason on which S causes the object in his hand to be lit if and only if (1) *R* obtains (i.e., S desires to smoke and takes the object in his hand to be a cigarette); and (2) S causes the object in his hand to be lit *with the purpose* of smoking.

I will call this the *teleological thesis.*

Causing an object to have some property purposively is, like causing rationally and causing intentionally, apparently translucent.

> If S causes the cigarette in his hand to be lit with the purpose of smoking, then

1. There is an object such that S causes it to be lit with the purpose that he smoke, and that object is a cigarette; but

2. If the cigarette in his hand is identical with the cigarette-bomb, it does not follow that S causes the cigarette-bomb to be lit with the purpose of smoking.

I want, next, to try to account for the apparent translucency of causing purposively, and to suggest that all intentional and rational causing is purposive causing.

## IV

What sort of structure should we postulate to account for the apparent translucency of causing purposively? We should consider first the simple sort of case I have been discussing.

There will be at least the following two elements: (1) the fact, or true singular proposition, that an agent S causes some object to have some property, and (2) the possible fact, i.e., the proposition (be it true or false) for the sake of which the agent causes the object to have the property. This latter proposition will be general, either particular or universal. It will be the propositional object of a desire on which S acts in causing the object to have the property, if he acts on an antecedently existing desire.[9] For example, if S desires to smoke and acts on this desire, the possible fact that is his goal will be the existential proposition, there being something *x* that is a smokable (a cigarette, cigar, pipe, hooka, or whatever) and *x* being smoked by S.

We may think of purposiveness as a relation that relates at least these two elements.

But these two elements are not enough to account for the apparent translucency of causing purposively, for S may cause the object in his hand to be lit with the purpose that there be an *x* such that *x* is smokable and *x* is smoked by S, but the object may be a firecracker or a cigarette-bomb, and he will not have caused the firecracker or the cigarette-bomb to be lit with the purpose of smoking.

I suggested earlier that knowledge of the setting of an intentional action is implied by an agent's acting intentionally; i.e., if S causes the cigarette in his hand to be lit intentionally, then he perceives the object in his hand to be a cigarette. Let me now suggest that teleological action requires, not knowledge of the setting, but belief or taking of the setting.

The third element in the structure of purposive causing would then be (3) at least one singular proposition which is the object of S's perceptual taking of the object that he causes to have the property. This proposition may be true or it may be false. In the example I have been discussing it will be the proposition that the object in S's hand is a cigarette. If S is acting on his perceptual belief and his desire to smoke, then this third element will be S's "practical minor."

Purposiveness, then, we might think of as a relation among at least these three elements: (1) the fact that an agent S causes some object to have some property, (2) the singular proposition which is the propositional object of S's perceptual taking of the object, and (3) some general proposition which is the object of S's desire, if he has one, but which, at least, is what we refer to as "the purpose with which S acts." If we so construe purposiveness, then its apparent translucency both is accounted for and disappears.

Purposiveness, I suggest, is a modality of propositions, some of whose special features are that it relates at least three propositions, that at least two are singular, and that at least one must be a true causal proposition. In each of these features the modality of purposiveness differs markedly from the standard modality of necessity, which may modify just one proposition, never modifies singular propositions, and may modify propositions none of which are causal.

Since it relates at least two singular propositions, the modality of purposiveness may be quantified into from the outside. Thus, we may say that being caused purposively to have some property is itself sometimes a property of objects in the world, even of cigarette-bombs.

Causing purposively may be considerably more complex than the simple case I have been considering.

Suppose I cause the mousetrap in my hand to be set with the purpose of catching a mouse. This will involve the elements I have so far mentioned, but it will involve more besides. A further element in such a case is my belief that there are some mice around. The propositional object of this belief is not singular, though clearly I am acting on the belief when I set the trap.

Furthermore, in causing purposively, normally, there is more than one purpose. I may cause the mousetrap to be set, taking *it* to be a mousetrap, believing there are some mice around, with the purpose that there be a mouse in the trap. But, also with the purpose that I have mouse for dinner.

These complications can be accommodated, however.

Let us say that purposiveness is a relation among (1) a true singular proposition, that S causes some object *o* to have some property, (2) a set of propositions believed, at least one of which will be a singular proposition about the object *o*, and (3) a set of propositions "aimed at." I will not elaborate this accommodation further here.

An intentional action, I would suggest, is a purposive action in which the perceptual takings of the object caused to have some property are correct takings. S causes the cigarette in his hand to be lit intentionally if and only if S causes the object in his hand to be lit purposively, and the object in S's hand is a cigarette.

I will conclude this paper with some remarks about the Aristotelian "practical syllogism," which I take to be an explication of our idea of acting on reasons.

According to Aristotle, the practical syllogism has at least these features:

1. Its major premise is general and is something "aimed at" or "wished" or "desired."

2. Its minor premise is a perception or an "opinion" and is singular.
3. Its conclusion is an action.
4. Given the premises, the agent must act; he "straightway" acts. (Though, sometimes, Aristotle says, the agent must act if he is not prevented.)
5. It (the practical syllogism) is a nondeductive inference.

A valid deductive inference, for Aristotle, is a structure with three propositions as elements. All the propositions in the structure are general, but at least one must be universal. And all the propositions in the structure may be false. The one requirement as far as truth combinations go is that, if the first two elements, the premises, are true, then the conclusion must be true.

A practical syllogism, however, is a structure with at least three elements, two of which must be singular, one of which is something "perceived," the other of which "is an action," and none of which has to be universal. Nevertheless, given the premises, the agent must act.

The structure that I have attributed to causing purposively reproduces these characteristics which Aristotle attributes to the practical syllogism,[10] if we are willing to call the true singular causal proposition the "conclusion," the true or false singular perceptual proposition the minor, and the general proposition that is the aim, the major.

On this hypothesis, the sense in which an agent must act, given the "practical premises," is not, it would appear, that the psychological states of which the premises are propositional objects cause him to act or that the propositions entail that he acts. It is simply that the practical syllogism, i.e., the relation of purposiveness, does not hold unless it is true that the agent acts.

## Notes

1. Part of what we mean when we say it is *events* that are caused is shown in the fact that quantifiers do not follow, but precede the verb 'to cause'. Thus, it is never true that S causes $(\exists x)$ ($x$ is a cigarette and is lit).

2. Translucency as being something, figuratively, between opacity and transparency.

3. For example, by H. L. A. Hart, in "The Ascription of Responsibility and Rights."

4. For example, by G. E. M. Anscombe, in *Intention* (Oxford: Basil Blackwell, 1957), and by Donald Davidson in "Actions, Reasons and Causes," *The Journal of Philosophy*, 60, 23 (Nov. 7, 1963): 685–700. [The latter reprinted in this volume.]

5. It seems doubtful to me that '$(\exists x)$ $S$ knows (or takes) $x$ to be $F$' *entails* 'S knows (or believes) $(\exists x)$ ($x$ is $F$)'; i.e., that all knowledge of objects or events (of singulars) requires knowledge of some general proposition. However, this question is not of central importance to my argument. The claim that is important to my argument is the anti-Platonic claim that we sometimes have knowledge of objects or events.

6. There are restrictions on the transitiveness of cause, probably, but these do not affect my point.

7. I shall assume that it is *not* a necessary condition for premises being "practical" that at least one of them contain some value-term ('good', 'desirable', 'ought', etc.), but that it is a necessary condition that at least one of them be something *desired*, or "aimed at."

8. I leave the question open whether there ever *are* desires that are properties of the objects desired.

9. Someone might hold, as Sartre does, for example, that there are no antecedently existing desires when an agent acts with a certain purpose; that an expression of the form: 'the agent S's desire that so and so', never has a referent. This view is, perhaps, an exaggeration.

10. The structure of purposiveness also has the characteristics that Sartre attributes to what he calls "The Project." Sartre's claim that Projects are "situated" seems to be equivalent to the claim that the purposiveness relation can always be quantified into. Also, Projects are triadic.

# Part III ~ The Concept of Action in History, Ethics, and Law

WILLIAM DRAY

# The Rationale of Actions*

## 1. *Historical Understanding as 'Empathetic'*

I . . . want to direct attention to the kind of explanation historians generally give of the *actions* of those individuals who are important enough to be mentioned in the course of historical narrative. It will be my thesis that the explanation of individual human behaviour as it is usually given in history has features which make the covering law model peculiarly inept.

What I wish to say may be regarded as an attempt to rehabilitate to some extent a traditional doctrine of idealist philosophers of history: the view that the objects of historical study are fundamentally different from those, for example, of the natural sciences, because they are the actions of beings like ourselves; and that even if (for the sake of argument) we allow that natural events may be explained by subsuming them under empirical laws, it would still be true that this procedure is inappropriate in history. Sometimes such a view is supported by the belief that human actions—at any rate the ones we call 'free'—do not fall under law at all. Sometimes it is alleged only that even if they do fall under law, discovery of the law would still not enable us to understand them in the sense proper to this special subject-matter. It is the second of these claims which I especially want to consider here.

* Sections 1 through 5 (section 1 slightly revised) of Chapter V of *Laws and Explanation in History* (1957) by William Dray. Reprinted by permission of the author and the Clarendon Press, Oxford.

The doctrine is commonly expressed with the aid of a characteristic set of terms. To understand a human action, it will be said, it is necessary for the inquirer somehow to discover its 'thought-side'; it is not sufficient merely to know the pattern of overt behaviour. The historian must *penetrate* behind appearances, achieve *insight* into the situation, *identify* himself sympathetically with the protagonist, *project* himself imaginatively into his situation. He must *revive, re-enact, re-think, re-experience* the hopes, fears, plans, desires, views, intentions, &c., of those he seeks to understand. To explain action in terms of covering law would be to achieve, at most, an external kind of understanding. The historian, by the very nature of his self-imposed task, seeks to do more than this.

It is worth noticing that historians themselves, and not just professional philosophers of history, often describe their task in these terms. Professor Butterfield is representative of a large group of his professional colleagues when he insists that "the only understanding we ever reach in history is but a refinement, more or less subtle and sensitive, of the difficult—and sometimes deceptive—process of imagining oneself in another person's place". And elsewhere in *History and Human Relations,* he writes:

Our traditional historical writing . . . has refused to be satisfied with any merely causal or stand-offish attitude towards the personalities of the past. It does not treat them as mere things, or just measure such features of them as the scientist might measure; and it does not content itself with merely reporting about them in the way an external observer would do. It insists that the story cannot be told correctly unless we see the personalities from the inside, feeling with them as an actor might feel the part he is playing—thinking their thoughts over again and sitting in the position not of the observer but of the doer of the action. If it is argued that this is impossible—as indeed it is—not merely does it still remain the thing to aspire to, but in any case the historian must put himself in the place of the historical personage, must feel his predicament, must think as though he were that man. Without this art not only is it impossible to tell the story correctly but it is impossible to interpret the very documents on which the reconstruction depends. Traditional historical writing emphasizes the importance of sympathetic imagination for the purpose of getting inside human beings. We may even say that this is part of the science of history for it produces communicable results—the insight of one historian may be ratified by scholars in general, who then give currency to the interpretation that is produced. . . .[1]

Among covering law logicians there is an 'official' answer to philosophers or historians who talk in this way about the peculiarities of 'historical understanding'. The answer is that although there is something right about it, the element of truth in such an account is not a point of logic; it is a mixture of psychological description and methodological precept. As a psychological description of the historian's state of mind when he succeeds in explaining the action of one of his characters, the notion of 'empathy' or 'imaginative understanding', as it is often called, will be allowed some merit—although it will be represented as involving us all too easily in the philosophical error of thinking that merely having certain experiences, or thinking certain thoughts similar to those of the historical agents, itself constitutes understanding or explaining. Similarly, as a suggestion as to how to go about discovering what the agent's motives were, the 'empathy' theory will be admitted to have a certain methodological point—although the reservation will be made that the principle involved often leads the investigator astray. Professor Hempel puts the position succinctly in the following passage:

> The historian, we are told, imagines himself in the place of the persons involved in the events which he wants to explain; he tries to realize as completely as possible the circumstances under which they acted, and the motives which influenced their actions; and by this imaginary self-identification with his heroes, he arrives at an understanding and thus at an adequate explanation of the events with which he is concerned.
>
> This method of empathy is, no doubt, frequently applied by laymen and by experts in history. But it does not in itself constitute an explanation; it rather is essentially a heuristic device; its function is to suggest certain psychological hypotheses which might serve as explanatory principles in the case under consideration. Stated in crude

terms, the idea underlying this function is the following: the historian tries to realize how he himself would act under the given conditions, and under the particular motivations of his heroes; he tentatively generalizes his findings into a general rule and uses the latter as an explanatory principle in accounting for the actions of the persons involved. Now, this procedure may sometimes prove heuristically helpful; but its use does not guarantee the soundness of the historical explanation to which it leads. The latter rather depends upon the factual correctness of the empirical generalizations which the method of understanding may have suggested.

Nor is the use of this method indispensable for historical explanation. A historian may, for example, be incapable of feeling himself into the role of a paranoiac historic personality, and yet be able to explain certain of his actions; notably by reference to the principles of abnormal psychology. Thus whether the historian is or is not in a position to identify himself with his historical hero, is irrelevant for the correctness of his explanation; what counts, is the soundness of the general hypotheses involved, no matter whether they were suggested by empathy, or by a strictly behaviouristic procedure.[2]

Now I do not wish to deny that there is any value at all in this sort of objection. But I think it important to show that the argument does not cut as deeply as covering law theorists commonly assume. For in recognizing the mixture of psychological and methodological elements in many statements of the idealist position, and in denying that these amount to an analysis of logical structure, these theorists fail to notice what it is about explanations of human actions in history which make the idealists want to say what they do—albeit in a quasi-psychological and quasi-methodological way. And what is left out, I wish to maintain, should properly be taken into account in a *logical* analysis of explanation as it is given in history. I shall argue that idealist theory partially, and perhaps defectively, formulates a certain pragmatic criterion operating in explanations of action given by historians, and that when this is ignored, we are quite properly puzzled as to why certain alleged explanations, which meet the covering law requirements, would be dismissed by historians as unsatisfactory—perhaps even as 'no explanation at all'.

The discussion to follow may be regarded in part as an attempt to 'make sense' of what Collingwood, in particular, has to say about historical understanding—and I make no apology for this. But although some reference will be made to dicta of his, I shall not offer any close textual discussion of his account. I shall try, rather, to bring out independently, by reference to examples, features which covering law theory seems to me to miss, going on thereafter to discuss likely misunderstandings of, and objections to, the logical point which appears to emerge out of such an examination.

## 2. *Explaining and Justifying Actions*

The following extract from G. M. Trevelyan's *The English Revolution* is typical of a wide range of explanations of individual actions to be found in ordinary historical writing. In the course of an account of the invasion of England by William of Orange, Trevelyan asks: "Why did Louis make the greatest mistake of his life in withdrawing military pressure from Holland in the summer of 1688?" His answer is:

> He was vexed with James, who unwisely chose this moment of all, to refuse the help and advice of his French patron, upon whose friendship he had based his whole policy. But Louis was not entirely passion's slave. No doubt he felt irritation with James, but he also calculated that, even if William landed in England, there would be civil war and long troubles, as always in that factious island. Meanwhile, he could conquer Europe at leisure. "For twenty years," says Lord Acton, "it had been his desire to neutralize England by internal broils, and he was glad to have the Dutch out of the way (in England) while he dealt a blow at the Emperor Leopold (in Germany)." He thought "it was impossible that the conflict between James and William should not yield him an opportunity." This calculation was not as absurd as it looks after the event. It was only defeated by the unexpected solidity of a new type of Revolution.[3]

What Trevelyan here makes quite explicit is that, when we ask for the explanation of an action, what we very often want is a reconstruction of the agent's *calculation* of means to be adopted toward his chosen end in the light of the circumstances in which he found himself. To explain the action we need to know what considerations convinced him that he should act as he did.

But the notion of discovering the agent's calculation, it must be admitted, takes us no more than one preliminary step towards a satisfactory analysis of such explanations; and it may in itself be misleading. It must not be assumed, for instance, that the agent 'calculated' in the sense of deriving by strict deductive reasoning the practical conclusion he drew—i.e. that the various considerations are elements in a calculus. Indeed, Trevelyan's explanation provides an obvious example to the contrary. Nor should we assume that the explanatory calculation must have been recited in propositional form, either aloud or silently—a notion which one might be forgiven for extracting out of Collingwood's discussion of the way thought must be re-enacted by historians in order to understand intelligent, purposive actions. Not all high-grade actions are performed deliberately in the sense that they are undertaken with a plan consciously preformulated.

Indeed, it is tempting to say that in such cases there is *no* calculation to be *re*constructed by the historian. But such an admission need not affect the main point; for in so far as we say an action is purposive at all, no matter at what level of conscious deliberation, there is a calculation which could be constructed for it: the one the agent would have gone through if he had had time, if he had not seen what to do in a flash, if he had been called upon to account for what he did after the event, &c. And it is by eliciting some such calculation that we explain the action. It might be added that if the agent is to understand his *own* actions, i.e. after the event, he may have to do so by constructing a calculation in exactly the same way, although at the time he recited no propositions to himself. No doubt there are special dangers involved in such construction after the fact. But although we may have to examine very critically any particular example, the point is that when we do consider ourselves justified in accepting an explanation of an individual action, it will most often assume the general *form* of an agent's calculation.

Since the calculation gives what we should normally call the agent's *reasons* for acting as he did, I shall refer hereafter to this broad class of explanations as 'rational'. It should be clear that this use of the expression 'rational explanation' is a narrower one than is often found in philosophical and semi-philosophical literature. It is sometimes said, for instance, that all science, all systematic inquiry, seeks a rational explanation for what is observed, where all that is meant is an explanation which takes account of all the facts considered puzzling, and which does not violate, say, the canons of coherence and induction. I intend something much more restricted than this: an explanation which displays the *rationale* of what was done.

The goal of such explanation is to show that what was done was the thing to have done for the reasons given, rather than merely the thing that is done on such occasions, perhaps in accordance with certain laws (loose or otherwise). The phrase 'thing to have done' betrays a crucially important feature of explanations in terms of agent calculations—a feature quite different from any we have noticed so far. For the infinitive 'to do' here functions as a value term. I wish to claim therefore that there is an element of *appraisal* of what was done in such explanations; that what we want to know when we ask to have the action explained is in what way it was *appropriate*. In the ordinary course of affairs, a demand for explanation is often recognized to be at the same time a challenge to the agent to produce either justification of excuse for what was done. In history, too, I want to argue, it will often be found impossible to bring out the point of what is offered as explanation unless the overlapping of these notions, when it is human actions we are interested in, is explicitly recognized.

Once again, however, I must be on guard against overstating the point; for I do not wish to imply that anything that is explained on the rational model is thereby certified *without qualification* as the right, or proper, or intelligent thing to have done. In saying that the explanation must exhibit what was done as appropriate or justified it is always necessary to add the philosopher's proviso: 'in a sense.'

The sense in question may be clarified if we note a scale along which rational explanations can be ranged. The scale falls away from the simple case in which we can say: 'I find his action perfectly intelligible; he did exactly as I should have done.' It is a small step from such a case to one where we can understand an action when we see that it is what we should agree was the thing to do in view of the agent's peculiar circumstances. In such a case the explanation would consist of an account of these circumstances; they are the missing data which permit the construction of a calculation certifying the action as appropriate. Sometimes, of course, the agent is found to have been mistaken about the facts—including (as Trevelyan's example of Louis XIV shows) his views about what the results of certain lines of action will be. The agent is thus mistaken about the nature of his circumstances; yet his action can still be explained in the rational way so long as by bringing his erroneous beliefs to bear, the calculation can be satisfactorily constructed. It may also be necessary, at times, to take note explicitly of the agent's purposes, which may be quite different from the ones which the investigator would have had in the same circumstances, or even in the circumstances the agent envisaged. And the calculation may also have to take into account certain peculiar principles of the agent; for the action is rationally explained if it is in accordance with the agent's principles—no matter what we think of these.

There are thus gradations of rational explanation, depending on the amount of 'foreign' data which the investigator must bring in to complete the calculation: beliefs, purposes, principles, &c., of the agent which are different from those we might have assumed in absence of evidence to the contrary. Rational explanation may be regarded as an attempt to reach a kind of logical equilibrium at which point an action is *matched* with a calculation. A demand for explanation arises when the equilibrium is upset—when from the 'considerations' obvious to the investigator it is impossible to see the point of what was done. The function of the historian's explanatory story will in many cases be to sketch in the corrections to these 'obvious' considerations which require to be made if the reader is to be able to say: 'Now I understand what he was about.'

In the light of this account, it should be clear how restricted is the sense in which a rational explanation, as I use the term here, must show that what was done was the appropriate or right thing to have done. It is not necessary for the historian to show that the agent had reason for what he did; it is sufficient for explanation to show that he had reasons. But the element of appraisal remains in that what the historian declares to have been the agent's reasons must really *be* reasons (from the agent's point of view). To record what the agent *said* his reasons were would not be enough to provide a rational explanation unless the cogency of such reported reasons could be appreciated by the historian, when any peculiar beliefs, purposes, or principles of the agent were taken into account. Reported reasons, if they are to be explanatory in the rational way, must be *good* reasons at least in the sense that *if* the situation had been as the agent envisaged it (whether or not we, from our point of vantage, concur in his view of it), then what was done would have been the thing to have done. The historian must be able to 'work' the agent's calculation.

### 3. *The Point of the 'Identification' Metaphor*

If my account of rational explanation is correct, what should we say about the view that historical understanding is 'empathetic'? It seems to me that our being able to range rational explanations along a scale in the way described above gives a real point to the 'projection' metaphors used by empathy theorists. Perhaps it is because the scale has been either ignored or misunderstood that what such theorists have said has been so easily written off as obvious but uninteresting, or as interesting but dangerous.

Covering law logicians commonly speak of empathy as a 'methodological dodge'. And it might, I suppose, be claimed that if an old, practised historian were to say to a novice: 'You will never understand the way medieval knights behaved unless you drop your 20th century prejudices and try to see things from their point of view', he *may* be telling the novice how to get on with his job, and thus be making a point which might be called 'methodological'. But I cannot believe that what the old hand offers his young colleague is (in Hempel's words) "a heuristic device" whose function is "to suggest certain psychological hypotheses which might serve as explanatory principles in the case under consideration". As Hempel goes on to explain, by this he means that the historian, since he lacks empirically tested psychological laws which fit, say, the behaviour of medieval knights, must do something about repairing the deficiency if he is ever to give an explanation of knightly activities; for according to the covering law theory there is no explanation without empirical laws. Clearly the historian, especially the novice, is in no position to work over the whole field himself in search of the required laws. So, according to Hempel, he takes a short cut; he imagines himself in the knight's position, asks himself what *he* would have done, generalizes the answer as an empirical law covering knights (i.e. from a single imaginary case), and in this way sastisfies the logical requirements of the model.

Hempel warns us, of course, that the use of the 'device' does not "guarantee the soundness of the historical explanation to which it leads", which depends rather "upon the factual correctness of the empirical generalizations which the method of understanding may have suggested". That is, we may presume, further empirical confirmation of the generalization must come in before we can regard the explanation as anything more than an inspired guess. In Hempel's terminology, the generalization is only a "hypothesis" until it has received the sort of empirical confirmation and testing that any respectable scientific law must undergo, losing in the process the marks of its Athena-like origin.

In the light of what was said in the previous section, it should be clear how misleading this is as an account of 'empathetic understanding'. No doubt there *is* a methodological side to the doctrine; and it might be formulated in some such way as: 'Only by putting yourself in the agent's position can you *find out* why he did what he did.' Here the suggestion is admittedly that by an imaginative technique we shall discover some *new information*—the agent's motives or reasons for acting. When Collingwood says that historical understanding consists of penetrating to the thought-side of actions—discovering the thought and nothing further—the temptation to interpret this in the methodological way is understandably strong. But there is another way in which the doctrine can be formulated: 'Only by putting yourself in the agent's position can you *understand* why he did what he did.' The point of the 'projection' metaphor is, in this case, more plausibly interpreted as a logical one. Its function is not to remind us of *how we come to know* certain facts, but to formulate, however tentatively, certain *conditions which must be satisfied* before a historian is prepared to say: 'Now I have the explanation.'

To dismiss 'empathy' as a mere 'methodological dodge' is to assume, falsely, that all there is to notice when rational explanations are given is a second-rate method of obtaining the same sort of result as can be obtained more reliably by direct attempts to subsume what is to be explained under an empirical covering law. But, as I have tried to show, at least part of what is meant by talking about the 'need to project', &c., is not achievable at all by the method recommended by covering law theorists. To accept Hempel's argument against 'empathy' is to obliterate a distinction between explanation types: a distinction between representing something as the thing generally done, and representing it as the appropriate thing to have done. Thus, when Hempel, after the passage quoted, goes on to say: "The kind of understanding thus conveyed must be clearly separated from scientific understanding", I have no objection to make, provided that by 'scientific understanding' is meant 'knowing to fall under an empirical law'. But Hempel's account of the alternative is quite unsatisfactory. For 'empathetic understanding', interpreted as 'rational explanation', is *not* a matter of "presenting the phenomena in question as somehow 'plausible' or 'natural' to us . . . by means of attractively worded metaphors".

No doubt the widespread resistance to admitting the need to cite anything more than antecedent conditions and a general law in explaining actions owes something to the air of mystery surrounding the language in which 'empathy' theory is often framed: 'projection', 'identification', 'imagination', 'insight', 'intuition', &c. Such words arouse the suspicion that, if the conditions of the covering law theory are not met, it will be necessary to claim that the historian's explanation somehow goes beyond the limits of empirical inquiry into the realm of the unverifiable. As Gardiner puts it, historians often seem to be credited with "an additional power of knowing which allows them to 'penetrate into' the minds of the subjects of their study and take, as it were, psychological X-ray photographs".[4] And in [a] bulletin of the American Social Science Research Council . . . , historians are warned against a view of 'historical understanding' supposed to be "achieved not by introducing general laws or relevant antecedent events, but by an act of 'intuition', 'imaginative identification', 'empathy' or 'valuation' which makes the historical occurrence plausible or intelligible", and whose adequacy is determined by "a self-certifying insight".[5] To allow the legitimacy of empathy appears to many of its opponents as the granting of a license to eke out scanty evidence with imaginative filler.

It is therefore worth my denying explicitly that what I have called rational explanation is in any damaging sense beyond empirical inquiry. As I have pointed out already, it has an inductive, empirical side, for we build up to explanatory equilibrium *from the evidence*. To get inside Disraeli's shoes the historian does not simply ask himself: 'What would I have done?'; he reads Disraeli's dispatches, his letters, his speeches, &c.—and not with the purpose of discovering antecedent conditions falling under some empirically validated law, but rather in the hope of appreciating the problem as Disraeli saw it. The attempt to provide rational explanation is thus—if you like the term—'scientific' explanation in a broad sense; there is no question of the investigator letting his imagination run riot. Indeed, many 'empathy' theorists have expressly guarded against such a misinterpretation of their views. To Butterfield, for instance, historical understanding is not a deliberate commission of the sin of anachronism; it is a "process of emptying oneself in order to catch the outlook and feelings of men not like-minded with oneself".[6]

It is true, of course, that the *direction* of inquiry in the explanation of actions is generally from what the inquirer presumes the relevant agent calculation to be—using his own, or his society's conception of rational purposes and principles—to what he discovers to be the peculiar data of the historical agent: a direction suggested by the scale already indicated. In view of this, Butterfield's admonition to 'empty ourselves' is a little sweeping. In achieving rational explanation of an action we do project—but we project from our own point of view. In each case, the inclusion of 'foreign' data in the calculation requires positive evidence that the agent was *not* like-minded with us. The historian does not build up to explanatory equilibrium from scratch. But this is far from admitting the covering law objection that the whole direction of the inquiry amounts to a vicious methodology. The procedure is self-corrective.

There is thus no reason to think that what I am calling 'rational' explanations are put forward as self-evidently true, as some philosophers who talk of 'insight' may seem to imply. Collingwood has sometimes been thought to provide justification for those who attack empathy theory on this account—e.g. when he represents the understanding of an action as an immediate leap to the discovery of its 'inside', without the aid of any general laws, and (it may appear) without the use of any inductive reasoning at all.[7] But it is always possible that a mistake has been made in the inductive reasoning which provided the factual information for the calculation. It is always possible that further data may come in which will upset the logical equilibrium—perhaps evidence that the agent did not know something which it was at first thought he did. The ability of the historian to go through what he takes to be a relevant calculation does not guarantee the correctness of the explanation given; correct *form* is never a guarantee of correct *content*. But this is nothing more than the normal hazard of any empirical inquiry.

4. *Generalizations and Principles of Action*

Some exponents of the covering law model, while accepting the thesis of the two preceding sections, may object that this only amounts to recognizing an additional condition of a pragmatic sort which explanations must often satisfy in ordinary historical writing. It may be held, therefore, that what I say about rational explanation affects the claims of covering law theory only on its sufficient condition side. It seems to me, however, that in cases where we want to elicit the rationale of what was done, there are special reasons for regarding the model as false or misleading on its necessary condition side as well. For in an important sense, rational explanation falls short of, as well as goes beyond, subsuming a case under a general empirical law.

Any argument to the effect that a satisfactory or complete rational explanation must subsume what is explained under an empirically ascertainable 'regularity' depends on treating the data of the agent's calculation as 'antecedent conditions' (no doubt a very complicated set). It will be said that no matter what *else* is said about these conditions, they must be data from which what was done could have been predicted; and that the only difficulties we should encounter in trying to formulate the implicit covering law linking these to actions of the kind performed would be the ones discussed in Chapter II above (which I propose to ignore here). If we say: 'Disraeli attacked Peel because Peel was ruining the landed class', we mean *inter alia* that anyone like Disraeli in certain respects would have done the same thing in a situation similar in certain respects—the respects in question being discovered by pressing for amplification of the single reason given.

Now this objection is an important one, because its plausibility arises out of a genuine characteristic of rational explanation which ought to be made clear. For it is quite true that 'reasons for acting' as well as 'conditions for predicting' have a kind of generality or universality. If *y* is a good reason for *A* to do *x*, then *y* would be a good reason for anyone sufficiently like *A* to do *x* under sufficiently similar circumstances. But this universality of reasons is unlike the generality of an empirically validated law in a way which makes it especially hazardous to say that by giving a rational explanation, an historian commits himself to the truth of a corresponding law. For if a negative instance is found for a general empirical law, the law itself must be modified or rejected, since it states that people *do* behave in a certain way under certain circumstances. But if a negative instance is found for the sort of general statement which might be extracted out of a rational explanation, the latter would not necessarily be falsified. For that statement would express a judgement of the form: 'When in a situation of type $C_1 \ldots C_n$ the thing to do is *x*.' The 'implict law' in such explanation is better called a *principle of action* than a generalization (or even a principle of inference).

It is true that finding a large number of negative instances —finding that people often do not act in accordance with it— would create a presumption against the claim of a given principle to universal validity. But it would not *compel* its withdrawal; and if it was not withdrawn, the explanatory value of the principle for those actions which *were* in accordance with it would remain. It is true, too, that if a particular person often acted at variance with a principle which he was said to hold, the statement that he held that principle would come into question. But that statement would not *necessarily* be falsified; and if it were retained, we could still explain in the rational way those of his actions which *were* in accordance with it. The connexion between a principle of action and the 'cases' falling under it is thus intentionally and peculiarly loose.

I do not deny, of course, that we often *can* predict successfully a person's response to a situation if we know, among other things, what his principles are (in so far as they are peculiar). In representing the action as the thing to have done, even in the extended sense required for rational explanation, we to some extent license the conclusion that it was the thing to have expected. Having said '*A* did *x* because of *y*', where *y* is *A*'s reason for doing *x*, we could also say that a bystander who knew the fact *y*, and also knew what *A*'s purposes and principles were, should not be surprised at *A*'s doing *x*. It is thus easy enough, under the guidance of a general theory of explanation which requires it, to slip into believing that the real force of the original explanation resides in alleviating such surprise; that its point is to show that this is the kind of thing we can expect to be done by such a person in such circumstances, and that the justification for the expectation must be found in experience of similar cases.

The widespread failure to distinguish between explanations which 'apply' empirical laws and those which 'apply' principles of action may owe something to the fact that the word 'because' is systematically ambiguous in this connexion. Taken in isolation, it is very seldom beyond all doubt whether a given explanatory statement of the form 'He did *x* because of *y*' is to be taken in the rational sense or not, i.e. whether the 'because' derives its explanatory force from an empirical law or a principle. The particular 'because' does not carry its language level on its face; this has to be determined by other means. It is thus often possible to interpret an explanation at the wrong level for a long time without committing any obvious logical errors. And this leaves plenty of room for manœuvring by philosophers who have a thesis to maintain which requires that only one level be recognized.

Whether an explanation of a piece of behaviour is to be interpreted rationally or not will often depend on the context of utterance; we may have to ask how the explanation would be argued for, what else would be said if it were expanded, &c. Take the following example from Trevelyan's discussion of the problem of the early eighteenth-century smog in London:

> On days when the north-east wind carried the smoke-cloud, even Chelsea became dangerous to the asthmatic, as the mild philosopher Earl of Shaftesbury had reason to complain. There is no wonder that King William with his weak lungs had lived at Hampton Court when he could, and at Kensington when he must.[8]

The explanation offered can easily be reduced to a 'because' statement. But what exactly does the historian mean to imply: does he mean that any person *would* have done so, circumstances being what they were? Or does he mean that any *sensible* person would have done so? The explanation could surely be pushed either way, depending on how we cared to read it. And the explanation may be satisfactory (in the sense of 'adequate for its type') no matter which way it is read. Butterfield would no doubt elect to defend it in the second, or rational, way, while Gardiner, in the interests of his thesis, could choose the regularity way without obvious logical error. We cannot settle the issue between them until the writer gives us a more definite indication of what he intends. It is worth noticing, in this connexion, that many of the examples used by Gardiner to support the covering law model could be plausibly re-analyzed in the rational way. The force of the explanation of Louis XIV's unpopularity in terms of his policies being detrimental to French interests is very likely to be found in the detailed description of the aspirations, beliefs, and problems of Louis's subjects. Given these men and their situation, Louis and his policies, their dislike of the king was an *appropriate* response.

Nor is the ambiguity confined to the word 'because'; it can be traced through a wide variety of terms used to describe and explain actions. It can be found, for instance, in the terms 'natural' and 'humanly possible', which Mr. W. H. Walsh employs in *An Introduction to Philosophy of History,* when arguing that explanations of action in history are accomplished by means of basic non-technical generalizations.[9] "We are agreed", Walsh declares, "that to understand an historical situation we must bring some kind of general knowledge to bear on it, and the first question to ask here is clearly in what this general knowledge consists." Against the positivists he maintains that the most important generalizations used in an historian's explanations do not come from any of the sciences; they are fundamental judgments about human nature—"judgments about the characteristic responses human beings made to the various challenges set them in the course of their lives, whether by the natural conditions in which they live, or by their fellow beings". These constitute a 'science of human nature' distinguishable from scientific psychology; they provide the historian with a criterion of what is 'humanly possible', when he seeks to understand the past.

But the 'science of human nature' here described does not differ logically from scientific psychology; it is really just the common-sense psychology of the plain man. If left at that, Walsh's argument would make no other point against the positivists than Hempel's own admission that, because of the unfortunate backwardness of the science of psychology, historians must formulate many of the 'laws of human nature' required on the basis of their own experience. But the facts of historical writing which stimulate Walsh's sympathy with the idealists seem to me to require our drawing, not a distinction merely between different *sources* of empirical laws used, but between different *types* of explanation. For we sometimes want to explain actions not by representing them as instances of laws, but as the reasonable thing to have done; and when we do, if we appeal to 'general knowledge' at all, it is to principles of behaviour rather than empirical generalizations; to knowledge of what to do rather than of what is usually or always done.

Walsh does not put it this way, yet there are suggestions of the point in some of his remarks. For instance, in pointing out that the basic general knowledge which historians bring to their work differs from one historian to another, he includes both knowledge of how men *do* and (he adds 'perhaps') *should* behave.[10] And again, in a footnote, he considers favourably Ryle's term 'knowledge how' (i.e. practical knowledge of some kind) as a characterization of what is to be included in the envisaged 'science of human nature'.[11] There is a hint of the same view in his acceptance of the suggestion that the 'science' in question is continuous with common sense—which, it may be remarked, is generally taken to cover our knowledge of what to do, as well as of what is generally done.[12] And the use of 'challenge-response' terminology in describing the nature of the fundamental judgements concerned points roughly in the same direction.[13]

Walsh's terms 'humanly possible' and 'human nature' are located at the centre of the difficulty; they straddle the distinction between explanation types, or between the levels of language at which we talk about actions. Consider the following explanatory remark of Ramsey Muir about a political decision of George III. "The king", he writes, ". . . naturally chose Shelburne rather than the hated Whigs." [14] In a way, this word does, as Walsh might say, represent the action as a characteristic response, in that anyone with George III's political memories would have tried to keep the Whigs out. But there is a very strong suggestion, too, that this response was *appropriate* in a rational sense; to say the choice naturally went to Shelburne is to imply that this was obviously the right thing for the king to do—from his point of view. Similarly, saying that an historian has a keen appreciation of what is 'humanly possible' *may* refer to the sort of law-governed phenomenon Walsh cites, e.g. "that men who undergo great physical privations are for the most part lacking in mental energy". But I think it may just as well refer to the fundamental principles on which any man may be expected to order his activities.

## 5. *The Standpoint of Historical Writing*

I have argued that rational explanation is a recognizably distinct type of explanation; that it employs a criterion of intelligibility which is different from that formulated by the covering law model, and that there are special reasons for objecting to the claim that such explanations require the truth of corresponding empirical laws. Let me now ask what we can say about the relation between such explanation and other kinds, and what, in general, is its role in historical writing.

It seems to me that there is a general presumption that a given action will be explicable on the rational model if we study it closely enough. The general belief that people act for sufficient reason does not arise out of definite pieces of evidence in particular cases; it is a *standing* presumption which requires contrary evidence in a particular case to defeat. Acknowledging the presumption does not imply that all actions must ultimately be done for sufficient reasons—even in the weak sense sketched in the foregoing sections; but it does register the conviction that it will generally be worth while making a sustained effort to 'save the appearances' rationally. If the first calculation we try to match with an action fails to fit it, then we normally consider ourselves obliged to look for evidence of additional, and perhaps queer, beliefs, &c., of the agent which, when explicitly recognized, permit the construction of a calculation which enjoins what was done. On the other hand, if we have satisfactorily achieved an equilibrium, we tend to regard this as a proper stopping place. The rational explanation of an action at a particular level carries a certain degree of plausibility on its face.

It is impossible to set theoretical limits to the guiding force of the presumption of rationality. It may often, for instance, lead us into attributing unconscious motives for action. Psychoanalysts seem to find it therapeutically useful to extend the scope of the presumption beyond the limits which would be countenanced in ordinary historical writing. But although no firm boundary can be drawn here, it is nevertheless necessary to recognize the fact that there will be particular cases in which we find it impossible to rationalize what was done, so that if an explanation is to be given at all, it will have to be of another kind. To say *a priori* that all actions must have a rationale, no matter how hard to discover, is just a dogma—although we could make it analytically true by a suitable definition of 'action'. In the ordinary course of affairs, rational and non-rational explanations of actions are alternatives—and alternatives sought in a certain order. We give reasons if we can, and turn to empirical laws if we must.[15]

Not only is this done in the ordinary course of affairs; it is done, too, in ordinary historical writing. Historians, as well as plain men, tend to push their explanations as high up the 'scale of understanding' as possible. Proof for this assertion would have to rest upon a detailed examination of historical writing, which cannot be undertaken here. But the following quotation appears to me typical in what it reveals about the workaday approach of historians to the problem of explaining human actions. In *The English Revolution*, while describing the last years of the Interregnum, I. D. Jones remarks:

> It would be falsifying history to bring order out of the confusion of the year between the fall of Richard and the return of Charles II. *There is no logic or reason in it.* The resurrections and re-burials of the Rump: the meteoric energies and extinction of Lambert, now a Fifth Monarchist, now considered an eligible father-in-law to Charles Stuart: *the cryptic evolution of Monck* from the Cromwellian, Republican, Presbyterian to Royalist: the alliances of Fleetwood with Ludlow, Lambert, the Anabaptists and the Rump—all these events produce a tangled skein of desperation, irresolution and treachery *which needs a psychologist's rather than a historian's analysis.*[16]

The passage suggests that Jones has an ideal of explanation which he finds frustratingly inapplicable to the case of, for example, Monck's observed behaviour in 1658–9. He is so accustomed to using it in the course of his work that he appropriates it as *the* model of 'historical explanation', relegating the other kind (like Collingwood) to the attention of psychologists.[17] In so sharply repudiating any responsibility for giving a psychological explanation, Jones no doubt goes too far; for if a psychological theory were necessary and available to explain Monck's 'cryptic' behaviour, it would be the historian's business to use it, and it would be of interest to the reader to know it. But except in history deliberately written to a thesis, non-rational explanation only supplements, it does not replace, the rational sort.

In this respect history is logically continuous with literature rather than social science, if by the latter we mean something like a social 'physics'. This sort of claim has often been made, but usually for reasons which fail to reduce the cogency of the covering law theory as an account of the logical structure of all explanation. Trevelyan, for instance, seems to regard the use of narrative in the presentation of results as the feature which puts history among the humanities.[18] For to a narrative exposition, the canons of literary taste apply. The authors of the American Social Science Research Council's *Bulletin No. 64*, on the other hand, regard much historical writing as "in the tradition of the humanities" because, on their view, its conclusions lack empirical verification.[19] Both views leave the logical claims of the model intact. But my claim is rather that certain criteria of *what shall count as explanation* are applied throughout the humane studies which have, to say the least, a doubtful place in most programmes of social science. Even those who deplore this fact have often seen the point at issue. F. J. Teggart, a self-conscious reformer of history, in attacking the unregenerate kind, observes sourly: "The intelligibility which the historian thus introduces into the materials which he selects for his composition is of the same order as that provided by the author of a historical novel or drama." [20] The comparison is, of course, in Teggart's eyes quite damning.

What is at stake here is the proper 'standpoint' or 'approach' to at any rate a large part of the subject-matter of history. Collingwood declares that history is not a *spectacle*.[21] What he means could perhaps be put in terms of a distinction between two standpoints from which human actions can be studied. When we subsume an action under a law, our approach is that of a spectator of the action; we look for a pattern or regularity in it. But when we give an explanation in terms of the purpose which guided the action, the problem which it was intended to resolve, the principle which it applied, &c., we adopt the standpoint from which the action was done: the standpoint of an agent. In adopting this standpoint, the investigator appreciates the agent's problem and appraises his response to it. The importance in history of explanations given from the agent's standpoint gives some point to well-known idealist dicta like 'All history is contemporary history', and 'All history is history of thought'. Such slogans are exaggerated and paradoxical, but they do register an awareness that the problems of historical agents have to be faced by the reader and the investigator if they are to understand what was done.

It should, perhaps, be added that the historian's preference for the rational model sometimes leads him into making highly elliptical explanatory statements when group rather than individual behaviour is being considered—statements which have sometimes scandalized literal-minded philosophers when they have come to analyse them. In highly condensed general histories, classes and nations and societies are often personified and written about in a quasi-rational way. Thus Germany's attack on Russia in 1941 may be explained by citing the threat of Russian encirclement—as if a 'calculation' of this sort were relevant to the actions of a super-agent called 'Germany'. The precise analysis of such statements would, no doubt, often present difficulties; but I think it is clear that reference to the more detailed studies on which such general histories rest would show that what the 'calculation' in question really explains is the actions of those individuals who were authorized to act 'for Germany'. In other cases the actions of groups are explained on the rational model by means of a kind of 'typical' calculation—e.g. when an historian asks why the Puritans, in particular, became exercised about taxation in seventeenth-century England, or why the Slavs were especially hostile to the Hapsburg monarchy in the early years of the present century. Such extensions of rational explanation would appear to raise no problem other than the practical one of determining whether, in a particular case, the group concerned is homogeneous enough for this kind of treatment.

A different, although related, problem which is sometimes raised by the extension of what I have called rational explanation beyond the sphere of particular actions of particular individuals, is whether the motives, purposes, circumstances, &c., of historical agents afford *sufficient* explanation of large-scale historical phenomena. There is, as Whitehead has put it, a "senseless side" to history;[22] and by this he means more than that natural phenomena, which cannot, of course, be explained rationally, have to be taken into account by historians. For the 'senseless' also appears in larger-scale social results of individual actions which are not themselves explicable on the rational model because they are not what any individual—even one acting for a group—intended or even wanted to happen; and they may often, indeed, be quite the reverse. According to Mrs. K. Cornforth, it is precisely this sort of thing (e.g. "the introduction of steam in modern times, and the development of the cinema industry") which can be explained by general 'scientific' theories of the historical process; and she regards such explanations as the more profound and important ones.[23] M. R. Cohen, too, warns us against exaggerating the extent to which the notion of 'purpose' can be appealed to in explaining social phenomena.[24] The voyage of Columbus was a cause of the spread of European civilization to America, but the result is not explained by the voyage, nor did Columbus intend it.

What Cornforth and Cohen say has a certain point, but it can be misleading. For to say that the sort of phenomena they have in mind cannot be explained, or explained adequately, in purposive terms may mean one or another of two things. If it means merely that they cannot be explained in terms of the purposes of some individual who stage-managed the whole thing, then of course no objection need be raised at all. But if they mean that a perfectly adequate explanation of the gross event cannot be given in terms of the rationale of the activities of the various individuals involved—and this is strongly suggested—then it is surely necessary to disagree. An historian's explanation of the spread of European civilization to America will normally be what I called in Chapter II 'piecemeal'; and it will involve a detailed examination, mainly in rational terms, of the activities and motives of countless individuals and groups; the French Jesuits and the English Puritans as well as Columbus; Colbert and Raleigh as well as Philip II; fur traders, explorers, gold-seekers, land-hungry peasants, and a host of others. As for the question whether explanation can or cannot, should or should not, be given in terms of 'theories of the historical process' where these are available, all that needs to be said is that this would be uncharacteristic of ordinary historical writing. And I can see no reason to brand the more characteristic sort of thing less 'profound'.

## Notes

1. Pp. 145–46. See also pp. 116–17.

2. C. G. Hempel, "The Function of General Laws in History," reprinted in *Readings in Philosophical Analysis,* ed. H. Feigl and W. Sellars, New York, 1949, p. 467. A similar argument is used by R. M. Crawford, "History as Science," *Historical Studies, Australia and New Zealand,* 1947, p. 157; R. S. Peters, "Motives and Causes," *Proceedings of the Aristotelian Society, Supp. Vol.,* 1952, p. 143; Patrick Gardiner, *The Nature of Historical Explanation,* Oxford, 1952, p. 129; A. Danto, "Mere Chronicle and History Proper," *Journal of Philosophy,* 1953, p. 176.

3. Pp. 105–106.

4. Op. cit., p. 128.

5. *Bulletin No. 54,* p. 128.

6. Op. cit., p. 146.

7. E.g., "When [the historian] knows what happened, he already knows why it happened" (*The Idea of History,* p. 214).

8. *English Social History,* London, 1946, p. 337.

9. Chap. III, sections 4, 5.

10. P. 69.

11. P. 67.

12. P. 66.

13. P. 65.

14. *A Short History of the British Commonwealth,* vol. ii, p. 105.

15. The relation between giving the reasons for, and giving the causes of, an action is a little more complicated. I discuss this in section 7.

16. London, 1931, p. 106, my italics.

17. In *The Idea of History* (p. 29) Collingwood attacks history whose "chief purpose is to affirm laws, psychological laws". This, he says, is "not history at all, but natural science of a special kind".

18. *History and the Reader,* London, 1945, pp. 10 ff.; and Trevelyan's plea for 'literary history' in *Clio, A Muse,* London, 1930, pp. 140–76.

19. Pp. 130–1.

20. *Theory and Processes of History,* Berkeley and Los Angeles, 1941, p. 78.

21. Op. cit., pp. 164, 214.

22. *Adventures of Ideas,* Cambridge, 1933, p. 8.

23. 'Explanation in History', *Proceedings of the Aristotelian Society, Supp. Vol.,* 1935, p. 137.

24. 'The Social Sciences and the Natural Sciences', *The Social Sciences and their Interrelations,* eds. W. F. Ogburn and A. Goldenweiser, Boston, 1927, pp. 445–6.

CARL G. HEMPEL

# Rational Action*

## 1. Two aspects of the concept of rational action

To say of an action that it is rational is to put forward an empirical hypothesis and a critical appraisal. The hypothesis is to the effect that the action was done for certain reasons, that it can be *explained* as having been motivated by them; these reasons will include certain ends the agent sought to attain, and his beliefs about available means of attaining them. And the *critical appraisal* implied by the attribution of rationality is to the effect that, judged in the light of the agent's beliefs, his action constituted a reasonable or appropriate choice of means for the attainment of his ends.

Both the critical and the explanatory aspects of the concept of rational action give rise to various philosophical questions. The considerations that follow are an attempt to delineate and explore some of the most important among these.

---

* The Presidential Address delivered before the American Philosophical Association, Eastern Division, in December, 1961. Reprinted by permission of the author and the American Philosophical Association from *Proceedings and Addresses of the American Philosophical Association,* XXXV (1962).

## 2. Rationality of action as a critical concept

### 2.1. *General characterization*

Let us consider first the basic problem of explicating the critical, or normative, idea of rational action. This calls for the elaboration of precise criteria of rationality which might provide us with standards for appraising the rationality of particular actions, and which might thus also afford guidance in making rational decisions.

Rationality in the sense here intended is obviously a relative concept. Whether a given action—or the decision to perform it—is rational will depend on the objectives that the action is meant to achieve and on the relevant empirical information available at the time of the decision. Broadly speaking, an action will qualify as rational if, on the basis of the given information, it offers optimal prospects of achieving its objectives. I will now discuss more closely the key concepts invoked in this characterization: the concepts of the information basis and of the objectives of an action, and finally that of rationality relative to a given basis and given objectives.

### 2.2. *The information basis of rational decision and action*

If we are to choose a rational course of action in pursuit of given ends, we will have to take into account all available information concerning such matters as the particular circumstances in which the action is to be taken; the different means by which, in these circumstances, the given ends might be attained; and the side-effects that may be expected to result from the use of different available means.

The total empirical information that is available for a given decision may be thought of as represented by a set of sentences, which I will call the *information basis* of the decision or of the corresponding action. This construal of the empirical basis for a decision takes account of an obvious but important point: to judge the rationality of a decision, we have to consider, not what empirical facts—particular facts as well as general laws—are actually relevant to the success or failure of the action decided upon, but what information concerning such facts is available to the decision-maker. Indeed, a decision may clearly qualify as rational even though it is based on incomplete or on false empirical assumptions. For example, the historian, precisely in order to present an action by a historical figure as rational, will often have to assume—and may well be able to show on independent grounds—that the agent was incompletely informed, or even entertained false beliefs, concerning relevant empirical matters.

But while the information basis of a rational action thus need not be true, should there not at least be good reasons for believing it true? Should not the basis satisfy a requirement of adequate evidential support? Some writers do consider this a necessary condition of rational action; and this view is indeed quite plausible; for example, as one of its recent advocates, Quentin Gibson, points out, if "someone were, carefully and deliberately, to walk round a ladder because he believed, without evidence, that walking under it would bring him bad luck, we would not hesitate to say that he acted irrationally." [1]

No doubt we often understand rationality in this restricted sense. But if we wish to construct a concept of rational action that might later prove useful in explaining certain types of human behavior, then it seems preferable not to impose on it a requirement of evidential support; for in order to explain an action in terms of the agent's reasons, we need to know what the agent believed, but not necessarily on what grounds. For example, an explanation of the behavior of Gibson's ladder-shunner in terms of motivating reasons would have to invoke the man's superstitions beliefs, but not necessarily the grounds on which he holds them; and the man may well be said to be acting quite reasonably, given his beliefs.

### 2.3. *The objective of rational decision or action*

From the information basis of a decision let me now turn to its objectives. In very simple cases, an action might be construed simply as intended to bring about a particular state of affairs, which I will call the end state. But even in such simple cases, some of the courses of action which, according to the information basis, are available and are likely to achieve the end state, may nevertheless be ruled out because they violate certain general constraining principles, such as moral or legal norms, contractual commitments, social conventions, the rules of the game being played, or the like. Accordingly, the contemplated action will be aimed at achieving the end state without such violation; and what I will call its *total objective* may then be characterized by a set E of sentences describing the intended end-state, in conjunction with another set, N, of constraining norms.

Again, as in the case of the empirical basis, I will not impose the requirement that there must be "good reasons" for adopting the given ends and norms: rationality of an action will here be understood in a strictly relative sense, as its suitability, judged in the light of the given information, for achieving the specified objective.

### 2.4. *Basic criteria of rationality of action*

How can such suitability be defined? For decision situations of the simple kind just contemplated, a characterization can readily be given: If the information basis contains general laws by virtue of which certain of the available courses of action would be bound to achieve the total objective, then, clearly, any one of those actions will count as rational in the given context. If the information basis does not single out any available course of action as a sufficient means for attaining the objective, it may yet assign a numerical probability of success to each of the different available actions, and in this case, any one of those actions will count as rational whose probability of success is not exceeded by that of any available alternative.

### 2.5. *Broadened construal of objective and of rationality*

However for many problems of rational decision, the available information, the objectives, and the criteria of rationality cannot be construed in this simple manner. Our construal becomes inapplicable, in particular, when the objective of a proposed action does not consist in attaining a specified end-state; and this is quite frequently the case, as we will see.

To begin with, even when a particular end-state is to be attained, the available information will often indicate that there are several alternative ways of definitely or probably attaining it, and that these alternatives would be attended by different incidental consequences, such [as] side-effects, after-effects, and the like. Some of these might be regarded as more or less desirable, others as more or less undesirable. In a theoretical model of such situations the total goal must accordingly be indicated, not simply by describing the desired end-state, but by specifying the relative desirability of the different total outcomes that may result from the available courses of action.

In the mathematical theory of decision-making, various models of rational choice have been constructed in which those desirabilities are assumed to be specifiable in numerical terms, as the so-called utilities of the different total outcomes.

If the given information basis specifies the probabilities of the different outcomes, we have a case of what is called *decision-making under risk*. For this case, one criterion of rationality has gained wide acceptance, namely that of *maximizing expected utility*. The expected utility which, on the given information, is associated with a contemplated course of action is determined by multiplying, for each possible outcome of the action, its probability with its utility, and adding the products. An action then qualifies as rational if its expected utility is maximal in the sense of not being exceeded by the expected utility of any alternative action.

One more type of decision-situation deserves brief mention here because of its interesting philosophical implications. This is the case of *decision under uncertainty*. Here the formulation of the problem is assumed to specify the available courses of action, and for each of them its different possible outcomes with their utilities, but not their probabilities. By way of illustration, suppose that you are offered as a present a metal ball that you will obtain by one single drawing made, at your option, from one of two urns. You are given the information that the metal balls are of the same size, and that the first urn contains platinum balls and lead balls in an unspecified proportion; the second urn, gold and silver balls in an unspecified proportion. Suppose that the utilities you assign to platinum, gold, silver, and lead are in the ratio of 1000: 100: 10: 1; from which urn is it rational to draw? Interestingly, several quite different criteria of rational choice under uncertainty have been set forth in recent decision theory. Perhaps the best-known of them is *the maximin rule;* it directs us to maximize the minimum utility, that is to choose an action whose worst possible outcome is at least as good as the worst possible outcome of any alternative. In our example, this calls for a drawing from the second urn; for at worst, it will give you a silver ball, whereas the worst outcome of a drawing from the first urn would give you a lead ball. This rule clearly represents a policy of extreme caution, reflecting the pessimistic maxim: act on the assumption that the worst possible outcome will result from your action.

By contrast, the so-called *maximax rule* reflects an attitude of optimism; it directs us to act on the assumption that the best possible thing is going to happen, and hence to choose an action whose best possible outcome is at least as good as the best possible outcome of any alternative. In our example, the proper decision under this rule would be to draw from the first urn; for at best this will give us a platinum ball, whereas a drawing from the second urn can at best yield a gold ball.

Apart from the two rules just considered, several other rules of rational choice have been suggested for decision under uncertainty. The standards of rationality they reflect all have a certain plausibility, yet they conflict with one another: for one and the same decision situation, they will normally single out different choices as optimal.[2]

The mathematical models here briefly characterized do not offer us much help for a rational solution of the grave and complex decision problems that confront us in our daily affairs. For in these cases, we are usually far from having the data required by our models: we often have no clear idea of the available courses of action, nor can we specify the possible outcomes, let alone their probabilities and utilities. In contexts, however, where such information is available, mathematical decision theory has been applied quite successfully even to rather complex problems, for example in industrial quality control and some phases of strategic planning.

But whatever their practical promise, these models contribute, I think, to the analytic clarification of the concept of rational action. In particular, they throw into relief the complex, multiply relative, character of this concept; and they show that some of the characterizations of rational action which have been put forward in the philosophical literature are of a deceptive neatness and simplicity. For example, Gibson, in his careful and illuminating study, remarks: "there may be various alternative ways of achieving an end. To act rationally . . . is to select what on the evidence is *the best* way of achieving it;" [3] and he refers to "an elementary logical point—namely, that, given certain evidence, there can only be one correct solution to the problem as to the best way of achieving a given end." [4] Gibson offers no criterion for what constitutes the best solution. But surely, what he asserts here is not an elementary logical point, and indeed it is not true.

For, first, even when the decision situation is of a kind for which one definite criterion of rational choice may be assumed to be available and agreed upon—for example, the principle of maximizing expected utility—then that criterion may qualify several different courses of action as equally rational. Secondly, there are various kinds of decision—for example, decisions under uncertainty—for which there is not even agreement on a criterion of rationality, where maximin opposes maximax, and both are opposed by various alternative rules.

It is important to bear in mind that the different competing criteria of rationality of decision or action do not reflect differences in the evaluation of the various ends which, on the given information, are attainable; all the competing rules here referred to presuppose that the utilities of those ends have been antecedently fixed. Rather, the different decision rules or criteria of rationality reflect different inductive attitudes; different degrees of optimism or pessimism concerning what to expect of the world; and accordingly different degrees of venturesomeness or caution in deciding upon a course of action.

The considerations here outlined concerning the critical or normative notion of rationality have important implications for the explanatory use of the idea of rational action. I now turn to this second topic of my paper.

## 3. Rational action as an explanatory concept

Purposive human actions are often explained in terms of motivating reasons. The preceding discussion suggests that, if fully stated, a specification of such reasons will have to indicate the agent's objectives as well as his beliefs about such matters as the available means and their likely consequences. This conception is clearly reflected, for example, in R. S. Peters' remark that in such motivational explanations we "assume that *men are ra-*

*tional* in that they will take means which lead to ends if they have the information and want the ends." [5] Here, then, we have the idea of an *explanatory* use of the concept of rationality.

Let us now examine the logic of explanations by motivating reasons, and especially the rôle which the attribution of rationality to the agent plays in this context.

### 3.1. *Dray's concept of rational explanation*

As our point of departure, let us choose Professor William Dray's stimulating and lucid analysis of this kind of explanation: Dray calls it *rational explanation* because, as he says, it "displays the *rationale* of what was done" by offering "a reconstruction of the agent's *calculation* of means to be adopted toward his chosen end in the light of the circumstances in which he found himself. To explain the action we need to know what considerations convinced him that he should act as he did." [6] But Dray attributes to rational explanation a further characteristic, which clearly assigns an essential rôle to the evaluative or critical concept of rationality. According to him, the "goal of such explanation is to show that what was done was the thing to have done for the reasons given, rather than merely the thing that is done on such occasions, perhaps in accordance with certain laws." [7] Hence, "reported reasons, if they are to be explanatory in the rational way, must be *good* reasons at least in the sense that *if* the situation had been as the agent envisaged it . . . , then what was done would have been the thing to have done." [8] To show that the agent had good reasons for his action, a rational explanation must therefore invoke, not a general empirical law, but a "*principle of action,*" which expresses "a judgment of the form: 'When in a situation of type $C_1 \ldots C_n$ the thing to do is $x$'." [9] Thus, there is "an element of *appraisal* of what was done in such explanations." [10] And it is precisely in this reliance on a principle of action expressing an appraisal that Dray sees the essential difference between rational explanations and those explanatory accounts, familiar especially from the natural sciences, which explain a phenomenon by subsuming it under covering general laws that describe but do not appraise.

It appears then that according to Dray's conception a rational explanation answers the question 'Why did agent *A* do *x*?' by a statement of the form: '*A* was in a situation of type $C_1 \ldots C_n$; and in a situation of that type, the thing to do is *x*'; or briefly: '*A* was in a situation of type *C* (whose description would presumably include a specification of *A*'s objectives and relevant beliefs), and in such a situation, the rational thing to do is *x*'.

Now, this construal of rational explanation clearly presupposes that there is a criterion of rationality which, for the given kind of decision situation, uniquely singles out one particular course of action as "*the* thing to do." However, this assumption seems to be untenable, for reasons indicated earlier.

But, more importantly, even if such a criterion were granted, an account of the form Dray attributes to a rational explanation cannot, it seems to me, do the job of explaining why *A* did *x*. For any adequate answer to the question why a certain event occurred will surely have to provide us with information which, if accepted as true, would afford good grounds for believing that that event did indeed occur—even if there were no other evidence for its occurrence. This seems clearly a necessary condition for an adequate explanation—though of course by no means a sufficient one: producing evidence for the occurrence of an event is not the same thing as explaining it. Now, information to the effect that agent *A* was in a situation of kind *C*, and that in such a situation the rational thing to do is *x*, affords grounds for believing that it would have been *rational for A to do x*; but not for believing that *A* did *in fact* do *x*. To justify this latter belief, we clearly need a further explanatory assumption, namely that—at least at the time in question—*A* was a *rational agent* and thus was *disposed* to do whatever was rational under the circumstances.

But when this assumption is added, the answer to the question 'Why did *A* do *x*?' takes on the following form:

(Schema $R$)

$A$ was in a situation of type $C$
$A$ was a rational agent
In a situation of type $C$ any rational agent will do $x$

Therefore A did $x$.

This construal of rational explanation differs from Dray's in two respects: First, the assumption that $A$ was a rational agent is explicitly added; and secondly, the evaluative or appraising *principle of action,* which tells us what is the thing to do in situation $C$, is replaced by a *descriptive generalization* telling us how a rational agent will act in situations of that kind: but this restores the covering-law form to the explanation.

In thus disagreeing with Dray's analysis of rational explanation, I do not wish to deny that an explanatory account in terms of motivating reasons may well have evaluative overtones: what I maintain is only that whether a critical appraisal is included in, or suggested by, a given account, is irrevelant to its explanatory force: and that an appraisal alone, by means of what Dray calls a principle of action, does not explain at all why A did in fact do x.

### 3.2. *Explanation by reasons as broadly dispositional*

The alternative construal which I have so far sketched only in outline now requires a somewhat fuller statement.

The notion of rational agent invoked in Schema R above must of course be conceived as a descriptive-psychological concept governed by objective criteria of application; any normative or evaluative connotations it may carry with it are inessential for the explanatory force of the argument. To be sure, normative preconceptions as to how a truly rational person ought to behave may well influence the choice of descriptive criteria for a rational agent—just as the construction of tests providing objective criteria of intelligence, verbal aptitude, mathematical aptitude, and the like will be influenced by pre-systematic conceptions and norms. But the descriptive-psychological use of the term 'rational agent' (just like that of the terms 'IQ,' 'verbal aptitude,' 'mathematical aptitude,' *et cetera*) must then be governed by the objective empirical rules of application that have been adopted, irrespective of whether this or that person (for example, the proponent of a rational explanation or the person to whom it is addressed) happens to find those objective rules in accord with his own normative standards of rationality.

By whatever specific empirical criteria it may be characterized, rationality in the descriptive-psychological sense is what I will call a *broadly dispositional* trait: to say of someone that he is a rational agent is to attribute to him, by implication, a complex bundle of dispositions, each of them a tendency to behave in characteristic ways in certain kinds of situation (whose full specification would have to include information about the agent's objectives and beliefs, about other aspects of his psychological and biological state, about his environment, *et cetera*). To explain a given action by reference to the agent's reasons and his rationality is thus to present it as conforming to, as being an instance of, one of those general tendencies. Roughly speaking, therefore, explanations by motivating reasons have the character of dispositional explanations in the sense examined by Ryle in *The Concept of Mind.*[11] However, this rough characterization now must be elaborated a little and must also be qualified in certain respects.

To begin with, the dispositions implied by the psychological concept of rational agent are not simply dispositions to respond by certain characteristic overt behavior to specific external stimuli. They differ in this respect from at least some of the dispositions implied when we say of a person that he is allergic to ragweed pollen; for to say this is to imply, among other things, that he will exhibit the symptoms of a head cold when exposed to the pollen. When we call someone a rational agent, we assert by implication that he will behave in characteristic ways if he finds himself in certain kinds of situation; but—and this is a first point to note—those situations cannot be described simply in terms of certain environmental conditions and external stimuli; for characteristically they include the agent's having certain objectives and entertaining certain revelant beliefs. To mark this difference, we might say that the dispositions implied by attributing rationality to a person are *higher-order dispositions*; for the beliefs and ends-in-view in response to which, as it were, a rational agent acts in a characteristic way are not manifest external stimuli but rather, in turn, broadly dispositional features of the agent. Indeed, to attribute to someone a particular belief or end-in-view is to imply that in certain circumstances he will tend to behave in certain ways which are indicative or symptomatic of his belief or his end-in-view. When I say that belief-attributions or end-attributions "imply" certain dispositional statements, the implying in question will usually have to be conceived as being probabilistic in character; but in order not to complicate the discussion of our central problems, I will make no further explicit reference to this qualification.

There is yet another point I wish to indicate by saying that the ascription of a belief, of a goal, or of rationality to a person is only *broadly* dispositional in character; namely, that a statement expressing such an ascription may *imply, but is not tantamount to,* a set of other statements which attribute to the person certain clusters of dispositions. These dispositions constitute symptoms or indices of the person's beliefs, objectives, or rationality; but they do not suffice fully to specify the latter.

Let me try to support this view first by means of a parallel. To say of a physical body that it is electrically charged, or that it is magnetic, is to attribute to it, *by implication,* bundles of dispositions to respond in characteristic, or symptomatic, ways to various testing procedures. But this does not exhaust what is being asserted; for the concepts of electric charge, magnetization, and so on are governed by a network of theoretical principles interconnecting a large number of physical concepts. Conjointly, these theoretical principles determine an infinite set of empirical consequences, among them various dispositional statements which provide operational criteria for ascertaining whether a given body is electrically charged or magnetic or the like. Thus, the underlying theoretical assumptions contribute essentially to what is being asserted by the attribution of those physical properties. Indeed, it is only in conjunction with such theoretical background assumptions that a statement attributing an electric charge to a given body implies a set of dispositional statements; whereas the whole set of dispositional statements does not imply the statement about the charge, let alone the theoretical background principles.

Now, to be sure, the psychological concepts that serve to indicate a person's beliefs, objectives, moral standards, rationality, *et cetera*, do not function in a theoretical network comparable in scope or explicitness to that of electromagnetic theory. Nevertheless, we use those psychological concepts in a manner that clearly presupposes certain similar connections—we might call them *quasi-theoretical connections*. For example, we assume that the overt behavior shown by a person pursuing a certain *objective* will depend on his beliefs; and conversely. Thus, the attribution, to Henry, of the belief that the streets are slushy will be taken to imply that he will put on galoshes only on suitable further assumptions about his objectives and indeed about his further beliefs; such as that he wants to go out, wants to keep his feet dry, believes that his galoshes will serve the purpose, does not feel in too much of a hurry to put them on, *et cetera*: and this plainly reflects the assumption of many complex interdependencies between the psychological concepts in question. It is these assumptions which determine our expectations as to what behavioral manifestations, including overt action, a psychological trait will have in a particular case.

To reject the construal of those traits as simply bundles of dispositions is not to conjure up again the ghost in the machine, so deftly and subtly exorcised by Ryle and earlier—more summarily, but on basically similar grounds—by the logical behaviorism of Carnap. The point is rather that to characterize the psychological features in question, we have to consider not only their dispositional implications, which provide operational criteria for attributing certain beliefs and objectives to a person: we must also take account of the quasi-theoretical assumptions connecting them; for these, too, govern the use of those concepts, and they cannot be regarded as logical consequences of the sets of dispositional statements associated with them.

### 3.3. *Epistemic interdependence of belief attributions and goal attributions*

The quasi-theoretical connections just referred to give rise to a problem that requires at least brief consideration. For our purposes it will suffice to examine one form of it which is of fundamental importance to the idea of rational explanation.

What sorts of dispositions do we attribute to a person by implication when we assert that he has such and such objectives or beliefs? To begin with objectives or ends-in-view: The statement that Henry wants a drink of water implies, among other things, that Henry is disposed to drink a liquid offered him—provided that he *believes* it to be potable water (and provided he has no overriding reasons for refusing to accept it, *et cetera*). Thus, ascription of an objective here has implications concerning characteristic overt behavior only when taken in conjunction with ascriptions of appropriate beliefs. Similarly, in our earlier example, the hypothesis that Henry *believes* the streets to be slushy implies the occurrence of characteristic overt behavior only when taken in conjunction with suitable hypotheses about Henry's objectives.

And indeed it seems that generally a hypothesis about an agent's objectives can be taken to imply the occurrence of specific overt action only when conjoined with appropriate hypotheses about his beliefs; and *vice versa*. Hence, strictly speaking, an examination of an agent's behavior cannot serve to test assumptions about his beliefs or about his objectives separately, but only in suitable pairs, as it were; or briefly, belief attributions and goal attributions are *epistemically interdependent.*

This fact does not create insuperable difficulties in ascertaining a person's beliefs or his objectives. For often we have good antecedent information about one of the interdependent items and then a hypothesis about the other may be tested by ascertaining how the person acts in certain situations. For example, we may have good grounds for the assumption that our man is subjectively honest; then his answers to our questions may afford a reliable indication of his beliefs. Conversely, we are often able to test a hypothesis about a person's objectives by examining his behavior in certain critical situations because we have good reasons to assume that he has certain relevant beliefs.

But the epistemic interdependence of belief attributions and goal attributions does raise the question whether an explanation by motivating reasons ever requires the explanatory assumption that the acting person was, at least, at the time in question, a rational agent. How this question arises can be seen by a closer look at the criteria for belief- and goal attributions.

Suppose we know an agent's beliefs and wish to test the hypothesis that he wants to attain goal *G*. Just what sort of action is implied by this hypothesis? It seems clear that the criterion used in such cases is roughly this: If *A* actually wants to attain *G* then he will follow a course of action which, in the light of his beliefs, offers him the best chance of success. In the parlance of our earlier discussion, therefore, the test and the justification of our goal attribution appears to presuppose the assumption that *A* will choose an action that is rational relative to his objectives and beliefs. This would mean that the way in which we use a person's actions as evidence in ascertaining his goals has the presupposition of rationality built into it. An analogous comment applies to the way in which the actions of a person whose objectives we know are normally used as evidence in ascertaining his beliefs. But this seems to discredit the construal of rational explanation as involving, in the manner suggested in Schema *R*, an explanatory hypothesis to the effect that the person in question was a rational agent. For the considerations just outlined suggest that this hypothesis is always made true by a tacit convention governing our attribution of motivating reasons—that is, objectives and beliefs—to the agent. If this is generally the case, then the assumption of rationality could not possibly be violated; any apparent violation would be taken to show only that our conjectures about the agent's beliefs, or those about his objectives, or both, were in error. And undeniably, such will in fact often be our verdict.

But will it always be so? I think there are various kinds of circumstances in which we might well leave our belief- and goal attributions unchanged and abandon instead the assumption of rationality. First of all, in deciding upon his action, a person may well overlook certain relevant items of information which he clearly knows or at least believes to be true and which, if properly taken into account, would have called for a different course of action. Secondly, the agent may overlook certain items in the total goal he is clearly seeking to attain, and may thus decide upon an action that is not rational as judged by his objectives and beliefs. Thirdly, even if the agent were to take into account all aspects of his total goal as well as all the relevant information at his disposal, and even if he should go through a deliberate "calculation of means to be adopted toward his chosen end" (to repeat an earlier quotation from Dray), the result may still fail to be a rational decision because of some logical flaw in his calculation. It is quite clear that there could be strong evidence, in certain cases, that an agent had actually fallen short of rationality in one of the ways here suggested; and indeed, if his decision had been made under pressure of time or under emotional strain, fatigue, or other disturbing influences, such deviations from rationality would be regarded as quite likely.

(This reflects another one of the quasi-theoretical connections among the various psychological concepts that play a rôle in explanations by reasons or by motives.)

In sum then, rationality of human actions is not universally guaranteed by conventions governing the attribution of goals and beliefs in human agents; there may be very good grounds for ascribing to an agent certain goals and beliefs and yet acknowledging that his action was not rational as judged by those goals and beliefs.

### 3.4. *Rational action as an explanatory model concept*

So far I have argued three main points concerning the explanatory use of the concept of rational action, namely (i) that explanations by motivating reasons are broadly dispositional in character; (ii) that therefore they conform to the general conception of an explanation as subsuming its explanandum under covering laws (the laws may be of strictly universal or of statistical form, and the subsumption will accordingly be deductive or inductive-probabilistic in character[12]); and (iii) that in explanations by motivating beliefs and ends-in-view, the assumption that the acting individual was a rational agent is not, as it may appear to be, always made true by a tacit convention governing the attribution of beliefs and ends-in-view.

For further clarification of the rôle that the assumption of rationality plays in explanations by motivating reasons, it may be illuminating to ask whether the concept of rational agent might not be viewed as an idealized explanatory model comparable to the explanatory concept of an ideal gas, that is, a gas conforming exactly to Boyle's and Charles's laws. No actual gas strictly satisfies those laws; but there is a wide range of conditions within which many gases conform at least very closely to the account the model gives of the interrelations between temperature, pressure, and volume. Moreover, there are more general, but less simple laws, such as van der Waals', Clausius', and others, which explain to a large extent the deviations from the ideal model that are exhibited by actual gases under certain conditions.

Perhaps the concept of a rational agent can similarly be regarded as an explanatory model characterized by an "ideal law" to the effect that the agent's actions are strictly rational (in the sense of some specific criterion) relative to his objectives and beliefs. How could this programmatic conception be implemented? How could an explanatory model of rational action be precisely characterized, and how could it be applied and tested?

As noted earlier, the concept of rationality is by no means as clear and unequivocal as is sometimes implied in the literature on rational explanation. But let us assume that the proposed explanatory use of the concept of rational action is limited, to begin with, to cases of a relatively simple type for which some precise criterion of rationality can be formulated and incorporated into our model.

Then there is still the question of how to apply the model to particular instances, how to test whether a given action does in fact conform to the criterion of rationality the model incorporates. And this raises a perplexing problem. The problem is not just the practical one of how to *ascertain* an agent's beliefs and actions in a given case, but the conceptual one of what is to be *understood* by the beliefs and objectives of an agent at a given time, and what kind of logical device might serve to characterize them. Let me amplify this briefly.

First, a person must surely be taken to hold many beliefs which he is not consciously entertaining at the time, but which could be elicited by various means. Indeed, a person may be held to believe many things he has never thought of at all and perhaps never will think of as long as he lives. For example, if he believes that five and seven are twelve, we would surely take him to believe also that five speckled hens and seven more speckled hens make twelve speckled hens—although he might never consciously entertain this particular belief. Generally, a man will be taken to believe certain things that are consequences of other things he believes: but surely not all those consequences, since —to mention but one reason—his logical perspicacity is limited.

Hence, while in a theoretical model of the normative or critical concept of rational decision the information basis may be construed as a set of statements that is closed under an appropriate relation of logical derivability, this assumption definitely cannot be transferred to an explanatory model of rational decision. In particular, a person may well give his believing assent to one of a pair of logically equivalent statements but withhold it from the other—although, according to a familiar parlance, both express the same proposition. It seems clear, therefore, that the objects of a person's beliefs cannot be construed to be propositions each of which may be represented by any one of an infinite set of equivalent statements; in specifying an agent's beliefs, the mode of its formulation is essential. (This peculiarity seems closely akin to what Quine has called the referential opacity of belief sentences.[13])

Presumably, then, in an explanatory model concept of rational action, the agent's beliefs would have to be represented by some set of sentences that is not closed under logical derivability. But what set? For example: should the belief-set for an agent at a given time be taken to include all sentences assent to which could be elicited from him by pertinent questions and arguments, no matter how numerous or complex? Clearly such construal is unwarranted if we are interested in specifying a set of beliefs which can be regarded as motivating factors in explaining an action done by the agent. Where the boundary line of the belief set is to be drawn—conceptually, not just practically—is a puzzling and obscure question.

Quite similar observations apply to the problem of how to characterize an agent's total objectives in a given decision situation. Consequently, though in a normative-critical model of rational decision rationality is always judged by reference to the total information basis and the total objective specified, it would be self-defeating to incorporate into an explanatory model of rational action the principle that a rational agent acts optimally, as judged by specified criteria, on the basis of his total set of objectives and beliefs: this latter notion is simply too obscure.

### 3.5. *The model of a consciously rational agent*

A way out seems to be suggested by the observation that many rational explanations present an action as rationally determined by considerations which presumably the agent took consciously into account in making his decision. Let us say that a person is a *consciously rational agent* (at a certain time) if (at that time) his actions are rational relative to those of his objectives and beliefs which he consciously takes into account in arriving at his decision.

This "ideal model" of a consciously rational agent seems to yield approximate explanatory and predictive accounts of at least some types of decision or action.

Consider, for example, a competent engineer who seeks an optimal solution to a problem of design or of industrial quality control for which the range of permissible solutions is clearly delimited, the relevant probabilities and utilities are precisely specified, and even the criterion of rationality to be employed (for example, maximization of expected utilities) has been explicitly stated. In this case, the objectives and beliefs which determine the engineer's decision may be taken to be fully indicated by the specification of the problem; and by applying to the engineer the explanatory model of a consciously rational agent (whose standard of rationality is that specified in the given problem), we can explain—or predict—that he will come up with that solution, or set of solutions, which is the theoretically correct one.

The idea of a consciously rational agent, with its very limited scope of application, does not, however, represent the only way in which a model concept of rational decision might be put to explanatory and predictive use. One interesting alternative has been suggested in a study by Davidson, Suppes, and Siegel.[14]

These investigators present an empirical theory of human choice which is modeled on the mathematical model of decision under risk and incorporates the hypothesis that the choices made by human subjects will be rational in the precise sense of maximizing expected utilities.

As might be expected, the rigorously quantitative character of the theory has to be purchased at the price of limiting its applicability to decisions of a rather simple type which permit of strict experimental control. In the experiment designed by the authors to test the theory, the subjects had to make a series of decisions each of which called for a choice between two options. Each option offered the prospect of either gaining a specified small amount of money or losing some other specified small amount, depending on the outcome of a certain random experiment, such as rolling a regular die with peculiar markings on its faces. The random experiments, their possible outcomes, and the corresponding gains or losses were carefully described to the subjects, who then made their choices.

The results of the experiment conformed quite well to the hypothesis that subjects would choose the option with the greater expected utility, where the expected utility of an option is computed, in the standard manner, on the basis of theoretically postulated subjective probabilities and utilities which the different outcomes have for the choosing subject. The theory proposed by the authors provides an objective, if indirect, method for the simultaneous and independent measurement of such subjective probabilities and utilities for a given agent. Experimental study shows that the subjective probability which a specified outcome of a given random experiment possesses for a given subject is not, in general, equal to its objective probability, even though the subject may know the latter; nor are the subjective utilities proportional to the corresponding monetary gains or losses. Indeed a person will normally be entirely unaware of the subjective probabilities and utilities which, on the theory under consideration, the possible outcomes possess for him.

Thus, insofar as the theory is correct, it gives a quite peculiar twist to the idea of rational action. Though the subjects make their choices in clearly structured decision situations, with full opportunity for antecedent deliberation and even calculation, they act rationally (in a precisely refined quantitative sense) relative to subjective probabilities and utilities which they do not know, and which, therefore, they cannot take into account in their deliberations; they act rationally in the sense of acting *as if* they were trying to maximize expected utilities. We seem to have here a type of conscious choice which is non-consciously rational with quantitative precision. What might Freud have thought of this?

### 3.6. *Concluding remarks*

Obviously, the more familiar instances of explanation by motivating reasons do not conform to this special theoretical model. By intent, at least, they come closer to invoking the model of a consciously rational agent. In particular, many of the rational explanations offered in historical writings seem to imply that the given action was the outcome of rational deliberation based on specific beliefs and objectives which the historian, often on very good evidence, attributes to the agent. But since it is impossible for the historian, even under the best of conditions, to ascertain all the considerations that may have entered into the agent's deliberation and may thus have influenced his decision, the most favorable construal that can be given to the explanatory import of such arguments appears to be [to] this effect: The explanans includes the information that the agent had such and such goals and beliefs; and since he acted in a manner to be expected of a rational agent in these circumstances, it is plausible to suppose that whatever other considerations may have figured in his deliberation had no decisive influence on its outcome: in this sense, the agent's decision is accounted for by the specified beliefs and goals.

In explanations of this kind, the relevant sense of rationality is not explicitly defined; rather, it is left to our judgment to put an appropriate construal on the explanatory hypothesis of rationality and to recognize that what was done was rational relative to the adduced reasons.

Practically, this is no doubt often the best we can do by way of explaining an action. But I would not agree with the view that explanations of this kind are perfectly adequate for the purposes of history and that nothing further need be attempted. For since, in their explanations, historians make objective claims, they will have to take into account whatever relevant insights may be provided by the scientific study of motivation and action. And I think it likely that as a result the vague general procedure of explanation by reasons will gradually be replaced, at least in some areas, by the use of more specific explanatory hypotheses, in which our standard notions of rationality may play a less important rôle. The influence which some recent psychological theories, including the ideas of psychoanalysis, have had on the explanation of human action seems to me indicative of this trend.

If such theoretical developments should show that the explanatory power of the concept of rational action is in fact rather limited, we will have to accept this philosophically: after all, in the methodology of explanation we can ill afford to give a general advance endorsement to the saying: "Man is a rational being indeed: he can give reasons for *anything* he does."

## Notes

1. Quentin Gibson, *The Logic of Social Enquiry* (London and New York, 1960), p. 43.

2. For a lucid statement and comparative analysis of the criteria in question, see R. D. Luce and H. Raiffa, *Games and Decisions* (New York, 1957), Chap. 13.

3. Gibson, *loc. cit.*, p. 160 (italics the author's).

4. *Ibid.*, p. 162.

5. R. S. Peters, *The Concept of Motivation* (London and New York, 1958), p. 4 (Italics supplied).

6. William Dray, *Laws and Explanation in History* (Oxford, 1957), pp. 124 and 122 (italics the author's). [In this volume, pp. 261 and 259.]

7. *Ibid.*, p. 124. [In this volume, p. 261.]

8. *Ibid.*, p. 126 (italics the author's). [In this volume, p. 263.]

9. *Ibid.*, p. 132 (italics the author's). [In this volume, p. 269.]

10. *Ibid.*, p. 124 (italics the author's). [In this volume, p. 261.]

11. Gilbert Ryle, *The Concept of Mind* (London, 1949).

12. These two types of explanation by covering laws are discussed more fully in my essay "Deductive-Nomological vs. Statistical Explanation" in H. Feigl and G. Maxwell (eds.), *Minnesota Studies in the Philosophy of Science,* Vol. III (Minneapolis, 1962).

13. See, for example, W. V. Quine, *Word and Object* (New York, 1960), sec. 30. This section and the subsequent ones through sec. 45 contain incisive analyses of the basic logical problems raised by belief attributions and goal attributions and an illuminating discussion of recent philosophical literature on this subject.

14. Donald Davidson, Patrick Suppes, and Sidney Siegel, *Decision Making: An Experimental Approach* (Stanford, 1957).

JOHN RAWLS

# Two Concepts of Rules*

In this paper I want to show the importance of the distinction between justifying a practice[1] and justifying a particular action falling under it, and I want to explain the logical basis of this distinction and how it is possible to miss its significance. While the distinction has frequently been made,[2] and is now becoming commonplace, there remains the task of explaining the tendency either to overlook it altogether, or to fail to appreciate its importance.

To show the importance of the distinction I am going to defend utilitarianism against those objections which have traditionally been made against it in connection with punishment and the obligation to keep promises. I hope to show that if one uses the distinction in question then one can state utilitarianism in a way which makes it a much better explication of our considered moral judgments than these traditional objections would seem to admit.[3] Thus the importance of the distinction is shown by the way it strengthens the utilitarian view regardless of whether that view is completely defensible or not.

To explain how the significance of the distinction may be overlooked, I am going to discuss two conceptions of rules. One of these conceptions conceals the importance of distinguishing between the justification of a rule or practice and the justification of a particular action falling under it. The other conception

* Reprinted by permission of the author and the editors from *The Philosophical Review,* LXIV (1955).

makes it clear why this distinction must be made and what is its logical basis.

# I

The subject of punishment, in the sense of attaching legal penalties to the violation of legal rules, has always been a troubling moral question.[4] The trouble about it has not been that people disagree as to whether or not punishment is justifiable. Most people have held that, freed from certain abuses, it is an acceptable institution. Only a few have rejected punishment entirely, which is rather surprising when one considers all that can be said against it. The difficulty is with the justification of punishment: various arguments for it have been given by moral philosophers, but so far none of them has won any sort of general acceptance; no justification is without those who detest it. I hope to show that the use of the aforementioned distinction enables one to state the utilitarian view in a way which allows for the sound points of its critics.

For our purposes we may say that there are two justifications of punishment. What we may call the retributive view is that punishment is justified on the grounds that wrongdoing merits punishment. It is morally fitting that a person who does wrong should suffer in proportion to his wrongdoing. That a criminal should be punished follows from his guilt, and the severity of the appropriate punishment depends on the depravity of his act. The state of affairs where a wrongdoer suffers punishment is morally better than the state of affairs where he does not; and it is better irrespective of any of the consequences of punishing him.

What we may call the utilitarian view holds that on the principle that bygones are bygones and that only future consequences are material to present decisions, punishment is justifiable only by reference to the probable consequences of maintaining it as one of the devices of the social order. Wrongs committed in the past are, as such, not relevant considerations for deciding what to do. If punishment can be shown to promote effectively the interest of society it is justifiable, otherwise it is not.

I have stated these two competing views very roughly to make one feel the conflict between them: one feels the force of *both* arguments and one wonders how they can be reconciled. From my introductory remarks it is obvious that the resolution which I am going to propose is that in this case one must distinguish between justifying a practice as a system of rules to be applied and enforced, and justifying a particular action which falls under these rules; utilitarian arguments are appropriate with regard to questions about practices, while retributive arguments fit the application of particular rules to particular cases.

We might try to get clear about this distinction by imagining how a father might answer the question of his son. Suppose the son asks, "Why was *J* put in jail yesterday?" The father answers, "Because he robbed the bank at *B*. He was duly tried and found guilty. That's why he was put in jail yesterday." But suppose the son had asked a different question, namely, "Why do people put other people in jail?" Then the father might answer, "To protect good people from bad people" or "To stop people from doing things that would make it uneasy for all of us; for otherwise we wouldn't be able to go to bed at night and sleep in peace." There are two very different questions here. One question emphasizes the proper name: it asks why *J* was punished rather than someone else, or it asks what he was punished for. The other question asks why we have the institution of punishment: why do people punish one another rather than, say, always forgiving one another?

Thus the father says in effect that a particular man is punished, rather than some other man, because he is guilty, and he is guilty because he broke the law (past tense). In his case the law looks back, the judge looks back, the jury looks back, and a penalty is visited upon him for something he did. That a man is to be punished, and what his punishment is to be, is settled by its being shown that he broke the law and that the law assigns that penalty for the violation of it.

On the other hand we have the institution of punishment itself, and recommend and accept various changes in it, because it is thought by the (ideal) legislator and by those to whom the law applies that, as a part of a system of law impartially applied from case to case arising under it, it will have the consequence, in the long run, of furthering the interests of society.

One can say, then, that the judge and the legislator stand in different positions and look in different directions: one to the past, the other to the future. The justification of what the judge does, *qua* judge, sounds like the retributive view; the justification of what the (ideal) legislator does, *qua* legislator, sounds like the utilitarian view. Thus both views have a point (this is as it should be since intelligent and sensitive persons have been on both sides of the argument); and one's initial confusion disappears once one sees that these views apply to persons holding different offices with different duties, and situated differently with respect to the system of rules that make up the criminal law.[5]

One might say, however, that the utilitarian view is more fundamental since it applies to a more fundamental office, for the judge carries out the legislator's will so far as he can determine it. Once the legislator decides to have laws and to assign penalties for their violation (as things are there must be both the law and the penalty) an institution is set up which involves a retributive conception of particular cases. It is a part of the concept of the criminal law as a system of rules that the application and enforcement of these rules in particular cases should be justifiable by arguments of a retributive character. The decision whether or not to use law rather than some other mechanism of social control, and the decision as to what laws to have and what penalties to assign, may be settled by utilitarian arguments; but if one decides to have laws then one has decided on something whose working in particular cases is retributive in form.[6]

The answer, then, to the confusion engendered by the two views of punishment is quite simple: one distinguishes two offices, that of the judge and that of the legislator, and one distinguishes their different stations with respect to the system of rules which make up the law; and then one notes that the different sorts of considerations which would usually be offered as reasons for what is done under the cover of these offices can be paired off with the competing justifications of punishment. One reconciles the two views by the time-honored device of making them apply to different situations.

But can it really be this simple? Well, this answer allows for the apparent intent of each side. Does a person who advocates the retributive view necessarily advocate, as an *institution,* legal machinery whose essential purpose is to set up and preserve a correspondence between moral turpitude and suffering? Surely not.[7] What retributionists have rightly insisted upon is that no man can be punished unless he is guilty, that is, unless he has broken the law. Their fundamental criticism of the utilitarian account is that, as they interpret it, it sanctions an innocent person's being punished (if one may call it that) for the benefit of society.

On the other hand, utilitarians agree that punishment is to be inflicted only for the violation of law. They regard this much as understood from the concept of punishment itself.[8] The point of the utilitarian account concerns the institution as a system of rules: utilitarianism seeks to limit its use by declaring it justifiable only if it can be shown to foster effectively the good of society. Historically it is a protest against the indiscriminate and ineffective use of the criminal law.[9] It seeks to dissuade us from assigning to penal institutions the improper, if not sacrilegious, task of matching suffering with moral turpitude. Like others, utilitarians want penal institutions designed so that, as far as humanly possible, only those who break the law run afoul of it. They hold that no official should have discretionary power to inflict penalties whenever he thinks it for the benefit of society;

for on utilitarian grounds an institution granting such power could not be justified.[10]

The suggested way of reconciling the retributive and the utilitarian justifications of punishment seems to account for what both sides have wanted to say. There are, however, two further questions which arise, and I shall devote the remainder of this section to them.

First, will not a difference of opinion as to the proper criterion of just law make the proposed reconciliation unacceptable to retributionists? Will they not question whether, if the utilitarian principle is used as the criterion, it follows that those who have broken the law are guilty in a way which satisfies their demand that those punished deserve to be punished? To answer this difficulty, suppose that the rules of the criminal law are justified on utilitarian grounds (it is only for laws that meet his criterion that the utilitarian can be held responsible). Then it follows that the actions which the criminal law specifies as offenses are such that, if they were tolerated, terror and alarm would spread in society. Consequently, retributionists can only deny that those who are punished deserve to be punished if they deny that such actions are wrong. This they will not want to do.

The second question is whether utilitarianism doesn't justify too much. One pictures it as an engine of justification which, if consistently adopted, could be used to justify cruel and arbitrary institutions. Retributionists may be supposed to concede that utilitarians *intend* to reform the law and to make it more humane; that utilitarians do not *wish* to justify any such thing as punishment of the innocent; and that utilitarians may appeal to the fact that punishment presupposes guilt in the sense that by punishment one understands an institution attaching penalties to the infraction of legal rules, and therefore that it is logically absurd to suppose that utilitarians in justifying *punishment* might also have justified punishment (if we may call it that) of the innocent. The real question, however, is whether the utilitarian, in justifying punishment, hasn't used arguments which commit him to accepting the infliction of suffering on innocent persons if it is for the good of society (whether or not one calls this punishment). More generally, isn't the utilitarian committed in principle to accepting many practices which he, as a morally sensitive person, wouldn't want to accept? Retributionists are inclined to hold that there is no way to stop the utilitarian principle from justifying too much except by adding to it a principle which distributes certain rights to individuals. Then the amended criterion is not the greatest benefit of society *simpliciter*, but the greatest benefit of society subject to the constraint that no one's rights may be violated. Now while I think that the classical utilitarians proposed a criterion of this more complicated sort, I do not want to argue that point here.[11] What I want to show is that there is *another* way of preventing the utilitarian principle from justifying too much, or at least of making it much less likely to do so: namely, by stating utilitarianism in a way which accounts for the distinction between the justification of an institution and the justification of a particular action falling under it.

I begin by defining the institution of punishment as follows: a person is said to suffer punishment whenever he is legally deprived of some of the normal rights of a citizen on the ground that he has violated a rule of law, the violation having been established by trial according to the due process of law, provided that the deprivation is carried out by the recognized legal authorities of the state, that the rule of law clearly specifies both the offense and the attached penalty, that the courts construe statutes strictly, and that the statute was on the books prior to the time of the offense.[12] This definition specifies what I shall understand by punishment. The question is whether utilitarian arguments may be found to justify institutions widely different from this and such as one would find cruel and arbitrary.

This question is best answered, I think, by taking up a particular accusation. Consider the following from Carritt:

. . . the utilitarian must hold that we are justified in inflicting pain always and only to prevent worse pain or bring about greater happiness. This, then, is all we need to consider in so-called punishment, which must be purely preventive. But if some kind of very cruel crime becomes common, and none of the criminals can be caught, it might be highly expedient, as an example, to hang an innocent man, if a charge against him could be so framed that he were universally thought guilty; indeed this would only fail to be an ideal instance of utilitarian 'punishment' because the victim himself would not have been so likely as a real felon to commit such a crime in the future; in all other respects it would be perfectly deterrent and therefore felicific.[13]

Carritt is trying to show that there are occasions when a utilitarian argument would justify taking an action which would be generally condemned; and thus that utilitarianism justifies too much. But the failure of Carritt's argument lies in the fact that he makes no distinction between the justification of the general system of rules which constitutes penal institutions and the justification of particular applications of these rules to particular cases by the various officials whose job it is to administer them. This becomes perfectly clear when one asks who the "we" are of whom Carritt speaks. Who is this who has a sort of absolute authority on particular occasions to decide that an innocent man shall be "punished" if everyone can be convinced that he is guilty? Is this person the legislator, or the judge, or the body of private citizens, or what? It is utterly crucial to know who is to decide such matters, and by what authority, for all of this must be written into the rules of the institution. Until one knows these things one doesn't know what the institution is whose justification is being challenged; and as the utilitarian principle applies to the institution one doesn't know whether it is justifiable on utilitarian grounds or not.

Once this is understood it is clear what the countermove to Carritt's argument is. One must describe more carefully what the *institution* is which his example suggests, and then ask oneself whether or not it is likely that having this institution would be for the benefit of society in the long run. One must not content oneself with the vague thought that, when it's a question of *this* case, it would be a good thing if *somebody* did something even if an innocent person were to suffer.

Try to imagine, then, an institution (which we may call "telishment") which is such that the officials set up by it have authority to arrange a trial for the condemnation of an innocent man whenever they are of the opinion that doing so would be in the best interests of society. The discretion of officials is limited, however, by the rule that they may not condemn an innocent man to undergo such an ordeal unless there is, at the time, a wave of offenses similar to that with which they charge him and telish him for. We may imagine that the officials having the discretionary authority are the judges of the higher courts in consultation with the chief of police, the minister of justice, and a committee of the legislature.

Once one realizes that one is involved in setting up an *institution*, one sees that the hazards are very great. For example, what check is there on the officials? How is one to tell whether or not their actions are authorized? How is one to limit the risks involved in allowing such systematic deception? How is one to avoid giving anything short of complete discretion to the authorities to telish anyone they like? In addition to these considerations, it is obvious that people will come to have a very different attitude towards their penal system when telishment is adjoined to it. They will be uncertain as to whether a convicted man has been punished or telished. They will wonder whether or not they should feel sorry for him. They will wonder whether the same fate won't at any time fall on them. If one pictures how such an institution would actually work, and the enormous risks involved in it, it seems clear that it would serve no useful purpose. A utilitarian justification for this institution is most unlikely.

It happens in general that as one drops off the defining features of punishment one ends up with an institution whose utilitarian justification is highly doubtful. One reason for this is that punishment works like a kind of price system: by altering the prices one has to pay for the performance of actions it supplies a motive for avoiding some actions and doing others. The defining features are essential if punishment is to work in this way; so that an institution which lacks these features, e.g., an institution which is set up to "punish" the innocent, is likely to have about as much point as a price system (if one may call it that) where the prices of things change at random from day to day and one learns the price of something after one has agreed to buy it.[14]

If one is careful to apply the utilitarian principle to the institution which is to authorize particular actions, then there is *less* danger of its justifying too much. Carritt's example gains plausibility by its indefiniteness and by its concentration on the particular case. His argument will only hold if it can be shown that there are utilitarian arguments which justify an institution whose publicly ascertainable offices and powers are such as to permit officials to exercise that kind of discretion in particular cases. But the requirement of having to build the arbitrary features of the particular decision into the institutional practice makes the justification much less likely to go through.

## II

I shall now consider the question of promises. The objection to utilitarianism in connection with promises seems to be this: it is believed that on the utilitarian view when a person makes a promise the only ground upon which he should keep it, if he should keep it, is that by keeping it he will realize the most good on the whole. So that if one asks the question "Why should I keep *my* promise?" the utilitarian answer is understood to be that doing so in *this* case will have the best consequences. And this answer is said, quite rightly, to conflict with the way in which the obligation to keep promises is regarded.

Now of course critics of utilitarianism are not unaware that one defense sometimes attributed to utilitarians is the consideration involving the practice of promise-keeping.[15] In this connection they are supposed to argue something like this: it must be admitted that we feel strictly about keeping promises, more strictly than it might seem our view can account for. But when we consider the matter carefully it is always necessary to take into account the effect which our action will have on the practice of making promises. The promisor must weigh, not only the effects of breaking his promise on the particular case, but also the effect which his breaking his promise will have on the practice itself. Since the practice is of great utilitarian value, and since breaking one's promise always seriously damages it, one will seldom be justified in breaking one's promise. If we view our individual promises in the wider context of the practice of promising itself we can account for the strictness of the obligation to keep promises. There is always one very strong utilitarian consideration in favor of keeping them, and this will insure that when the question arises as to whether or not to keep a promise it will usually turn out that one should, even where the facts of the particular case taken by itself would seem to justify one's breaking it. In this way the strictness with which we view the obligation to keep promises is accounted for.

Ross has criticized this defense as follows:[16] however great the value of the practice of promising, on utilitarian grounds, there must be some value which is greater, and one can imagine it to be obtainable by breaking a promise. Therefore there might be a case where the promisor could argue that breaking his promise was justified as leading to a better state of affairs on the whole. And the promisor could argue in this way no matter how slight the advantage won by breaking the promise. If one were to challenge the promisor his defense would be that what he did was best on the whole in view of all the utilitarian considerations, which in this case *include* the importance of the practice. Ross feels that such a defense would be unacceptable. I think he is right insofar as he is protesting against the appeal to consequences in general and without further explanation. Yet it is extremely difficult to weigh the force of Ross's argument. The kind of case imagined seems unrealistic and one feels that it needs to be described. One is inclined to think that it would either turn out that such a case came under an exception defined by the practice itself, in which case there would not be an appeal to consequences in general on the particular case, or it would happen that the circumstances were so peculiar that the conditions which the practice presupposes no longer obtained. But certainly Ross is right in thinking that it strikes us as wrong for a person to defend breaking a promise by a general appeal to consequences. For a general utilitarian defense is not open to the promisor: it is not one of the defenses allowed by the practice of making promises.

Ross gives two further counterarguments:[17] First, he holds that it overestimates the damage done to the practice of promising by a failure to keep a promise. One who breaks a promise harms his own name certainly, but it isn't clear that a broken promise always damages the practice itself sufficiently to account for the strictness of the obligation. Second, and more important, I think, he raises the question of what one is to say of a promise which isn't known to have been made except to the promisor and the promisee, as in the case of a promise a son makes to his dying father concerning the handling of the estate.[18] In this sort of case the consideration relating to the practice doesn't weigh on the promisor at all, and yet one feels that this sort of promise is as binding as other promises. The question of the effect which breaking it has on the practice seems irrelevant. The only consequence seems to be that one can break the promise without running any risk of being censured; but the obligation itself seems not the least weakened. Hence it is doubtful whether the effect on the practice ever weighs in the particular case; certainly it cannot account for the strictness of the obligation where it fails to obtain. It seems to follow that a utilitarian account of the obligation to keep promises cannot be successfully carried out.

From what I have said in connection with punishment, one

can foresee what I am going to say about these arguments and counterarguments. They fail to make the distinction between the justification of a practice and the justification of a particular action falling under it, and therefore they fall into the mistake of taking it for granted that the promisor, like Carritt's official, is entitled without restriction to bring utilitarian considerations to bear in deciding whether to keep *his* promise. But if one considers what the practice of promising is one will see, I think, that it is such as not to allow this sort of general discretion to the promisor. Indeed, the point of the practice is to abdicate one's title to act in accordance with utilitarian and prudential considerations in order that the future may be tied down and plans coordinated in advance. There are obvious utilitarian advantages in having a practice which denies to the promisor, as a defense, any general appeal to the utilitarian principle in accordance with which the practice itself may be justified. There is nothing contradictory, or surprising, in this: utilitarian (or aesthetic) reasons might properly be given in arguing that the game of chess, or baseball, is satisfactory just as it is, or in arguing that it should be changed in various respects, but a player in a game cannot properly appeal to such considerations as reasons for his making one move rather than another. It is a mistake to think that if the practice is justified on utilitarian grounds then the promisor must have complete liberty to use utilitarian arguments to decide whether or not to keep his promise. The practice forbids this general defense; and it is a purpose of the practice to do this. Therefore what the above arguments presuppose—the idea that if the utilitarian view is accepted then the promisor is bound if, and only if, the application of the utilitarian principle to his own case shows that keeping it is best on the whole—is false. The promisor is bound because he promised: weighing the case on its merits is not open to him.[19]

Is this to say that in particular cases one cannot deliberate whether or not to keep one's promise? Of course not. But to do so is to deliberate whether the various excuses, exceptions and defenses, which are understood by, and which constitute an important part of, the practice, apply to one's own case.[20] Various defenses for not keeping one's promise are allowed, but among them there isn't the one that, on general utilitarian grounds, the promisor (truly) thought his action best on the whole, even though there may be the defense that the consequences of keeping one's promise would have been *extremely* severe. While there are too many complexities here to consider all the necessary details, one can see that the general defense isn't allowed if one asks the following question: what would one say of someone who, when asked why he broke his promise, replied simply that breaking it was best on the whole? Assuming that his reply is sincere, and that his belief was reasonable (i.e., one need not consider the possibility that he was mistaken), I think that one would question whether or not he knows what it means to say "I promise" (in the appropriate circumstances). It would be said of someone who used this excuse without further explanation that he didn't understand what defenses the practice, which defines a promise, allows to him. If a child were to use this excuse one would correct him; for it is part of the way one is taught the concept of a promise to be corrected if one uses this excuse. The point of having the practice would be lost if the practice did allow this excuse.

It is no doubt part of the utilitarian view that every practice should admit the defense that the consequences of abiding by it would have been extremely severe; and utilitarians would be inclined to hold that some reliance on people's good sense and some concession to hard cases is necessary. They would hold that a practice is justified by serving the interests of those who take part in it; and as with any set of rules there is understood a background of circumstances under which it is expected to be applied and which need not—indeed which cannot—be fully stated. Should these circumstances change, then even if there is no rule which provides for the case, it may still be in accordance with the practice that one be released from one's obligation. But this sort of defense allowed by a practice must not be confused with the general option to weigh each particular case on utilitarian grounds which critics of utilitarianism have thought it necessarily to involve.

The concern which utilitarianism raises by its justification of punishment is that it may justify too much. The question in connection with promises is different: it is how utilitarianism can account for the obligation to keep promises at all. One feels that the recognized obligation to keep one's promise and utilitarianism are incompatible. And to be sure, they are incompatible if one interprets the utilitarian view as necessarily holding that each person has complete liberty to weigh every particular action on general utilitarian grounds. But must one interpret utilitarianism in this way? I hope to show that, in the sorts of cases I have discussed, one cannot interpret it in this way.

## III

So far I have tried to show the importance of the distinction between the justification of a practice and the justification of a particular action falling under it by indicating how this distinction might be used to defend utilitarianism against two long-standing objections. One might be tempted to close the discussion at this point by saying that utilitarian considerations should be understood as applying to practices in the first instance and not to particular actions falling under them except insofar as the practices admit of it. One might say that in this modified form it is a better account of our considered moral opinions and let it go at that. But to stop here would be to neglect the interesting question as to how one can fail to appreciate the significance of this rather obvious distinction and can take it for granted that utilitarianism has the consequence that particular cases may always be decided on general utilitarian grounds.[21] I want to argue that this mistake may be connected with misconceiving the logical status of the rules of practices; and to show this I am going to examine two conceptions of rules, two ways of placing them within the utilitarian theory.

The conception which conceals from us the significance of the distinction I am going to call the summary view. It regards rules in the following way: one supposes that each person decides what he shall do in particular cases by applying the utilitarian principle; one supposes further that different people will decide the same particular case in the same way and that there will be recurrences of cases similar to those previously decided. Thus it will happen that in cases of certain kinds the same decision will be made either by the same person at different times or by different persons at the same time. If a case occurs frequently enough one supposes that a rule is formulated to cover that sort of case. I have called this conception the summary view because rules are pictured as summaries of past decisions arrived at by the *direct* application of the utilitarian principle to particular cases. Rules are regarded as reports that cases of a certain sort have been found on *other* grounds to be properly decided in a certain way (although, of course, they do not *say* this).

There are several things to notice about this way of placing rules within the utilitarian theory.[22]

1. The point of having rules derives from the fact that similar cases tend to recur and that one can decide cases more quickly if one records past decisions in the form of rules. If similar cases didn't occur, one would be required to apply the utilitarian principle directly, case by case, and rules reporting past decisions would be of no use.

2. The decisions made on particular cases are logically prior to rules. Since rules gain their point from the need to apply the utilitarian principle to many similar cases, it follows that a particular case (or several cases similar to it) may exist whether or not there is a rule covering that case. We are pictured as recognizing particular cases prior to there being a rule which covers them, for it is only if we meet with a number of cases of a certain sort that we formulate a rule. Thus we are able to describe a

particular case as a particular case of the requisite sort whether there is a rule regarding *that* sort of case or not. Put another way: what the *A*'s and the *B*'s refer to in rules of the form 'Whenever *A* do *B*' may be described as *A*'s and *B*'s whether or not there is the rule 'Whenever *A* do *B*', or whether or not there is any body of rules which make up a practice of which that rule is a part.

To illustrate this consider a rule, or maxim, which could arise in this way: suppose that a person is trying to decide whether to tell someone who is fatally ill what his illness is when he has been asked to do so. Suppose the person to reflect and then decide, on utilitarian grounds, that he should not answer truthfully; and suppose that on the basis of this and other like occasions he formulates a rule to the effect that when asked by someone fatally ill what his illness is, one should not tell him. The point to notice is that someone's being fatally ill and asking what his illness is, and someone's telling him, are things that can be described as such whether or not there is this rule. The performance of the action to which the rule refers doesn't require the stage-setting of a practice of which this rule is a part. This is what is meant by saying that on the summary view particular cases are logically prior to rules.

3. Each person is in principle always entitled to reconsider the correctness of a rule and to question whether or not it is proper to follow it in a particular case. As rules are guides and aids, one may ask whether in past decisions there might not have been a mistake in applying the utilitarian principle to get the rule in question, and wonder whether or not it is best in this case. The reason for rules is that people are not able to apply the utilitarian principle effortlessly and flawlessly; there is need to save time and to post a guide. On this view a society of rational utilitarians would be a society without rules in which each person applied the utilitarian principle directly and smoothly, and without error, case by case. On the other hand, ours is a society in which rules are formulated to serve as aids in reaching these ideally

rational decisions on particular cases, guides which have been built up and tested by the experience of generations. If one applies this view to rules, one is interpreting them as maxims, as "rules of thumb"; and it is doubtful that anything to which the summary conception did apply would be called a *rule.* Arguing as if one regarded rules in this way is a mistake one makes while doing philosophy.

4. The concept of a *general* rule takes the following form. One is pictured as estimating on what percentage of the cases likely to arise a given rule may be relied upon to express the correct decision, that is, the decision that would be arrived at if one were to correctly apply the utilitarian principle case by case. If one estimates that by and large the rule will give the correct decision, or if one estimates that the likelihood of making a mistake by applying the utilitarian principle directly on one's own is greater than the likelihood of making a mistake by following the rule, and if these considerations held of persons generally, then one would be justified in urging its adoption as a general rule. In this way *general* rules might be accounted for on the summary view. It will still make sense, however, to speak of applying the utilitarian principle case by case, for it was by trying to foresee the results of doing this that one got the initial estimates upon which acceptance of the rule depends. That one is taking a rule in accordance with the summary conception will show itself in the naturalness with which one speaks of the rule as a guide, or as a maxim, or as a generalization from experience, and as something to be laid aside in extraordinary cases where there is no assurance that the generalization will hold and the case must therefore be treated on its merits. Thus there goes with this conception the notion of a particular exception which renders a rule suspect on a particular occasion.

The other conception of rules I will call the practice conception. On this view rules are pictured as defining a practice. Practices are set up for various reasons, but one of them is that in many areas of conduct each person's deciding what to do on utilitarian grounds case by case leads to confusion, and that the attempt to coordinate behavior by trying to foresee how others will act is bound to fail. As an alternative one realizes that what is required is the establishment of a practice, the specification of a new form of activity; and from this one sees that a practice necessarily involves the abdication of full liberty to act on utilitarian and prudential grounds. It is the mark of a practice that being taught how to engage in it involves being instructed in the rules which define it, and that appeal is made to those rules to correct the behavior of those engaged in it. Those engaged in a practice recognize the rules as defining it. The rules cannot be taken as simply describing how those engaged in the practice in fact behave: it is not simply that they act as if they were obeying the rules. Thus it is essential to the notion of a practice that the rules are publicly known and understood as definitive; and it is essential also that the rules of a practice can be taught and can be acted upon to yield a coherent practice. On this conception, then, rules are not generalizations from the decisions of individuals applying the utilitarian principle directly and independently to recurrent particular cases. On the contrary, rules define a practice and are themselves the subject of the utilitarian principle.

To show the important differences between this way of fitting rules into the utilitarian theory and the previous way, I shall consider the differences between the two conceptions on the points previously discussed.

1. In contrast with the summary view, the rules of practices are logically prior to particular cases. This is so because there cannot be a particular case of an action falling under a rule of a practice unless there is the practice. This can be made clearer as follows: in a practice there are rules setting up offices, specifying certain forms of action appropriate to various offices, establishing penalties for the breach of rules, and so on. We may think of the rules of a practice as defining offices, moves, and offenses. Now what is meant by saying that the practice is logically prior to particular cases is this: given any rule which specifies a form of

action (a move), a particular action which would be taken as falling under this rule given that there is the practice would not be *described as* that sort of action unless there was the practice. In the case of actions specified by practices it is logically impossible to perform them outside the stage-setting provided by those practices, for unless there is the practice, and unless the requisite proprieties are fulfilled, whatever one does, whatever movements one makes, will fail to count as a form of action which the practice specifies. What one does will be described in some *other* way.

One may illustrate this point from the game of baseball. Many of the actions one performs in a game of baseball one can do by oneself or with others whether there is the game or not. For example, one can throw a ball, run, or swing a peculiarly shaped piece of wood. But one cannot steal base, or strike out, or draw a walk, or make an error, or balk; although one can do certain things which appear to resemble these actions such as sliding into a bag, missing a grounder and so on. Striking out, stealing a base, balking, etc., are all actions which can only happen in a game. No matter what a person did, what he did would not be described as stealing a base or striking out or drawing a walk unless he could also be described as playing baseball, and for him to be doing this presupposes the rule-like practice which constitutes the game. The practice is logically prior to particular cases: unless there is the practice the terms referring to actions specified by it lack a sense.[23]

2. The practice view leads to an entirely different conception of the authority which each person has to decide on the propriety of following a rule in particular cases. To engage in a practice, to perform those actions specified by a practice, means to follow the appropriate rules. If one wants to do an action which a certain practice specifies then there is no way to do it except to follow the rules which define it. Therefore, it doesn't make sense for a person to raise the question whether or not a rule of a practice correctly applies to *his* case where the action he contem-

plates is a form of action defined by a practice. If someone were to raise such a question, he would simply show that he didn't understand the situation in which he was acting. If one wants to perform an action specified by a practice, the only legitimate question concerns the nature of the practice itself ("How do I go about making a will?").

This point is illustrated by the behavior expected of a player in games. If one wants to play a game, one doesn't treat the rules of the game as guides as to what is best in particular cases. In a game of baseball if a batter were to ask "Can I have four strikes?" it would be assumed that he was asking what the rule was; and if, when told what the rule was, he were to say that he meant that on this occasion he thought it would be best on the whole for him to have four strikes rather than three, this would be most kindly taken as a joke. One might contend that baseball would be a better game if four strikes were allowed instead of three; but one cannot picture the rules as guides to what is best on the whole in particular cases, and question their applicability to particular cases as particular cases.

3 and 4. To complete the four points of comparison with the summary conception, it is clear from what has been said that rules of practices are not guides to help one decide particular cases correctly as judged by some higher ethical principle. And neither the quasi-statistical notion of generality, nor the notion of a particular exception, can apply to the rules of practices. A more or less general rule of a practice must be a rule which according to the structure of the practice applies to more or fewer of the kinds of cases arising under it; or it must be a rule which is more or less basic to the understanding of the practice. Again, a particular case cannot be an exception to a rule of a practice. An exception is rather a qualification or a further specification of the rule.

It follows from what we have said about the practice conception of rules that if a person is engaged in a practice, and if he is asked why *he* does what *he* does, or if he is asked to defend what he does, then his explanation, or defense, lies in referring the questioner to the practice. He cannot say of *his* action, if it is an action specified by a practice, that he does it rather than some other because he thinks it is best on the whole.[24] When a man engaged in a practice is queried about his action he must assume that the questioner either doesn't know that he is engaged in it ("Why are you in a hurry to pay him?" "I promised to pay him today") or doesn't know what the practice is. One doesn't so much justify one's particular action as explain, or show, that it is in accordance with the practice. The reason for this is that it is only against the stage-setting of the practice that one's particular action is described as it is. Only by reference to the practice can one *say* what one is doing. To explain or to defend one's own action, as a particular action, one fits it into the practice which defines it. If this is not accepted it's a sign that a different question is being raised as to whether one is justified in accepting the practice, or in tolerating it. When the challenge is to the practice, citing the rules (saying what the practice is) is naturally to no avail. But when the challenge is to the particular action defined by the practice, there is nothing one can do but refer to the rules. Concerning particular actions there is only a question for one who isn't clear as to what the practice is, or who doesn't know that it is being engaged in. This is to be contrasted with the case of a maxim which may be taken as pointing to the correct decision on the case as decided on *other* grounds, and so giving a challenge on the case a sense by having it question whether these other grounds really support the decision on this case.

If one compares the two conceptions of rules I have discussed, one can see how the summary conception misses the significance of the distinction between justifying a practice and justifying actions falling under it. On this view rules are regarded as guides whose purpose it is to indicate the ideally rational decision on the given particular case which the flawless application of the utilitarian principle would yield. One has, in principle, full option to use the guides or to discard them as the situation warrants without one's moral office being altered in any way: whether one discards the rules or not, one always holds the office of a rational person seeking case by case to realize the best on the whole. But on the practice conception, if one holds an office defined by a practice then questions regarding one's actions in this office are settled by reference to the rules which define the practice. If one seeks to question these rules, then one's office undergoes a fundamental change: one then assumes the office of one empowered to change and criticize the rules, or the office of a reformer, and so on. The summary conception does away with the distinction of offices and the various forms of argument appropriate to each. On that conception there is one office and so no offices at all. It therefore obscures the fact that the utilitarian principle must, in the case of actions and offices defined by a practice, apply to the practice, so that general utilitarian arguments are not available to those who act in offices so defined.[25]

Some qualifications are necessary in what I have said. First, I may have talked of the summary and the practice conceptions of rules as if only one of them could be true of rules, and if true of any rules, then necessarily true of *all* rules. I do not, of course, mean this. (It is the critics of utilitarianism who make this mistake insofar as their arguments against utilitarianism presuppose a summary conception of the rules of practices.) Some rules will fit one conception, some rules the other; and so there are rules of practices (rules in the strict sense), and maxims and "rules of thumb."

Secondly, there are further distinctions that can be made in classifying rules, distinctions which should be made if one were considering other questions. The distinctions which I have drawn are those most relevant for the rather special matter I have discussed, and are not intended to be exhaustive.

Finally, there will be many border-line cases about which it will be difficult, if not impossible, to decide which conception of rules is applicable. One expects border-line cases with any concept, and they are especially likely in connection with such involved concepts as those of a practice, institution, game, rule, and so on. Wittgenstein has shown how fluid these notions are.[26] What I have done is to emphasize and sharpen two conceptions for the limited purpose of this paper.

## IV

What I have tried to show by distinguishing between two conceptions of rules is that there is a way of regarding rules which allows the option to consider particular cases on general utilitarian grounds; whereas there is another conception which does not admit of such discretion except insofar as the rules themselves authorize it. I want to suggest that the tendency while doing philosophy to picture rules in accordance with the summary conception is what may have blinded moral philosophers to the significance of the distinction between justifying a practice and justifying a particular action falling under it; and it does so by misrepresenting the logical force of the reference to the rules in the case of a challenge to a particular action falling under a practice, and by obscuring the fact that where there is a practice, it is the practice itself that must be the subject of the utilitarian principle.

It is surely no accident that two of the traditional test cases of utilitarianism, punishment and promises, are clear cases of practices. Under the influence of the summary conception it is natural to suppose that the officials of a penal system, and one who has made a promise, may decide what to do in particular cases on utilitarian grounds. One fails to see that a general discretion to decide particular cases on utilitarian grounds is incompatible with the concept of a practice; and that what discretion one does have is itself defined by the practice (e.g., a judge may have discretion to determine the penalty within certain limits). The traditional objections to utilitariansm which I have discussed presuppose the attribution to judges, and to those who have made promises, of a plenitude of moral authority to decide particular cases on utilitarian grounds. But once one fits utilitarianism together with the notion of a practice, and notes that punishment and promising are practices, then one sees that this attribution is logically precluded.

That punishment and promising are practices is beyond question. In the case of promising this is shown by the fact that the form of words "I promise" is a performative utterance which presupposes the stage-setting of the practice and the proprieties defined by it. Saying the words "I promise" will only be promising given the existence of the practice. It would be absurd to interpret the rules about promising in accordance with the summary conception. It is absurd to say, for example, that the rule that promises should be kept could have arisen from its being found in past cases to be best on the whole to keep one's promise; for unless there were already the understanding that one keeps one's promises as part of the practice itself there couldn't have been any cases of promising.

It must, of course, be granted that the rules defining promising are not codified, and that one's conception of what they are necessarily depends on one's moral training. Therefore it is likely that there is considerable variation in the way people understand the practice, and room for argument as to how it is best set up. For example, differences as to how strictly various defenses are to be taken, or just what defenses are available, are likely to arise amongst persons with different backgrounds. But irrespective of these variations it belongs to the concept of the practice of promising that the general utilitarian defense is not available to the promisor. That this is so accounts for the force of the traditional objection which I have discussed. And the point I wish to make is that when one fits the utilitarian view together with the practice conception of rules, as one must in the appropriate cases, then there is nothing in that view which entails that there must be such a defense, either in the practice of promising, or in any other practice.

Punishment is also a clear case. There are many actions in the sequence of events which constitute someone's being punished which presuppose a practice. One can see this by considering the definition of punishment which I gave when discussing Carritt's criticism of utilitarianism. The definition there stated refers to such things as the normal rights of a citizen, rules of law, due process of law, trials and courts of law, statutes, etc., none of which can exist outside the elaborate stage-setting of a legal system. It is also the case that many of the actions for which people are punished presuppose practices. For example, one is punished for stealing, for trespassing, and the like, which presuppose the institution of property. It is impossible to say what punishment is, or to describe a particular instance of it, without referring to offices, actions, and offenses specified by practices. Punishment is a move in an elaborate legal game and presupposes the complex of practices which make up the legal order. The same thing is true of the less formal sorts of punishment: a parent or guardian or someone in proper authority may punish a child, but no one else can.

There is one mistaken interpretation of what I have been saying which it is worthwhile to warn against. One might think that the use I am making of the distinction between justifying a practice and justifying the particular actions falling under it involves one in a definite social and political attitude in that it leads to a kind of conservatism. It might seem that I am saying that for each person the social practices of his society provide the standard of justification for his actions; therefore let each person abide by them and his conduct will be justified.

This interpretation is entirely wrong. The point I have been making is rather a logical point. To be sure, it has consequences in matters of ethical theory; but in itself it leads to no particular social or political attitude. It is simply that where a form of action is specified by a practice there is no justification possible of the particular action of a particular person save by reference to the practice. In such cases the action is what it is in virtue of the practice and to explain it is to refer to the practice. There is no inference whatsoever to be drawn with respect to whether or not one should accept the practices of one's society. One can be as radical as one likes but in the case of actions specified by practices the objects of one's radicalism must be the social practices and people's acceptance of them.

I have tried to show that when we fit the utilitarian view together with the practice conception of rules, where this conception is appropriate,[27] we can formulate it in a way which saves it from several traditional objections. I have further tried to show how the logical force of the distinction between justifying a practice and justifying an action falling under it is connected with the practice conception of rules and cannot be understood as long as one regards the rules of practices in accordance with the summary view. Why, when doing philosophy, one may be inclined to so regard them, I have not discussed. The reasons for this are evidently very deep and would require another paper.

## Notes

1. I use the word "practice" throughout as a sort of technical term meaning any form of activity specified by a system of rules which defines offices, roles, moves, penalties, defenses, and so on, and which gives the activity its structure. As examples, one may think of games and rituals, trials and parliaments.

2. The distinction is central to Hume's discussion of justice in *A Treatise of Human Nature*, bk. III, pt. II, esp. secs. 2–4. It is clearly stated by John Austin in the second lecture of *Lectures on Jurisprudence* (4th ed.; London, 1873), I, 116 ff. (1st ed., 1832). Also it may be argued that J. S. Mill took it for granted in *Utilitarianism;* on this point cf. J. O. Urmson, "The Interpretation of the Moral Philosophy of J. S. Mill," *Philosophical Quarterly*, vol. III (1953). In addition to the arguments given by Urmson there are several clear statements of the distinction in *A System of Logic* (8th ed.; London,

1872), bk. VI, ch. xii pars. 2, 3, 7. The distinction is fundamental to J. D. Mabbott's important paper, "Punishment," *Mind,* n.s., vol. XLVIII (April, 1939). More recently the distinction has been stated with particular emphasis by S. E. Toulmin in *The Place of Reason in Ethics* (Cambridge, 1950), see esp. ch. xi, where it plays a major part in his account of moral reasoning. Toulmin doesn't explain the basis of the distinction, nor how one might overlook its importance, as I try to in this paper, and in my review of his book (*Philosophical Review,* vol. LX [October, 1951]), as some of my criticisms show, I failed to understand the force of it. See also H. D. Aiken, "The Levels of Moral Discourse," *Ethics,* vol. LXII (1952), A. M. Quinton, "Punishment," *Analysis,* vol. XIV (June, 1954), and P. H. Nowell-Smith, *Ethics* (London, 1954), pp. 236–239, 271–273.

3. On the concept of explication see the author's paper *Philosophical Review,* vol. LX (April, 1951).

4. While this paper was being revised, Quinton's appeared; footnote 2 supra. There are several respects in which my remarks are similar to his. Yet as I consider some further questions and rely on somewhat different arguments, I have retained the discussion of punishment and promises together as two test cases for utilitarianism.

5. Note the fact that different sorts of arguments are suited to different offices. One way of taking the differences between ethical theories is to regard them as accounts of the reasons expected in different offices.

6. In this connection see Mabbott, *op. cit.,* pp. 163–164.

7. On this point see Sir David Ross, *The Right and the Good* (Oxford, 1930), pp. 57–60.

8. See Hobbes's definition of punishment in *Leviathan,* ch. xxviii; and Bentham's definitions in *The Principle of Morals and Legislation,* ch. xii, par. 36, ch. xv, par. 28, and in *The Rationale of Punishment,* (London, 1830), bk. I, ch. i. They could agree with Bradley that: "Punishment is punishment only when it is deserved. We pay the penalty, because we owe it, and for no other reason; and if punishment is inflicted for any other reason whatever than because it is merited by wrong, it is a gross immorality, a crying injustice, an abominable crime, and not what it pretends to be." *Ethical Studies* (2nd ed.; Oxford, 1927), pp. 26–27. Certainly by definition it isn't what it pretends to be. The innocent can only be punished by mistake; deliberate "punishment" of the innocent necessarily involves fraud.

9. Cf. Leon Radzinowicz, *A History of English Criminal Law: The*

*Movement for Reform 1750–1833* (London, 1948), esp. ch. xi on Bentham.

10. Bentham discusses how corresponding to a punitory provision of a criminal law there is another provision which stands to it as an antagonist and which needs a name as much as the punitory. He calls it, as one might expect, the *anaetiosostic,* and of it he says: "The punishment of guilt is the object of the former one: the preservation of innocence that of the latter." In the same connection he asserts that it is never thought fit to give the judge the option of deciding whether a thief (that is, a person whom he believes to be a thief, for the judge's belief is what the question must always turn upon) should hang or not, and so the law writes the provision: "The judge shall not cause a thief to be hanged unless he have been duly convicted and sentenced in course of law" (*The Limits of Jurisprudence Defined,* ed. C. W. Everett [New York, 1945], pp. 238–239).

11. By the classical utilitarians I understand Hobbes, Hume, Bentham, J. S. Mill, and Sidgwick.

12. All these features of punishment are mentioned by Hobbes; cf. *Leviathan,* ch. xxviii.

13. *Ethical and Political Thinking* (Oxford, 1947), p. 65.

14. The analogy with the price system suggests an answer to the question how utilitarian considerations insure that punishment is proportional to the offense. It is interesting to note that Sir David Ross, after making the distinction between justifying a penal law and justifying a particular application of it, and after stating that utilitarian considerations have a large place in determining the former, still holds back from accepting the utilitarian justification of punishment on the grounds that justice requires that punishment be proportional to the offense, and that utilitarianism is unable to account for this. Cf. *The Right and the Good,* pp. 61–62. I do not claim that utilitarianism can account for this requirement as Sir David might wish, but it happens, nevertheless, that if utilitarian considerations are followed penalties will be proportional to offenses in this sense: the order of offenses according to seriousness can be paired off with the order of penalties according to severity. Also the absolute level of penalties will be as low as possible. This follows from the assumption that people are rational (i.e., that they are able to take into account the "prices" the state puts on actions), the utilitarian rule that a penal system should provide a motive for preferring the less serious offense, and the principle that punishment as such is an evil. All this was care-

fully worked out by Bentham in *The Principles of Morals and Legislation,* chs. xiii–xv.

15. Ross, *The Right and the Good,* pp. 37–39, and *Foundations of Ethics* (Oxford, 1939), pp. 92–94. I know of no utilitarian who has used this argument except W. A. Pickard-Cambridge in "Two Problems about Duty," *Mind,* n.s., XLI (April, 1932), 153–157, although the argument goes with G. E. Moore's version of utilitarianism in *Principia Ethica* (Cambridge, 1903). To my knowledge it does not appear in the classical utilitarians; and if one interprets their view correctly this is no accident.

16. Ross, *The Right and the Good,* pp. 38–39.

17. Ross, *ibid.,* p. 39. The case of the nonpublic promise is discussed again in *Foundations of Ethics,* pp. 95–96, 104–105. It occurs also in Mabbott, "Punishment," *op. cit.,* pp. 155–157, and in A. I. Melden, "Two Comments on Utilitarianism," *Philosophical Review,* LX (October, 1951), 519–523, which discusses Carritt's example in *Ethical and Political Thinking,* p. 64.

18. Ross's example is described simply as that of two men dying alone where one makes a promise to the other. Carritt's example (cf. n. 17 supra) is that of two men at the North Pole. The example in the text is more realistic and is similar to Mabbott's. Another example is that of being told something in confidence by one who subsequently dies. Such cases need not be "desert-island arguments" as Nowell-Smith seems to believe (cf. his *Ethics,* pp. 239–244).

19. What I have said in this paragraph seems to me to coincide with Hume's important discussion in the *Treatise of Human Nature,* bk. III, pt. II, sec. 5; and also sec. 6, par. 8.

20. For a discussion of these, see H. Sidgwick, *The Methods of Ethics* (6th ed.; London, 1901), bk. III, ch. vi.

21. So far as I can see it is not until Moore that the doctrine is expressly stated in this way. See, for example, *Principia Ethica,* p. 147, where it is said that the statement "I am morally bound to perform this action" is identical with the statement "*This* action will produce the greatest possible amount of good in the Universe" (my italics). It is important to remember that those whom I have called the classical utilitarians were largely interested in social institutions. They were among the leading economists and political theorists of their day, and they were not infrequently reformers interested in practical affairs. Utilitarianism historically goes together with a coherent view of society, and is not simply an ethical theory, much less

an attempt at philosophical analysis in the modern sense. The utilitarian principle was quite naturally thought of, and used, as a criterion for judging social institutions (practices) and as a basis for urging reforms. It is not clear, therefore, how far it is necessary to amend utilitarianism in its classical form. For a discussion of utilitarianism as an integral part of a theory of society, see L. Robbins, *The Theory of Economic Policy in English Classical Political Economy* (London, 1952).

22. This footnote should be read after sec. 3 and presupposes what I have said there. It provides a few references to statements by leading utilitarians of the summary conception. In general it appears that when they discussed the logical features of rules the summary conception prevailed and that it was typical of the way they talked about moral rules. I cite a rather lengthy group of passages from Austin as a full illustration.

John Austin in his *Lectures on Jurisprudence* meets the objection that deciding in accordance with the utilitarian principle case by case is impractical by saying that this is a misinterpretation of utilitarianism. According to the utilitarian view ". . . our conduct would conform to *rules* inferred from the tendencies of actions, but would not be determined by a direct resort to the principle of general utility. Utility would be the test of our conduct, ultimately, but not immediately: the immediate test of the rules to which our conduct would conform, but not the immediate test of specific or individual actions. Our rules would be fashioned on utility; our conduct, on our rules" (vol. I, p. 116). As to how one decides on the tendency of an action he says: "If we would try the tendency of a specific or individual act, we must not contemplate the act as if it were single and insulated, but most look at the class of acts to which it belongs. We must suppose that acts of the class were generally done or omitted, and consider the probable effect upon the general happiness or good. We must guess the consequences which would follow, if the class of acts were general; and also the consequences which would follow, if they were generally omitted. We must then compare the consequences on the positive and negative sides, and determine on which of the two the *balance* of advantage lies. . . . If we truly try the tendency of a specific or individual act, we try the tendency of the class to which that act belongs. The *particular* conclusion which we draw, with regard to the single act, implies a *general* conclusion embracing all similar acts. . . . To the rules thus inferred, and lodged in the memory, our conduct would conform *immediately* if it were truly adjusted to utility" (*ibid.*, p. 117). One might think that Austin meets the objection by stating the practice conception of rules; and perhaps he did intend to. But it is not clear that he has stated this conception. Is the generality he refers to of the statistical sort? This is suggested by the notion of tendency. Or does he refer to the utility of setting up a practice? I don't know; but what suggests the summary view is his subsequent remarks. He says: "To consider the specific consequences of single or individual acts, would *seldom* [my italics] consist with that ultimate principle" (*ibid.*, p. 117). But would one ever do this? He continues: ". . . this being admitted, the necessity of pausing and calculating, which the objection in question supposes, is an imagined necessity. To preface each act or forbearance by a conjecture and comparison of consequences, were clearly *superfluous* [my italics] and mischievous. It were clearly superfluous, inasmuch as the *result of that process* [my italics] would be embodied in a known *rule*. It were clearly mischievous, inasmuch as the *true* result would be expressed by that rule, whilst the process would probably be faulty, if it were done on the spur of the occasion" (*ibid.*, pp. 117–118). He goes on: "If our experience and observation of particulars were not *generalized*, our experience and observation of particulars would seldom avail us in *practice*. . . . The inferences suggested to our minds by repeated experience and observation are, therefore, drawn into *principles*, or compressed into *maxims*. These we carry about us ready for use, and apply to individual cases promptly . . . without reverting to the process by which they were obtained; or without recalling, and arraying before our minds, the numerous and intricate considerations of which they are *handy abridgments* [my italics]. . . . True theory is a *compendium* of particular truths. . . . Speaking then, generally, human conduct is inevitably *guided* [my italics] by *rules*, or by *principles* or *maxims*" (*ibid.*, pp. 117–118). I need not trouble to show how all these remarks incline to the summary view. Further, when Austin comes to deal with cases "of comparatively rare occurrence" he holds that specific considerations may outweigh the general. "Looking at the reasons from which we had inferred the rule, it were absurd to think it inflexible. We should therefore dismiss the *rule;* resort directly to the *principle* upon which our rules were fashioned; and calculate *specific* consequences to the best of our knowledge and ability" (*ibid.*, pp. 120–121). Austin's view is interesting because it shows how one may come close to the practice conception and then slide away from it.

In *A System of Logic*, bk. VI, ch. xii, par. 2, Mill distinguishes clearly between the position of judge and legislator and in doing so suggests the distinction between the two concepts of rules. However, he distinguishes the two positions to illustrate the difference between cases where one is to apply a rule already established and cases where one must formulate a rule to govern subsequent conduct. It's the latter case that interests him and he takes the "maxim of policy" of a legislator as typical of rules. In par. 3 the summary conception is very clearly stated. For example, he says of rules of conduct that they should be taken provisionally, as they are made for the most numerous cases. He says that they "point out" the manner in which it is least perilous to act; they serve as an "admonition" that a certain mode of conduct has been found suited to the most common occurrences. In *Utilitarianism,* ch. ii, par. 24, the summary conception appears in Mill's answer to the same objection Austin considered. Here he speaks of rules as "corollaries" from the principle of utility; these "secondary" rules are compared to "landmarks" and "direction-posts." They are based on long experience and so make it unnecessary to apply the utilitarian principle to each case. In par. 25 Mill refers to the task of the utilitarian principle in adjudicating between competing moral rules. He talks here as if one then applies the utilitarian principle directly to the particular case. On the practice view one would rather use the principle to decide which of the ways that make the practice consistent is the best. It should be noted that while in par. 10 Mill's definition of utilitarianism makes the utilitarian principle apply to morality, i.e., to the rules and precepts of human conduct, the definition in par. 2 uses the phrase "actions are right in *proportion* as they *tend* to promote happiness" [my italics] and this inclines towards the summary view. In the last paragraph of the essay "On the Definition of Political Economy," *Westminster Review* (October, 1836), Mill says that it is only in art, as distinguished from science, that one can properly speak of exceptions. In a question of practice, if something is fit to be done "in the majority of cases" then it is made the rule. "We may . . . in talking of art *unobjectionably* speak of the *rule* and the *exception,* meaning by the rule the cases in which there exists a preponderance . . . of inducements for acting in a particular way; and by the exception, the cases in which the preponderance is on the contrary side." These remarks, too, suggest the summary view.

In Moore's *Principia Ethica,* ch. v, there is a complicated and difficult discussion of moral rules. I will not examine it here except to express my suspicion that the summary conception prevails. To be sure, Moore speaks frequently of the utility of rules as generally followed, and of actions as generally practiced, but it is possible that these passages fit the statistical notion of generality which the summary conception allows. This conception is suggested by Moore's taking the utilitarian principle as applying directly to particular actions (pp. 147–148) and by his notion of a rule as something indicating which of the few alternatives likely to occur to anyone will generally produce a greater total good in the immediate future (p. 154). He talks of an "ethical law" as a prediction, and as a generalization (pp. 146, 155). The summary conception is also suggested by his discussion of exceptions (pp. 162–163) and of the force of examples of breaching a rule (pp. 163–164).

23. One might feel that it is a mistake to say that a practice is logically prior to the forms of action it specifies on the grounds that if there were never any instances of actions falling under a practice then we should be strongly inclined to say that there wasn't the practice either. Blue-prints for a practice do not make a practice. That there is a practice entails that there are instances of people having been engaged and now being engaged in it (with suitable qualifications). This is correct, but it doesn't hurt the claim that any given particular instance of a form of action specified by a practice presupposes the practice. This isn't so on the summary picture, as each instance must be "there" prior to the rules, so to speak, as something from which one gets the rule by applying the utilitarian principle to it directly.

24. A philosophical joke (in the mouth of Jeremy Bentham): "When I run to the other wicket after my partner has struck a good ball I do so because it is best on the whole."

25. How do these remarks apply to the case of the promise known only to father and son? Well, at first sight the son certainly holds the office of promisor, and so he isn't allowed by the practice to weigh the particular case on general utilitarian grounds. Suppose instead that he wishes to consider himself in the office of one empowered to criticize and change the practice, leaving aside the question as to his right to move from his previously assumed office to another. Then he may consider utilitarian arguments as applied to the practice; but once he does this he will see that there are such arguments for not allowing a general utilitarian defense in the practice for this sort of case. For to do so would make it impossible to ask for and to give a kind of promise which one often wants to be able to ask for and to give. Therefore he will not want to change the practice, and so as a promisor he has no option but to keep his promise.

26. *Philosophical Investigations* (Oxford, 1953), I, pars. 65–71, for example.

27. As I have already stated, it is not always easy to say where the conception is appropriate. Nor do I care to discuss at this point the general sorts of cases to which it does apply except to say that one should not take it for granted that it applies to many so-called "moral rules." It is my feeling that relatively few actions of the moral life are defined by practices and that the practice conception is more relevant to understanding legal and legal-like arguments than it is to the more complex sort of moral arguments. Utilitarianism must be fitted to different conceptions of rules depending on the case, and no doubt the failure to do this has been one source of difficulty in interpreting it correctly.

B. J. DIGGS

# Rules and Utilitarianism*

Although moral rules have had a prominent place in recent moral philosophy, their character is not clear. One reason for this is the vagueness and ambiguity which infect the use of the term "rule": Philosophers tend to conceive of moral rules on some particular model, sometimes in a confused way, often innocently and without a clear view of the alternatives. J. Rawls called attention to one important instance of this: He pointed out that the tendency to regard rules as convenient guides, or as summaries of earlier experiences, seems to have blinded some philosophers ". . . to the significance of the distinction between justifying a practice and justifying a particular action falling under it. . . ." [1]

Partly as a consequence, utilitarianism has been interpreted in a special way, as asserting that the rightness and wrongness of particular acts is decidable on general utilitarian grounds. This form of utilitarianism, so-called "act utilitarianism," is open to serious and well-known objections.[2]

The appeal of the recently more popular "rule utilitarianism" is that it is able to meet some of these objections, and still retain the tie between morality and "the general welfare," which is one of the most attractive characteristics of utilitarianism. I shall argue in this paper, however, that rule utilitarians (and some of their critics, and many others who view moral rules in the same

* Reprinted by permission of the author and the editor from *American Philosophical Quarterly*, I (1964).

general way) have also tended unwittingly to adopt a particular kind of rule as the model of a moral rule. When this kind of rule has been delineated, and alternatives noted, I think rule utilitarianism loses much of its initial appeal.

My object in this paper, however, is not so much to refute rule utilitarianism as to contribute to the clarification of moral rules. By distinguishing two kinds of rules I shall try to illuminate one of the fundamental options (as well as one of the fundamental confusions) open to moral theory. (1) The first kind of rule is exemplified by the rules which workers follow as part of their jobs; these rules may be used to describe a job. (2) The other kind of rule characterizes such common games as baseball, chess, and the like. Both kinds of rule define "practices," but the practices are very different. I think the easy tendency to confuse them may have blinded moral philosophers to significant distinctions between justifying a system of rules designed to contribute to some goal or product, justifying a system of rules which defines a "form of life," and justifying moral rules. Marking these distinctions should help clarify certain steps taken in recent moral philosophy: One should be able to appreciate more fully the point of Baier's assertion that although moral rules are "for the good of everyone alike," they are not designed to promote the greatest good of everyone.[3] One should also be able to see more clearly why Rawls maintains that the decision on the rules of justice is not properly conceived on the utilitarian model, as an administrative decision on how to promote the greatest happiness.[4] The analysis of rules is illuminating, moreover, not only because it helps mark major differences of this kind, but also because it shows what is behind some of the twists and turns of moral theory.

# I

*1.0* The first kind of rule which I shall describe belongs to a large class of rules which I call "instrumental." All rules in this large class are adopted or followed as a means to an end, in order to "accomplish a purpose" or "get a job done." The simplest of these rules is the "practical maxim" which one ordinarily follows at his own pleasure, such as "Be sure the surface to be painted is thoroughly dry" or "Do not plant tomatoes until after the last frost." [5]

The instrumental rule to which I call attention is more complex. On many occasions when one wants a job done, either he is not in a position or not able or not willing to do the job himself. If he is in a position of power or authority, or if he has money, he may simply order or hire others to "do the job" and leave it to them. In numerous cases, however, he himself lays down rules of procedure, and establishes "jobs" or "roles" in the institutional sense. A "job" in this latter sense is not a job to be "done," but a job to be "offered to" or "given" to a person. If a person "takes" or is "assigned" "the job" then we often think of him as under an obligation to "do his job," and this partly consists in his following rules. Instrumental rules of this kind, unlike practical maxims, have a social dimension: It *makes sense* to ask whether a job-holder (or role-taker) is *obligated* to follow a particular rule, or whether this is one of his *duties,* and the penalty attaching to a breach of the rules does not consist simply in his not "getting the job done."

Rules of this kind are found in very different institutions. Some are rules of a "job" in the ordinary sense. Others apply to anyone who voluntarily assumes a "role," such as "automobile driver." Others characterize a position which one is obliged to take by law, for example, that of private in the army. The goals which the rules are designed to serve may be ordinary products of labor, such as houses, steel beams, etc.; or fairly specific social goals such as "getting vehicles to their destinations safely and expeditiously"; or goals as general as "the national defense." In some cases the rules, differing from job to job, mark a division of labor, as the rules which say what factory workers, or the members of a platoon, are to do. In other cases, the same rules apply more or less equally to all, as in the case of (at least some) rules regulating traffic.

Notwithstanding their variety, these rules can be classified together because they share two fundamental characteristics: (1) The rules prescribe action which is thought to contribute to the attainment of a goal. This is the "design" of such rules, at least in the sense that if the prescribed action does not effectively contribute to the attainment of the goal, for the most part, then the rule itself is subject to criticism. (2) The rules are "laid down" or "legislated" or "made the rule" by a party which has power or authority of some kind; one cannot learn "what the rules are" simply by determining what general procedures most effectively promote the goal. This latter characteristic sharply differentiates these rules from what I have called practical maxims, although both share the first characteristic and are "instrumental." [6]

I shall now consider each of these two characteristics in turn.

*1.1* Since rules of this kind are designed to serve a goal, the "best" set of rules is that set, *other things equal,* which is most effective in promoting the goal. The qualification is important: One ordinarily asks the question, "Is this a good rule?" in order to determine whether or not the action to be prescribed by the rule, together with other acts, will most efficiently produce the goal, without violating certain other rules, and in a way that harmonizes best with other aims, assuming persons can be persuaded to follow the rule.[7]

Consider a factory planner designing an assembly line, or an army officer considering platoon reorganization, or a traffic planning commission trying to decide whether a street should be made a throughway. In each case rules are proposed, but there is no contradiction in saying that action on the rules will not contribute to the goal. Within its context the question "Is this a good rule?" is one of practical fact and experience. This indicates one sense in saying that the goal is "over and beyond" the action and the rules.

There is another sense in saying this: In practice a goal is often described in terms of rules or procedures which are thought to produce it (when, for example, a beam is to be built according to procedural specifications). Moreover, at the time of action one may not be able to say just what he wants in other terms. Nevertheless, there is no contradiction, explicit or implied, in saying that this person got the goal (in the sense that he can truthfully say "This has all the desirable features of what I wanted") without anyone's having laid down or followed rules. Although the beam was not constructed according to specifications, tests may now show that it is as strong as one could have wished for. In this sense it is *logically* possible for one to attain the goal which a set of instrumental rules is designed to serve without these rules having been followed. I shall refer to this characteristic by saying that the goal of any set of instrumental rules is "logically independent" of these rules.

Although an instrumental action is *properly* described in many ways, depending on the context, it can always be *truthfully* described in terms of a goal, as a "trying to get or produce G." For a goal is essential to such action, and to the rules which guide it. Nevertheless, it is clear that it is logically possible to act and follow instrumental rules without attaining the goal, and to attain the goal without following rules.

Moreover, although obviously one cannot act *on* a rule of any kind if there is no rule, one can act *in the way* specified by a set of instrumental rules (as well as attain a desired result) without *these* rules having been adopted. A group of workers, for example, may hit upon certain procedures which are so effective that they are made "the rule"; in such a case we may say, somewhat misleadingly, that one discovered a good rule by observing the actual results of a line of action. In complex cases it is very unlikely that men will act in the way rules would prescribe if the rules have not in fact been enacted. Nevertheless, there is no contradiction in saying that men acted in this way but there were no rules prescribing this course of action.[8]

Thus in the case of instrumental rules the action as well as the goal may be said to be logically independent of the rules.

*1.2* Now consider the second major characteristic of rules of this kind, namely, that they are "laid down," "legislated," "made," or "adopted."

It is clear enough that an employer, for example, who "informs" his employee of the rules, is not simply "giving information." Moreover, this act or performance is very different from one's "adopting" a practical maxim or making a rule "a rule for himself." Note that in the case of a maxim the adoption of the rule is "incomplete" so long as one simply resolves to follow it. Rules of the present kind, however, are normally made for others to follow: To make their adoption complete, one must get at least some of these others "to agree," in some sense, to follow the rules.

This is so in spite of our sometimes speaking, in the sense indicated earlier, of one's "discovering a good rule" of this kind. We also speak of an administrator's "thinking of a good rule," "deciding on a rule," and "informing an employee of the rules decided on." It is quite clear, however, that "thinking of a rule" and "deciding on it" are steps taken *in the direction of* adopting a rule; the latter corresponds roughly to the stage of "resolution" in the case of a maxim. They are only steps; the rule will not become effective, and strictly speaking, will not *be* a rule, until it is "put in force" or "made a rule."

Legislation is one way of putting such a rule in force. In this case parents and guardians "teach" their children what the laws are; they do not ask for consent. In other cases the members of a group, working co-operatively, "decide on the rules," or an employer or a sergeant "tells one the rules." By such an act those subject to the rules are "directed to follow them," and the rules are then "in force." The rules serve on the one hand as guides to action—they tell one what to do—and on the other as criteria of correctness of action—acts in accord with them are said to be *right* and breaches of them are said to be *wrong*. The rules thus tell one both *what* to do, and *that* he should do it. They are useful just on this account: One may lay down rules of this kind to make use of unskilled labor, or to gain the benefits of a division of labor, or simply to coordinate activity as in the case of an efficient traffic system.

The analysis of what the various cases of adopting a rule have in common, and what it is to be subject to rules, takes one to the difficult problem of what constitutes an authority. For our purpose the following will suffice: A party seems to be constituted as a *de facto* authority when one accepts the fact, that this party prescribes an act, as a *reason* for following the prescription (a rule of the present kind being one form of prescription). This indicates the somewhat technical sense of saying that the rule follower "agrees to" follow the rules.[9] In the case of rules of the present kind authority is ordinarily constituted, and agreement to follow the rules obtained, by contract, law, convention, or the like. Some such arrangement is necessary to induce a person to follow rules of this kind, since persons other than the rule-follower "are interested in" the goal, and normally he himself does not get (more than a share of) the product of his labor. The contract, law, or convention both promises some reward to the rule-follower, and at the same time converts others' "being interested in" the goal to their "having an interest in it"—in a legal or quasi-legal sense. This, of course, is why one who follows rules of this kind, unlike one who adopts a maxim as his guide, is not free to alter or follow the rules "at his pleasure."

The point which needs particular emphasis here, however, is that the contract, law, or convention is essential to the rule's being a rule; it is not "external" to the rule, since without it one's "laying down the rules" would be only so much rhetoric. When a contract is simply "to do a job," notice that the criterion of correctness is simply "getting the job done." If I hire a person to paint a house, he has done what he is supposed to do when the house is painted. On the other hand, to the extent to which a contract lays down rules specifying how the job is to be done, the rules are the criterion. If a painter contracts to follow certain procedures, and then fails to follow them, he has not done what he is supposed to do. This should make it quite clear that it is the contract, law, or convention which determines in a given case that rules will be the criterion of correctness. The "agreement" secured by contract, law, or convention thus makes a rule a rule, and without something like it there could be no rules of this kind.

*1.3* The discussion of the two major characteristics of these rules reveals two criteria of correctness. On the one hand, there is the criterion of a "good" rule. On the other, there are rules *in force* constituting a criterion in certain respects of the *right thing to do.* In the case of these rules there is thus a clear distinction between the justification of a rule or practice and the justification of a particular action falling under it. Perhaps on this very account some have been led to view moral rules as rules of this kind.

*1.3.1* Before going on to moral rules let us notice that this distinction is not important simply because acts are judged by rules which are judged in turn in another manner, in this case by reference to a goal. The significance of the distinction derives more from the fact that the two criteria are "independent" in the following way: One may do the thing which most contributes to the goal, yet violate the rules in force; and one may act according to the rule in force when the rule is a poor one.

Moreover, the rules *in force,* not the rules which are *best,* constitute (at least under certain conditions) the criterion of right and wrong acts. This is evident in practice: A worker who does his job is *entitled* to his pay, whether or not the rules he follows in doing his job are *good* rules. This question, whether or not the rules in force are "good," ordinarily does not have to be settled for them to serve as a criterion of right action. Normally it does not even arise.

Of course, one might criticize the rules *in force* as "illegitimate" or as laid down by one who lacks rightful or proper authority, and *on this account* argue that they are not the "true" criterion of right action. However, the question of the "legitimacy" of the rules is not settled by determining which rules are best. To try to have it this way would be to invite disagreement concerning which rules *are* best, and to have no effective rule at all.[10] It would be wholly impractical to accept as authoritative or binding, and as the criterion of right action, only "the rules which are best." Who, for example, would lay down, or contract to follow under penalty, rules characterized only in this way?

Thus, even though rules of the present kind are explicitly designed to promote a goal, the rule follower is not generally at liberty to use the goal as his criterion of the right thing to do. The distinction between the two criteria so far remains firm.

*1.3.2* Nevertheless, the independence of these two criteria can be overemphasized. For one thing, the criterion of a good rule, in virtue of its being used by those who adopt rules, is an indirect criterion of right action. The rules which are the criterion of right and wrong action do not prescribe action which just *as a matter of fact* contributes or fails to contribute to the goal; the rules are *criticizable* if they are not good rules. Thus it does not "just so happen" that the right act *tends* to contribute to the goal. If it did not generally do this it would not be called "right," for there would be no such rules.

Second, no statement of a rule includes reference to all conditions pertinent to its application; one would not wish so to encumber it, even if every contingency could be foreseen. This implies that every rule follower is expected to know "what he is doing" in a sense larger than "following the rules"; and if the rules are instrumental he is often expected to know the goal to which his rule-directed action supposedly contributes—to know "what he is doing" in this sense. Not always, to be sure, but often he could not make a sound judgment of when and how to apply the rule without this knowledge.

For both of these reasons it is a mistake to say, in a pedestrian and casuistical way, that "the criterion of right acts is the rules." It is a mistake to think of *every* exception and *every* case as somehow included in the rule. The motive for doing so, presumably to preserve the authority of rules, is mistaken: There is an important difference between interpreting a rule, or violating it *in special circumstances,* and deciding each individual case just as if there were no rules. A person subject to rules who follows the latter course merits a special kind of criticism. Although it is difficult to specify conditions in which the violation of an instrumental rule is proper, surely the bare fact, "that by doing so one can better promote the goal," is not sufficient. The rule follower is not the sole or final authority on the propriety of breaking a rule, even when it is for the benefit of the other party.

This brings us back to the independence of the two criteria. However, it should now be clear that these criteria are interrelated and operate together. Moreover, since there are two criteria in the case of rules of the present kind, it always *makes sense* to ask if an action right by the rules is also right in the respect that it is good that a rule prescribes it. It not only *makes sense* to speak of its being proper to violate a rule, "successful violations" tend to be commended.

## II

*2.0* As soon as rules of the foregoing kind have been described it is rather obvious that many moral theorists, intentionally or not, have cut moral rules to their pattern. Anyone who regards the standard of morally right action as itself a means to an end will have this tendency, and this is typically true of rule utilitarians: The distinctive characteristic of their theory is that a system of rules is the criterion of morally right action, and these rules in turn are to be judged good or bad according to the consequences which action on the rules either generally produces as a matter of fact, or would produce if people could be persuaded to follow them.[11] The consequence which has been thought to be critical in assessing the soundness of a system of rules has been variously identified, as "the happiness of all," "public utility," "security," "the general welfare," etc. Nevertheless, in spite of the difference in name and even in conception, this has been taken to be a consequence, real or possible, and as an end or goal which a good system of rules would first promote and then ensure. The question of which system of rules will be most successful in this respect generally has been thought to be, at least broadly speaking, empirical: Fact and practical experience will decide which system is best. The theory thus implies that the goal, and goal promoting action, both, in senses indicated earlier, are *logically* independent of any system of rules. This fundamentally instrumental and telic character of the system of rules, and indirectly of rule-directed action as well, is a distinctive feature of utilitarianism.[12] Moreover, as I pointed out above, it is an essential feature of rules of the foregoing kind that persons other than the rule follower are "interested" in the product; this "interest" is expressed in some kind of contract, convention, or law which gives the rules authority. In utilitarian theory the "party-in-authority" tends to be "the people"; directly or indirectly they enter conventions, "adopt" rules, then enforce them, so that all may share the fruits of the rule-directed action. The product is shared, the goal is the good of all.

*2.1* Moral rules on the rule utilitarian view thus have the basic characteristics of the rules which I discussed in (1). When the two are compared, and the analysis in (1) is brought to bear, it quickly reveals that rule utilitarianism is faced with a fundamental problem. If the position is to have the advantage over act utilitarianism that is claimed for it, then the criterion of right action must be a system of rules and not general utility. Rules are a criterion of right action, however, only on condition that they are "rules-in-force" and in some sense "agreed to." But obviously the rules which are "in force" or "agreed to" may or may not be the rules which maximize utility; and to the extent that they are not, then the "best rules" by the utilitarian standard, not having been "adopted," are not the criterion of right action. The best rules may not even be known. The "rules" and the "utilitarianism" in "rule utilitarianism" thus constitute two independent criteria, and they may not be in much accord.

*2.1.1* The analysis in (1) not only clearly shows the nature of this difficulty, but also helps one to understand some of the directions in which utilitarianism has moved in an effort to avoid it. Some good utilitarians, mindful of evil in ordinary conventions, tend to say that just as men *ought* to adopt a rule only if it maximizes utility, so one is *obligated* to follow a rule only if it maximizes utility. This doctrine implies that one may freely disregard a rule if ever he discovers that action on the rule is not maximally felicific, and in this respect makes moral rules like "practical maxims." It deprives social and moral rules of their authority and naturally is in sharp conflict with practice. On this alternative rule utilitarianism collapses into act utilitarianism.[13]

*2.1.2* Other rule utilitarians, equally concerned to avoid an ethical conventionalism, either close their eyes to the difficulty or else overlook it. They either just declare an ideal set of rules to be the criterion, or else say that the criterion of right action is the system of rules which, *if* adopted, *would* maximize utility, or something of the sort. Such a formulation clearly does not acknowledge that rules must be adopted if they are to be rules: The "if adopted" is only a way of describing the ideal and actually obscures the necessity of a rule's being adopted.

The fact that it is commonly the case that some moral principles and rules to which a person subscribes are not "in force" in his society raises important issues for *any* moral philosophy of rules. I cannot even try to do them justice here. Nevertheless, surely it is a mistake to maintain that a set of rules, thought to be ideally utilitarian or felicific, is the criterion of right action. If the rules are simply described in this way, and are not enumerated, we so far do not have any rules and are not likely to get any.[14] On the other hand, if we are presented with a list, but these are not rules in practice, the most one could reasonably do is to try to get them adopted. A manager in the quiet of his office may dream of a system of rules which will maximize production, and a utilitarian may build a theory around the set of rules which will maximize utility. Surely the latter would be as foolish as the former if he said that these ideal rules are the criterion of right and wrong acts. As previous analysis has shown, acts are not judged by proposed rules, ideal rules, and rules-in-theory: for these do not fully qualify as rules.[15]

*2.1.3* Other rule utilitarians show a finer appreciation of the logic of their position: They interpret moral rules on analogy with the rules in (1), even if it forces them to admit that the criterion of right action is not the set of rules which maximizes utility. This alternative seems to be popular with those whose primary allegiance is to a "morality of rules," and who are utilitarian only because they suppose that "welfare" *must* have something to do with morality. (After all, what else *can* serve as a criterion of rules?)

On this alternative it always makes sense to ask whether or not a "moral or social convention" subscribed to in practice is best, and this gives sense to the question, sometimes asked, whether a people who follow their conventions act in the best way they could. At the same time the question, whether an individual ought to do something in particular—for example, repay money borrowed—is quite a different question, to be answered by referring, at least in part, to the practices and conventions of that society. Such a view does not make the blunder of taking an ideal system of rules as the criterion of which particular acts are right, and yet it does not endorse conventions which are obviously questionable. One may seek earnestly to reform the moral conventions of a people, and yet insist that these conventions, some of which are in need of reform, are the general criterion by which a man must decide what in particular he ought to do, and by which his acts are to be judged. At the same time, such a view need not dichotomize the two criteria. As we found above, rules of this kind have an open texture which permits the criterion of the rules to enter into their proper interpretation. I think we may presume, moreover, that there are instances in which one should violate the letter of a moral rule when following it would clearly be to the detriment of the general welfare, or the welfare of all parties concerned. Rule utilitarians could no doubt take instances of this sort to support their theory. As we also found above, one may admit this without depriving rules of their authority.[16]

## III

*3.0* A careful development and criticism of rule utilitarianism, as just outlined, would be worth while, but it is outside the range of this paper. Even without this development, however, it can be shown that rule utilitarians, by using the kind of rule in (1) as a model, have exercised a definite option, and I want to indicate the general character of this option. To do this, I shall first consider briefly the rules of certain kinds of games.[17]

*3.1* Rules of common competitive games, such as baseball, chess, and the like, say how a game is to be played. They state the "object of the game," "the moves," "how the counting should go," etc. Often they are stated in "rule books," and sometimes they are enforced by referees appointed by an acknowledged authority. These formalities, however, are not at all necessary. The rules must be "laid down" or "adopted" in some sense, but all that is required (in the case of those games being discussed) is that a group of players "agree" on a set of rules. This agreement may consist simply in their following and enforcing rules which they all have learned: Think, for example, of a group of small boys playing baseball, and think of the difference between one's knowing the rules and playing the game. In such cases there is no formally agreed-upon authority; each player—in principle—is both rule-follower and rule-enforcer. No player has the authority to modify the rules at will, but the players together can change them in any way they see fit. As one should expect, there are many variations.

In the latter respects game rules of this kind are quite like the rules in (1). These game rules, however, noticeably lack the first major characteristic of those rules: They are not designed to yield a product. More precisely, they are not adopted to promote the attainment of a goal which, in the senses indicated earlier, is "over and beyond" the rules.[18] They do not serve a goal which is "logically independent" of the game which they define.

*3.1.1* Of course people who play games do so with various motives, and some of the goals which motivate them are logically independent of the game: for example, exercise, recreation, the opportunity to talk to friends or make a conquest. Undoubtedly games are popular because they serve so many ends. Nevertheless, motives and goals of this kind are not essential. Many players participate (so far as can be determined without psychoanalyzing them) "just because they want to" or simply "from love of the game." Actually this kind of motive, even if it is not typical, is that which is most distinctive of players: One who "loves a game" commonly regards another, who lacks the motive, as poorly appreciating "the quality of the game." This is apt to be missed just because games have been turned into instruments, for exercise, diversion, etc., to such a great degree. The point is, they *need* not be.

Moreover, games *qua* games do not seem to have a design or goal *different* from the motives of the rule-followers, in the way rules of jobs commonly do. What is this goal? One who most appreciates a game speaks about it rather as if it were an aesthetic object, worth playing on its own account and apart from any product or result; and if he is asked to justify his claim that it is good, he seems to have a problem analogous to that of justifying an aesthetic judgment.[19] Sometimes, to be sure, the rules of games are changed, and in particular instances violated, in order to change the consequences. Many official rules, for example, have been changed in order to lessen player injuries; and particular persons may find a game played by the official rules too strenuous, or pursuit of the ball after a bad drive too troublesome. These facts, however, do not imply that the rules are designed to produce consequences, such as the right amount of exercise or exertion, or the good health of the players. Changes of the kind mentioned simply indicate that the rules of a game, like the rules of a job, are adopted in a context by persons who have many desires and many obligations other than "to play the game" and "follow its rules." Games are often altered to make them harmonize better with such contextual features. It is true, of course, that persons who have turned games into instruments change or violate the rules more readily. As we say, these people do not take the game as seriously.

Some philosophers are inclined to say that even when one plays a game "just because he wants to" or "for love of the game," the game is still an instrument—to "his enjoyment" or "pleasure." This stand depends for its cogency on our being able to describe this pleasure or enjoyment without referring to the game, which should be possible if the pleasure or enjoyment really were something separate from playing the game. However, although it is clearly possible to play a game and not enjoy it, the converse does not appear plausible. To be sure, one sometimes says that he gets about the same enjoyment from one game as another, especially when the two are similar. But this is apt to mean that he has no strong preference for one game over another, that he likes one as well as the other, not that there is a kind of pleasurable feeling which in fact results from both, more or less equally, and which *conceivably* could be had from very different activities or even from being acted *on* in some way. (Similarly, when one says that he "likes to talk to one person about as much as another," this clearly does not mean that talking to the two persons produces the same kind of pleasure in him.) Moreover, when we speak of getting about the same enjoyment from two games, sometimes the "enjoyment" does not appear to be, strictly speaking, the enjoyment "of playing the game," but rather the enjoyment of exercising, talking to friends, etc. I do not deny, however, that games can become instruments. I want to argue that they need not be, often are not, and that in calling them games we do not imply that they are instruments.

The kind of goal the pursuit of which to some degree *is* essential to the playing of the game is the "object of the game," as defined by the rules, and the various sub-goals which promote this object according to the rules. Such goals as these, for example, "to score the most runs," "to get the batter out at second base," obviously are not logically independent of the rules of the game—if there were no rules it would be logically impossible to try to do these things. It is just nonsense to speak of changing the rules so that one can better attain the object of the game.

*3.1.2* Since the action within a game is designed to attain goals defined by the rules, the action as well as the goal logically depends on the rules: In important respects a move in the game has the consequences it has because the rules say it has; *in these respects* the rules define the consequences and determine the character of the action.[20] Since the character of instrumental action is fixed at least partly by the goal which the action is designed to serve, the action can be described in this essential respect, as a "trying to get the goal," without referring to or presupposing rules. In the case of play in a game, unless the game has become an instrument, this is not possible; if one describes the action in a game apart from the rules, as a "trying to catch a ball," he leaves out the design. On account of this difference one may feel inclined to say that whereas rules of the kind described in (1) *may* be used to describe an action, game rules by defining new kinds of action just constitute "forms of life."[21]

*3.2* However, this is but one side of the story, and if it were the only one it is not likely that the two kinds of rules would be confused. To see the other side, which is equally important, one should attend to the fact that the play in a game is not wholly defined by the rules of the game. "The kind of game he plays" ordinarily does not refer to the game as defined by the rules; "to play a game" ordinarily means more than following the rules. The point is that although the object of the game is defined by the rules, since the action in a game normally consists in "trying to attain that object," and since the game rules do not determine success in this respect, the action in *this* respect is instrumental. Players often develop tactics and strategies and skills in playing. Sometimes they follow what I have called practical maxims, and at other times they follow team rules agreed on among themselves or laid down by the "manager." The latter are, of course, examples of the rules described in (1). Obviously they should not be confused with rules of games, as I have described them. For one can be said to play a game without his following any particular set of instrumental rules.

The point of greatest importance here is that although game rules are not themselves instruments, they support, as it were, a considerable amount of instrumental activity, much of which logically could not be carried on without them. To play a game is typically to follow the rules of the game *and* engage in this instrumental activity; a "good player" does more than just follow the rules. Even one who "loves the game for its own sake" derives his satisfaction from the kind of *instrumental* activity which the rules of the game make possible. Games make new goals, new pursuits, and new skills available to men.

In this situation it is not surprising that some should regard games themselves as instruments. To regard them in this way, however, would be to confuse their function.

## IV

*4.0* The rules of games just considered differ most significantly from the rules described in (1) because they are, by our criterion, "non-instrumental." This point of difference between the two kinds of rules is one of the most important to be found. I have been concerned to mark it here to focus attention on the thesis, maintained by many utilitarians, that moral rules and social institutions are instruments designed to promote a goal logically independent of the rules and institutions. The thesis is only rarely discussed, and I think that failure to discuss it helps account for the recurrent popularity of utilitarianism. However, morality is obviously not a game, and if the thesis is to be fully assessed, moral rules must be carefully analyzed and alternatives considered. This is out of the question here. In the remainder of this paper I shall note a complexity which is too often overlooked, and just indicate the critical force of certain recently developed lines of argument. However, the fundamental issue here is not at all new.[22]

*4.1* Consider the rule "Do not cheat." Often it is taught in the context of a game, and it acquires a rather specific sense in this context. The rule in this use can be paraphrased as "Do not violate the rules of the game in order to gain an advantage for yourself." In this use the rule logically presupposes games as social institutions; if there were no games, the rule could not have this use and this meaning.

The same general point applies to many other moral rules, such as "Keep your promises," "Do not steal," and "Do not lie." Each of these logically presupposes institutions and practices, such as "promising," "a system of property," "a language." Since these moral rules presuppose such practices, they cannot be understood apart from them; the practice, constituted by its own rules, makes the moral rule meaningful. Philosophical analyses which have attempted to clarify moral rules apart from institutionalized practices have surrounded them with theoretical perplexities and turned them into "mere forms" of morality.[23]

However, the fact that these moral rules presuppose institutions or practices does not *in itself* decide the question whether or not they are instrumental and utilitarian. In some respects the rules "Do not cheat," "Do not lie," etc., are like the rules "Do not violate traffic lights," "Do not drive on the wrong side," etc. These rules obviously presuppose practices, and the rules and practices appear to be primarily instrumental and utilitarian. We can easily conceive of the practices being changed in order to provide a more effective system of traffic control.

On the utilitarian view moral rules and the institutions which they presuppose are rather like a system of this kind. The assumption is that men have various destinations which they want to reach and the social aim is to provide the system of institutions which will be most effective in helping them along. As men together devise such public instruments as roads and bridges, which no one alone could construct, and then regulate the use of these instruments for the "public good," so on this view men together have developed such institutions as "promising," "a system of property," etc. These institutions may not have arisen through deliberate design, although (there often seems to be the assumption that) if an institution or practice has arisen, then it *must* have been rewarding, and consequently *must* have served some purpose. The instrumental character of these institutions is evidenced more directly, however, by the fact that persons hold and dispose of property, make promises, and, quite generally, engage in the life of their institutions with goals in mind. If these reasons are decisive, moreover, one's language, too, should be viewed as a social tool.[24] Certainly men have purposes in speaking.

As in the case of a traffic system, however, on occasion it is to a person's advantage to break the rules of their institutions. Men must be taught not to; they must be made to realize that temporary advantage is far outweighed by the more permanent benefits to be gained if all can be depended on to follow the rules. Moral rules, such as "Keep your promises," "Do not steal," "Do not lie," like the rules "Always obey traffic signals," "Do not drive on the wrong side," seem to be conceived as deriving from the occasional but recurrent conflict between private advantage and public institutions. Utilitarians commonly make the point that if a person in his own interest is sometimes led to violate a rule, he will nevertheless insist, also in his own interest, that others follow the rule: The "security" which derives from a system of public institutions is given an important place in moral theory. Moral rules of this kind thus seem to be conceived as supports for and ancillary to the public institutions which they presuppose. If these rules could only be made to serve a system of truly *rational* (i.e., utilitarian) institutions, the aforementioned conflict would be minimized, as the happiness of all was promoted. The negative morality of rules would be lost in liberal affection for the general welfare.

4.2 Moral rules of this kind in a sense do *tend* to support the institutions and practices which they presuppose: They *tend* to receive their effective interpretation from the character of the institutions, and they are both taught and reaffirmed most vigorously when persons from self-interest show an inclination to violate the rules of the institutions. As a consequence (and for an additional reason which will soon be apparent[25]) these institutions and practices have, as it were, a "moral dimension" or a "moral part." Nevertheless, in assessing rule utilitarianism it is important to distinguish moral rules on the one hand from other rules which also define and characterize the underlying institutions and practices. For it is possible to learn the rules of a game, and to play the game, without being tempted to cheat, without grasping the concept of "cheating," and without learning the moral rule "Do not cheat." It is not uncommon for children to do this. Children ordinarily also learn to speak correctly, in the sense of learning many rules of the language, without learning the rule "Do not lie," thus without grasping the moral concept of a lie. It may not be so evident, but it is also the case that one can learn many rules governing property, can learn to make a promise, etc., without grasping the moral force of the rules "Do not steal," "Keep your promises," etc. There are surely legal experts on property and contract who have, as we say, very little moral understanding.[26]

In considering the soundness of rule utilitarianism, there are thus two interrelated questions. The first is whether or not the institutions of promising, property, language, etc., are instruments serving goals logically independent of these institutions. This bears on the question of the soundness of utilitarianism not only as a *moral* but as a *social* theory. Then there is the more restricted question whether rule utilitarianism offers a sound account of moral rules.

*4.3.1* Several lines of thought, some recently developed, bear on these questions. To take one example, primarily as it applies to the first of the questions: Utilitarians, as already indicated, have put considerable emphasis on "security," if not as *the* goal, nevertheless as an important "part" of the goal. A person cannot be "secure," however, without being able to *count on* others to act and refrain from acting in a variety of ways. His counting on others, moreover, is in a great many cases not "an expectation" based on an ordinary induction. For most often the expectation involved in one's counting on another is based on the fact that the action or restraint in question is governed by rules which define rights, obligations, duties, etc.: One can count on another because the other (presumably) is acting on such rules.[27] For this reason the expression "counting on another" in many occasions of its use makes no more sense apart from rules than "deciding to act" or "acting" makes apart from reasons for acting. There is also the related point that the action which one counts on another to do, itself, in many cases presupposes rules; for example, just as one could not count on a person to "play first base" if there were no game of baseball, so one could not count on another to "keep his promise" or "respect property" if there were no practice of promising or institution of property.[28] Although "security" is an ambiguous term, in the sense in which it refers to a significant social goal it could not mean what it does without rules which define institutions and practices.

For both these reasons "security" just does not appear to be a goal which is logically independent of the rules of institutions and practices like property, promising, language, etc. Moreover, it would seem very strange to think of the greatest number having the greatest happiness or pleasure or welfare without being fairly secure. The utilitarian position thus appears to be quite vulnerable, even apart from the fact that its proponents have notoriously failed to give "happiness," "pleasure," "welfare," and the like the clarity of meaning which they must have to function as goals.

4.3.2 Furthermore, as the earlier analysis of games revealed, the fact that one does many things as a means to an end when engaging in a practice gives no support to the claim that the practice itself is a means. The fact that one uses various devices to win a game does not imply that the game is an instrument, and similarly, the fact that one uses words as tools, or makes a promise or deals in property for some purpose, does not support the view that institutions and practices such as language, promising, and property are instruments for the promotion of goals logically independent of these institutions and practices. Nor does this appear plausible: It seems rather to be the case that institutions and practices create or establish most of the goals which men pursue, in the sense that these goals, like the object of a game, would be logically impossible without the institutions and practices. It also appears that persons who engage in business, or make speeches, or follow intellectual pursuits ultimately because "they just enjoy doing these things" are rather like players who enjoy a game for its own sake—in the respect that they derive their enjoyment from instrumental activity which is also made possible by institutions and practices.

At this point, however, it becomes apparent that much requires to be worked out before one can replace the utilitarian view of social institutions with another which is more adequate.

4.4 When one turns to consider utilitarianism as a theory of moral rules, *to some extent* the same arguments apply. For some moral rules *are* in some respects ancillary to the practices and institutions which they presuppose, and in so far as this is the case, then generally speaking moral rules are just as utilitarian as, and no more utilitarian than, these practices and institutions.

Notice that the most common uses of the moral rules "Do not lie," "Do not steal," and the like presuppose not only underlying institutions and practices, but also, as suggested above, a tendency or inclination of some persons at some times not to conform to the institutions and practices. This seems to explain why persons living in a law-abiding community use these moral rules so little. This in turn suggests that moral rules are "protective devices," rather like a police system, which also is little used in a law-abiding community and which also presupposes both institutions and an inclination on the part of some persons to violate them. The "police" view of moral rules is partial, but it is also partly true: It helps one see why moral rules are so often conceived as "external" to an individual, imposing restraints on him (and why some philosophers tend to pattern moral rules on rules in a prison!). At the same time it helps one understand why some people "internalize" moral rules in the way they do. For some insist on the importance of following moral rules only because they value a system of institutions and the "happiness and security" which the institutions afford. Seeing that valued institutions would cease to exist if people generally did not act in the way moral rules prescribe, they teach these rules—although morality for them is primarily a matter of promoting individual or public welfare, and it would be better if moral rules had little use. This interest in morality is epitomized in the person who regards moral rules as a protector of life, liberty, and property; breaking the rules breeds fear, ruins business, and disrupts the game. This is the internalization of moral rules as ancillary to institutions; it tends to characterize utilitarians past and present.

*4.5* Moral rules, however, may be internalized in quite another way, and on this account utilitarianism as a *moral* theory is open to an additional criticism specific to itself.

For a person who values an institution constituted by rules may come to see that rules by nature apply to all members of a class. One who sees this may then be led to look upon the rules which characterize some particular institutions and practices not simply as "applying to all," but at the same time as constituting "a common standard of correctness." And in this way one may be led to the abstract but practical conception of "a community of men living under the idea of law," of which particular institutions afford so many possible examples. In so far as one thinks that others as well as himself act under this conception, he will no doubt value a particular game or language or any other such institution not only *qua* game, *qua* language, etc., but also as a particular instance and a particular form of such a community.

When the idea of such a community is attained and made to govern practice (as it seems to have been, for example, by the Socrates of the *Crito*) then the moral rules "Do not lie," "Do not steal," etc., will appear in a new light. One who acts under such an idea will teach these rules neither as primarily negative and restraining, nor primarily as supports or protections for particular institutions. For although he may view the rules in these ways, he will regard them primarily as affirming in so many different ways the fundamental principle "Live under the idea of law." The principle may be stated negatively, in the form "Do not make an exception of oneself," but his primary aim in teaching the rules will be to raise one to the conception of a moral community. Since such a community potentially includes all men, part of the challenge may be to find particular institutions in which the conception can be realized.

Moral rules regarded in this way of course still presuppose particular institutions and practices. However, they are no longer, properly speaking, "ancillary to" the institutions and practices: They now "add something" to the institutions and practices which they presuppose; the institutions and practices now have a new dimension. Cheating comes to be deplored not primarily because it tends to disrupt a game but because it detracts from the quality which a game can have. If there is cheating, one may simply prefer not to play. In a similar way, lying may be deplored because it detracts from the quality of speech, theft because it detracts from the quality of exchange, etc. Put affirmatively, the idea of a moral community is realizable analogically—only in a variety of forms—in sportsmanship, morally mature speech, honest argument, etc. It should be evident that common institutions and practices are often not in fact logically independent of morality; one has to form a limited or abstract conception of them to make them so.

When moral rules are regarded in this way,[29] then obviously they do not serve a goal logically independent of themselves. In the language of Mill, virtue has now become a "part" of the end, a "part of happiness." Only it is clear that when Mill said this, with his usual willingness to sacrifice theory to good sense, he deserted utilitarianism. The instrumental and utilitarian pattern just will not fit.

## V

Further discussion of moral rules is beyond the aim of this paper. My primary purpose has been to contribute to the clarification of moral rules by clarifying a fundamental option open to moral theory. To this end I have both analyzed the general utilitarian view of social rules and practices, along with some variations, and I have tried to lay bare the (largely implicit) utilitarian view of moral rules. I have analyzed moral rules, however, only to the point where the character and significance of the option, and the force of some of the arguments which apply, will be fairly clear. I do not want to suggest that all moral rules are like those which I have considered. The analysis of games, in distinguishing the moral player from the good player, may remind one that there are two traditions in the history of ethics, one emphasizing an exoteric ethic and a moral law known to all, the other an esoteric ethic and a virtue reserved for the wise. I have been concerned, almost exclusively, with the former, and not all of that.

In the course of the discussion attention has been called to the fact that moral rules can be (and thus tend to be) conceived as summaries, reports, practical maxims, rules designed to promote a goal, rules which define institutions, rules which protect institutions, and as particular forms of the fundamental principle of justice.[30] Marking the important differences between these alternatives should remove more than one confusion and at the same time provide *some* of the subtlety which will be needed if the discussion of moral rules is to make genuine advances in the future.

## Notes

1. "Two Concepts of Rules," *Philosophical Review,* vol. 64 (1955), pp. 29–30. [In this volume, p. 327.]
2. Cf. e.g., R. B. Brandt, *Ethical Theory* (Englewood Cliffs, N.J., 1959), chap. 15.
3. K. Baier, *The Moral Point of View* (Ithaca, N.Y., 1958), pp. 200–204.
4. "Justice as Fairness," *Philosophical Review,* vol. 67 (April, 1958), pp. 164–194. It will be clear that Rawls's analysis in "Two Concepts of Rules" does not support a utilitarian theory.
5. Cf. Max Black, "Notes on the Meaning of 'Rule'," *Theoria,* vol. 24 (1958), pp. 121–122; reprinted in his *Models and Metaphors* (Ithaca, N.Y., 1962), pp. 95–139.
6. Practical maxims should not be dismissed, however, as "mere rules of thumb" on the one hand, or as "simply stating relations between means and ends" on the other. When one follows a maxim the rule *directs* action and is a *criterion* of certain kinds of rightness and wrongness in acting.

In passing note that Rawls's "summary conception," as a whole, does not properly apply to practical maxims, although several features of this conception do apply. Rawls's analysis, admirable as it is, is very apt to mislead. For the "summary view," as he calls it, is a blend of two quite distinct conceptions: In part it is a confused conception or a misconception of a rule, as a summary or report. In other respects it is an accurate conception of what I have called a practical maxim. This may account for an ambivalence in Rawls's article: Cf. ". . . it is doubtful that anything to which the summary conception did apply would be called a *rule.*" [(p. 23) "Two Concepts . . ." (In this volume, p. 323)] with "Some rules will fit one conception, some rules the other; and so there are rules of practices (rules in the strict sense), and maxims and 'rules of thumb.'" (p. 29) [In this volume, p. 328.] The point is that maxims are rules in a *different* sense from other kinds of rules, whereas no rule, *qua rule,* is a summary or report.

The importance of this point is that there are two possible confusions here, not one: A person may conceive moral rules as summaries or reports, or he may conceive moral rules on the model of maxims. The texts of Austin and Mill, which Rawls cites, together with Rawls's discussion, suggest that the latter, more than the former, was their mistake. *V.*, however, note 13 below.

7. Cf. my "Technical Ought," *Mind,* vol. 69 (1960), July issue.

8. Cf. Rawls, ibid., p. 22.

9. Cf. Black, pp. 120–121. Black's analysis of the "laying down of rules" in terms of "promulgator activities" and "subject activities" (pp. 139–146) is illuminating, as is H. L. A. Hart's recent analysis of the complex idea of "acceptance" in the case of the law. *V. The Concept of Law* (Oxford, 1961), chaps. IV–VI, esp. pp. 107–114.

10. Cf. Hume's remarks on the need of a "determinate rule of conduct," or "general rules," in his discussions of justice, both in the *Treatise* and *Inquiry.* Hume, however, does not make precisely the same point.

11. See, for example, J. O. Urmson's "The Interpretation of the Moral Philosophy of J. S. Mill," *Philosophical Quarterly,* vol. 3 (1953), pp. 33–39. By and large I agree with this interpretation of Mill, although Mill showed other tendencies, not only toward a more radical utilitarianism but, in the opposite direction, toward the ethics of Bradley. John Austin is sometimes said to be a good representative of this point of view, but his conception of moral rules as commands, learned in the way we learn practical maxims, is a hodgepodge (see *The Province of Jurisprudence Determined,* Lectures I-III). In *some* respects Hume's discussion of the artificial virtues, especially justice, is a much better (and perhaps the best) classical example of this type of theory.

Among contemporaries (and apart from useful textbook presentations: see Brandt, loc. cit., and J. Hospers, *Human Conduct*) S. Toulmin in *The Place of Reason in Ethics* and P. H. Nowell-Smith in *Ethics* have come closest to an explicit statement of the theory.

An examination of actual cases of this kind of theory, with all the proper qualifications, especially if the theory is extended beyond utilitarianism, would require considerable space. I do not undertake the historical investigation here. In my judgment, the theory has a popularity which exceeds its merit, and some tendencies which are pernicious (see Section IV below). By isolating the germ, the disease may be better understood—its valuable antibodies notwithstanding.

12. It would be a mistake to say that utilitarians maintained this deliberately, after considering alternatives, or even that they did so consistently. John Stuart Mill, in Chapter IV of *Utilitarianism,* seems to have been unaware of the issue when he discussed happiness as "a concrete whole" and virtue as one of its "parts." Cf. below 4.5.

13. For a clear recent statement of this position, see J. J. C. Smart, "Extreme and Restricted Utilitarianism," *Philosophical Quarterly,* vol. 6 (1956), pp. 344–354. Notice that Smart argues explicitly that moral rules are "rules of thumb."

14. Cf. above, *1.3.1.*

15. See *1.2* and *1.3.1* above. Since utilitarianism is rather often associated with reform, it tends to be formulated in ideal terms. See, for example, J. S. Mill's most explicit statement of his position in Ch. II, paragraph 10 of *Utilitarianism.* ". . . the standard of morality, which may accordingly be defined 'the rules and precepts for human conduct', by the observance of which an existence such as has been described might be, to the greatest extent possible, secured to all mankind . . ." In this passage, how is "possible" to be taken? Does it mean "possible, within the framework of existing institutions?" For one attempt to avoid in this way the difficulties inherent in an ideal formulation, see R. B. Brandt, op. cit., pp. 396–400. This attempt goes only part of the way in meeting the difficulty. On the difficulty itself cf. H. J. McCloskey, "An Examination of Restricted Utilitarianism," *Philosophical Review,* vol. 66 (1957), esp. pp. 475–481; and J. Austin, op. cit., Lecture III.

16. I think this is the most favorable interpretation which can be given to the utilitarianism of the nineteenth century reformers: They framed a theory which would make sense of reform, but at the same time had too much practical (if not always philosophical) sense to advocate the use of the criterion of rules as the criterion of acts. It is as if they perceived the importance of moral rules and practices but were unable fully to accommodate these to their theory. I think that the presence of the two criteria, which the analysis of the rules in (1) clearly reveals, explains for example the "tension" between chapter two of Mill's *Utilitarianism* on the one hand, and chapters three and five on the other.

17. I can be brief because rules of this kind have been discussed

by others. I shall mostly confine myself to points not previously mentioned, or at least not emphasized. I am perhaps most indebted to Rawls's acute analysis of what he calls the "practice conception," and on the whole agree with it. The name is misleading since very many "practices," as we ordinarily think of them, are defined by rules (e.g. by job rules) which are quite unlike those to which his "practice conception of rules" properly applies. Although unimportant in itself, it is just this kind of thing, I suspect, which has led moral philosophers into serious error. One can sympathize since it is almost impossible to find a conventional expression which is not misleading in some important respect.

18. Some games have become instruments to such a considerable degree, and some instrumental activities have become so much like games, that no description will prevent the intrusion of dubious and borderline cases.

19. This reminds one of the ancient distinctions between "doing" and "making," and between (what the medievals called) "immanent" and "transitive" activity. I do not mean to deny that some jobs are worth doing "on their own account," but even when "one enjoys a job," there is a discernible purpose which it is designed to promote.

20. This is the point which Rawls emphasized.

21. Cf. A. I. Melden, "Action," *Philosophical Review*, vol. 65 (1956), pp. 523–541. [Reprinted in this volume.]

22. Historically one perhaps first senses the issue in his reading of Plato and Aristotle. Is man's end somehow "writ in his nature" in such a way that it can be determined apart from a determination of virtue? If so, it might be reasonable to regard virtue as a *means* to the end, and instruction in virtue as a matter of learning from practical experience the best means. On the other hand, if man's end cannot be determined without the determination of virtue—if man's end is properly defined in terms of virtue, as activity in accordance with it, and man's nature is defined as potentialities for this end—then virtue is not a means and its discovery in practical experience must be understood differently. Although the second interpretation is the sounder, there were tendencies in medieval thought to favor the first—undoubtedly deriving from the fact that God, who is certainly different from man, was said to be man's end. Moreover, the desire of God was said to be implanted in man's nature. This inclination was said to be a natural participation of the eternal law, and natural virtue was said to be an insufficient means to God. I think myself, however,

that the second interpretation gives a sounder account of the ethics not only of Augustine but also of Aquinas. Yet it is not surprising that out of this tradition there should have come the contrary (Lockian) doctrine that natural law applies to man in a "state of nature," and that men by compact make societies as a remedy for natural evils and as a means to natural goals. This doctrine in turn, by way of reaction, stimulated theories according to which the distinction of right and wrong is not founded in nature, but in contract, convention, or rules. In the nineteenth century the opposition between the two general points of view assumed more of its original form when idealists worked out their own interpretation of the social contract, and opposed utilitarianism. (See, for example, Bradley's "Pleasure for Pleasure's Sake" in *Ethical Studies* and Bosanquet's *Philosophical Theory of the State.*) Very recent philosophy in some respects strongly resembles idealism, undoubtedly because it itself is a reaction to a kind of philosophy which arose in reaction to idealism. For one example, cf. Bosanquet, op. cit., with A. I. Melden, *Rights and Right Conduct* (Oxford, 1959).

This is, of course, only a fragmentary account of the historical origins of the issue.

23. This misinterpretation accounts for some criticisms of a morality of rules. Cf. A. Macbeath, *Experiments in Living* (London, 1952), Lecture XIII.

24. Cf. Hume's *Treatise,* III, II, II. Esp. p. 490 in Selby-Bigge edition.

25. See 4.5 below.

26. Although an adequate description of property and promising in a sense implies that theft and promise-breaking are morally wrong, a person may fail to "see" the implication. When we teach a child what property and promising are, we commonly say that it is wrong for him to take what belongs to another and wrong for him not to do what he has promised to do. So far, however, the child is not guilty of theft or promise-breaking, and until he has witnessed them, or an inclination thereto, in himself or another (since he has not yet had occasion to *use* the rules "Do not steal" and "Keep your promises"), he will have little practical understanding of these rules. Before he reaches this point, however, he may have learned enough of the underlying rules to exchange property, make promises, etc. Growth in moral understanding is long and complex and participation in ordinary practices does not wait upon it.

27. Cf. Hart, op. cit., pp. 54–7.

28. Cf. Hume, loc. cit. Black and many others make the same point.

29. Cf. K. Baier, op. cit., pp. 200–204, and W. D. Falk's comments on "natural obligation" and "mature moral thinking" in "Morality and Convention," *Journal of Philosophy,* vol. 57 (1960), pp. 675–685.

30. The list is not meant to be exhaustive. Cf. e.g., D. S. Shwayder, "Moral Rules and Moral Maxims," *Ethics,* vol. 67 (1957), pp. 269–285.

P. J. FITZGERALD

# Voluntary and Involuntary Acts*

The problem of defining an act owes its importance partly to the constant recurrence throughout the common law of a certain theme, namely the requirement of an act. This is exemplified in the Law of Contract by the proposition that acceptance must be something more than a mere mental assent; it must be by words or conduct.[1] In the Law of Torts we find that a man who has been carried bodily and against his will onto the land of another has been held not liable in trespass because there was no act on his part;[2] and in fact it has been suggested that in general a tort consists in some act done by the defendant whereby he has without just cause or excuse caused some form of harm to the plaintiff.[3] But nowhere is this requirement so clearly seen as in the Criminal Law, where it manifests itself in the rule that *mens rea* by itself is not enough to constitute a crime: there must be an *actus reus*. Even in the case of attempts to commit crimes where the criminal intent is the dominant factor, the prosecution must prove the commission of an *actus reus* sufficient to amount to an attempt.

This problem of defining an act gains further significance from the recognition by the Common Law that certain conduct, involuntary conduct, does not involve the actor in any responsibility because it is said there is in reality no act on his part. For this reason it becomes necessary to define the term 'act' to

* From *Oxford Essays in Jurisprudence* (1961) edited by A. G. Guest. Reprinted by permission of the author and the Clarendon Press, Oxford.

provide the test by which we can decide whether a man's conduct should involve him in any responsibility.

Difficulties arise, however, when jurists try to produce a satisfactory definition, and these difficulties are generated by the confusion of two separate questions: (1) what is an act?; and (2) when is conduct involuntary? The answer to (1) will not provide a complete solution to (2), if for no other reason than that it takes no account of the problems of involuntary omission. Nor will the answer to (2) give us the whole answer to (1), since this question includes such problems as the place and time of an act. To answer (1), we must consider the use lawyers make of the word, and examine how far this use diverges from the ordinary usage of the word.

## The Need for an Act

This notion of the need for an act is a complex thread and at the outset we should do well to try and disentangle some of the various strands.

### (1) *Physical and mental acts*

One such strand is the distinction between physical acts on the one hand, and thoughts, intentions, etc. on the other. This is the distinction that is being made when it is said that acceptance in the Law of Contract must be more than just a mere mental assent. Here what one might call mental acts are being excluded as not sufficient for the purpose of the law. The same is true to some extent of the need in Criminal Law for an *actus reus,* which also rules out as insufficient mere thoughts and intentions. One reason advanced for this requirement of an act is the difficulty of proof of such thoughts; as Bryan C.J. remarked, 'The intention (*l'entent*) of a man cannot be tried.' But this could hardly be a conclusive reason, for the Courts frequently decide what the accused thought and intended, and they could infer this from what he did and said. Every jury that convicts a person of larceny must be satisfied that he intended, at the time of taking, to deprive the owner permanently of the property. Another reason that is put forward is the need for objectivity. Unless there were some external, observable conduct on the part of the offeree, no-one (and especially the offeror) could tell whether the offer had been accepted or not. For, as Bryan C.J. continued, 'The devil himself knows not the intention of a man'. So until disputes and litigation arise on the matter, no-one can know (save the offeree) whether there is a contract or not.

But so far as Criminal Law is concerned, the reason why there must be an *actus reus* is partly something more important, namely, the idea that to punish mere intention, and make offences of 'thought crime', is too great an intrusion into individual liberty and privacy. Although the law seeks to protect society from harmful conduct, and intentions to commit crimes are potentially harmful in that they may lead to the commission of crimes, yet the interests of the individual must be weighed and a balance must be struck between the freedom of the citizen and the safety of the community. There is, however, a further difficulty that even if it were thought desirable to have such control over men's thoughts, the enforcement of such control might well be impossible.

## (2) *Acts and omissions*

Another strand in this notion is the distinction between acts and omissions. Only rarely does the law impose a positive duty to act. For instance a bystander has no legal duty to save a small child from drowning. The finder of a lost article has no duty to restore it to its owner, even though he knows who the owner is. The duty not to misrepresent in the Law of Contract does not normally amount to a positive duty to disclose all the information you have. In general, the law is content to say

'Thou shalt not kill, steal or deceive'. It will not take the further step and say 'Thou shalt preserve life, restore goods to the owner, disclose all the information you have'. Before this further step is taken there must usually be shown to exist some special relationship between the parties, which gives rise to this extra positive duty. For example, the bystander must be in charge of the child. The contact must be *uberrimae fidei.* The basis of this attitude seems again to be this same reluctance of the law to encroach too much on individual liberty. While ready to penalize conduct that harms a man's neighbours, the Courts feel that to ordain the performance of conduct that will benefit one's neighbours would restrict freedom unduly and place too great a burden on the individual. So the rule that you are to love your neighbour (a positive command) is narrowed in law to the prohibition, you must not injure your neighbour.

### (3) *Control*

The most difficult distinction, however, is that between acts over which a man has control, and happenings over which he has no control. There is a general principle that a man should not be punished, or have to pay damages, for occurrences over which he could exercise no control. To penalize him in this way would seem not only unfair, because he had no choice in the matter, but also inefficacious, because it would not prevent similar occurrences in the future.

Accordingly the law does not generally hold someone responsible for the operations of nature or the acts of third parties, since both these are outside his control. To hold *A* responsible for whatever harm befalls *B*, either because of the act of *C* or because of some natural event such as the falling of a tree, would be wholly unreasonable, in the absence of special circumstances, since it would be to constitute *A* an insurer of *B*'s safety. Even where *A* has himself been negligent in the first place, he may escape liability on the ground that *C*'s act, or the falling of the tree, amounted to a *novus actus interveniens.* On the other hand, there are exceptions. On some occasions, despite *C*'s act or the natural event, *A* may still be held responsible:

(i) Perhaps he should have foreseen that *C* might have done what he did, and have taken precautions to guard against this, *e.g.*, a man who leaves a horse unattended in a street should foresee that mischievous children might play with it.[4] A person who leaves the door of a house open should foresee that thieves might enter and steal things from the house.[5]

(ii) Or it may be that the situation created by *A* is so fraught with danger that he must become the insurer of *B*. If *A* chooses to keep a lion and *C* wrongfully lets it loose so that it mauls *B*, *A* will still have to compensate *B* for his injuries.[6]

(iii) Or the third party may in fact be someone over whom *A* has control. *A* may for instance be already liable in negligence for failing to keep under control his small child, if that child subsequently injures *B*. Or the third party may be the servant of *A*, acting in the course of his employment.

Nor is the law in general concerned with what a man is, but only with what he does, since he may choose what he does, but not what he is. As Holmes observed, 'It is felt to be impolitic and unjust to make a man answerable for harm unless he might have chosen otherwise'.[7] Here again the law is refusing to hold a man liable for something outside his control. Being found by night in a building with intention to commit a felony therein, and kindred offences against Section 28 of the Larceny Act, 1916, are not complete exceptions to this principle, since even here there is this much choice, that the prisoner need not have gone to or have been in that building with that intention. This is why so much dissatisfaction was aroused by the case of *Larsonneur*,[8] who was convicted of being found in the United Kingdom contrary to orders made under the Aliens Restriction Act, when in fact she had been brought to England under police custody and was found in a police cell, since she indeed had no choice at all in the matter.

The third and most difficult species of event over which the defendant has no control is the class of involuntary acts: the bodily movements outside his control such as reflex actions, heart beats, etc. It is chiefly this type of involuntary act that has given rise to the problem and led to the various attempts to formulate a satisfactory definition of an act in order to exclude these involuntary occurrences from liability on the ground that they are less than acts. Whereas in the first type of case where *B*'s injury results from *C*'s act, we say of *A* that it is not *his* act; in this type of case, if *B*'s injury results from a reflex action on *A*'s part, we say that it is not his *act.* So instead of asking what makes conduct involuntary, jurists have asked what exactly is an act.

## The Definition of an Act

Holmes' celebrated definition of an act as a willed muscular contraction, in which he followed Austin, contains two noteworthy features. The first of these seems at first sight, if perhaps unhelpful, at least innocuous: namely, the requirement that the muscular contraction should be willed. For a spasm, he argues, is not an act.[9] The other curious feature is the way Holmes restricts the term 'act' to cover only the movement of the actor's muscles or limbs, and excludes from his definition everything that follows. If *A* shoots and kills *B*, according to Holmes, *A*'s act is the willed contraction of his finger on the trigger of the gun. The firing of the gun, the bullet leaving the barrel and hitting *B*, and *B*'s falling dead, these are all consequences of *A*'s act, but not actually part of it. The reason for this oddly narrow interpretation of the term 'act', is perhaps the search for something for which to hold the actor absolutely responsible, something over which he has absolute power of control, and so complete choice. Over the firing of the gun, the bullet's hitting *B*, and *B*'s falling dead, he clearly lacks this complete control, for the gun may jam; the bullet may be deflected by a sudden gust of wind; and *B* may be saved by the bullet lodging in the bible given to him by his great-grandmother. What Holmes calls consequences are not so entirely dependent on *A*, it seems, as the original act of pulling the trigger.

But if we want something completely dependent on the will of the actor, may we not be forced logically to take a further step and claim that the only thing over which *A* has complete control is his process of willing? He lacks this control over the firing of the gun. It is something that usually ensues, but may on occasion fail, for the gun may jam. But the same could be said, surely, of *A*'s muscular contraction when he pulls the trigger. This 'motion of the body consequent on the determination of the will,' as Austin termed it, usually succeeds the act of willing (whatever that may be), but in one case in a million perhaps it might not do so, and we should recognize the onset of paralysis. Though such failure to follow may be exceedingly rare, the important fact is not the rarity, but the possibility of failure, since this suggests that the difference between *A*'s control over the firing of the gun and his control over the contraction of his finger is only one of degree. *A* can be much more sure that the finger will contract than he can that the gun will fire; but he cannot be absolutely certain of either. Indeed Holmes marvelled at the 'mysterious accuracy with which the adult, who is master of himself, foresees the outward adjustment which would follow his inward effort',[10] but his view of what an act is seems to lead to the result that no adult is really master of himself at all, and that since he only *foresees* but is not certain that his muscles will obey his will, his only control is over what goes on inside his mind. But if it is only with regard to these mental acts that *A* is in real control, should we not then have to conclude (if we still demand that *A* should only be punished for actions over which he has control) that he should only be punished for his mental acts; and that it is these mental occurrences with which the law is really concerned. It is as though it were not the man we see in the dock in whom we are really interested, but rather some inner figure who pulls the strings that cause (usually) the prisoner's muscles to contract. So that we should inquire not whether *A* shot and killed *B*, nor even whether *A*'s finger contracted and pulled the trigger due to an exercise of will on *A*'s part, but rather whether there was a determination of the will that took place in *A*'s mind. Yet clearly this is not the investigation that we make in the Courts. Nor does common sense dictate that it should be. Jurists have examined the notion of an act in order to illuminate the investigation we should make when faced with the problem of involuntary behaviour. The procedure should be reversed. Closer attention to the investigation we do make in cases of involuntary acts will help in effect to illuminate the notion of an act.

It might be objected that Holmes never meant to put forward a complete theory which would be thoroughly satisfactory from a philosophical point of view. All he aimed at providing us with was a rough test of what an act was; and this suffices for practical purposes. But it is for practical purposes precisely that this definition is unhelpful, because it conflicts with the general notion of what an act is. Whatever an act is, both in and out of court, we use the term in a way quite different from Holmes' way. 'Caught in the act', for example, conjures up a picture of the burglar creeping away with the swag over his shoulder; of the murderer standing over his victim, bloody knife in hand: not of a criminal contracting various muscles. So we speak of the act of stealing, and the act of shooting, and of a thousand other kinds of act. The 'act of contracting the finger' describes only the rare case when the accused tried to pull the trigger, but failed, and even here the normal description is "the act of attempting to shoot". This is why we demur at Holmes' conclusion that all acts are indifferent *per se* legally. Of course in his sense they must be (unless there were a statute prohibiting a certain willed muscular contraction) until we take into account the surrounding circumstances and the consequences of the contraction. But in the way we normally talk of acts it is quite untrue to say that they are legally indifferent *per se*. The reason why the act of stealing, the act of murdering, or the act of dangerous driving, are not so legally indifferent is precisely because the act in each of these cases includes all the surrounding circumstances and consequences which attract the condemnation of the law.

This restricted definition of an act is also liable to create difficulties in connection with the question of the locality of an act. Suppose *A*, standing in state *X*, shoots at and kills *B*, standing in state *Y*, to decide whether the courts of either state have jurisdiction to try *A*, it may be necessary to decide where the murder took place. The restricted definition might lead to the conclusion that it took place in state *X*, because it was there that *A* pulled the trigger. Whereas the ordinary use of the term 'act', may allow us to say that the act was begun in state *X* and completed in state *Y*, and therefore the courts of state *Y* should have jurisdiction in such a case. And it has been held that murder is committed in the place where the death occurs.[11] This can be reconciled with Holmes' theory only by distinguishing between the crime of murder and the act (pulling the trigger) which is only part of the crime. Yet the courts do not seem to distinguish in this way, as may be seen perhaps from the case of *R.* v. *Jarmain.*[12] Here the argument was that since the accused's gun fired without his consciously pulling the trigger, there was no act on his part and therefore he was not guilty of murder. The Court of Criminal Appeal, however, held that there was an act on his part, namely the act of robbery with violence and that as death resulted the accused was guilty.

Hence Salmond asserted that 'an act has no *natural* boundaries, any more than an event or a place has. Its limits must be artificially defined for the purpose in hand for the time being. It is for the law to determine, in each particular case, what circumstances and what consequences shall be counted within the compass of the act with which it is concerned. To ask what act a man has done is like asking in what place he lives.'[13] He also argued that the distinction between an act and its consequences is merely a verbal one; a matter of convenience of speech. But the fact that the question may be verbal does not entail that it is trivial. If the word 'act' were used in such a way that without a willed muscular contraction there is no act, Jarmain might not have been hanged. Indeed, it is true to say that many of the problems facing the courts are verbal problems. Once the facts have been found, *e.g.* that *A* stabbed *B* and Dr. *C* failed to treat *B* adequately, and *B* died, then the Court has to decide whether on these facts it would be right to say that *A* caused *B*'s death. Similarly, if *A*, intending to burn *B*'s haystack, takes out of his pocket a box of matches and runs over to the stack and then does no more, the court must decide whether, if these facts are proved, they amount to attempted arson. In all these cases, after the factual dispute has been settled, there then arises what may be called the verbal dispute, the problem of classifying the defendant's conduct—is what he did to count as murder, attempted arson, etc.? But none of these disputes are any the less difficult, or important, for being verbal.

The difficulty of such verbal disputes stems from the fact that the general meaning of the terms, *e.g.* 'attempt', 'murder', 'cause', has been set and, though it may be hard to draw the line in a given case, it is easy to find cases well to one side or other of the line. What the courts have to decide is whether the features of the border-line case are more akin to the cases on the one side or to those on the other. And remembering the important consequences that will follow from their decision, they must be guided by various principles in deciding with which group of cases to classify the border-line case. What the court is not free to do is to define the word (attempt, murder, cause) as it pleases. With regard to the problem of defining an act, it has been said that a person is free to define a word as he pleases.[14] One is free to do so, provided one remembers (and one never does) that this arbitrary way of using the word is different from the usual way of using it, and that when lawyers ask what is an act, they are concerned with the way the term is used in legal argument, and not with any special use that some writer might decide to make of the term.

One reason for the unhelpfulness of trying to elucidate criteria of responsibility by demanding an act on the defendant's part, and then by defining what an act is, is that it reverses to some extent the procedure of ordinary language, because in ordinary speech the word 'act', together with such allied expressions as '*A* did it', is used not so much to describe what has happened, as to ascribe responsibility.[15] In so far as the word 'act' is not being used to mark such distinctions as those referred to above, *e.g.* the distinction between acts and omissions; between acts and words (actions speak louder than words); or between acts, words and thoughts (we sin in thought, word and deed) the word is used to impute responsibility. '*A*'s act caused *B*'s death' is less a way of describing what has happened, than another way of saying that it was *A*'s fault. 'It was not *A*'s act at all' (*e.g.* because he was having an epileptic fit) is another way of saying that we should not blame *A* in this case because of some special feature in the situation.

Holmes suggested that the special feature was the lack of volition. One drawback of this approach is that it suggests that what we investigate in each case is whether the bodily movement was preceded or accompanied by some interior process. In certain cases it may be that before a man does something he goes through some such process of setting himself to do it, *e.g.* if it is something very difficult to do, but the vast majority of cases where a man does something do not contain any such feature, nor do we look for one when we consider his conduct, whether in court or out of court.

A further difficulty arises with regard to omissions. In those cases where a man is held criminally or civilly liable for an omission, it is quite clear that he may be held liable even though he never applied his mind to the matter at all. In fact he may be held liable just for not having applied his mind.

There may be, of course, the rare case where he might deliberately refuse to apply his mind, or where he might deliberately refrain from doing what the law enjoins; but the usual case of omission is that of the man who just fails to act without thinking about it at all. And here it is quite untrue to say that there has been any process of willing. Any test of responsibility must surely take into account the case of omissions, and just as there are cases where a man may not be held responsible for what he has done, *e.g.* while asleep, so there are cases where he may not be held responsible for what he has omitted to do; and the principle seems to be the same in both types of case. The real problem here is to see what is the minimum requirement of the law before a man can be held responsible, either for his act or for his omission.

## Voluntary and Involuntary Acts

The common method of stating this minimum requirement is to assert that there must be a voluntary act on the defendant's part.[16] This attempt to solve the problem, however, is no more helpful with regard to omissions, than is the definition of an act put forward by Holmes. It is a curious description of a thoughtless omission, to say that it is something voluntary on the part of the defendant. In any such cases of omission, there has been nothing on his part at all: so that it is difficult to see how one can sensibly talk here of a voluntary nothing.[17] The demand that the act should be voluntary confuses two different distinctions.

There is, it is true, a very important distinction between what a man does voluntarily and what he does under compulsion, duress, necessity, etc. Before admitting a confession in evidence, for example, the Judge may have to determine whether it was voluntary, or whether it was obtained by some threat or inducement. Or again, we may excuse someone of a crime on the ground that the accused was not acting voluntarily, but under duress. A woman's husband may have coerced her into acting as she did. In these cases the accused did have a choice; there was no need to make the confession, or to do what was done. But the choice was so difficult that we feel that the confession should be not admitted. For the inducement of bail, for example, may have led the accused to make a false confession. Or the husband's coercion may have made it difficult for the wife to choose to act otherwise than as she did.

But there is a totally different distinction: the distinction between normal conduct and involuntary movements of the body, such as the beating of one's heart, spasms, what one does in sleep, etc. In these cases there is no question of choice at all. Now the voluntary act theory blurs this important difference[18] and obscures the real question, namely, why it is that the courts refuse to hold a person liable in certain cases on the ground that his act or omission was involuntary. What is the test by which we distinguish these acts and omissions from the normal acts and omissions?

The search for the answer to these questions may best be conducted by first considering the types of behaviour that have been recognized as involuntary by the courts in different branches of the law. Then we may inquire whether there is any common criterion for determining whether in general behaviour is involuntary. Thirdly, there will arise the question why different branches of the law do, and should, treat these types of involuntary behaviour differently from normal behaviour.

## Types of Involuntary Action Recognized by Law

These fall into two main categories.

(*a*) Where the defendant is compelled to do what he does by some external force; and
(*b*) Where he is compelled by some internal force, or where at least the compulsion is not due to any external cause.

Where the defendant is physically compelled by some external force, either by some other person or by some force of nature to act as he does, courts have recognized this type of case as exonerating the defendant from liability. So in the Criminal Law 'If *A* takes *B*'s arm and the weapon in his hand and stabs *C*, *B* would be not guilty because there was no voluntary act on his part'.[19] Such a defence would also be raised in the case of an omission, where, for example, *A*, a parent, under a legal duty to rescue *B*, his child, from drowning, is forcibly prevented by *C* from so doing. In tort the same rule has been applied: where for instance a defendant was carried by a gang of armed men on to the plaintiff's premises, he was held not liable in trespass.[20] It is important to distinguish this case of physical compulsion, as it is sometimes called, from the case of duress. If the defence is duress, then the defendant is pleading that, though he had a choice, the alternative to doing what he did was so hard that it is too much to ask of any man that he should choose the alternative. The accused has no say in how his arm moves: it is moved for him. This is the difference between the case suggested by Hale and the case of *R.* v. *Bourne*,[21] the decision in which is only explicable on the basis that the wife herself had committed a crime. Similarly, in *Gilbert* v. *Stone*[22] a defendant compelled by threat of injury to enter the plaintiff's premises was held liable in trespass.

That people's acts may be involuntary without the compulsion of any external force is a fact that has become increasingly clearer with the growth of medical science. As Paton observed,[23] 'medicine, psychoanalysis and psychiatry are opening new doors and the law will gradually be forced to reconsider the theories on which its analysis of an act is based'. The best known of these internally motivated involuntary acts are those of epileptics undergoing fits of convulsions, and it is no accident that the word 'epileptic' was coined by the Greeks to signify something that might fall on a man, something that seized him from within himself.[24] These involuntary acts may be roughly divided into (*a*) movements over which nobody has control; and (*b*) movements over which people normally do have control, but over which a particular defendant lacks control because of some abnormality.[25]

There is little authority in law on the first class of involuntary acts, partly because it is unlikely that such uncontrollable movements should result in any harm, and even if they did, it is so clear that a person would not be held liable for such harm that prosecution would hardly be launched. Since the tort of trespass to the person now would seem to require intention or negligence on the part of the defendant,[26] it is unlikely that a defendant in such circumstances would be sued in tort either. Writers such as Austin, Bentham and Stephen, agree in classifying all these movements as involuntary and not deserving of punishment.[27] The American Law Institute's Model Penal Code defines certain types of acts as not voluntary, among which are reflexes or convulsions, and the Code contains a final omnibus class excluding as not voluntary any bodily movements that otherwise are not products of the effort or determination of the actor, either conscious or habitual.[28]

With regard to the type of movements over which people do normally have control, but over which a particular defendant lacked control because of some abnormality, the abnormality may be his unconsciousness, *e.g.* he may be merely asleep, and in sleep, it is said, there is no sin. 'Acts done by a person asleep cannot be criminal, there being no consciousness.'[29] Similarly, it is unlikely for instance, in the law of tort that a man would be held liable for slander, for defamatory words spoken in his sleep.[30] Likewise, the acts of a man under somnambulism will not render him guilty of any crime.[31] But the abnormality may be that the defendant's behavior is due to disease or injury. In *R.* v. *Charlson*[32] a father who in a fit of automatism seriously injured his small son was found not guilty of any crime since the jury was not satisfied that he might not have been acting as he did on account of a brain tumour; and so they were not satisfied that he had any choice as to his actions. Similarly, a man who killed his mother when his consciousness was clouded as a result of hypoglycaemia, was found not guilty of murder.[33] In these cases the lack of control arises because of lack of consciousness, as in cases of sleep-walking where the defendant does not know what he is doing. It may be, however, that he knows what he is doing and is yet quite incapable of exercising any control. Sufferers from fits of ictal or post-ictal conditions arising from epilepsy or injury have been known to describe their experiences by saying that though they knew in a sort of way what they were doing, yet they felt that all their actions were being controlled by some external force, as though by some remote control station.[34]

A very difficult problem is posed where the abnormal lack of control is due not to disease or injury, but to drunkenness or drugs. Involuntary drunkenness, *i.e.* where *A* secretly and against *B*'s will administers intoxicating liquor to *B*, is always said to be a defence.[35] Where, however, the accused himself was responsible for getting drunk, he will only be excused either if he is so drunk as to be insane within the McNaghten rules, or if he is incapable of forming a specific intent required by the courts. It is no defence that his intoxication made him more easily lose control of himself.[36] As to acts done under hypnotism or post-hypnotic suggestion, there is little authority.[37] The American Law Institute classifies 'conduct during hypnosis, or resulting from hypnotic suggestion' as involuntary. But the difficulty is that it is not clear how far a hypnotized person can be tricked into doing something dishonest or felonious.[38] On the other hand, such a subject might well be tricked into doing some dangerous act by being persuaded that he was in fact doing an act of quite a different kind, *e.g.*, the hypnotist might tell him to shoot someone with a water pistol while placing in his hand a real loaded pistol. But here the defence would not be so much that the defendant had no ability to control his movements, as that he did not fully appreciate the nature of his act.

What emerges from a survey of these different types of case

is that the common minimal requirement of the law seems to be that the accused should have had the ability to control his movements.

## Criminal Law

The most important field of law where problems arise with regard to involuntary acts is the Criminal Law. The attraction of stating the defence of involuntariness in terms of there being no act on the part of the accused is that this will be a defence even in cases of strict liability. To group this minimal requirement of power of control with the *actus reus* instead of with *mens rea,* means that a person who fails to conform to a halt sign because of a fit of automatism is not guilty of an offence, whereas one who fails because his brakes failed, or because he could not see the sign, would be guilty.[39]

The reason for the Criminal Law's insistence on this minimal requirement of ability of control is that the way in which the Criminal Law seeks to protect society from harmful conduct is in general by imposing penalties to deter would-be criminals. The imposition of penalties for involuntary acts cannot, of course, serve to prevent people from committing such involuntary acts. Furthermore, in the case of involuntary acts there arises no question of what Bentham termed the secondary mischief, *i.e.* the general effect on the community of the wrongful act, since in general if the accused acted involuntarily, there is no reason for the public to be apprehensive as to his future conduct in the same way as if he had behaved freely and willingly. Consequently, to use Bentham's phraseology, punishment would be both inefficacious and groundless. Inefficacious in that it could not prevent the primary mischief (since we cannot help our involuntary acts), and groundless because there is no secondary mischief to prevent.[40]

But not only is it therefore impolitic to punish such conduct, it is also unjust. Without inquiring too deeply into the moral justification for punishment, we may recognize the existence of a moral principle that we should not blame or punish one who could not help doing what he did. That this is a separate matter from that of deterrence can be seen from the following consideration. One can imagine that the punishment of involuntary conduct might possibly serve to deter would-be criminals in this way: While not preventing future involuntary conduct, it might prevent conduct that is not involuntary, if potential criminals said to themselves: 'See, this Draconian code even punishes those who cannot help stealing—the kleptomaniacs too. We, therefore, who can help stealing would be shown no mercy, so we had better refrain from committing crimes altogether'. Yet nobody would deny that, even if crimes could be prevented in this way, it would be unjust to punish those who cannot help what they do; and this it seems is the flaw in any theory of punishment based wholly on deterrence.

On the other hand there are cases where although the accused lacks the ability to control what he does, secondary mischief will arise and the community will be apprehensive about his future behaviour. Such cases are those where the accused's condition resulted from earlier conduct of his, over which he did have control. Stephen made this point clearly when he urged that the law ought to be that no act is a crime if the person who does it is at the time when it is done prevented, either by defective mental power or by disease affecting his mind, from controlling his own conduct, unless the absence of power of control is brought about by his own fault.[41] For this reason the courts have always leaned against allowing drunkenness as a defence when the accused allowed himself to get into a state of intoxication. Here it is felt that if he did this once he might well do it again, and men must be deterred from allowing themselves to get into such a condition. It is precisely because there was an earlier stage when the accused could have helped what he did, that punishment will serve some purpose. Likewise, if fumes suddenly overcome the driver of a motor car and the car swerves across the road into another vehicle, the driver will not be guilty of dangerous driving. But if he falls asleep at the wheel without any such external cause, then we could say that there was an earlier stage when he was driving dangerously, in that he continued to drive although he felt himself becoming drowsy. At this point he could have taken action either to ensure that he kept awake, or he could have stopped driving and waited until his somnolence had passed. This technique of moving back to a stage at which the defendant had a choice will sometimes enable lawyers to differentiate between cases where no blame should attach to the defendant because he could not help doing what he did, and cases where he is culpable because he could have avoided getting into the state where he was unable to help acting as he did. So we can say in a case such as *Hill* v. *Baxter*[42] that if the defendant was to blame for not forcing himself to stay awake, or for not stopping until he felt fit to drive, it was at this earlier stage that he was committing the crime of dangerous driving, rather than at the later stage when he actually was asleep. But this technique runs into difficulties with regard to omissions. For if the defendant argues that he is not guilty of failing to conform to a traffic sign because he was unconscious, we can hardly differentiate between the case where fumes suddenly bereft him of consciousness, and the case where he just fell asleep, by saying that in the latter case there was an earlier point of time where he was failing to conform. It is not yet clear how the courts will distinguish between these two types of case, but perhaps it can be suggested that where fumes overcome the driver he should be acquitted, not on the ground that there was no act on his part, but on the ground that he was unable to prevent himself from falling asleep, and at the same time there was no warning of what was going to happen, so that both his dangerous driving and his failure to conform to the traffic signs were involuntary. Where, however, he realizes he is falling asleep, has some warning, and yet takes no precautions, then this defence should not be open to him. The term 'involuntary' can then be reserved for those cases where no ability to control his actions arises at any stage;[43] and this defence of involuntariness should be excluded in cases where the accused either brought about his own lack of power of control, or foresaw that he might lack control and took no precautions. Here culpability and deterrence go hand-in-hand, for we feel that where there was the power of choice at an earlier stage, and the defendant could have helped it, he is culpable; and we also feel that punishment will serve to deter people from similar behaviour in the future. This, to some extent, supports the decision in *Jarmain's case*.[44] Even if he had no choice as to whether the gun went off or not, nevertheless he did have some say in the question whether or not to commit armed robbery, so that he was to some extent responsible, and his punishment would deter others from committing this crime.

There are, however, cases where there is no choice at all on the defendant's part, but his condition is such that he is liable to cause harm to others. Epileptics, for example, cannot help the fits they have. But if they know that they are likely to injure others in the course of these fits, it may not be wholly unreasonable to demand that they refrain from engaging in activities where the onset of a fit might lead to disastrous injury to other people. Such harm could clearly ensue if a fit overtook an epileptic in the course of driving a car, and for this reason the Motor Vehicle (Driving License) Regulations, 1950, prohibit epileptics from obtaining a driving license.[45] Similarly a diabetic who fails to take sufficient food and suffers from an insulin reaction may not unreasonably be convicted of driving under the influence of drugs, even though this was not perhaps the type of case originally envisaged by the Road Traffic Acts.[46] In these cases the defendant could not help the onset of the fits, or the insulin reaction. Nor is it true to say that his lack of control of his action is in any way due to anything he has done. But since he knows of the possible dangers, he should refrain from certain types of activity: and here choice does come into play, for he can choose, for instance, whether or not to drive a motor-car in the first place. He is not, therefore, absolutely justified in saying, 'I could not help what happened'. Here too, therefore, there is a stage at which we can say that he had some choice as to what has occurred.

There may, however, even be cases where there is no choice at all on the part of the accused. So far we have discussed two cases where a man cannot help acting as he does:

(*a*) where his inability arose from previous behaviour which he could have helped; and

(*b*) where his inability is no fault of his but, knowing that he is unable to help behaving as he does, he should avoid putting himself in a position where his involuntary behaviour may injure others; and he could so avoid putting himself into this position.

There is, however, the third case: that of the man who cannot help his involuntary behaviour, and cannot avoid putting himself in the position where his involuntary behaviour may injure others; and whose involuntary actions may be so dangerous to the community that deterrence gives place to prevention. The fits of an epileptic may be so dangerous that we no longer merely feel that he ought to refrain from certain activities requiring special care and skill, such as driving. It may even be necessary to confine him in order to prevent him altogether from mixing with other people. At this stage we begin to leave the question of punishment and turn to the question of what we should do to protect society from possible danger. Deterrents and correction no longer have any effect, and prevention is the only remedy.[47]

## Civil Liability

The way that the courts deal with involuntary acts with regard to civil liability is not necessarily the same as the way of the

Criminal Law. How far lack of ability to control one's movements exempts a defendant from liability in tort is bound up with the question whether liability in tort is based on fault or not. In so far as liability depends on fault, clearly involuntary acts or omissions on the part of the defendant should not render him liable, for a person is not at fault for doing what he cannot help doing. Accordingly, nobody should be held liable in negligence for an act or omission which he could not help, unless his inability to avoid the act or omission is due to some previous act or omission over which he does have control. A lunatic, therefore, could plead as a defence to negligence that he was not guilty of a breach of duty of care owing to the plaintiff, since the act or omission complained of was involuntary, and therefore could not constitute such a breach.[48] (It is submitted that this is a more satisfactory approach to the problem than to contend that the lunatic does not owe the same duty of care as the reasonable man.) An intoxicated man could not put forward such an argument because, if his breach of duty of care was involuntary, it resulted from his previous negligence in allowing himself to get into a state of intoxication.[49]

How far, however, is the fact that the defendant's behaviour was involuntary, a defense to torts of strict liability? Since the courts appear inclined to restrict trespass to the person to intentional or negligent acts,[50] and since inevitable accident is accepted as a defence to trespass to goods,[51] clearly an involuntary trespass would be a defence to either of these actions: though the courts may well have to distinguish between the case where this was due to no fault of the defendant, and the case where the defendant brought about his own inability to control his movements. With regard to trespass to land, it has been held that involuntary trespass, where the defendant could not help what he was doing, is a defence.[52] Even in those cases of strict liability, therefore, the lack of ability to control one's movements seems to operate as a defence. For liability may be so strict as not to allow a defendant to plead that he was mistaken, *e.g.* that he did not know that the land was not his own, but it does not force the courts to award damages against a man who had no choice at all as to what he did. This gives point to the above quoted defence of tort, that it is in general an act, for as Holmes remarked, an act implies choice.[53]

Even where the law of tort appears to be based purely on the need to compensate the plaintiff for the injury he has suffered, as in the ruling on *Rylands* v. *Fletcher* (though even here, the defence of act of God, or act of a third party, will avail), or in the Scienter action (where the wrongful act of a third party will not avail the defendant as a defence), nevertheless it seems that there must be some power of control exercisable at some stage by the defendant. The principle is, in these cases, that the defendant has created the dangerous situation and should therefore compensate a plaintiff who suffers harm as a result. The defendant need not have brought in and accumulated the water on his land. He need not have kept a ferocious animal. But where the bringing in of the water, or the keeping of the animal was not done by the defendant, it would be contrary to common sense to hold him responsible. Otherwise, 'Why need the defendant have acted at all, and why is it not enough that his existence has been at the expense of the plaintiff?' [54]

Involuntary conduct also raises problems with regard to causation. A conscious act on the part of the plaintiff will in general snap the chain of causation, whereas if the act is involuntary, the resulting harm may still be laid at the door of the defendant. So if *A* injures *B* who, as a result of the injury, commits suicide, *A* may be liable to *B*'s dependants under the Fatal Accidents Act, provided the deceased's condition was such that his act is regarded as involuntary.[55] Similarly, if *A* puts *B* in such a position of peril that he acts involuntarily, and so makes matters worse, *A* will be both civilly and criminally liable for the harm resulting to *B*.[56] This same principle is found at work in the rescue cases.

## Evidence

In the law of evidence, however, different questions arise with regard to involuntary acts which, in this context, comprise involuntary statements. The question is no longer whether the defendant should be held responsible for his involuntary behaviour, but whether any admission made involuntarily should be allowed in evidence against a party. The generally accepted reason for excluding statements made out of court as evidence to prove the truth of what they assert, is twofold:[57] (*a*) because such statements were not made on oath, and therefore may not be trustworthy; and (*b*) because there is no possibility of their veracity or correctness being decided by cross-examination. Admissions are, however, allowed as evidence against a party because (i) though not on oath, they are likely to be true since they were against the interest of the man who made them; and (ii) because the party who made them will have an opportunity by his own evidence to explain the circumstances, and show how much reliance is to be placed on them; and this will serve the purpose normally served by cross-examination. Admissions made in sleep, therefore, or in delirium, or under hypnosis, could it seems be admissible on this reasoning. Suppose, for example, the prisoner is charged with burgling premises, and denies ever having visited these premises; if he talks in his sleep and describes these premises, should this admission necessarily be excluded? The prisoner will be able to explain the statement and these circumstances (so that the objection of lack of cross-examination is met), and there is no reason to suppose that the statement (if against interest) is untrue. Such admissions have been received.[58] On the other hand, when the prisoner is arrested he must be cautioned that he need not say anything; consequently if he is in a state of delirium and cannot help saying what he does, perhaps it is only fair that anything he says in custody in such conditions should not be received in evidence against him. Otherwise he would be denied the choice offered to him by the law, the right not to say anything.[59]

Confessions, on the other hand, raise a different problem. Here the law of evidence lays down that a confession must be voluntary, *i.e.* it must not be obtained by force, threats, or inducement, since in such cases there is always the danger that such confessions may be false. That this is the principle seems to emerge from the fact that where the confession is obtained by fraud (as opposed to threats or inducement) it is not thereby excluded, because it is not thereby any the more likely to be untrue.[60] A confession that is involuntary, however, in that it is obtained by means of hypnosis or truth drugs cannot be excluded on this ground, for so far from the prisoners being induced to speak falsely, it may be that he is being forced to speak the truth. At present, however, medical experts are not agreed as to the success of hypnosis or the truth drug.[61] The former, it is suggested, involves the danger that the accused may agree to anything that is suggested to him. A confession made while drunk has been received in evidence,[62] but in an American case where the Sheriff deliberately made a prisoner drunk in order to obtain the confession, it was excluded.[63] This suggests the existence of another principle, that confessions obtained by removing from the defendant any choice as to what he says, should be excluded, not because they are any the less likely to be true, but because of the interference with personal liberty. To allow in evidence confessions obtained in such a manner would not only be serving to facilitate just the sort of police activity which the courts are astute to prevent, but would be inconsistent with the general principle of our legal system, which gives the prisoner the choice of whether to give evidence in court or not. It would be inconsistent with this principle to force the prisoner to make a confession and give evidence against himself outside the court, when you cannot force him to give evidence in the witness box. Indeed, in England, the Judges' rules require that a prisoner should first be cautioned that he need not say anything.[64] To get a confession from him against his will (even though the confession were clearly true) would contravene this principle of giving the prisoner the option of silence.

## Conclusion

In conclusion, it may be said:

(1) that the correct definition of the word 'act' is to be found by looking at the use made of the word by lawyers. It is used partly to mark certain distinctions and partly to ascribe responsibility.

(2) that this question should be kept separate from the other question, namely, in what circumstances does an act or omission fail to attract liability (criminal or civil) on the ground that it is involuntary. The answer to this may be found by examining the types of behaviour recognized as involuntary, by searching for a connecting quality, and by considering how far different branches of the law treat such involuntary behaviour differently from normal behaviour. The common quality connecting all these types of behaviour would seem to be inability to control one's bodily movements, *i.e.* in the case of an act, inability to avoid doing it; in the case of an omission, inability to do the act prescribed by law, provided that this inability is not the result of previous behaviour which was under the actor's control. How far the law treats, or ought to treat, such behaviour differently depends upon the purposes and principles of different branches of the law. It must be remembered that the considerations to be borne in mind in criminal cases are not necessarily the same as in actions in tort or in divorce, or yet again in the cases referred to above raised by the law of evidence.

## Notes

1. Anson, *Law of Contract* (21st ed.), p. 41.
2. *Smith* v. *Stone* (1647), Sty. 65.

3. Salmond, *Law of Torts* (12th ed.), p. 14.

4. *Lynch* v. *Nurdin* (1841), 1 Q.B. 29.

5. *Stansbie* v. *Troman*, [1948] 2 K.B. 48.

6. *Baker* v. *Snell*, [1908] 2 K.B. 352; *Bertram* v. *Bertram Mills Circus, Ltd.* [1957], 2 Q.B. 1.

7. Holmes, *The Common Law*, p. 45.

8. 24 Cr. App. Rep. 74. This dissatisfaction was not felt, however, in Northern Ireland, where the case was followed in the unreported case of *Kasriel* v. *Neumann* (1947): *vid.*, (1956), 12 N.I.L.Q., p. 61.

9. Holmes, *op. cit.*, p. 54.

10. Holmes, *op. cit.*, p. 54.

11. *R.* v. *Coombes* (1786), 1 Leach 388; Salmond, *Jurisprudence* (11th ed.), p. 406.

12. [1946] K.B. 74.

13. Salmond, *Jurisprudence* (11th ed.), pp. 401–2.

14. Dias and Hughes, *Jurisprudence*, p. 202.

15. H. L. A. Hart, *The Ascription of Responsibility and Rights* (1948–9), Proc. Arist. Soc. 179.

16. Cross and Jones, *Criminal Law* (3rd ed.), p. 32; Kenny, *Outlines of Criminal Law* (17th ed.), pp. 26–7; American Law Institute's *Model Penal Code, Tentative Draft No. 4*, Art. 2, s. 2.0 (1); *cf.*, Queensland Code, s. 23; Tasmanian Code, s. 13 (1); Stephen, *History of the Criminal Law of England*, Vol. II, p. 97; Barry, Paton and Sawer, *Criminal Law in Australia* (1948), p. 48.

17. *Cf.*, Perkins (1939), 52 Harv. L.R. 912; Glanville Williams, *Criminal Law*, p. 15. Nevertheless it is not true to say that the idea of a voluntary omission makes no sense—one can be compelled to omit to do something, and equally one can omit to do it voluntarily.

18. 'Voluntary' and 'Involuntary' are not opposites, as was pointed out by J. L. Austin in '*A Plea for Excuses*' (1956–7), Proc. Arist. Soc. *Cf.*, Bentham, *Principles of Morals and Legislation*, p. 82; see also Jerome Hall, *Principles of Criminal Law*, p. 522. Stephen opposed 'voluntary' to 'involuntary', however, and not to 'compelled', *op. cit.*, pp. 101–2.

19. 1 Hale. P.C. 434, 472; Blackstone, *Commentaries on the Laws of England*, Vol. IV, p. 27; *cp.*, 1 Hawk. P.C., ch. 29, s. 3.

20. *Smith* v. *Stone* (1647), Sty. 65.

21. (1952), 36 Cr. App. Rep. 125. See Cross in (1953), 69 L.Q.R., p. 354, but Lord Goddard stresses at p. 128 that '(the plea of duress) means that she admits that she has committed the crime', and at p. 129 that 'the offence of buggery . . . does not depend on consent:

it depends on the act, and if an act of buggery is committed, the felony is committed'.

22. (1647), Sty. 72; Aleyn 35.

23. Paton, *Jurisprudence* (2nd ed.), p. 243.

24. For a useful medical account of such conditions see Penfield and Jasper, *Epilepsy and the Functional Anatomy of the Human Brain* (1954). See also Gowers, *Diseases of the Nervous System,* II (1893), pp. 746–9; Henderson and Gillespie, *A Textbook of Psychiatry* (8th ed.).

25. The first sub-class may be sub-divided into:

(i) the movement of his body of which a man knows nothing without observation, *e.g.* heart beats, the peristaltic movement of the gut;

(ii) movements which he does know about without observation, *e.g.* twitches, ticks, jerks, etc. (where the cause itself, however, is known only by observation and reflex actions, such as the jerking of one's knee when it is tapped by a doctor, or a sudden leaping back when attacked by a wild animal).

See G. E. Anscombe, *Intention,* p. 13 ff.

26. *Fowler* v. *Lanning,* [1959] 1 Q.B. 426.

27. Austin, *Jurisprudence,* I. 360, 415, 419, 498; Bentham, *op. cit.*, p. 164, 171, 174–5; Stephen *op. cit.* p. 99.

28. Model Penal Code, Art. 2, s. 2.0 (2) (d).

29. MacDonald, *The Criminal Law of Scotland* (5th ed.), p. 11.

30. Pollock on Torts (15th ed.), p. 47.

31. Wharton, *Criminal Law* (12th ed.), I, s. 84; Russell on Crime (11th ed.), p. 40; Glanville Williams, *op. cit.*, p. 14. See *R.* v. *Minor* (1955), 112 Can.C.C. 29.

32. [1955] 1 All E.R. 859.

33. *Lancet* (1943), Vol. I, pp. 526–7.

34. *Cf.*, defendant's account in *Buckley & T.T.C.* v. *Smith Transport,* [1946] 4 D.L.R. 721.

35. *R.* v. *Pearson* (1835), 2 Lew. C.C. 144; 1 Hale 32.

36. *D.P.P.* v. *Beard,* [1920] A.C. 479; *R.* v. *McCarthy,* [1954] 2 Q.B. 105.

37. Glanville Williams, *op. cit.*, p. 12.

38. See Taylor, *Principles and Practice of Medical Jurisprudence* (11th ed.). Experiments were carried out on 50 subjects, all of whom awoke rather than perform some repugnant act: J. R. Rees, *Modern Practice in Psychiatric Medicine* (1949), p. 391.

39. *Hill* v. *Baxter,* [1958] 1 Q.B. 277; Edwards (1958), 21 M.L.R. 375; there are also repercussions from this grouping in the law of evidence, as was shown by *R.* v. *Harrison-Owen,* [1951] 2 All E.R. 726; see Cowen & Carter, *Essays on the Law of Evidence,* pp. 111–4; Cross, *Evidence,* 287–8; Glanville Williams, *op. cit.,* p. 14. The latter suggests that there are few offences of strict liability where the defence of involuntariness could apply, but road traffic offences are an exception to this contention.

40. Bentham, *op. cit.,* pp. 164, 171, 174–5, 315. It could be argued that punishment would be equally inefficacious in the case of the motorist whose brakes failed or who failed to observe the halt sign, but surely here the justification could be that punishment might cause him to test his brakes regularly and keep a keener look-out in future.

41. Stephen, *op. cit.,* p. 168. *Cp.,* Wharton, *Criminal Law* (12th ed.), I, s. 84; *Lewis* v. *State* (1943), 196 Ga. 755.

42. [1958] 1 Q.B. 277.

43. *i.e.,* once he has commenced a course of conduct, for otherwise the suggested test would exclude even the case of the motorist overcome by fumes, since he could have always abstained from driving, and so the test would become vacuous.

44. *Supra,* p. 9.

45. Regulation 5.

46. See *The New Scientist,* 4th June, 1959, p. 1244.

47. Prevention can often be seen as the basis of punishment, *e.g.,* in preventive detention, imposed when a court concludes from the prisoner's record that he is beyond reform and the only course is to lock him up so that he can no longer get at other people's property; in the incarceration of the guilty but insane; in the death penalty, and in the older penalties of transportation and mutilation; and in the more modern penalty of disqualification from driving. On the ground that the community must be protected, it may not be unreasonable that a man suffering so frequently from epileptic fits as to be dangerous should, if he raises a defence of automatism, run the risk of the prosecution contending that his condition brings him within the McNaghten Rules, as in *R.* v. *Kemp,* [1957] 1 Q.B. 399. *Cf.,* Henderson and Gillespie, *op. cit.,* p. 683, where it is contended that it is not justifiable to certify a man in the course of an epileptic fit. Contrast the South African decision *R.* v. *Mkize,* 1959 (2) S.A. 260 (N).

48. Clerk & Lindsell on Torts (11th ed.), pp. 92–3; Salmond, *Law of Torts* (12 ed.), 76; Street, *Law of Torts,* p. 500; Pollock, *Law of Torts* (15th ed.), p. 47; Winfield, *Law of Tort* (6th ed.), p. 130;

*Morriss* v. *Marsden,* [1952] 1 All E.R. 925; Todd (1952), 15 M.L.R. 486. *Cf.*, *White* v. *White,* [1950] p. 39, at p. 52.

49. Even in Negligence, however, liability is not wholly dependent on fault, as can be seen from the objective standard, whereby an abnormally stupid or abnormally clumsy man cannot be heard to say that, being unable to help being stupid or clumsy, he should not be held liable. See Holmes, *op. cit.*, 107 ff., Prosser, *Torts* (2nd ed.), 118, 29, and American Restatement of the Law of Torts, 1, 2.

50. *Fowler* v. *Lanning, supra,* p. 15.

51. *N.C.B.* v. *Evans,* [1951] 2 K.B. 861.

52. *Smith* v. *Stone* (*supra*); *cf.*, *Beckwith* v. *Shordike* (1767), 4 Burr. 2092.

53. Holmes, *op. cit.*, p. 54; *cf.*, Pollock, *op. cit.*, p. 47.

54. *Ibid.*, p. 95.

55. *Pigney* v. *Pointer's Transport Services,* [1957] 2 All E.R. 807.

56. *R.* v. *Pitts* (1482), Car. & M. 284; Hart & Honoré (1956), 72 L.Q.R. 272; Salmond, *Law of Torts,* p. 735, and cases there noted.

57. Cross, *Evidence,* p. 350; Wigmore on Evidence, s. 1048.

58. Wigmore, *op. cit.*, s. 500. *Cp.*, Gardiner and Landsdown, *South African Criminal Law and Procedure* (6th ed.), I, pp. 597, 603, 605; in S. Africa confessions to be admissible, must be made by the accused in sound and sober senses. But *cf. R.* v. *Lincoln,* 1950 P.H., H. 68 (A.D.) Contrast Indian Evidence Act, 1872, s. 29—a confession is not irrelevant because the accused is drunk or has been deceived.

59. Wigmore, *op. cit.*, s. 841; Indian Evidence Act, 1872, s. 29.

60. See Inbau, *Journal of Criminal Law and Criminology* (1934), XXIV, 1153; Mosier and Hames, *ibid.* (1935), XXVI, 431.

61. In *R.* v. *Booher,* [1928] 4 D.L.R. 795 a confession following an alleged hypnotic suggestion was excluded.

62. *Vaughan's Trial* (1696), 13 How. St. Tr. 507; *R.* v. *Spilsbury* (1835), 7 C. & P. 187.

63. *McNutt* v. *State* (1903), 68 Nebr. 207.

64. Archbold, *Criminal Pleading, Evidence and Practice* (33rd ed.), p. 414, Rules 4 & 5. See Silving (1956), 69 Harv. L.R. 693.

# Selected Bibliography

What follows is a listing of recent books, articles, and anthologies relevant to the theory of action. We have selected only a part of the considerable contemporary philosophical literature that seems to bear directly upon the various concerns of the essays collected in this volume. We have not included materials from classical sources. The following abbreviations are used for titles of certain of the professional journals:

| | |
|---|---|
| *JOP* | *Journal of Philosophy* |
| *PAS* | *Proceedings of the Aristotelian Society* |
| *PQ* | *Philosophical Quarterly* |
| *PR* | *Philosophical Review* |
| *ROM* | *Review of Metaphysics* |


R. Abelson, "Because I Want To," in *Mind*, 74 (1965).

Virgil C. Aldrich, "Behavior, Simulating and Nonsimulating," in *JOP*, 63 (1966).

G.E.M. Anscombe, "Intention," in *PAS*, 57 ns (1956–57).

———, *Intention*. Oxford: Blackwell, 1957.

———, "Pretending," in *PAS*, Supp. Vol. 32 (1958).

———, "The Two Kinds of Error in Action," in *JOP*, 60 (1963).

P. S. Ardal, "Motives, Intentions and Responsibility," in *PQ*, 15 (1965).

Bruce Aune, "Feelings, Moods, and Introspection," in *Mind*, 72 (1963).

J. L. Austin, *Philosophical Papers* (edited by J. O. Urmson and G. J. Warnock). Oxford: Clarendon Press, 1961. See especially the papers "A Plea for Excuses," "Pretending," and "Ifs and Cans."

———, "Three Ways of Spilling Ink," in *PR*, 75 (1966).

A. J. Ayer, *The Problem of Knowledge*. London: Penguin, 1956.

Kurt Baier, "Action and Agent," in *Monist*, 49 (1965).

———, "Good reasons," in *Philosophical Studies*, 4 (1953).

———, *The Moral Point of View.* Ithaca, N.Y.: Cornell University Press, 1958.

J. Balmuth, "Psychoanalytic Explanation," in *Mind,* 74 (1965).

W. H. F. Barnes, W. D. Falk, and A. E. Duncan-Jones, Symposium: "Intention, Motive, and Responsibility," in *PAS,* Supp. Vol. SV 19 (1945).

L. White Beck, "Conscious and Unconscious Motives," in *Mind,* 75 (1966).

Errol Bedford, "Emotions," in *PAS,* 57 (1956–57).

John Benson, "The Characterization of Action and the Virtuous Agent," in *PAS,* 63 ns (1962–63).

S. I. Benn and R. S. Peters, *Social Principles and the Democratic State.* London: George Allen & Unwin Ltd., 1959. (American title: *The Principles of Political Thought.* New York: The Free Press, 1965.)

Isaiah Berlin, "History and Theory: The Concept of Scientific History," in *History and Theory,* 1 (1960).

Max Black, "Notes on the Meaning of 'Rule,'" in *Theoria,* 24 (1958).

Karl Britton, "Feelings and Their Expression," in *Philosophy,* 32 (1957).

F. Broadie, "Knowing That I am Doing," in *PQ,* 17 (1967).

———, "Trying and Doing," in *PAS,* 66 ns (1965–66).

May Brodbeck, "Explanation, Prediction, and 'Imperfect' Knowledge" in *Minnesota Studies in the Philosophy of Science,* III (edited by Herbert Feigl and Grover Maxwell). Minneapolis: University of Minnesota Press, 1962.

Robert Brown, *Explanation in Social Science.* London: Routledge & Kegan Paul, 1963.

D. Browning, "Acts," in *ROM,* 14 (1960).

———, "The Moral Act," in *PQ,* 12 (1962).

C. A. Campbell, "Is 'Freewill' a Pseudo-Problem?" in *Mind,* 60 (1951).

Norman S. Care, "On Avowing Reasons," in *Mind,* 76 (1967).

James Cargile, "On Having Reasons," in *Analysis,* 26 (1965–66).

Hector Neri Castañeda, "Outline of a Theory on the General Logical Structure of the Language of Action," in *Theoria,* 26 (1960).

Arthur Child, "Doing and Knowing," in *ROM,* 9 (1955–56).

Roderick Chisholm, "The Descriptive Element in the Concept of Action," in *JOP,* 61 (1964).

Noam Chomsky, *Cartesian Linguistics.* New York: Harper and Row, 1966.

Y. N. Chopra, "The Consequences of Human Actions," in *PAS,* 65 ns (1964–65).

R. G. Collingwood, *The Idea of History.* Oxford: Clarendon Press, 1946.

Eric D'Arcy, *Human Acts, An Essay in Their Moral Evaluation.* Oxford: Clarendon Press, 1963.

T. F. Daveney, "Intentions and Causes," in *Analysis,* 27 (1966).

Donald Davidson, Patrick Suppes, and Sidney Siegel, *Decision Making: An Experimental Approach.* Stanford, Cal.: Stanford University Press, 1957.

P. E. Davis, " 'Action' and 'Cause of Action,' " in *Mind,* 71 (1962).

B. J. Diggs, "Technical Ought," in *Mind,* 69 (1960).

P. C. Dodwell, "Causes of Behaviour and Explanation in Psychology," in *Mind,* 69 (1960).

Alan Donagan, "Explanation in History," in *Mind,* 56 (1957).

Keith S. Donnellan, "Knowing What I am Doing," in *JOP,* 60 (1963).

William H. Dray, *Laws and Explanation in History.* Oxford: Clarendon Press, 1957.

——— (ed.), *Philosophical Analysis and History.* New York: Harper and Row, 1966.

Jonathan Edwards, *Freedom of the Will* (edited by Paul Ramsey). New Haven, Conn.: Yale University Press, 1957.

J. L. Evans, "Knowledge and Behaviour," in *PAS,* 54 (1953–54).

A. C. Ewing, O. S. Franks, and J. Macmurray, Symposium: "What is Action?" in *PAS,* Supp. Vol. 17 (1938).

W. D. Falk, "Action-guiding Reasons," in *JOP,* 60 (1963).

B. A. Farrell, P. M. Turquet, and J. O. Wisdom, Symposium: "The Criteria for a Psychoanalytic Interpretation," in *PAS,* Supp. Vol. 36 (1962).

Joel Feinberg, "Action and Responsibility," in *Philosophy in America* (edited by Max Black). Ithaca, N.Y.: Cornell University Press, 1965.

———, "Causing Voluntary Actions," in *Metaphysics and Explanation* (edited by W. H. Capitan and D. D. Merrill). Pittsburg: University of Pittsburgh Press, n. d. (1964 Oberlin Colloquium). With comments by Keith S. Donnellan and Keith Lehrer, and rejoinders by Feinberg.

Paul Feyerabend, "Materialism and the Mind-Body Problem," in *ROM,* 17 (1963).

Milton Fisk, "Causation and Action," in *ROM,* 19 (1965).

P. J. Fitzgerald, "Acting and Refraining," in *Analysis,* 27 (1967).

Brice Noel Fleming, "On Intention," in *PR,* 73 (1964).

Antony Flew, "Motives and The Unconscious," in *Minnesota Studies in the Philosophy of Science,* I (edited by Herbert Feigl and Mi-

chael Scriven). Minneapolis: University of Minnesota Press, 1956.
Jerry A. Fodor, "Explanations in Psychology," in *Philosophy in America* (edited by Max Black). Ithaca, N.Y.: Cornell University Press, 1965.
Patrick Gardiner, *The Nature of Historical Explanation.* London: Oxford University Press, 1952.
——— (ed.), *Theories of History.* Glencoe, Illinois: The Free Press, 1959.
D. P. Gauthier, "How Decisions are Caused," in *JOP,* 64 (1967).
P. T. Geach, "Ascriptivism," in *PR,* 69 (1960).
———, *Mental Acts.* London: Routledge & Kegan Paul, 1957.
W. D. Gean, "Reasons and Causes," in *ROM,* 19 (1965–66).
Quentin Gibson, *The Logic of Social Enquiry.* London: Routledge & Kegan Paul, 1960.
Carl Ginet, "Can the Will be Caused?" in *PR,* 71 (1962).
Bruce Goldberg, "Can a Desire be a Cause?" in *Analysis,* 25 (1964–65).
A. P. Griffiths, "Acting with Reason," in *PQ,* 8 (1958).
D. W. Hamlyn, "Behaviour," in *Philosophy,* 28 (1953).
Stuart Hampshire, *Feeling and Expression.* London: H. K. Lewis & Co. Ltd., 1960.
———, *Thought and Action.* London: Chatto and Windus, 1960.
H. L. A. Hart, "The Ascription of Responsibility and Rights," in *PAS,* 49 (1948–49). (Reprinted in *Logic and Language, First Series* (edited by Antony Flew). Oxford: Blackwell, 1955.)
——— and Stuart Hampshire, "Decision, Intention and Certainty," in *Mind,* 67 (1958).
——— and A. M. Honoré, *Causation in the Law.* London: Oxford University Press, 1959.
D. O. Hebb, *The Organization of Behavior.* New York: Wiley, 1949.
Carl G. Hempel, "Deductive-Nomological vs. Statistical Explanation," in *Minnesota Studies in the Philosophy of Science,* III (edited by Herbert Feigl and Grover Maxwell). Minneapolis: University of Minnesota Press, 1962.
———, "Explanation in Science and in History," in *Frontiers of Science and Philosophy* (edited by Robert G. Colodny). Pittsburgh: University of Pittsburgh Press, 1962.
———, "The Function of General Laws in History," in *JOP,* 39 (1942). (Reprinted in *Theories of History* [edited by Patrick Gardiner]. Glencoe, Illinois: The Free Press, 1959.)
———, *Fundamentals of Concept Formation in Empirical Science.* Chicago: University of Chicago Press, 1952.

——— and Paul Oppenheim, "The Logic of Explanation," in *Philosophy of Science,* 15 (1948). (Reprinted in *Readings in the Philosophy of Science* [edited by Herbert Feigl and May Brodbeck]. New York: Appleton-Century-Crofts, 1953.)

A. M. Honoré, "Can and Can't," in *Mind,* 73 (1964).

Sidney Hook (ed.), *Dimensions of Mind.* New York: New York University Press, 1960.

——— (ed.), *Psychoanalysis, Scientific Method and Philosophy.* New York: New York University Press, 1959.

R. A. Imlay, "Do I Ever Directly Raise My Arm?" in *Philosophy,* 42 (1967).

J. J. Jenkins, "Motive and Intention," in *PQ,* 15 (1965).

Jerrold J. Katz, *The Philosophy of Language.* New York: Harper and Row, 1966.

Arnold S. Kaufman, "Ability," in *JOP,* 60 (1963).

Anthony Kenny, *Action, Emotion, and Will.* London: Routledge & Kegan Paul, 1963.

John Ladd, "The Ethical Dimension of the Concept of Action," in *JOP,* 62 (1965).

Charles Landesman, "The New Dualism in the Philosophy of Mind," in *ROM,* 19 (1965).

Keith Lehrer (ed.), *Freedom and Determinism.* New York: Random House, 1966.

A. R. Louch, *Explanation and Human Action.* Berkeley and Los Angeles: University of California Press, 1966.

R. D. Luce and H. Raiffa, *Games and Decisions.* New York: Wiley, 1957.

D. J. McCracken, R. S. Peters, and J. O. Urmson, Symposium: "Motives and Causes," in *PAS,* Supp. Vol. 26 (1952).

Margaret Macdonald (ed.), *Philosophy and Analysis.* Oxford: Blackwell, 1954. See the papers by S. Toulmin and A. Flew on psychoanalytic explanation.

C. A. Mace and R. S. Peters, "Emotions and the Category of Passivity," in *PAS,* 62 (1961–62).

A. C. MacIntyre, "The Antecedents of Action," in *British Analytical Philosophy* (edited by Bernard Williams and Alan Montefiore). London: Routledge & Kegan Paul, 1966.

———, "Determinism," in *Mind,* 66 (1957).

———, "A Mistake about Causality in Social Science," in *Philosophy, Politics, and Society, Second Series* (edited by Peter Laslett and W. G. Runciman). Oxford: Blackwell, 1962.

———, *The Unconscious.* London: Routledge & Kegan Paul, 1958.

——— and Peter Alexander, Symposium: "Cause and Cure in Psychotherapy," in *PAS*, Supp. Vol. 29 (1955).
——— and P. H. Nowell-Smith, Symposium: "Purpose and Intelligent Action," in *PAS*, Supp. Vol. 34 (1960).
G. Madell, "Action and Causal Explanation," in *Mind*, 76 (1967).
Norman Malcolm, *Dreaming*. New York: The Humanities Press, 1959.
D. S. Mannison, "My Motive and Its Reason," in *Mind*, 73 (1964).
B. Mayo, "Commitments and Reasons," in *Mind*, 64 (1955).
J. W. Meiland, "Are There Unintentional Actions," in *PR*, 72 (1963).
A. I. Melden, *Free Action*. London: Routledge & Kegan Paul, 1961.
———, "Philosophy and the Understanding of Human Fact," in *Epistemology* (edited by Avrum Stroll). New York: Harper and Row, 1967.
———, "Reasons for Action and Matters of Fact," in *Proceedings and Addresses of the American Philosophical Association*, 35 (1962).
———, *Rights and Right Conduct*. Oxford: Blackwell, 1959.
Theodore Mischel, "Concerning Rational Behaviour and Psychoanalytic Explanation," in *Mind*, 74 (1965).
———, "Pragmatic Aspects of Explanation," in *Philosophy of Science*, 33 (1966).
G. E. Myers, "Motives and Wants," in *Mind*, 73 (1964).
Ernest Nagel, *The Structure of Science*. New York: Harcourt, Brace, 1961.
P. H. Nowell-Smith, "Choosing, Deciding and Doing," in *Analysis*, 18 (1957–58).
———, *Ethics*. London: Penguin, 1954.
Harold Ofsted, "Can We Produce Decisions?" in *PR*, 56 (1959).
Brian O'Shaughnessy, "Observation and the Will," in *JOP*, 60 (1963).
Talcott Parsons and Edward A. Shils (eds.), *Toward a General Theory of Action*. Cambridge, Mass.: Harvard University Press, 1951.
J. A. Passmore, "Intentions," in *PAS*, Supp. Vol. 29 (1955).
D. F. Pears, "Are Reasons for Actions Causes?" in *Epistemology* (edited by Avrum Stroll). New York: Harper and Row, 1967.
——— (ed.), *Freedom and the Will*. New York: St. Martin's Press, 1963.
Stephen Pepper, *The Sources of Value*. Berkeley and Los Angeles: University of California Press, 1958.
Moreland Perkins, "Emotion and Feeling," in *PR*, 75 (1966).
———, "Emotion and the Concept of Behavior," in *American Philosophical Quarterly*, 3 (1966).
R. S. Peters, "Cause, Cure and Motive," in *Analysis*, 10 (1949–50).

———, *The Concept of Motivation.* London: Routledge & Kegan Paul, 1958.

———, "More about Motives," in *Mind,* 76 (1967).

———, "Motives and Motivation," in *Philosophy,* 31 (1956).

———, "Observationalism in Psychology," in *Mind,* 60 (1951).

George Pitcher, "Hart on Action and Responsibility," in *PR,* 69 (1960).

——— (ed.), *Wittgenstein, The Philosophical Investigations.* Garden City, N.Y.: Doubleday (Anchor Books), 1966.

Karl Popper, *Conjectures and Refutations.* New York: Basic Books, 1962.

Betty Powell, "Uncharacteristic Actions," in *Mind,* 68 (1959).

———, *Knowledge of Actions.* London: Allen and Unwin, 1967.

H. A. Prichard, *Moral Obligation.* London: Oxford University Press, 1949. See especially the paper "Acting, Willing, and Desiring."

A. N. Prior and D. D. Raphael, Symposium: "The Consequences of Action," in *PAS,* Supp. Vol. 30 (1956).

W. V. O. Quine, *Word and Object.* Cambridge, Mass.: The M. I. T. Press, 1960.

K. W. Rankin, "Doer and Doing," in *Mind,* 69 (1960).

Anatol Rapoport, *Fights, Games, and Debates.* Ann Arbor, Michigan: University of Michigan Press, 1960.

N. Rescher, "Values and the Explanation of Behavior," in *PQ,* 17 (1967).

——— (ed.), *The Logic of Desision and Action.* Pittsburgh: U. of Pittsburgh Press, n.d.

A. D. Ritchie, "Agent and Act in Theory of Mind," in *PAS,* 52 ns (1951–52).

Richard Rorty, "Mind-Body Identity, Privacy, and Categories," in *ROM,* 19 (1965).

Amelie O. Rorty, "Wants and Justifications," in *JOP,* 63 (1966).

Gilbert Ryle, *The Concept of Mind.* London: Hutchinson, 1949. New York: Barnes and Noble, 1949.

David Sachs, "A Few Morals About Acts," in *PR,* 75 (1966).

Wilfrid Sellars, "Mind, Meaning, and Behavior," in *Philosophical Studies,* 3 (1953).

———, *Science, Perception and Reality.* London: Routledge & Kegan Paul, 1963. See especially chs. 1, 4, 5, 10, and 11.

David Shwayder, *The Stratification of Behaviour.* London: Routledge & Kegan Paul, 1965.

B. F. Skinner, *Science and Human Behavior.* New York: The Macmillan Company, 1953.

J. J. C. Smart, *An Outline of a System of Utilitarian Ethics.* Melbourne: Melbourne University Press, 1961.

———, "Sensations and Brain Processes," in *PR,* 68 (1959).

P. F. Strawson, *Individuals.* London: Methuen and Co. Ltd., 1959.

N. S. Sutherland, "Motives as Explanations," in *Mind,* 68 (1959).

Peter Swiggart, "Doing and Deciding to Do," in *Analysis,* 23 (1962–63).

Charles Taylor, *The Explanation of Behaviour.* London: Routledge & Kegan Paul, 1964.

Richard Taylor, " 'I can,' " in *PR,* 69 (1958).

———, *Action and Purpose.* Englewood Cliffs, N.J.: Prentice-Hall, 1966.

Irving Thalberg, "Do We Cause Our Own Actions?" in *Analysis,* 27 (1967).

———, "Freedom of Action and Freedom of Will," in *JOP,* 61 (1964).

J. Teichmann, "Mental Cause and Effect," in *Mind,* 70 (1961).

E. J. Tolman, *Behavior and Psychological Man.* Berkeley and Los Angeles: University of California Press, 1961.

———, *Purposive Behavior in Animals and Men.* Berkeley and Los Angeles: University of California Press, 1949.

G. N. A. Vesey, "Volition," in *Philosophy,* 36 (1961).

Georg Henrik Von Wright, *Norm and Action.* London: Routledge & Kegan Paul, 1963.

Alan R. White, "Different Kinds of Heed Concepts," in *Analysis,* 20 (1959–60).

———, "Inclination," in *Analysis,* 21 (1960–61).

———, "The Language of Motives," in *Mind,* 67 (1958).

———, *The Philosophy of Mind.* New York: Random House, 1967.

Morton White, *Foundations of Historical Knowledge.* New York: Harper and Row, 1965.

C. H. Whiteley, "Behaviorism," in *Mind,* 70 (1961).

B. T. Wilkins, "The Thing to Do," in *Mind,* 75 (1966).

Peter Winch, *The Idea of a Social Science.* London: Routledge & Kegan Paul, 1963.

Ludwig Wittgenstein, *Philosophical Investigations* (translated by G. E. M. Anscombe). New York: The Macmillan Company, 1953.

John Yolton, "Act and Circumstances," in *JOP,* 59 (1962).

———, "Agent Causality," in *American Philosophical Quarterly,* 3 (1966).